Twice round

Or, The hours of the day and night in London

George Augustus Sala

Alpha Editions

This edition published in 2024

ISBN : 9789362512918

Design and Setting By
Alpha Editions
www.alphaedis.com
Email - info@alphaedis.com

As per information held with us this book is in Public Domain.
This book is a reproduction of an important historical work. Alpha Editions uses the best technology to reproduce historical work in the same manner it was first published to preserve its original nature. Any marks or number seen are left intentionally to preserve its true form.

Contents

PREFACE. ....- 1 -
FOUR O'CLOCK A.M.—BILLINGSGATE MARKET. ....- 7 -
FIVE O'CLOCK A.M.—THE PUBLICATION OF THE "TIMES" NEWSPAPER. ....- 21 -
SIX O'CLOCK A.M.—COVENT GARDEN MARKET. ....- 31 -
SEVEN O'CLOCK A.M.—A PARLIAMENTARY TRAIN. .- 41 -
EIGHT O'CLOCK A.M.—ST. JAMES'S PARK—THE MALL. ....- 55 -
NINE O'CLOCK A.M.—THE CLERKS AT THE BANK, AND THE BOATS ON THE RIVER. ....- 65 -
TEN O'CLOCK A.M.—THE COURT OF QUEEN'S BENCH, AND THE "BENCH" ITSELF. ....- 74 -
ELEVEN O'CLOCK A.M.—TROOPING THE GUARD, AND A MARRIAGE IN HIGH LIFE. ....- 87 -
NOON.—THE JUSTICE-ROOM AT THE MANSION-HOUSE, AND THE "BAY TREE." ....- 97 -
ONE P.M.—DOCK LONDON AND DINING LONDON....- 107 -
TWO P.M.—FROM REGENT STREET TO HIGH CHANGE. ....- 119 -
THREE P.M.—DEBENHAM AND STORR'S AUCTION-ROOMS, AND THE PANTHEON BAZAAR. ....- 133 -
FOUR P.M.—TATTERSALL'S, AND THE PARK. ....- 156 -
FIVE O'CLOCK P.M.—THE FASHIONABLE CLUB, AND THE PRISONERS' VAN. ....- 168 -
SIX P.M.—A CHARITY DINNER, AND THE NEWSPAPER WINDOW AT THE GENERAL POST-OFFICE. ....- 183 -
SEVEN O'CLOCK P.M.—A THEATRICAL GREEN-ROOM, AND "BEHIND THE SCENES." ....- 198 -

EIGHT O'CLOCK P.M.—HER MAJESTY'S THEATRE, AND A PAWNBROKER'S SHOP. ....- 212 -

NINE O'CLOCK P.M.—HALF-PRICE IN THE NEW CUT, AND A DANCING ACADEMY. ....- 226 -

TEN O'CLOCK P.M.—A DISCUSSION AT THE "BELVIDERE," AND AN ORATORIO AT EXETER HALL. ....- 239 -

ELEVEN O'CLOCK P.M.—A SCIENTIFIC CONVERSAZIONE, AND AN EVENING PARTY..............- 250 -

MIDNIGHT.—THE HAYMARKET, AND THE SUB-EDITOR'S ROOM. ....- 267 -

ONE O'CLOCK A.M.—EVANS'S SUPPER-ROOMS, AND A FIRE. ....- 278 -

TWO O'CLOCK A.M.—A LATE DEBATE IN THE HOUSE OF COMMONS, AND THE TURNSTILE OF WATERLOO BRIDGE. ....- 301 -

HOUR THE TWENTY-FOURTH AND LAST—THREE A.M.—A BAL MASQUE, AND THE NIGHT CHARGES AT BOW STREET. ....- 315 -

FOOTNOTES ....- 331 -

PREFACE.

TO AUGUSTUS MAYHEW.

Had I not fifty other valid reasons—did I not feel myself impelled to such a course by the long years of affectionate intercourse which have cast sunshine on that highway of life, of which the shadier side of the road has been apportioned to me, I should still, my dear Augustus, dedicate this book to you. I could show, I hope, my affection and esteem in other ways; but to address to you the Epistle Dedicatory of "Twice Round the Clock" is only your due, in justice and in courtesy. Civility is not so common a quality among the Eminent British Authors of the day, and mutual admiration is not so plentifully displayed by our Fieldings and Smolletts of 1859, that we middling and middle-class ink-spillers can afford to throw away a chance of saying a kind or civil thing to one another in the right way and in the right place. Do you, therefore, say something neat and complimentary about me in the preface to your next book; and I only trust that the task will confer as sincere a pleasure on you as it confers on me at this moment.

But I might still, I must admit, admire you very much, without that admiration giving you a Right to the Dedication of a Book relating exclusively to London Life and London Manners in the nineteenth century. Herein, however, rests, I think, your claim: That you are the author of a capital book called "Paved with Gold," replete with[vi] the finest and shrewdest observation drawn from the scenes we have both delighted to survey, to study, and to describe, and of which book, although the basis was romantic fiction, the numerous episodes were picturesque but eminently faithful photographs of fact. I should have liked, myself, to tell the story of a prize fight, of a ratting match, or of a boy's low lodging-house, in my own way, and in these pages; but I shrank from the attempt after your graphic narratives in "Paved with Gold." And, again, have you not been for years the fellow-labourer of your brother Henry, in those deeply-tinted but unalterably-veracious studies of London Life, of which we have the results in "Labour and the Poor" and in the "Great World of London?" Of how many prisons, workhouses, factories, work-rooms, have you not told the tale? of how many dramas of misery and poverty have you not been the chronicler? Let us bow to the great ones of letters, and, reading their books with a hearty, honest admiration, confess that the capacity to produce such master-pieces is not given to us; but let us, on our own parts, put in a modest claim to the recognition and approval of the public. Please remember the reporters. Please not to forget the bone-grubbers. Fling a pennyworth of praise to the excavators and night-watchmen who have at least industriously laboured to collect materials wherefrom better painters may execute glowing tableaux of London Life. At least, we have toiled to bring together our tale of bricks, that by the hand of genius they may be erected some day into a Pyramid. At least, we have endeavoured to our utmost to describe the London of our day as we have seen it, and as we know it; and, in the words of the judicious Master Hooker—of whose works, my Augustus, I am afraid you are not a very sedulous student—we have worked early and late on London, and have done our best to paint the infinitely-varied characteristics of its streets and its population, "Tho' for no other cause, yet for this, that Posteritie may know we have not looselie, thro' silence, permitted thinges to pass away as in a dreame; there shall be for men's information extant thus much concerning the present state of"—London.

So you see, my dear friend, that I have dedicated my work to you; and that, *bon grè, mal grè*, you have been saddled with the dignity of its Patron. I might have addressed you in heroic verse, and with[vii] your name in capitals; and, in the manner of Mr. Alexander Pope, bidden you:—

"Awake, my MAYHEW: leave all meaner things

To low ambition and the pride of kings."

I believe your present ambition extends only to few-acre farming and the rearing of poultry, and I might well exhort you to return to your literary pursuits, and to leave the Dorkings and Cochin Chinas alone. But I refrain. Am I to insult my Patron with advice? Do I expect any reward for my dedication? Will your Lordship send me a handful of broad-pieces for my flattery's sake by the hands of your gentleman's gentleman? Will you put me down for the next vacancy as a Commissioner of Hackney Coaches, or the next reversion for a snug sinecure connected with the Virginia Plantations or the Leeward Islands? Will your Lordship invite me to dinner at your country-seat, and place me between Lady Betty and the domestic chaplain? May I write rhyming epitaphs for her ladyship's pug-dog, untimely deceased from excess of cream and chicken? Or will you speak to Mr. Secretary in my behalf, lest that last paper of mine against Ministers in "Mist's Weekly Journal" should draw down on me the *ex-officio* wrath of Mr. Attorney-General, and cause my ears to be nailed to the pillory? Can I ever hope to crack a bottle in your Lordship's society at Button's, or to see your Lordship's coach-and-six before my lodgings in Little Britain? Let us be thankful, rather, that the species of literary patronage at which I have hinted exists no longer, and that an Author has no need to toady his Patron in order to make him his friend. For what more in cordiality and kind-fellowship I could say, you will, I am sure, give me credit. When friendship is paraded too much in public, its entire sincerity may be open to doubt. I am afraid that Orestes, so affectionate on the stage, has often declined in the green-room to lend Pylades sixpence; and

I am given to understand, that Damon has often come down from the platform, where he has been saying such flourishing fine things about Pythias, and in private life has spoken somewhat harshly of that worthy.

You will observe that, with the economy which we should all strive to inculcate in an age of Financial Reform, I have made these remarks to serve two ends. You are to take them, if you please,[viii] as a Dedication. The public will be good enough to accept them as a Preface. But as the dedicatory has hitherto disproportionately exceeded the prefatory matter, a few words on my part are due to that great body-corporate of Patrons whom some delight to call the "many-headed monster;" some the "million;" some the fickle, ungrateful, and exigent—and some the generous, forbearing, and discerning British Public.

The papers I have now collected into a volume under the title of "Twice Round the Clock, or the Hours of the Day and Night in London," were originally published in the pages of the "Welcome Guest," a weekly periodical whose first and surprising success must be mainly ascribed to the taste and spirit of its original proprietor, Mr. Henry Vizetelly. I confess that I thought as little of "Twice Round the Clock" in the earlier hours of its publication as the critics of the *Saturday Review*—who, because I contributed for six years to another periodical whose conductor they hold in hatred, have been pleased to pursue me with an *acharnement* quite exciting to experience—may think of it, now. I looked upon the articles as mere ephemeral essays, of a description of which I had thrown off hundreds during a desultory, albeit industrious, literary career. But I found ere long that I had committed myself to a task whose items were to form an Entirety in the end; that I had begun the first act of a Drama which imperatively demanded working out to its catastrophe. I grew more interested in the thing; I took more pains; I felt myself spurred to accuracy by the conscientious zeal of the admirable artist, Mr. William M'Connell, whose graphic and truthful designs embellished my often halting text. I found, to my great surprise, that the scenes and characters I had endeavoured to embody were awakening feelings of curiosity and interest among the many thousand readers of the journal to which I contributed. The work, such as it is, was in the outset not very deliberately planned. I can only regret now, when it is terminated, that the details I have sometimes only glanced at were not more elaborately and completely carried out.

It would be a sorry piece of vanity on my part to imagine that the conception of the History of a Day and Night in London is original.[ix] I will tell you how I came to think of the scheme of "Twice Round the Clock." Four years ago, in Paris, my then Master in literature, Mr. Charles Dickens, lent me a little thin octavo volume, which, I believe, had been presented to him by another Master of the craft, Mr. Thackeray, entitled—but I will transcribe the title-page in full.

LOW LIFE;
OR, ONE HALF THE WORLD KNOWS NOT HOW THE OTHER HALF LIVE.

Being a Critical Account of what is Transacted by People of almost all Religions, Nations, Circumstances, and Sizes of Understanding, in the

TWENTY-FOUR HOURS,
BETWEEN
SATURDAY NIGHT AND MONDAY MORNING.
In a true Description of a
SUNDAY,

As it is usually spent within the Bills of Mortality, calculated for the twenty-first of June.

WITH AN ADDRESS TO THE INGENIOUS AND INGENUOUS MR. HOGARTH.

Let Fancy guess the rest.—*Buckingham*.

The date of publication is not given; but internal evidence proves the Opuscule to have been written during the latter part of the reign of George the Second; and in the copy I now possess, and which I bought at a "rarity" price, at a sale where it was ignorantly labelled among the "*facetiæ*"—it is the saddest book, perhaps, that ever was written—in my copy, which is bound up among some rascally pamphlets, there is written on the fly-leaf the date 1759. Just one hundred years ago, you see. The work is anonymous; but in a manuscript table of contents to the collection of miscellanies of which it forms part, I find written "By Tom Legge." The epigraph says that it "is printed for the author, and is to be sold by T. Legg, at the Parrot, Green Arbour Court, in the Little Old Bailey." Was the authorship mere guess-work on the part of the owner of the book, or was "Tom Legge" really the writer of "Low Life," and, if so, who was "Tom Legge?" Mr. Peter Cunningham, or a contributor to "Notes and Queries," may be able to inform us. I have been thus particular, for a reason: that this thin octavo is one of the minutest, the most graphic—and while in parts coarse as a scene from the "Rake's Progress,"—the[x] most pathetic, picture of London life a century since that has ever been written. There are passages in it irresistibly reminding one of Goldsmith; but the offensive and gratuitous coarseness in the next page destroys *that* theory. Our Oliver was pure. But for the dedicatory epistle to the great painter prefixed, and which is merely a screed of fulsome flattery, I could take an affidavit that "Low Life" was written by William Hogarth. And why not, granting even the fulsome dedication? Hogarth could have more easily written this calendar of Town Life than the "Analysis of Beauty;" and the sturdy grandiloquent little painter was vain enough to have employed some hack to write the prefatory epistle, if, in a work of satire, he had chosen to assume the anonymous. Perhaps, after all, the book was written by some clever, observant, deboshed man out of Grub Street, who had been wallowing in the weary London trough for years, and had eliminated at last some pearls which the other swine were too piggish to discern. There, however, is "Low Life." If you want to know what London was really like in 1759, you should study it by night and study it by day; and then you may go with redoubled zest to your Fielding, Smollett, and Richardson, as one, after a vigorous grind at his Greek verbs, may go to his Euripides, refreshed. From this thin little octavo I need not say I borrowed the notion of "Twice Round the Clock." I chose a week-day instead of a Sunday, partly for the sake of variety, partly because Sunday in London has become so decorous as to be simply dull, and many of the hours would have been utterly devoid of interest. I brooded fitfully over the scheme for many months. At first I proposed to take my stand (in imagination) at King Charles's Statue, Charing Cross, and describe the Life revolving round me during the twenty-four hours; but I should have trenched upon sameness by confinement to singularity; and I chose at last all London as the theme of description—

"A mighty maze, but not without a plan."

As a literary performance, this book must take its chance; and I fear that the chance will not be a very favourable one. Flippant, pretentious, superficial and yet arrogant of knowledge; verbose without being eloquent; crabbed without being quaint; redundant without[xi] being copious in illustration; full of paradoxes not extenuated by originality; and of jocular expressions not relieved by humour—the style in which these pages are written, combines the worst characteristics of the comic writers who have been the "guides, philosophers and friends" of a whole school of *quasi* youthful authors in this era. I have reviewed too many would-be comic books in my time, not to be able to pounce on the unsuccessful attempts at humour in "Twice Round the Clock;" I have sufficient admiration and respect for the genuine models of literary vigour and elegance extant, not to feel occasionally disgusted with myself when I have found the most serious topics discussed with a grotesque grimace the while. It is a bad sign of the age—this turning of "cart-wheels" by the side of a hearse, this throwing of somersaults over grave-stones. The style we write in is popular now; but a few years, I hope, will see a re-action, when a literary man must be either clown or undertaker, and grinning through a horse-collar will not be tolerated in the case of a mountebank otherwise attired in a shroud. Meanwhile, I cannot accuse myself of pandering to a depraved taste. I neither follow nor lead it. I cannot write otherwise than I do write. The leopard cannot change his spots. Born in England, I am neither by parentage nor education an Englishman; and in my childhood I browsed on a salad of languages, which I would willingly exchange now for a plain English lettuce or potato. Better to feed on hips and haws than on gangrened green-gages and mouldy pine-apples. I read Sterne and Charles Lamb, Burton and Tom Brown, Scarron and Brantôme, Boccaccio and Pigault-le-Brun, instead of Mrs. Barbauld, and the Stories from the Spelling-book. I was pitchforked into a French college before I had been through Pinnock in English; and I declare that to this day I do not know one rule out of five in Lindley Murray's grammar. I can spell decently, because I can draw; and the power (not the knowledge) in spelling correctly is concurrent with the capacity for expressing the images before us more or less graphically and symmetrically. It isn't how a word *ought* to be spelt: it is how it *looks* on paper, that decides the speller. I began to look upon the quaint side of things almost as soon as I could see things at all; for I was alone and Blind for a long time in childhood. I had so[xii] much to whimper about, poor miserable object, that I began to grin and chuckle at the things I saw, so soon as good Doctor Curée, the homœopathist, gave me back my eyes. It is too late to mend now. While I am yet babbling, I feel that I have nearly said my say. This book, as a Book, will go, and be forgotten; but it will, years hence, acquire comparative value when disinterred, from the "two-penny-box" at a bookstall. Old Directories, Road Books, Court-Guides, Gazetteers, of half a century since, are worth something now. They are as the straw that enters into the composition of new bricks or books. Let us bide our time, then, my Augustus, humbly but cheerfully. *You* may have better fortune. You write novels and tales: and the chronicles of Love never die. But if in the year 1959, some historian of the state of manners in England during the reign of Queen Victoria, points an allusion in a foot note by a reference to an old book called "Twice Round the Clock," and which professes to be a series of essays on the manners and customs of the Londoners in 1859, that reference will be quite enough of reward for your friend. Macaulay quotes broadsides and Grub Street ballads. Carlyle does not disdain to put the obscurest of North German pamphleteers into the witness-box; albeit he often dismisses him with a cuff and a kick. At all events, we may be quoted some of these days, dear Gus, even if we are kicked into the bargain.

GEORGE AUGUSTUS SALA.

FOUR O'CLOCK A.M.—BILLINGSGATE MARKET.

Reader, were you ever up all night? You may answer that you are neither a newspaper editor, a market gardener, a journeyman baker, the driver of the Liverpool night mail, Mrs. Gamp the sicknurse, the commander of the Calais packet, Professor Airey, Sir James South, nor a member of the House of Commons. It may be that you live at Clapham, that one of the golden rules of your domestic economy is "gruel at ten, bed at eleven," and that you consider keeping late hours to be an essentially immoral and wicked habit,— the immediate prelude to the career and the forerunner of the fate of the late George Barnwell. I am very sorry for your prejudices and your susceptibilities. I respect them, but I must do them violence. I intend that— *bon gré, mal gré*—in spirit, if not in actual corporeality, you should stop out not only all night but all day with me; in fact, for the space of twenty-four hours, it is my resolve to prohibit your going to bed at all. I wish you to see the monster LONDON in the varied phases of its outer and inner life, at every hour of the day-season and the night-season; I wish you to consider with me the giant sleeping and the giant waking; to watch him in his mad noonday rages, and in his sparse moments of unquiet repose. You must travel TWICE ROUND THE CLOCK with me; and together we will explore this London mystery to its remotest recesses—its innermost arcana. To others the downy couch, the tasselled nightcap, the cushioned sofa, the luxurious ease of night-and-day rest. Ours be the staff and the sandalled shoon, the cord to gird up the lions, the palmer's wallet and cockle-shells. For, believe me, the pilgrimage will repay fatigue, and the shrine is rich in relics.

Four o'clock in the morning. The deep bass voice of Paul's, the Staudigl of bells, has growlingly proclaimed the fact. Bow church confirms the information in a respectable baritone. St. Clement's Danes has sung forth acquiescence with the well-known chest-note of his tenor voice, sonorous and mellifluous as Tamberlik's. St. Margaret's, Westminster, murmurs a confession of the soft impeachment in a contralto rich as Alboni's in "Stridi la vampa;" and all around and about the pert bells of the new churches, from evangelical Hackney to Puseyite Pimlico, echo the announcement in their shrill treble and soprani.

Four o'clock in the morning. Greenwich awards it,—the Horse Guards allow it—Bennett, arbiter of chronometers and clocks that, with much striking, have grown blue in the face, has nothing to say against it. And that self-same hour shall never strike again this side the trumpet's sound. The hour itself being consigned to the innermost pigeon-hole of the Dead Hour office—(a melancholy charnel-house of misspent time is that, my friend)—you and I have close upon sixty minutes before us ere the grim old scythe-bearer, the saturnine child-eater, who marks the seconds and the minutes of which the infinite subdivision is a pulsation of eternity, will tell us that the term of another hour has come. That hour will be five a.m., and at five it is high market at Billingsgate. To that great piscatorial Bourse we, an't please you, are bound.

It is useless to disguise the fact that you, my shadowy, but not the less beloved companion, are about to keep very bad hours. Good to hear the chimes at midnight, as Justice Shallow and Falstaff oft did when they were students in Gray's Inn; but four and five in the morning! these be small hours indeed: this is beating the town with a vengeance. Were it winter, our bedlessness would be indefensible; but this is still sweet summer time.

But why, the inquisitive may ask—the child-man who is for ever cutting up the bellows to discover the reservoir of the wind—why four o'clock a.m.? Why not begin our pilgrimage at one a.m., and finish the first half at midnight, in the orthodox get-up-and-go-to-bed manner? Simply because four a.m. is in reality the first hour of the working London day. The giant is wide awake at midnight; he sinks into a fitful slumber about two in the morning: short is his rest, for at four he is up again and at work, the busiest bee in the world's hive.

The child of the Sun, the gorgeous golden peacock, strutting in a farmyard full of the Hours, his hens, now triumphs. It is summer; and more than that, a lovely summer morning. The brown night has retired, and the meek-eyed moon, mother of dews, has disappeared: the young day pours in apace; the mountains' misty tops are swelling on the sight, and brightening in the sun. It is the cool, the fragrant, and the silent hour, to meditation due and sacred song; the air is coloured, the efflux divine turns hovels into palaces, and shoots with gold the rags of beggars.

"The city now doth like a garment wear

The beauty of the morning....

Never did Sun more beautifully steep

In his first splendour, valley, rock, or hill.

Ne'er saw I, never felt, a calm so deep.

The River glideth at its own sweet will;

Dear God! the very houses seem asleep,

And all that mighty Heart is lying still."

I know that the acknowledgment of one's quotations or authorities is going out of fashion. Still, as I murmur the foregoing lines as I wander round about the Monument and in and out of Thames Street, waiting for Billingsgate-market time to begin, a conviction grows upon me that the poetry is not my own; and in justice to the dead, as well as with a view of sparing the printer a flood of inverted commas, I may as well confess that I have been reading Mr. James Thomson and Mr. William Wordsworth on the subject of summer lately, and that very many of the flowery allusions to be found above, have been culled from the works of those pleasing writers.

Non omnis moriar. Though the so oft-mentioned hours be asleep, and the river glideth in peace, undisturbed by penny steamboats, the mighty heart of Thames Street is anything but still. The great warehouses are closed, 'tis true; the long wall of the Custom House is a huge dead wall, full of blind windows. The Coal Exchange (which edifice, with its gate down among the dead men in Thames Street, and its cupola, like a middle-sized bully, lifting its head to about the level of the base of that taller bully the Monument, is the neatest example of an architectural "getting up stairs" that I know)—the Coal Exchange troubles not its head as yet about Stewarts or Lambtons, Sutherlands or Wallsend. The moist wharfs, teeming with tubs and crates of potter's ware packed with fruity store, and often deliciously perfumed with the smell of oranges, bulging and almost bursting through their thin prison bars of wooden laths, are yet securely grated and barred up. The wharfingers are sleeping cosily far away. But there are shops and shops wide open, staringly open, defiantly open, with never a pane of glass in their fronts, but yawning with a jolly ha! ha! of open-windowedness on the bye-strollers. These are the shops to make you thirsty; these are the shops to make your incandescent coppers hiss; these are the shops devoted to the apotheosis and apodeiknensis (I quote Wordsworth again, but Christopher, not William) of Salt Fish—

"Spend Herring first, save Salt Fish last,

For Salt Fish is good when Lent is past."

So old Tusser. What piles of salted fish salute the eye, and make the mouth water, in these open-breasted shops! Dried herrings, real Yarmouth bloaters, kippered herrings, not forgetting the old original, unpretending red herring, the modest but savoury "soldier" of the chandler's-shop! What flaps of salt cod and cured fishes to me unknown, but which may be, for aught I know, the poll of ling which King James the First wished to give the enemy of mankind when he dined with him, together with the pig and the pipe of tobacco; or it may be Coob or Haberdine! What are Coob and Haberdine? Tell me, Groves, tell me, Polonius, erst chamberlain and first fishmonger to the court of Denmark. Great creels and hampers are there too, full of mussels and periwinkles, and myriads of dried sprats and cured pilchards—shrunken, piscatorial anatomies, their once burnished green and yellow panoplies now blurred and tarnished. On the whole, each dried-fish shop is a most thirst-provoking emporium, and I cannot wonder much if the blue-aproned fishmongers occasionally sally forth from the midst of their fishy mummy pits and make short darts "round the corner" to certain houses of entertainment, kept open, it would seem, chiefly for their accommodation, and where the favourite morning beverage is, I am given to understand, gin mingled with milk. It is refreshing, however, to find that the fragrant berry of Mocha (more or less adequately represented by chicory, burnt horse-beans, and roasted corn)—that coffee, the nurse of Voltaire's wit, the inspirer of Balzac's brain; coffee, which Madame de Sevigné pertly predicted would "go out" with Racine, but which nevertheless has, with astonishing tenacity of vitality, "kept in" while the pert Sevigné and the meek Racine have quite gone out into the darkness of literary limbo—is in great request among the fishy men of Billingsgate. Huge, massive, blue and white earthenware mugs full of some brown decoction, which to these not too exigent critics need but to steam, and to be sweet, to be the "coffee as in France," whose odoriferous "percolations" the advertising tradesmen tell us of, are lifted in quick succession to the thirsty lips of the fishmen. Observe, too, that all market men drink and order their coffee by the "pint," even as the scandal-loving old ladies of the last century (ladies don't love scandal now-a-days) drank their tea by the "dish." I can realise the contempt of a genuine Billingsgate marketeer for the little thimble-sized filagree cups with the bitter Mocha grouts at the bottom, which, with a suffocating Turkish chibouque, Turkish pachas and attar-of-roses dealers in the Bezesteen, offer as a mark of courtesy to a Frank traveller when they want to cheat him.

Close adjacent is a narrow passage called Darkhouse Lane, and here properly should be a traditional Billingsgate tavern called the "Darkhouse." There is one, open all night, under the same designation, in Newgate Market. Hither came another chronicler of "twice round the clock" with another neophyte, to show him the wonders of the town, one hundred and fifty years ago. Hither, when pursy, fubsy, good-natured Queen Anne reigned in England, and followed the hounds in Windsor's Park, driving two piebald ponies in a chaise, and touched children for the "evil," awing childish Sam Johnson with her black velvet and her diamonds, came jovial, brutal, vulgar, graphic Ned Ward, the "London Spy." Here, in the "Darkhouse," he saw a waterman knock down his wife with a stretcher, and subsequently witnessed the edifying spectacle of the recreant husband being tried for his offence by a jury of fishwomen. Scant mercy, but signal justice, got he from those fresh-water Minoses and Rhadamanthuses. Forthwith was he "cobbed"—a punishment invented by sleeveboard-wielding tailors, and which subsequently became very popular in her Majesty's navy. Here he saw "fat, motherly flatcaps, with fish-baskets hanging over their heads instead of riding-hoods," with silver rings on their thumbs, and pipes charged with "mundungus" in their mouths, sitting on inverted eel-baskets, and strewing the flowers of their exuberant eloquence over dashing young town rakes who had stumbled into Billingsgate to finish the night—disorderly blades in laced velvet coats, with, torn ruffles, and silver-hilted swords, and plumed hats battered in scuffles with the watch. But the town-rakes kept comparatively civil tongues in their heads when they entered the precincts of the Darkhouse. An amazon of the market, otherwise known as a Billingsgate fish-fag, was more than a match for a Mohock. And here Ned Ward saw young city couples waiting for the tide to carry them in a tilt-boat to Gravesend; and here he saw bargemen eating broiled red-herrings, and Welshmen "louscobby" (whatever that doubtless savoury dish may have been, but there *must* have been cheese in it); and here he heard the frightful roaring of the waters among the mechanism of the piers of old London Bridge. There are no waterworks there now; the old bridge itself is gone; the Mohocks are extinct; and we go to Gravesend by the steamer, instead of the tilt-boat; yet still, as I enter the market, a pleasant cataract of "chaff" between a fishwoman and a costermonger comes plashing down—even as Mr. Southey tells us that the waters come down at Lodore—upon my amused ears; and the conviction grows on me that the flowers of Billingsgate eloquence are evergreens. Mem.: To write a philosophical dissertation on the connection between markets and voluble vituperation which has existed in all countries and in all ages. 'Twas only from his immense mastery of Campanian slang that Menenius Agrippa obtained such influence over the Roman commons; and one of the gaudiest feathers in Daniel O'Connell's cap of eloquence was his having "slanged" an Irish market-woman down by calling her a crabbed old hypothenuse!

Billingsgate has been one of the watergates or ports of the city from time immemorial. Geoffrey of Monmouth's fabulous history of the spot acquaints us that "Belin, a king of the Britons, about four hundred years before Christ's nativity, built this gate and called it 'Belinsgate,' after his own calling;" and that when he was dead, his body being burnt, the ashes in a vessel of brass were set on a high pinnacle of stone over the said gate. Stowe very sensibly observes, that the name was most probably derived from some previous owner, "happily named Beling or Biling, as Somars' Key, Smart's Wharf, and others, thereby took the names of their owners." When he was engaged in collecting materials for his "Survey," Billingsgate was a "large Watergate port, or harborough for ships and boats commonly arriving there with fish, both fresh and salt, shellfish, salt, oranges, onions, and other fruits and roots, wheat, rye, and grain of divers sorts, for the service of the city, and the parts of this realm adjoining." Queenhithe, anciently the more important watering-place, had yielded its pretensions to its rival. Each gives its name to one of the city wards.

Some of the regulations concerning the "mystery" of the fishmongers in old times are sufficiently interesting for a brief notice. In the reign of Edward I. the prices of fish were fixed—for the best soles, 3*d.* per dozen; the best turbot, 6*d.* each; the best pickled herrings, 1*d.* a score; fresh oysters, 2*d.* a gallon; the best eels, 2*d.* per quarter of a hundred. In a statute of Edward I. it was forbidden to offer for sale any fish except salt fish after the second day. In the city assize of fish the profits of the London fishmongers were fixed at one penny in twelve. They were not to sell their fish secretly, within doors, but in plain market-place. In 1320 a combination was formed against the fishmongers of Fish-wharf, to prevent them from selling by retail; but Edward II. ordered the mayor and sheriffs to interfere, and the opposition was unsuccessful. The mayor issued his orders to these fishmongers of Bridge Street and Old Fish Street, to permit their brethren in the trade to "stand at stall;" to merchandise with them, and freely obtain their share of merchandise, as was fit and just, and as the freedom of the city required. A few years later some of the fishmongers again attempted to establish a monopoly; but it was ordered that the "billestres," or poor persons who cried or sold fish in the streets, "provided they buy of free fishmongers, and do not keep a stall, or make a stay in the streets, shall not be hindered;" and also that persons and women coming from the uplands with fish caught by them or their servants in the waters of the Thames or other neighbouring streams, were to be allowed to frequent the market. With these exceptions, none but members of the Fishmongers' Company were to be allowed to sell fish in the city, lest the commodity should be made dear by persons dealing in it who were unskilful in the mystery.

The old churches of London in the immediate vicinity of the fish-markets contained numerous monuments to fishmongers. That the stock-fishmongers, or dealers in dried or salted fish, should have formed so important a portion of the trade is deserving of notice, as a peculiarity of the times. Lovekin and Walworth, who both acquired wealth, were stock-fishmongers. The nature of the commodity was such as to render the dealers in it a superior class to the other fishmongers. A great store might be accumulated, and more capital was required than by the other fishmongers, who only purchased from hand to mouth.

In 1699, an act was passed for making it a free market for the sale of fish—though the very commencement of the preamble alludes to Billingsgate having been time out of mind a free market for all kinds of floating and salt fish, as also for all manner of floating and shellfish. The necessity of a new act had arisen, as the preamble recites, from various abuses, one of which was that the fishmongers would not permit the street hawkers of fish to buy of the fishermen, by which means the fishmongers bought at their own prices. The extraordinary dream of making the country wealthy, and draining the ocean of its riches by means of fisheries, had for above a century been one of the fondest illusions of the English people; and about the time that the act was passed, "ways to consume more fish" were once more attracting the popular attention. The price of fish at the time was said to be beyond the reach of the poor and even of the middling classes; and for many days together the quantity received at Billingsgate was very inconsiderable. To remedy these evils, carriages were to be constructed, to be drawn by two post-horses, which were to convey the fish to market at a rate of speed which was then thought to be lightning rapidity. But though the project was much talked about, it never came to a head, and ultimately fell through, the projectors consoling themselves with the axiomatic reflection—that there are more fish in the sea than ever came out of it.

But while I am rummaging among the dusty corners of my memory, and dragging forth worm-eaten old books to the light; while I have suffered the hare of the minute-hand, and the tortoise of the hour-hand (the tortoise wins the race), to crawl or scamper at least half round the clock, Billingsgate Market itself—the modern—the renovated—a far different place to that uncleanly old batch of sheds and hovels, reeking with fishy smells, and more or less beset by ruffianly company, which was our only fish market twenty years ago—New Billingsgate, with a real fountain in the centre, which during the day plays real water, is now in full life and bustle and activity. Not so much in the market area itself, where porters are silently busied in clearing piles of baskets away, setting forms and stools in order, and otherwise preparing for the coming business of the fish auction, as on the wharf, in front of the tavern known to fame as Simpson's, and where the eighteenpenny fish ordinary is held twice every day, except Sunday, in each year of grace. This wharf is covered with fish, and the scaly things themselves are being landed, with prodigious celerity, and in quantities almost as prodigious, from vessels moored in triple tier before the market. Here are Dutch boats that bring eels, and boats from the north sea that bring lobsters, and boats from Hartlepool, Whitstable, Harwich, Great Grimsby, and other English seaports and fishing stations. They are all called "boats," though many are of a size that would render the term ship, or at least vessel, far more applicable. They are mostly square and squat in rigging, and somewhat tubby in build, and have an unmistakeably fishy appearance. Communications are opened between the vessels, each other, and the shore, by means of planks placed from bulwark to bulwark; and these bulwarks are now trodden by legions of porters carrying the fish ashore. Nautical terms are mingled with London street vernacular; fresh mackerel competes in odour with pitch and tar; the tight strained rigging cuts in dark indigo-relief against the pale-blue sky; the whole is a confusion, slightly dirty but eminently picturesque, of ropes, spars, baskets, oakum, tarpaulin, fish, canvas trousers, osier baskets, loud voices, tramping feet, and "perfumed gales," not exactly from "Araby the blest," but from the holds of the fishing-craft.

BILLINGSGATE MARKET: CARRYING FISH ASHORE.

Upon my word, the clock has struck five, and the great gong of Billingsgate booms forth market-time. Uprouse ye, then, my merry, merry fishmongers, for this is your opening day! And the merry fishmongers uprouse themselves with a vengeance. The only comparison I can find for the aspect, the sights, and sounds of the place, is—a Rush. A rush hither and thither at helter-skelter speed, apparently blindly, apparently without motive, but really with a business-like and engrossing pre-occupation, for fish and all things fishy. Baskets full of turbot, borne on the shoulders of the *facchini* of the place, skim through the air with such rapidity that you might take them to be flying fish. Out of the way! here is an animated salmon leap. Stand on one side! a shoal of fresh herrings will swallow you up else. There is a rush to the tribunes of the auctioneers; forums surrounded by wooden forms—I mean no pun—laden with fish, and dominated by the rostra of the salesmen, who, with long account-books in their hands, which they use instead of hammers, knock down the lots with marvellous rapidity. An eager crowd of purchasers hedge in the scaly merchandise. They are substantial-looking, hearty, rosy-gilled men—for the sale of fish appears to make these merchants thrive in person as well as in purse. Why, though, should fishmongers have, as a body, small eyes? Can there be any mysterious sympathy between them and the finny things they sell?—and do they, like the husband and wife who loved each other so much, and lived together so long, that, although at first totally dissimilar in appearance, they grew at last to resemble one another feature for feature—become smaller and smaller-eyed as their acquaintance with the small-eyed fishes lengthens? I throw this supposition out as a subject for speculation for some future Lavater. Among the buyers I notice one remarkable individual, unpretending as to facial development, but whose costume presents a singular mixture of the equine and the piscine. Lo! his hat is tall and shiny, even as the hat of a frequenter of Newmarket and an *habitué* of Aldridge's Repository, and his eminently sporting-looking neckcloth is fastened with a horse-shoe pin; but then his sleeves are as the sleeves of a fishmonger, and his loins are girt with the orthodox blue apron appertaining, by a sort of masonic prescription, to his craft and mystery! His nether man, as far as the spring of the calf, is clad in the galligaskins of an ordinary citizen; but below the knee commence a pair of straight tight boots of undeniably sporting cut. Who is this marvellous compound of the fishy and "horsey" idiosyncrasies? Is he John Scott disguised as Izaak Walton? is he Flatman or Chifney? Tell me, Mr. Chubb, proprietor of the "Golden Perch;" tell me, "Ruff," mythical author of the "Guide to the Turf"—for knowing not to which authority especially to appeal, I appeal to both, even as did the Roman maid-servant, who burnt one end of the candle to St. Catherine and the other to St. Nicholas (old St. Nicholas I mean, sometimes familiarised into "Nick"), in order to be on the safe side.

There are eight auctioneers or fish salesmen attached to the market, and they meet every morning between four and five o'clock at one of the principal public-houses, to discuss the quantity and quality of fish about to be offered for sale. The three taverns are known as Bowler's, Bacon's, and Simpson's. The second of these is situated in the centre of the market, and is habitually used by the auctioneers, probably on account of the son of the proprietor being the largest consignee at Billingsgate.

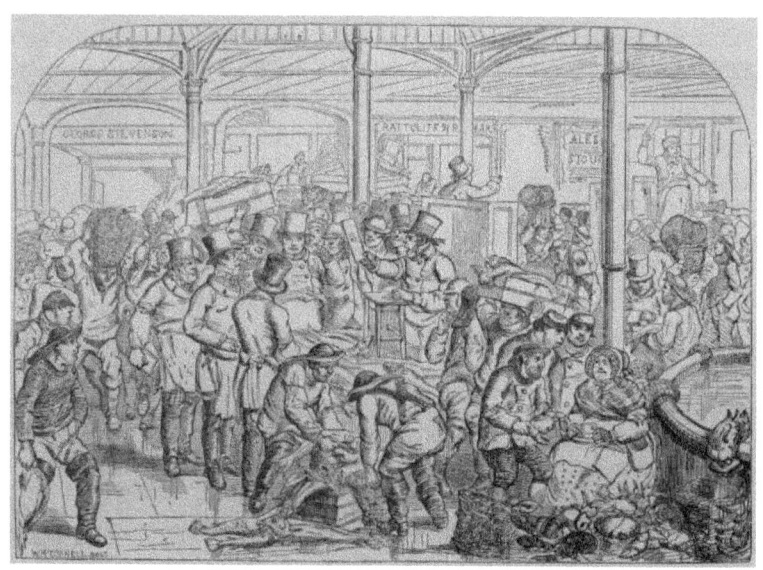

BILLINGSGATE: THE FISH SOLD BY AUCTION.

As the clock strikes five, the auctioneers disperse to their various boxes. Below each box are piled on "forms" or bulks the "doubles" of plaice, soles, haddock, whiting, and "offal." A "double" is an oblong basket tapering to the bottom, and containing from three to four dozen of fish; "offal" means odd lots of different kinds of fish, mostly small and broken, but always fresh and wholesome. When the auctioneer is ready, a porter catches up a couple of "doubles," and swings one on to each shoulder, and then the bids begin. Soles have been sold as low as four shillings the "double," and have fetched as high as three pounds. There is one traditional bid on record, which took place in the early part of the present century, of forty guineas per hundred for mackerel. Plaice ranges from one-and-sixpence to four shillings the double. The sale is conducted on the principle of what is termed a "Dutch auction," purchasers not being allowed to inspect the fish in the doubles before they bid. Offal is bought only by the "fryers." You may see, almost every market morning, a long, gaunt, greasy man, of that dubious age that you hesitate whether to call him youngish or oldish, with a signet ring on one little finger, and a staring crimson and yellow handkerchief round the collar of his not very clean checked shirt, buy from fifteen to twenty doubles of one kind or another; and in the season the *habitués* of the market say that he will purchase from twenty-five to thirty bushels of periwinkles and whelks. This monumental "doubler," this Rothschild of the offal tribe, resides in Somers Town. To him resort to purchase stock those innumerable purveyors of fried fish who make our courts and bye-streets redolent with the oleaginous perfumes of their hissing cauldrons. For the convenience of small dealers, who cannot afford to buy an entire double, stands are erected at different parts of the market for "bumbarees." We may ask in vain, *undè derivatur*, for the meaning of the term, though it is probably of Dutch origin. Any one can be a bumbaree: it requires neither apprenticeship, diploma, nor license, and it is the *pons asinorum* of the "mystery of fishmongers." The career is open to all; which, considering the difficulty of settling one's children in life, must be rather a gratifying reflection for parents. The process of bumbareeing is very simple. It consists in buying as largely as your means will afford of an auctioneer, hiring a stall for sixpence, and retailing the fish at a swingeing profit. I think that if I were not a landed gentleman, a Middlesex magistrate, and a member of the Court of Lieutenancy—vainly endeavouring, meanwhile, to ascertain my parochial settlement, in order to obtain admission to a workhouse as an unable-bodied pauper—that I should like to be a bumbaree.

Plaice, soles, haddocks (fresh), skate, maids, cod, and ling (the two last-mentioned fish in batches of threes and fours, with a string passed through the gills), are the only fish sold by auction. Fresh herrings are sold from the vessel by the long hundred (130). They are counted from the hold to the buyers in "warp" fives. Twopence per hundred is charged to bring them on shore. Eels are sold by the "draft" of twenty pounds weight—the price of the draft varying from three shillings to fifteen. Twopence per draft is paid for "shoreing" or landing the fish from the vessels. Sprats are sold on board the ships by the bushel. A "tindal" is a thousand bushels of sprats. When we come to consider the vast number of these oily, savoury little fishes that a bushel will contain, the idea of a "tindal" of them seems perfectly Garagantuan; yet many "tindals" of them are sold every week during the winter season—for the consumption of sprats among the poorer classes is enormous. What says the Muse of the Bull at Somers Town—what sweet stanzas issue from the anthology of Seven Dials?—

"O! 'tis my delight on a Friday night,

When sprats they isn't dear,

To fry a couple of score or so

Upon a fire clear.

"They eats so well, they bears the bell

From all the fish I knows:

Then let us eat them while we can,

Before the price is rose."

(Chorus—ad libitum) "O! 'tis my delight," &c.

The last two lines are replete with the poetry and philosophy of the poorer classes: "Let us eat them while we can, before the price is rose;" for even sprats are sometimes luxuries unattainable by the humble. Exceedingly succulent sprats labour under the disadvantage of being slightly unwholesome. To quote Mr. Samuel Weller's anecdote of the remark made by the young lady when remonstrating with the pastrycook who had sold her a pork pie which was all fat, sprats are "rayther too rich." And yet how delicious they are! I have had some passably good dinners in my time; I have partaken of *turbôt à la crême* at the Trois Frères Provençaux; I have eaten a *filet à la Chateaubriand* at Bignon's: yet I don't think there is a banquet in the whole repertory of Lucullus and Apicius—a more charming red-letter night in the calendar of gastronomy, than a sprat supper. You must have three pennyworth of sprats, a large tablecloth is indispensable for finger-wiping purposes—for he who would eat sprats with a knife and fork is unworthy the name of an epicure—and after the banquet I should recommend, for purely hygienic and antibilious reasons, the absorption of a *petit verre* of the best Hollands.

To return. As regards salmon, nine-tenths of the aristocratic fish are brought up by rail in barrels, and in summer packed in ice. Salmon and salmon-trout are not subjected to the humiliation of being "knocked down" by an auctioneer. They are disposed of "by private contract" at so much per pound.

Of dried and smoked fish of all kinds the best come from Yarmouth; but as regards the costermonger and street-vender—the modern "billestres," of dried haddocks, smoked sprats and herrings, entire or kippered—they are little affected by the state of the cured fish market so long as they can buy plenty of the fresh kind. The costermonger cures his fish himself in the following manner:—He builds a little shed like a watch-box, with wires across the upper part; and on this grating he threads his fish. Then he makes a fire on the floor of his impromptu curing-house with coal or mahogany dust, and smokes the fish "till done," as the old cookery books say. There is a dealer in the market to whom all fish-sellers bring the skins of departed soles. He gives fourpence-halfpenny a pound for them. They are used for refining purposes. And now for a word concerning the crustacea and the molluscs. Of oysters there are several kinds: Native Pearls, Jerseys, Old Barleys, and Commons. On board every oyster-boat a business-like gentleman is present, who takes care that every buyer of a bushel of oysters pays him fourpence. No buyer may carry his oysters ashore himself, be he ever so able and willing. There are regular "shoremen," who charge fourpence a bushel for their services; so that whatever may be the market-price of oysters, the purchaser must pay, *nolens volens*, eightpence a bushel over and above the quoted rate.

Of mussels there are three kinds: Dutch, Exeters, and Shorehams. They are brought to market in bags, of the average weight of three hundredweight; each bag containing about one hundred and sixty quarts, inclusive of dirt and stones. They are sold at from five shillings to seven shillings a bag. Of periwinkles—or, as they are more popularly and familiarly termed, "winkles"—there are four sorts: Scotch, Clays, Isle of Wights, and Maidens. They are sold by the bushel, or by the "level" or gallon. Crabs are sold by the "kit" (a long shallow basket) and by the score. Lobsters by the score and the double.

At the "Cock," in Love Lane, and at the "White Hart," in Botolph Lane, there is a boiling-house in the rear of the premises. Each boiling-house consists of a spacious kitchen filled with immense cauldrons. Here winkle and whelk buyers, who have neither utensils nor convenient premises sufficient to boil at home, can have it done for them for fourpence a bushel. Each boiling is performed separately in a wicker-basket; crabs and lobsters may likewise be boiled at these houses. Half-a-dozen scores of the fish are packed in a large basket, shaped like a strawberry-pottle, a lid is put between each lot, and the hot-water torture is inflicted at the rate of sixpence a score.

If your servant, the writer, were not precluded by the terms of his contract from taking any natural rest, he might, pleading fatigue, retire to bed; and, tossing on an unquiet couch, as men must do who slip between the sheets when the blessed sun is shining, have fantastic dreams of Ned Ward and Sir William Walworth: dream of the market-scene in "Masaniello," and hum a dream-reminiscence of "Behold, how brightly beams the morning!" which, of course, like all things appertaining to dreams, has no more resemblance to the original air than the tune the cow died of. Then fancy that he is a supernumerary in a pantomime, and that Mr. Flexmore, the clown, has jumped upon his shoulders, and is beating him about the ears with a "property" codfish. Then he might be Jonah, swallowed by the whale; and then Tobit's fish. Then he would find himself half awake, and repeating some lines he remembered reading years ago, scrawled in ink on a huge placard outside the shop of Mr. Taylor, the famous fishmonger, in Lombard Street. Yes: they ran thus—

"So the 'Times' takes an interest in the case of Geils;

I wish it would take some in my eels!"

What a queer fish Mr. Taylor must have been! Where is he now? Why, he (your servant) is Taylor—Jeremy Taylor—Tom Taylor—Taylor the water-poet—Billy Taylor—the Three Tailors of Tooley Street—Mr. Toole, the toast-master of arts and buttered toast; and—he is asleep!

FIVE O'CLOCK A.M.—THE PUBLICATION OF THE "TIMES" NEWSPAPER.

"There she is—the great engine—she never sleeps. She has her ambassadors in every quarter of the world—her couriers upon every road. Her officers march along with armies, and her envoys walk into statesmen's cabinets. They are ubiquitous. Yonder Journal has an agent at this minute giving bribes at Madrid; and another inspecting the price of potatoes at Covent Garden."

"Pendennis."

If you have no objection to the statement of the fact, I would beg to observe that our present station on the clock face, twice round which we have to go, is now five in the morning; and that at five a.m. the publication of the "Times" newspaper is, to use a north-country mining expression, in "full blast." You abhor the politics of the journal in question, you say: you consider the "Times" and "Evening Mail" to be the organ of a company, with limited liability, composed of the Emperor Alexander, Cardinal Wiseman, Baron Rothschild, Prince Aali Pacha, Metternich, Doctor Cumming, Baring Brothers, Lord Palmerston, Mr. Disraeli, Mr. W. J. Fox, and Miss Martineau. You are offended with the "Times" because the editor declined to insert that last six-paged letter from you against organ grinding. Never mind, you must come all the same to see the paper published. For the publication of the "Times" is a great, an enormous, a marvellous fact: none the less wonderful for being repeated three hundred and thirteen times a-year. It is a pulsation of London's mighty heart, that should not be neglected. It is the daily booming of a tocsin, which, year after year, proclaims progress, and still progress to the nations; which is the joy bell to the good, the passing bell to the bad, the world is blessed or cursed with; which rings out ignorance and prejudice and superstition, and rings in knowledge and enlightenment and truth. The "Times" is not alone in the possession of a peal of bells of this kind; and many daily, more weekly, papers ring out, loud and clear, to eager listeners; were your vassal not one of the modestest of men, he would hint that for the last dozen years he has been agitating daily and weekly a little tintinnabulum with what lustiness his nerveless arm will let him. But hard by St. Paul's, the cathedral of Anglicanism, is Printing House Square, the cathedral of Journalism, and in it hangs a bell to which Great Tom of Lincoln, Peter of York, the Kolokol of Moscow, and our own defunct "Big Ben," are but as tinkling muffineers. For though the sides of the bell are only paper, the clapper is the great public tongue; the booming sound that fills the city every morning, and, to use the words of Mr. Walter Whitman, "utters its barbaric youp over the house-tops of creation," is the great Public Voice. Bottle up your animosities, then, stifle your prejudices, and come and hear the voice's first faint murmur at five o'clock in the morning.

The office of the "Times" and "Evening Mail" is, as all civilised men should know, situated in Printing House Square and Playhouse Yard, in the parish of St. Ann's, Blackfriars, in the city of London. Now this is very pleasant and comfortable information, and is fit matter for a studious man to lay to heart; and there exists but one little drawback to mar the felicity which one must naturally feel at having the style and title of the press's great champions' *habitat* so patly at one's fingers' ends. The drawback—the kink in the cable, the hyssop in the wine-cup, the thorn to the rose—is that, with the exception of Honey Lane market and Little Chester Street, Pimlico, Printing House Square is the most difficult locality to find in all London. It is not much use asking your way to it; a map of London, however elaborate, would not be of the slightest assistance to you in discovering it: it will avail you little even to be told that it is close to Apothecaries' Hall, for where, I should like to know, is that huge musty caravanserai of drugs, and who is to find it at a short notice? And the intimation that Printing House Square is not far from Puddle Dock, would not, I opine, render you great service, intimate as might be your acquaintance with the shores of the river, both above and below bridge, and would be scarcely more lucid a direction than the intimation that the London terminus of the South-Western Railway was close to Pedlars' Acre. The "Times" newspaper is somewhere near all these places; and it is likewise within a stone's throw from Ludgate Hill, and not far from St. Paul's, and within a minute's walk of Fleet Street, and contiguous to Blackfriars Bridge, close handy to Earl Street, and no great distance from Chatham Place. Yet, for all this, the "Times" office might be, to the uninitiated, just as well placed in the centre of the Cretan labyrinth, or the maze at Hampton Court, or the budget of a Chancellor of the Exchequer. The best way to reach the office is to take any turning to the south side of London Bridge, or the east of Bridge Street, Blackfriars, and then trust to chance. The probabilities are varied. Very likely you will find yourself entangled in a seemingly hopeless net-work of narrow streets; you will be jostled into chandlers' shops, vilified by boys unctuous, black, and reeking from the printing-machine; pursued by costermongers importuning you to purchase small parcels of vegetables; and, particularly after sundown, your life will be placed in jeopardy by a Hansom cab bouncing up or down the narrow thoroughfare, of course on its way to the "Times" office, and on an errand of life and death; the excited politician inside, frantically offering the cabman (he, even, doesn't know the way to the "Times," and has just asked it of a grimy cynic, smoking a pipe in front of a coal and potato shed) extra shillings for speed. The grimy cynic, perhaps from sheer malevolence of disposition, perhaps from the ruffling of his temper naturally incidental to his being asked the same question about five hundred times every day, answers morosely that he believes the Hoffice is in Bummondsey, but he's blest if he knows hanything more about it. He will have bad times of it, that grimy cynic, I perpend, for telling such fibs. Still struggle on manfully, always like the nautical gentleman in the blue pilot jacket who had had so many domestic afflictions, and exhorted the passenger to "go down, go down." Never mind the regiments of gallinacea that board in the gutter and lodge in the adjacent coal-cellars, and peck at your feet as though they could relish your corns. Never mind the infants of tender years who come tumbling between your legs, sprawl, howling, at your feet, and cast around appealing glances, which draw cries of "shame!" from vengeful family-men who have never set eyes on you before, but who evidently regard you as a peripatetic ogre, going about, of malice prepense, to trip up children. Never mind the suffocating odour of second-hand fish, vegetables, fruit, coal-dust, potato sacks, the adjacent gasworks, gum-benzoin, hartshorn, opium, and other medicaments from Apothecaries' Hall. Never mind the noises of dogs barking, of children that are smacked by their parents or guardians for crying, and then, of course, roar louder; of boys yelling the insufferable "Old Dog Tray," the abominable "Keemo Kimo," the hideous "Hoomtoomdoodendoo," and rattling those abhorrent instruments of discord, the "bones;" of women scolding, quarrelling, or shrieking domestic calumnies of Mrs. Armstrong in connection with Bill Boosker, nicknamed the "Lively Flea," from garret-windows across the street; of men growling, and wagon-wheels rumbling, and from distant forges the yell of the indignant anvil as the ruthless hammer smites it, and the great bar of iron is beaten flat, the sparks flying up, rejoicing in a red "ha-ha!" at the ferruginous defeat. Never mind the dangers of hoop, "hopscotch," "fly-the-garter," "thread-the-needle," "trip-the-baker," "tipcat," and "shove-halfpenny," for the carrying out of which exciting and amusing games the juvenile population entirely monopolise what spare strips of pavement there are. Trust on, be not afraid, keep struggling; and it is five hundred to one that you will eventually turn up Printing House Square, over against the "Times" office. How ever the leviathan of the press manages to breathe in this close, stifling, elbow-hampering neighbourhood, has always puzzled me, and has puzzled, I daresay, a great many wiser than I. How do the archbishops in their coaches and six (it is well known that those gorgeous prelates write the leading articles, carrying the necessary stationery in their mitres, and wiping their pens on their black silk aprons—the B—p of O—x—d, however, always writes with a pastoral crozier, dipped in milk and honey, or a lamb's fleece—and come down to the office at a quarter past nine every evening to correct their proofs) contrive to squeeze their broad-shouldered equipages through these bye-lanes? How can the sub-editor's four-in-hand pass, the city correspondent's comfortable yellow chariot, nay, even the modest broughams of the compositors? Why does not the "Times" burst forth from the shell it has grown too large for, and plant its standard on the hill of Ludgate, or by the side of Cheap,—if it must needs be in the city? The area of Lincoln's Inn Fields would be perhaps the most suitable locality for a new office; but it is indubitable that unless the "leading journal" retrogress and contract its operation, they will have, some day, to pull down the choking little nests of back-streets which surround and hem it in, even as they had to pull down the wall of the dock, bodily, in order to let the *Great Britain* steamship out.

What a contrast sequestered Printing House Square, with its old-fashioned aspect, its quiet, dingy-looking houses, its clump of green trees within a railing to the left, presents to the gurgling, gasping neighbourhood which stands in such close propinquity to it! Here is the great brainpan of journalism; the centre of newspaper activity, the prefecture of police of the public press. Absolutely necessary is it that it should be entirely a secret police, the "awful, shadowy, irresponsible, and yet *puissant* we" should dominate over the columns of the daily journal. Will a time ever come, I wonder, when a man will sign his own articles in a newspaper; receive his reward for honesty, his censure for tergiversation, from the public? Will a strange day of revolution ever arrive, when the mystic "we" shall be merged into the responsible, tax-paying, tangible, palpable, shootable, suicidable, and kickable "I?" Perhaps never; perhaps such a consummation would be disastrous. Old Cobbett, in one of his screeds of passionate contempt in his "gridiron" paper the "Register," once said that he should like to have all the newspaper editors and correspondents in London assembled in Hyde Park, in order that from their personal appearance the public might judge by what a disreputable-looking set of fellows they were hoodwinked and nose-led. There would be no need to hold such a gathering in this scene-painting age. Walk but into any fashionable photographic studio, and you shall find all the "sommités" of the press neatly collectionised, and stuck on pasteboard in the show-room portfolio; and if you entreat the photographer's pretty wife civilly, she will point out to you Doctor Copperbolt of the "Thunderer," and Bill Hornblower of the "Penny Trumpet," in their habit as they live.

Printing House Square is to me interesting at all times of the day and night. In the afternoon, the dullest period of its existence, when the compositors are gone away, the editors not come, the last number of the last edition of the day's sheet printed, and the mighty steam-engine for a time hushed, I wander into its precincts often; make some small pretexts of taking out a slip of paper, and wending my way towards the advertising department; but soon retrace my steps, and, to tell the truth, moon about the square in such a suspicious and prowling manner, that if they kept any spoons on the premises, I should most probably be ordered off by the compositor on duty. This was Playhouse Yard too, once, was it—nay, is still; but where is the old playhouse—the Globe Theatre, Blackfriars, if I mistake not? Not a vestige, not a particle remains. The fourth estate has swallowed it all up. The Press Dragon of Wantley has devoured everything; and the "Times" seems omnipotent in its home by Puddle Dock. Look over the door of the advertisement office. Above that portal is a handsome marble slab, a votive tablet, in commemoration of a great victory the "Times" once gained, not a legal victory, but one of power and influence with the people, and especially with the commercial community, by its exposure, anent the trial of Bogle *v.* Lawson, of the most extensive and remarkable fraudulent conspiracy ever brought to light in the mercantile world. The "Times" refused to be reimbursed for the heavy costs with which its proprietors had been saddled in defending the action brought by Mr. Bogle, a banker at Florence, against the publisher of the "Times," Mr. Lawson. But a subscription, amounting to £2,700, had been raised, and this handsome sum, which the "Times" proprietors refused to accept, was at last laid out in the foundation of two scholarships at Christ's Hospital and the City of London School, for the benefit of pupils of those institutions proceeding to the universities of Oxford and Cambridge. Do you remember—are you old enough to remember—the famous case of Bogle *versus* Lawson, reader? It would take me five times the space I can spare for this paper to give you even the outline of the history of the monstrous fraud from which that action grew. Suffice it now to say, that Mr. Bogle had been mixed up—it has been since established innocently—in the great continental letter of credit forging system, invented, carried out, and pursued with consummate success by an accomplished scoundrel, the Marquis de Bourbel, who, when the felonious bubble at length burst, and the fraud was detected, was in nowise cast down or abashed by that discovery that had come, and the punishment that seemed imminent, but with admirable strategy called in his outlying pickets of countesses, actresses—*demi-monde* adventuresses—couriers, and sham English milords, who had been scouring the Continent changing his forged letters of credit, and, after the unutterable impudence of an appearance in court during the "Times" trial, gracefully retired into private life. I, the scribe, *moi qui vous parle*, have lived in the same house with this great man. It was at a hairdresser's shop in the Regent's Quadrant, and in an upper chamber of the house in question did the gallant marquis, assisted by a distinguished countess, who had formerly danced on stilts, and an English copper-plate engraver, work off the proofs of his wicked paper money from the counterfeited plates. I should like to know what became eventually of the Marquis de Bourbel: whether his lordship was, in the ripeness of his time, guillotined, garotted, hanged, or knouted. I go for Siberia and the knout, for, from the peculiar conformation of his lordship's character, I don't think it possible that he could have refrained for long from forgery. We should have heard of him, I think, had he come to grief in Western Europe; but Russian bank-notes are very easy to forge, and Russian prisons and prisoners are seldom brought before the public eye. They manage those little things better, and keep them nice and cozy and quiet; and so I go for Siberia and the knout.

It is, however, as the shades of evening gather round the *Cour des Miracles* which encompasses the "Times" office, that the scene which it and the Square present becomes more interesting. For early in the evening that giant steam-engine begins to throb, and, as the hour advances, the monster is fed with reams on reams of stout white paper, which he devours as though they were so many wafers.[1] It gets late at Printing House Square; the sub-editors have been for some time in their rooms; the ineffable mysteries of the "Times"—editors, proprietors, cabinet ministers, lord chancellors, generals of the Jesuits, for aught I know, have arrived from their clubs in broughams and in cabs. Who shall tell? That stout good-humoured looking gentleman with the umbrella and the ecclesiastical neckcloth, may be the writer of the comic leading articles, just arrived with his copy. No; he has vainly tried the door of the advertisement office, which is closed. Perhaps he is only X. Y. Z., who, in the second column, entreats P. Q. R. to return to his disconsolate parents; or the inventor of some new tooth-powder with a Greek name, or the discoverer of the "fourteen shilling trousers." It is getting later, and the windows of the great office are all blazing with gas. The steam-engine not only throbs; it pants, it groans, it puffs, it snorts, it bursts into a wild, clanging pæan of printing. Sub-editors are now hard at work cutting down "flimsy," ramming sheets of "copy" on files, endlessly conferring with perspiring foremen. Ineffable mysteries (I presume) are writing terribly slaughtering articles in carpeted rooms, by the light of Argand lamps. Do they have cake and wine, I wonder, in those rooms? Sherry and sandwiches, perhaps, and on field-nights lobsters. It is getting later, but there is no sign of diminution yet in the stream of cabs that drive into the Square. Every one who is in debt, and every one who is in difficulties, and everybody who fancies that he, or any friend, relation, or connection of his, has a grievance, and can put pen to paper, four letters together in orthography and four words in syntax, must needs write a letter to the "Times;" and of the metropolitan correspondents of that journal, the immense majority themselves bring their letters down to the office, thinking, haply, that they might meet the editor standing "promiscuous" on the door-step, and after some five minutes' button-holding, secure, irrevocably, the insertion of their communications. I don't at all envy the gentleman whose duty it is to open and read (do they read them all?) the letters addressed to the editor of the "Times". What quires of insane complaints, on matters running from the misdelivery of a letter to the misgovernment of India, from the iniquities of the income-tax to an overcharge for a sandwich in a country inn, that editor must have to wade through; what reams of silly compliments about "your influential journal," and "your world-known paper," he must have to read, and grin in his sleeve at! What a multitudinous army, what a Persian host, these correspondents must be! Who are they?—the anonymous ones—what are they like? Who is "Verax?" who "Paterfamilias?" who "Indophilus?" who "The London

Scoundrel?" who "A Thirsty Soul?" When will Mr. Herbert Watkins photograph me a collection of portraits of "Constant Readers," "Englishmen," and "Hertfordshire Incumbents?" Where is the incumbency of that brilliant writer? Who is "*Habitans in Sicco*," and how came he first to date from the "Broad Phylactery?" and where does "Jacob Omnium" live when he is at home? I should like to study the physiognomy of these inveterate letter writers; to be acquainted with the circumstances which first led them to put pen to paper in correspondence with the "Times;" to know how they like to see themselves in print, and also how they feel, when, as happens with lamentable frequency, their lucubrations don't get printed at all.

PUBLICATION OF THE "TIMES" NEWSPAPER: INSIDE THE OFFICE.

PUBLICATION OF THE "TIMES" NEWSPAPER: OUTSIDE THE OFFICE.

It is getting later and later, oh! anxious waiters for to-morrow's news. The "Times" has its secrets by this time. State secrets, literary secrets, secrets artistic and dramatic; secrets of robbery, and fire, and murder—it holds them all fast now, admitting none to its confidence but the Ineffables, the printers, and the ever-throbbing steam-engine; but it will divulge its secrets to millions at five o'clock to-morrow morning. Later and later still. The last report from the late debate in the Commons has come in; the last paragraph of interesting news, dropped into the box by a stealthy penny-a-liner, has been eliminated from a mass of flimsy on its probation, and for the most part rejected; the foreign telegrams are in type; the slaughtering leaders glare in their "chases," presaging woe and disaster to ministers to-morrow; the last critic, in a white neckcloth, has hurried down with his column and a-half on the last new spectacle at the Princess's; or has, which very frequently happens, despatched that manuscript from the box at the "Albion," where he has been snugly supping, bidding the messenger hasten, and giving him to procure a cab the sum of one extra shilling, which that messenger never by any chance expends in vehicular conveyance, but runs instead with the art-criticism, swift as the timid roe, so swift indeed, that policemen are only deterred through chronic laziness from pursuing and asking whether he hasn't been stealing anything. By this time the "Times" has become tight and replete with matter, as one who has dined well and copiously. Nothing is wanting: city correspondence, sporting intelligence, markets, state of the weather, prices of stocks and railway shares, parliamentary summary, law and police reports, mysterious advertisements, and births, deaths, and marriages. Now let the nations wonder, and the conductors of the mangy little continental fly-sheets of newspapers hide their heads in shame, for the "Times"—the mighty "Times"—has "gone to bed." The "forms," or iron-framed and wedged-up masses of type, are, in other words, on the machine; and, at the rate of twelve thousand an hour, the damp broad sheets roll from the grim iron instrument of the dissemination of light throughout the world.

At five o'clock a.m., the first phase of the publication of the "Times" newspaper commences. In a large bare room—something like the receiving ward of an hospital—with a pay counter at one end, and lined throughout with parallel rows of bare deal tables, the "leading journal" first sees the light of publicity. The tables are covered with huge piles of newspapers spread out the full size of the sheet. These are, with dazzling celerity, folded by legions of stout porters, and straightway carried to the door, where cabs, and carts, and light express phæton-like vehicles, are in readiness to convey them to the railway stations. The quantity of papers borne to the carriages outside by the stout porters seems, and truly is, prodigious; but your astonishment will be increased when I tell you that this only forms the stock purchased every morning by those gigantic newsagents, Messrs. Smith and Son, of the Strand. As the largest consumers, the "Times" naturally allows them a priority of supply, and it is not for a considerable period after they have received their orders that the great body of newsagents and newsvenders—the "trade," as they are generically termed—are admitted, grumbling intensely, to buy the number of quires or copies which they expect to sell or lend that day. The scene outside then becomes one of baffling noise and confusion. There is a cobweb of wheeled vehicles of all sorts, from a cab to a hybrid construction something between a wheelbarrow and a costermonger's shallow. There is much bawling and flinging, shoving, hoisting, pulling and dragging of parcels; all the horses' heads seem to be turned the wrong way; everybody's off-wheel seems locked in somebody else's; but the proceedings on the whole are characterised by much good-humour and some fun. The mob of boys—all engaged in the news-trade—is something wonderful: fat boys, lean boys, sandy-haired and red-haired boys, tall boys and short boys, boys with red comforters (though it is summer), and boys with sacks on their backs and money-bags in their hands; boys with turn-down collars; and boys whose extreme buttonedupness renders the fact of their having any shirts to put collars to, turn-down or stuck-up, grievously problematical. Hard-working boys are these juvenile Bashi-Bazouks of the newspaper trade. And I am glad to observe, for the edification of social economists, with scarcely an exception, very honest boys. I don't exactly say that they are trusted with untold gold, but of the gold that is told, to say nothing of the silver and copper, they give a generally entirely satisfactory account. At about half-past seven the cohorts of newsvenders, infantry and cavalry, gradually disperse, and the "Times" is left to the agonies of its second edition.

As you walk away from Printing House Square in the cool of the morning, and reflect, I hope with salutary results, upon the busy scene you have witnessed, just bestow one thought, and mingle with it a large meed of admiration, for the man who, in his generation, truly made the "Times" what it is now—John Walter, of Bearwood, Member of Parliament. Foul-mouthed old Cobbett called him "Jack Walters," and him and his newspaper many ungenteel names, predicting that he should live to see him "earthed," and to "spit upon his grave;" but he survived the vituperative old man's coarse epithets. He put flesh on the dry bones of an almost moribund newspaper. He, by untiring and indomitable energy and perseverance, raised the circulation of the "Times" twenty-fold, and put it in the way of attaining the gigantic publicity and popularity which it has now achieved. It is true that Mr. Walter realised a princely fortune by his connection with the "Times," and left to his son, the present Mr. John Walter, M.P., a lion's share in the magnificent inheritance he had created. But he did much solid good to others besides himself. This brave old pressman, who, when an express came in from Paris—the French king's speech to the Chambers in 1835—and when there were neither contributors nor compositors to be found at hand, bravely took off his coat, and in his shirt-sleeves first translated, and then, taking "a turn at case," proceeded to set up in type his own manuscript. Mr. Walter was one of the pioneers of liberal knowledge; and men like him do more to clear the atmosphere of ignorance and prejudice, than whole colleges full of scholiasts and dialecticians.

SIX O'CLOCK A.M.—COVENT GARDEN MARKET.

An Emperor will always be called Cæsar, and a dog "poor old fellow," in whatever country they may reign or bark, I suppose; and I should be very much surprised if any men of Anglo-Saxon lineage, from this time forward to the millennium, could build a new city in any part of either hemisphere without a street or streets named after certain London localities, dear and familiar to us all. There is a Pall Mall in Liverpool, though but an unsavoury little thoroughfare, and a Piccadilly in Manchester—a very murky, bricky street indeed, compared with that unequalled hill of London, skirted on one side by the mansions of the nobles, and on the other by the great green parks. Brighton has its Bond Street—*mutatus ab ille*, certainly, being a fourth-rate skimping little place, smelling of oyster-shells, sand, recently-washed linen, and babies. I question not but in far-off Melbourne and Sydney, and scarcely yet planned cities of the Bush, the dear old names are springing up, like shoots from famous trees. Antipodean legislators have a refreshment room they call "Bellamy's;" merchants in far-off lands have their "Lloyd's;" there are coffee-houses and taverns, thousands of miles away, christened "Joe's," and "Tom's," and "Sam's," though the original "Joe," the primeval "Tom," the first "Sam," most bald-headed and courteous of old port-wine-wise waiters, have long since slept the sleep of the just in quiet mouldy London graveyards, closed years ago by the Board of Health. On very many names, and names alone, we stamp *esto perpetua*; and English hearts would ill brook the alteration of their favourite designations. Long, long may it be, I hope, before the great Lord Mayor of London shall be called the Prefect of the Thames, or the Secretary of State for the Home Department be known as the Minister of the Interior!

Foremost among names familiar to British mouths is Covent Garden. The provincial knows it; the American knows it; Lord Macaulay's New Zealander will come to meditate among the moss-grown arcades, when he makes that celebrated sketching excursion we have so long been promised. To the playgoer Covent Garden is suggestive of the glories of Kemble and Siddons; old book-a-bosom studious men, who live among musty volumes, remember that Harry Fielding wrote the "Covent Garden Journal;" that Mr. Wycherley lived in Bow Street; and that Mr. Dryden was cudgelled in Rose Street hard by. Politicians remember the *fasti* of the Westminster election, and how Mr. Sheridan, beset by bailiffs on the hustings, escaped through the churchyard. Artists know that Inigo Jones built that same church of St. Paul, in compliance with the mandate of his patron, the Earl of Bedford. "Build me a barn," said the Earl. Quoth Inigo, "My lord, I will build you the handsomest barn in England;" and the church is in the market to this day, with its barn-like roof, to see. Old stagers who have led jovial London lives, have yet chuckling memories of how in Covent Garden they were wont to hear the chimes at midnight in the days when they were eating their terms, and lay over against the "Windmill" in Moorfields, and consorted with the Bona Robas. Those days, Sir John Falstaff—those days, Justice Shallow, shall return no more to you. There was the "Finish,"—a vulgar, noisy place enough; but stamped with undying gentility by the patronage of his late Royal Highness the Prince of Wales. Great George "finished" in Covent Garden purlieus; Major Hanger told his stories, Captain Morris sang his songs, there. In a peaceable gutter in front of the "Finish," Richard Brinsley Sheridan, Esq., M.P., lay down overtaken in foreign wines, and told the guardian of the night that his name was Wilberforce. A wild place, that "Finish;" yet a better one than Great George's other "Finish" at Windsor, with the actress to read plays to him, the servants anxious for him to quit the stage, that they might sell his frogged, furred coats, and white kid pantaloons: the sorry end in a mean chair—unfriended, unloved, save by hirelings deserted. When the Hope of England is old enough to wear on his fair head the coronal and the three ostrich feathers, will *he* patronise a "Finish?" shall we have another wild young Prince and Poins, I wonder. To be sure, Mr. Thackeray tells us that the young nobles of the present age have "Spratts" and the "back kitchen" to finish up a night in; but, pshaw! the Hope of England takes the chair at the Royal Institution to hear Mr. Faraday lecture, and sits on the bench beside John Lord Campbell to see rogues tried.

Covent Garden is a very chain, and its links are pleasant reminiscences. They are somewhat dangerous to me, for my business is not antiquarian, nor even topographical, just now; and I have but to do with the sixth hour of the morning, and the vegetable market that is held in the monks' old garden. I will dismiss the noble house of Bedford, though Covent Garden, &c., are the richest appanage of that ducal entity—simply recording a wish that you or I, my friend, had one tithe of the fat revenues that ooze from between the bricks of the Bedford estate. You should not dig, nor I delve, then. We would drink brown ale, and pay the reckoning on the nail, and no man for debt should go to jail, that we could help, from Garryowen to glory. I will say nothing to you of the old theatre: how it was burnt again and again, and always re-appeared, with great success on the part of Phœnix. Of Bow Street, even, will I be silent, and proffer nought of Sir Richard Birnie, or that famed runner, Townsend. Nor of the Garrick Club, in King Street, will I discourse; indeed, I don't know that I am qualified to say anything pertinent respecting that establishment. I am not a member of the club; and I am afraid of the men in plush, who, albeit aristocratic, have yet a certain "Garrick" look about them, and must be, I surmise, the prosperous brothers of the "green-coats" who sweep and water the stage, and pick up Sir Anthony Absolute's hat and crutch in the play. And scant dissertations shall you have from me on those dim days of old, when Covent Garden was in verity the garden of a convent; when matins and vespers, complins and benedictions, were tinkled out in mellow tintinnabulations through the leafy aisles of fruit trees; when my Lord Abbot trod the green sward, stately, his signet-ring flashing in the evening sun; and Brother Austin hated Friar Lawrence, and cursed him softly as he paced the gravel walks demurely, his hands in his brown sleeves, his eyes ever and anon cast up to count the peaches on the wall. Solemn old conventual days, with shrill-voiced choir-boys singing from breves and minims as big as latch-keys, scored in black and red on brave parchment music-tomes. Lazy old conventual days, when the cellarer brewed October that would give Messrs. Bass and Allsopp vertigo; when the poor were fed with a manchet and stoup at the gate, without seeking the relieving officer, or an order for the stoneyard. Comfortable old days, when the Abbot's *venator* brought in a fat buck from Sheen or Chertsey, the *piscator* fresh salmon (the water-drops looked like pearls on their silvery backs). Comfortable old days of softly-saddled palfreys, venison pasties, and Malvoisie, sandalled feet, and shaven crowns, bead-telling, and censor-swinging. These were the days of the lazy monks in their Covent Garden. Lazy! They were lazy enough to illuminate the exquisitely beautiful missals and books of hours you may see in the British Museum; to feed, and tend, and comfort the poor, and heal them when they were sick; to keep art and learning from decay and death in a dark age; to build cathedrals, whose smallest buttress shall make your children's children, Sir Charles Barry, blush; but they were the lazy monks—so let us cry havoc upon them. They were shavelings. They didn't wash their feet, they aided and abetted Guy Fawkes, Ignatius Loyola, and the Cardinal Archbishop of ——.

It is six o'clock on a glorious summer's morning; the lazy monks fade away like the shadows of the night, and leave me in Covent Garden, and in high market. Every morning during the summer may be called market morning; but in the winter the special mornings are Tuesday, Thursday, and Saturday. It is a strange sight then in the winter blackness to see the gas glimmering among huge piles of vegetables hoisted high on carts, and slowly moving like Birnam Woods coming to a Dunsinane of marketdom. When the snow is on the ground, or when the rain it raineth, the glare of lights and black shadows; the rushing figures of men with burdens; the great heaving masses of baskets that are tumbled from steep heights; the brilliantly-lighted shops in the grand arcade, where, winter or summer, glow the oranges and the hot-house fruits and flowers; all these make up a series of pictures, strange and sometimes almost terrible. There are yawning cellars, that vomit green stuff; there are tall potato-sacks, propped up in dark corners, that might contain corpses of murdered men; there are wondrous masses of light and shade, and dazzling effects of candlelight, enough to make old Schkalken's ghost rise, crayon and sketch-book in hand, and the *eidolon* of Paul Rembrandt to take lodgings in the Piazza, over against the market.

COVENT GARDEN MARKET: THE WEST END.

But six o'clock in the glorious summer time! The London smoke is not out of bed yet, and indeed Covent Garden market would at all times seem to possess an exemption from over fumigation. If you consider the fronts of the houses, and the arches of the Piazza, you will see that though tinted by age, they have not that sooty grimness that degrades St. Paul's cathedral into the similitude of a temple dedicated to the worship of the goddess of chimney-sweepers, and makes the East India House (what will they do with the India House when the directors are demolished?) look like the outside of the black-hole at Calcutta. Smoke has been merciful to Covent Garden market, and its cornucopia is not as dingy as a ramoneur's sack. All night long the heavily-laden wagons—mountains of cabbages, cauliflowers, brocoli, asparagus, carrots, turnips, and seakale; Egyptian pyramids of red-huddled baskets full of apples and pears, hecatombs of cherries, holocausts of strawberry pottles, chair wicker bosoms crimsoned by sanguinolent spots; and above all, piles, heaps—Pelions on Ossas, Atlases on Olympuses, Chimborazos on Himalayas, Mount Aboras on Mont Blancs—of PEAS, have been creaking and rumbling and heavily wheezing along suburban roads, and through the main streets of the never-sleeping city. You heard those broad groaning wheels, perturbed man, as your head tossed uneasily on the pillow, and you thought of the bill that was to come due on the morrow. You too heard them, pretty maiden, in the laced night cap, as you bedewed that delicate border of dentelle with tears, coursing from the eyes which should have been closed in sleep two hours since, tears evoked by the atrocious behaviour of Edward (a monster and member of the Stock Exchange) towards Clara (a designing, wicked, artful thing, whose papa lives in Torrington Square) during the last *deux temps*. That dull heavy sound was distinct above the sharp rattle of the night cabmen's wheels; the steady revolving clatter of the home-returning brougham: for the sound of wheels in London are as the waves of a sea that is never still. The policemen met the market wagons as they trudged along, and eyed them critically, as though a neat case of lurking about with intent to commit a felony might be concealed in a strawberry-pottle, or a drunk and incapable lying perdu in a pea-basket. Roaring blades, addicted to asserting in chorus that they would not go home till morning—a needless vaunt, for it was morning already—hailed the bluff-visaged market carters, interchanged lively jocularities with them bearing on the syrup giving rhubarb and the succulent carrot, and lighted their pipes at the blackened calumets of the vegetarians. Young Tom Buffalo, who had been out at a christening party at Hammersmith, and had made the welkin ring (whatever and wherever the welkin may be, and howsoever the process of making it ring be effected) met a gigantic cabbage-chariot, as home returning, precisely at that part of Knightsbridge where Old Padlock House used to stand, and struck a bargain with the charioteer for conveyance to Charing Cross, for fourpence, a libation of milk, qualified by some spirituous admixture, and a pipeful of the best Bristol bird's-eye. And so from all outlying nursery-grounds and market-gardens about London: from Brompton, Fulham, Brentford, Chiswick, Turnham Green, and Kew; from sober Hackney, and Dalston, and Kingsland, bank-clerk beloved; from Tottenham, and Edmonton, sacred to John Gilpin, his hat and wig; from saintly Clapham and Brixton, equally interested in piety, sugar-baking, and the funds, come, too heavy to gallop, too proud to trot, but sternly stalking in elephantine dignity of progression, the great carts bound to Covent Garden. One would think that all the vegetable-dishes in the world would not be able to hold the cabbage, to say nothing of the other verdant esculents.

Delude not yourself with the notion that the market-carts alone can bring, or the suburban market-gardens furnish, a sufficient quantity of green meat for the great, insatiable, hungry, ravenous monster that men call (and none know why) London. Stand here with me in Covent Garden market-place, and let your eyes follow whither my finger points. Do you see those great vans, long, heavily-built, hoisted on high springs, and with immense wheels—vans drawn by horses of tremendous size and strength, but which, for all their bulk and weight, seem to move at a lightning pace compared with the snail crawl of the ancient market-carts? Their drivers are robust men, fresh-coloured, full-whiskered, strong-limbed, clad in corduroy shining at the seams, with bulging pockets, from which peep blotting-paper, interleaved books of invoices, and parcels receipts. They are always wiping their hot foreheads with red cotton pocket-handkerchiefs. They are always in such a hurry. They never can wait. Alert in movement, strong in action, hardy in speech, curt and quick in reply, setting not much store by policemen, and bidding the wealthiest potatoe salesman "look sharp;" these vigorous mortals discharge from their vans such a shower of vegetable missiles that you might almost fancy the bombardment of a new Sebastopol. "Troy," the old ballad tells us, "had a breed of stout bold men;" but these seem stouter and bolder. And they drive away, these stalwart, bold-spoken varlets, standing erect in their huge vans, and adjuring, by the name of "slow coach," seemingly immoveable market-carts to "mind their eye;" wearing out the London macadam with their fierce wheels, to the despair of the commissioners of paving (though my private opinion is, that the paving commissioners like to see the paving worn out, in order that they may have the "street up" again); threading their way in a surprisingly dexterous though apparently reckless manner through the maze of vehicles, and finding themselves, in an astonishingly short space of time, in Tottenham Court Road, and Union Street, Borough. What gives these men their almost superhuman velocity, strength, confidence? They do but carry cabbages, like other market-folk; but look on the legends inscribed on these vans, and the mystery is at once explained. "Chaplin and Home," "Pickford and Co.," railway carriers. These vegetable Titans are of the rail, and raily. They have brought their horns of plenty from the termini of the great iron roads. Carts and carts, trucks and trucks have journeyed through the dense night, laden with vegetable produce; locomotives have shrieked over Chatmoss, dragging cabbages and carrots after them; the most distant counties have poured the fatness of their lands at the feet of the Queen-city; but she, like the daughter of the horse-leech, still cryeth, "Give! give!" and, like Oliver Twist, "asks for more." So they send her more, even from strange countries beyond the sea. Black steamers from Rotterdam and Antwerp belch forth volumes of smoke at the Tower stairs, and discharge cargoes of peas and potatoes. The Queen-city is an hungered, and must be fed; and it is no joke, I need scarcely tell you, to feed London. When the King of Siam has resolved upon the ruin of a courtier, he makes him a present of a white elephant. As the animal is thrice sacred in Siamese eyes, the luckless baillee, or garnishee, or possessor of the brute, dare neither sell, kill, nor neglect it; and the daily ration of rice, hay, and sugar which the albino monster devours, soon reduces the courtier to irremediable bankruptcy. Moral: avoid courts. If this were a despotic country, and her Majesty the Empress of Britain should take it into her head to ruin Baron Rothschild or the Marquis of Westminster (and indeed I have heard that the impoverished nobleman last mentioned is haunted by the fear of dying in a workhouse), I don't think she could more easily effect her purpose than by giving him LONDON and bidding him feed it for a week.

COVENT GARDEN MARKET: EARLY BREAKFAST STALL.

Very sweet is the smell of the green peas this summer morning; and very picturesque is it to see the market-women ranged in circles, and busily employed in shelling those delicious edibles. Some fastidious persons might perhaps object that the fingers of the shellers are somewhat coarse, and that the vessels into which the peas fall are rudely fashioned. What does it matter? If we took this fastidiousness with us into an analysis of all the things we eat and drink, we should soon fill up the measure of the title of Dr. Culverwell's book, by "avoiding" eating and drinking altogether. The delicate Havannah cigar has been rolled between the hot palms of oleaginous niggers; nay, some travellers declare, upon the bare thighs of sable wenches. The snowy lump-sugar has been refined by means of unutterable nastinesses of a sanguineous nature; the very daily bread we eat has, in a state of dough, formed the flooring for a vigorous polka, performed by journeymen bakers with bare feet. Food is a gift from heaven's free bounty: take Sancho Panza's advice, and don't look the gift-horse in the mouth. He may have false teeth. We ought to be very much obliged, of course, to those disinterested medical gentlemen who formed themselves into a sanitary commission, and analysing our dinners under a microscope, found that one-half was poison, and the other half rubbish; but, for my part, I like anchovies to be red and pickles green, and I think that coffee without chicory in it is exceedingly nasty. As for the peas, I have so fond a love for those delicious pulse that I could partake of them even if I knew they had been shelled by Miss Julia Pastrana. I could eat the shucks; I have eaten them indeed in Russia, where they stew pea-shells in a sweet sauce, and make them amazingly relishing.

But sweeter even than the smell of the peas, and more delightful than the odour of the strawberries, is the delicious perfume of the innumerable flowers which crowd the north-western angle of the market, from the corner of King Street to the entrance of the grand avenue. These are not hot-house plants, not rare exotics; such do not arrive so soon, and their aristocratic purchasers will not be out of bed for hours. These are simply hundreds upon hundreds of flower-pots, blooming with roses and geraniums, with pinks and lilacs, with heartsease and fuschias. There are long boxes full of mignionette and jessamine; there are little pet vases full of peculiar roses with strange names; there are rose-trees, roots and all, reft from the earth by some floral Milo who cared not for the rebound. The cut flowers, too, in every variety of dazzling hue, in every gradation of sweet odour, are here, jewelling wooden boards, and making humble wicker-baskets iridescent. The violets have whole rows of baskets to themselves. Who is it that calls the violet humble, modest? He (I will call him he) is nothing of the sort. He is as bold as brass. He comes the earliest and goes away the latest of all his lovely companions; like a guest who is determined to make the most of a banquet. When the last rose of summer, tired of blooming alone, takes his hat and skulks home, the modest violet, who has been under the table for a great part of the evening, wakes up, and calls for another bottle of dew—and the right sort.

It seems early for so many persons to be abroad, not only to sell but to purchase flowers, yet there is no lack of buyers for the perfumed stores which meet the eye, and well nigh impede the footsteps. Young sempstresses and milliner's girls, barmaids and shopwomen, pent up all day in a hot and close atmosphere, have risen an hour or two earlier, and make a party of pleasure to come to Covent Garden market to buy flowers. It is one of heaven's mercies that the very poorest manage somehow to buy these treasures; and he who is steeped to the lips in misery will have a morsel of mignionette in his window, or a bunch of violets in a cracked jug on his mantelshelf, even as the great lady has rich, savage, blooming plants in her conservatory, and camelias and magnolias in porphyry vases on marble slabs. It is a thin, a very thin, line that divides the independent poor from the pauper in his hideous whitewashed union ward: the power of buying flowers and of keeping a dog. How the halfpence are scraped together to procure the violets or mignionette, whence comes the coin that purchases the scrap of paunch, it puzzles me to say: but go where you will among the *pauperum tabernas* and you will find the dog and the flowers. Crowds more of purchasers are there yet around the violet baskets; but these are buyers to sell again. Wretched-looking little buyers are they, half-starved Bedouin children, mostly Irish, in faded and tattered garments, with ragged hair and bare feet. They have tramped miles with their scanty stock-money laid up in a corner of their patched shawls, daring not to think of breakfast till their purchases be made; and then they will tramp miles again through the cruel streets of London town, penetrating into courts and alleys where the sun never shines, peering into doorways, selling their wares to creatures almost as ragged and forlorn as themselves. They cry violets! They cried violets in good Master Herrick's time. There are some worthy gentlemen, householders and ratepayers, who would put all such street-cries down by Act of Parliament. Indeed, it must an intolerable sin, this piping little voice of an eight-years old child, wheezing out a supplication to buy a ha'porth of violets. But then mouthy gentlemen are all Sir Oracles; and where they are, no dogs must bark nor violets be cried.

It is past six o'clock, and high 'Change in the market. What gabbling! what shouting! what rushing and pushing! what confusion of tongues and men and horses and carts! The roadway of the adjacent streets is littered with fragments of vegetables. You need pick your way with care and circumspection through the crowd, for it is by no means pleasant to be tripped up by a porter staggering under a load of baskets, that look like a Leaning Tower of Pisa. Bow Street is blocked up by a triple line of costermongers' "shallows," drawn by woe-begone donkies; their masters are in the market purchasing that "sparrergrass" which they will so sonorously cry throughout the suburbs in the afternoon. They are also, I believe, to be put down by the worthy gentlemen who do not like noise. I wish they could put down, while they are about it, the chaffering of the money-changers in the temple, and the noise of the Pharisees' brushes as they whiten those sepulchres of theirs, and the clanging of the bells that summon men to thank Heaven that they are not "as that publican," and to burn their neighbour because he objects to shovel hats. King Street, Southampton Street, Russell Street, are full of carts and men. Early coffee-shops and taverns are gorged with customers, for the Covent Gardeners are essentially jolly gardeners, and besides, being stalwart men, are naturally hungry and athirst after their nights' labour. There are public-houses in the market itself, where they give you hot shoulder of mutton for breakfast at seven o'clock in the morning! Hot coffee and gigantic piles of bread-and-butter disappear with astounding rapidity. Foaming tankards are quaffed, "nips" of alcohol "to keep the cold out" (though it is May) are tossed off; and among the hale, hearty, fresh-coloured market-people, you may see, here and there, some tardy lingerer at "the halls of dazzling light," who has just crawled away from the enchanted scene, and, cooling his fevered throat with soda-water, or whipping up his jaded nerves with brandy and milk, fancies, because he is abroad at six o'clock in the morning, that he is "seeing life." Crouching and lurking about, too, for anything they can beg, or anything they can borrow, or, I am afraid, for anything they can steal, are some homeless, shirtless vagabonds, who have slept all night under baskets or tarpaulins in the market, and now prowl in and out of the coffee-shops and taverns, with red eyes and unshaven chins. I grieve to have to notice such unsightly blots upon the Arcadia I have endeavoured to depict; but, alas! these things ARE! You have seen a caterpillar crawling on the fairest rose; and this glorious summer sun must have spots on its face. There are worse on London's brow at six o'clock in the morning.

SEVEN O'CLOCK A.M.—A PARLIAMENTARY TRAIN.

I know that the part which I have proposed to myself in these papers is that of a chronological Asmodeus; you, reader, I have enlisted, *nolens volens*, to accompany me in my flights about town, at all hours of the day and night; and you must, perforce, hold on by the skirts of my cloak as I wing my way from quarter to quarter of the immense city, to which the Madrid which the lame fiend showed his friend was but a nut-shell. And yet, when I look my self-appointed task in the face, I am astounded, humiliated, almost disheartened, by its magnitude. How can I hope to complete it within the compass of this book, within the time allotted for daily literary labour? For work ever so hard as we penmen may, and rob ever so many hours from sleep as you may choose to compute—as we are forced to do sometimes—that you may have your pabulum of printed matter, more or less amusing and instructive, at breakfast time, or at afternoon club reading hour, we must yet eat, and drink, and sleep, and go into the world soliciting bread or favours, we must quarrel with our wives, if married, and look out the things for the wash, if single—all of which are operations requiring a certain expenditure of time. We must, we authors, even have time, an't please you, to grow ambitious, and to save money, stand for the borough, attend the board-room, and be appointed consuls-general to the Baratarian Islands. The old Grub Street tradition of the author is defunct. The man of letters is no longer supposed to write moral essays from Mount Scoundrel in the Fleet, to dine at twopenny ordinaries, and pass his leisure hours in night-cellars. Translators of Herodotus no longer lie three in a bed; nor is the gentleman who is correcting the proof-sheets of the Sanscrit dictionary to be found in a hay-loft over a tripe shop in Little Britain, or to be heard of at the bar of the Green Dragon. Another, and as erroneous, an idea of the author has sprung up in the minds of burgesses. He wears, according to some wiseacres, a shawl dressing-gown, and lies all day on a sofa, puffing a perfumed *narghilè*, penning paragraphs in violet ink on cream-laid paper at intervals; or he is a lettered Intriguer, who merely courts the Muses as the shortest way to the Treasury bench, and writes May Fair novels or Della Cruscan tragedies that he may the sooner become Prime Minister. There is another literary idea that may with greater reason become prevalent—that of the author-manufacturer, who produces such an amount of merchandise, takes it into the market, and sells it according to demand and the latest quotations, and the smoke of whose short cutty pipe, as he spins his literary yarn, is as natural a consequence of manufacture as the black cloud which gusts from Mr. Billyroller's hundred-feet-high brick chimney as he spins *his* yarns for madapolams and "domestics." The author-manufacturer has to keep his books, to pay his men, to watch the course of the market, and to suit his wares to the prevailing caprice. And, like the cotton-spinner, he sometimes goes into the "Gazette," paying but an infinitesimal dividend in the pound.

Did I not struggle midway into a phrase, some page or so since, and did it not waltz away from me on the nimble feet of a parenthesis? I fear that such was the case. How can I hope, I reiterate, to give you anything like a complete picture of the doings in London while still the clock goes round? I might take one house and unroof it, one street and unpave it, one man and disclose to you the secrets of twenty-four hours of his daily and nightly life; but it is London, in its entirety, that I have presumed to "time"—forgetting, oh! egregious and inconsistent!—that every minute over which the clock hand passes is as the shake of the wrist applied to a kaleidoscope, and that the whole aspect of the city changes with as magical rapidity.

I should be Briareus multiplied by ten thousand, and not Asmodeus at all, if I could set down in writing a tithe of London's sayings and doings, acts and deeds, seemings and aspects, at seven o'clock in the morning. Only consider. Drumming with your finger on a map of the metropolis; just measure a few palms' lengths, say from Camberwell Gate to the "Mother Redcap," on the one hand—from Limehouse Church to Kensington Gravel Pits, on the other. Take the cubic dimensions, my dear sir; think of the mean area; rub up those mathematics, for proficiency in whose more recondite branches you so narrowly escaped being second wrangler, twenty years since; out with your logarithms, your conic sections, your fluxions, and calculate the thousands upon thousands of little dramas that must be taking place in London as the clock strikes seven. Let me glance at a few, as I travel with you towards that railway terminus which is our destination. Camberwell Gate: tollbar-keeper, who has been up all night, going to bed, very cross; tollbar-keeper's wife gets up to mind the gate, also very cross. Woodendesk Grove, Grosvenor Park, Camberwell: Mr. Dockett, wharfage clerk in Messrs. Charter Party and Co.'s shipping house, Lower Thames Street, is shaving. He breakfasts at half-past seven, and has to be in the city by nine. Precisely at the same time that he is passing Mr. Mappin's razor over his commercial countenance, Mr. Flybynight, aged twenty-two, also a clerk, but attached to the Lost-Monkey-and-Mislaid-Poodle-Department (Inland Revenue), Somerset House, lets himself into No. 7, Woodendesk Grove, next door to Mr. Dockett's, by means of a Chubb's key. Mr. Flybynight is in evening costume, considerably the worst for the concussion of pale ale bottle corks. On his elegant tie are the stains of the dressing of some lobster salad, and about half-a-pint of the crimson stream of life, formerly the joint property of Mr. Flybynight's nose and of a cabman's upper lip, both injured during a "knock-down and drag-out" fight, supervening on the disputed question of the right of a passenger to carry a live turkey (purchased in Leadenhall market) with him in a hackney cab. Mr. Flybynight has been to two evening parties, a public ball (admission sixpence), where he created a great sensation among the ladies and gentlemen present, by appearing with a lady's cap on his head, a raw shoulder of mutton in one hand, and a pound of rushlights in the other; and to two suppers— one of roasted potatoes in Whitechapel High Street, the second of scolloped oysters in the Haymarket. He paid a visit to the Vine Street station-house, too, to clear up a misunderstanding as to a bell which was rung by accident, and a policeman's hat which was knocked off by mistake. The inspector on duty was so charmed with Mr. Flybynight's engaging demeanour and affable manners, that it was with difficulty that he was dissuaded from keeping him by him all night, and assigning him as a sleeping apartment a private parlour with a very strong lock, and remarkably well ventilated. He only consented to tear himself away from Mr. Flybynight's society on the undertaking that the latter would convey home his friend Mr. Keepitup, who, though he persistently repeated to all comers that he was "all right," appeared, if unsteadiness of gait and thickness of utterance were to be accepted as evidence, to be altogether wrong. Mr. Flybynight, faithful to his promise, took Mr. Keepitup (who was in the Customs) home; at least he took him as far as he would go—his own doorstep, namely, on which somewhat frigid pedestal he sat, informing the "milk," a passing dustman, and a lady in pink, who had lost her way, and seemed to think that the best way to find it was to consult the pavement by falling prone thereupon every dozen yards or so—that though circumstances had compelled him to serve his country in a civil capacity, he was at heart and by predilection a soldier. In proof of which Mr. Keepitup struck his breast, volunteered a choice of martial airs, beginning with the "Death of Nelson," and ending with a long howl, intermingled with passionate tears and ejaculations bearing reference to the infidelity of a certain Caroline, surname unknown, through whose cruelty he "would never be the same man again." Mr. Flybynight, safely arrived at Woodendesk Grove, after these varied peripatetics, is due at the Lost-Monkey-and-Mislaid-Poodle Office at ten; but he will have a violent attack of lumbago this morning, which will unavoidably prevent him from reaching Somerset House before noon. His name will show somewhat unfavourably in the official book, and the Commissioners will look him up sharply, and shortly too, if he doesn't take care. Mr. Keepitup, who, however eccentric may have been his previous nocturnal vagaries, possesses the faculty of appearing at the Custom-house gates as the clock strikes the half-hour after nine, with a very large and stiff shirt-collar, a microscopically shaven face, and the most irreproachable shirt, will go to work at his desk in the Long Room, with a steady hand and the countenance of a candidate for the Wesleyan ministry; but Mr. Flybynight will require a good deal of soda-water and sal-volatile, and perhaps a little tincture of opium, before he is equal to the resumption of his arduous duties. Wild lads, these clerks; and yet they don't do such a vast amount of harm, Flybynight and Keepitup! They are very young; they don't beat the town every night; they are honest lads at bottom, and have a contempt for meanness and are not lost to shame. They have not grown so vicious as to be ashamed and remorseful without any good resulting therefrom; and you will be astonished five years hence to see Keepitup high up in the Customs, and Flybynight married to a pretty girl, to whom he is the most exemplary of husbands. Let me edge in this little morsel of morality at seven o'clock in the morning. I know the virtue of steadiness, lectures, tracts, latch-key-prohibitions, strict parents, young men's Christian associations, serious tea-parties and electrifying machines; but I have seen the world in my time, and its ways. Youth *will* be youth, and youthful blood *will* run riot. There is no morality so false as that which ignores the existence of immorality. Let us keep on preaching to the prodigals, and point with grim menace to the draff and husks, and the fatted calf which never shall be theirs if they do not reform; let us thunder against their dissipation, their late hours, their vain "larks," their unseemly "sprees." It is our duty; youth must be reproved, admonished, restrained by its elders. It has been so ever since the world began; but do not let us in our own hearts think every wild young man is bound hopelessly to perdition. Some there are, indeed, (and they are in evil case,) who have come to irremediable grief, and must sit aloof—spirits fallen never to rise again—and watch the struggling souls. But it must rejoice even those callous ones to see how many pecks of wild oats are sown every day, and what goodly harvests of home virtues and domestic joys are reaped on all sides, from the most unpromising soil. Let us not despair of the tendencies of the age. Young men will be young men, but they should be taught and led with gentle and wise counsels, with forbearance and moderation, to abandon the follies of youth, and to become staid and decorous. Flybynight, with such counsels, and good examples from his elders—ah, ye seniors! what examples are not due from you!—will leave off sack and live cleanly like a gentleman; and Keepitup will not bring his parents' gray hairs with sorrow to the grave.

Seven o'clock in the morning! I have already ventured a passing allusion to the "milk." The poor little children who sell violets and water-cresses debouch from the great thoroughfares, and ply their humble trade in by-streets full of private houses. The newsvenders' shops in the Strand, Holywell Street, and Fleet Street, are all in full activity. Legions of assistants crowd behind the broad counters, folding the still damp sheets of the morning newspapers, and, with fingers moving in swift legerdemain, tell off "quires" and "dozens" of cheap periodicals. If it happen to be seven o'clock, and a Friday morning, not only the doors of the great newsvenders—such as Messrs. Smith and Son and Mr. Vickers—but the portals of all the newspaper offices, will be crowded with newsmen's carts and newsmen's trucks; and from the gaping gates themselves will issue hordes of newsmen and flying cohorts of newsboys—boys with parcels, boys with bags, boys with satchels, men staggering under the weight of great piles of printed paper. Mercy on us! what a plethora of brainwork is about, and what a poor criterion of its quality the quantity manifestly affords! Yon tiny urchin with the red comforter has but half-a-dozen copies tucked beneath his arm of a journal sparkling with wit, and radiant in learning, and scathing in its satire, and Titanic in its vigour; yet, treading on his heels, comes a colossus in corduroy, eclipsed by a quadrangular mountain of closely-packed paper, quires—nay, whole reams—of some ragamuffin print, full of details of the last murder and abuse of some wise and good statesman because he happens to be a lord.

Seven, still seven! Potboys, rubbing their eyes, take down the shutters of taverns in leading thoroughfares, and then fall to rubbing the pewter pots till they assume a transcendent sheen. Within, the young ladies who officiate in the bar, and who look very drowsy in their curl-papers and cotton-print dresses, are rubbing the pewter counters and the brass-work of the beer-engines, the funnels and the whisky noggins, washing the glasses, polishing up the mahogany, cutting up the pork pies which Mr. Watling's man has just left, displaying the Banbury cakes and Epping sausages under crystal canopies. The early customers—matutinal *habitués*—drop in for small measures of cordials or glasses of peculiarly mild ale; and the freshest news of last night's fire in Holborn, or last night's division in the House, or last night's opera at Her Majesty's, are fished up from the columns of the "Morning Advertiser." By intercommunication with the early customers, who all have a paternal and respectful fondness for her, the barmaid becomes *au courant* with the news of the day. As a rule, the barmaid does not read the newspaper. On the second day of publication, she lends it to the dissenting washerwoman or the radical tailor in the court round the corner, who send small children, whose heads scarcely reach to the top of the counter, for it. When it is returned, she cuts it up for tobacco screws and for curl papers. I like the barmaid, for she is often pretty, always civil, works about fourteen hours a day for her keep and from eighteen to twenty pounds a year, is frequently a kinless orphan out of that admirable Licensed Victuallers' School, and is, in nine cases out of ten, as chaste as Diana.

I should be grossly misleading you, were I to attempt to inculcate the supposition that at seven o'clock in the morning only the humbler classes, or those who have stopped up all night, are again up and doing. The Prime Minister is dressed, and poring over a savage leader in the "Times," denouncing his policy, sneering at his latest measure, and insulting him personally in a facetious manner. The noble officers told off for duty of her Majesty's regiment of Guards are up and fully equipped, though perchance they have spent the small hours in amusements not wholly dissimilar from those employed by the daring Flybynight and the intrepid Keepitup to kill time, and have devoted their vast energies to the absorbing requirements of morning parade. Many of the infant and juvenile scions of the aristocracy have left their downy couches ere this, and are undergoing a lavatory purgatory in the nursery. Many meek-faced, plainly-dressed young ladies, of native and foreign extraction, attached as governesses to the aristocratic families in question, are already in the school-room, sorting their pupils' copy-books, or preparing for the early repetition of the music lesson, which is drummed and thrummed over in the morning pending the arrival of Signor Papadaggi or Herr Hammerer, who comes for an hour and earns a guinea. The governess, Miss Grissel, does not work more than twelve hours a day, and she earns perhaps fifty guineas a year against Papadaggi's fifteen hundred and Hammerer's two thousand. But then she is only a governess. Her life is somewhat hard, and lonely, and miserable, and might afford, to an ill-regulated mind, some cause for grumbling; but it is her duty to be patient, and not to repine. What says the pleasing poet?

"O! let us love our occupations,

Bless the squire and his relations,

Live upon our daily rations,

And always know our proper stations."[2]

Let us trust Miss Grissel knows her proper station, and is satisfied.

Seven o'clock in the morning; but there are more governesses, and governesses out of bed, than Miss Grissel and her companions in woe, in the mansions of the nobility. Doctor Wackerbarth's young gentlemen, from Towellem House, New Road, are gone to bathe at Peerless Pool, under escort of the writing-master. The Misses Gimps' establishment for young ladies, at Bayswater, is already in full activity; and the eight and thirty boarders (among whom there are at present, and have been for the last ten years, two, and positively only two, vacancies. N.B.—The daughters of gentlemen only are received)—the eight and thirty boarders, in curl papers and brown Holland pinafores, are floundering through sloughs of despond in the endeavour to convey, in the English language, the fact that Calypso was unable to console herself for the departure of Ulysses; and into the French vernacular, the information that, in order to be disabused respecting the phantoms of hope and the whisperings of fancy, it is desirable to listen to the history of Rasselas, Prince of Abyssinia. In Charterhouse and Merchant Taylors' and St. Paul's, the boys are already at their lessons, and the cruel anger of Juno towards Æneas, together with the shameful conduct of Clytemnestra to Agamemnon, are matters of public (though unwilling) discussion; some private conversations going on surreptitiously, meanwhile, touching the price of alleytaws as compared with agates, and the relative merits of almond-rock and candied horehound. After all, the poor have their privileges—their immunities; and the couch of the rich is not altogether a bed of roses. Polly Rabbets, the charity girl, lies snugly in bed, while the honourable Clementina St. Maur is standing in the stocks, or is having her knuckles rapped for speaking English instead of French. Polly has a run in the Dials before breakfast, an expedition to buy a red herring for father, and perchance a penny for disbursement at the apple-stall. She is not wanted at school till nine. The most noble the Marquis of Millefleurs, aged ten, at Eton, has to rise at six; he is fag to Tom Tucker, the army clothier's son. He has to clean his master's boots, fry bacon, and toast bread for his breakfast. If he doesn't know his lesson in school, the most noble the Marquis of Millefleurs is liable to be birched; but no such danger menaces Jemmy Allbones at the National, or Tommy Grimes at the Ragged School. If the schoolmaster were to beat them, their parents would have the *plagosus Orbilius* up at the police-court in a trice, and the Sunday newspapers would be full of details of the "atrocious cruelty of a schoolmaster."

One more peep at seven o'clock doings, and we will move further afield. Though sundry are up and doing, the great mass of London is yet sleeping. Sleeps the cosy tradesman, sleeps the linendraper's shopman (till eight), sleeps the merchant, the dandy, the actor, the author, the *petite maitresse*. Hold fast while I wheel in my flight and hover over Pimlico. There is Millbank, where the boarders and lodgers, clad in hodden gray, with masks on their faces and numbers on their backs, have been up and stirring since six. And there, north-west of Millbank, is the palace, almost as ugly as the prison, where dwells the Great Governess of the Land. She is there, for you may see the standard floating in the morning breeze; and at seven in the morning, she, too, is up and doing. If she were at Osborne she would be strolling very likely on the white-beached shore, listening to the sea murmuring "your gracious Majesty," and "your Majesty's ever faithful subject and servant," and "your petitioner will ever pray;" for it is thus doubtless that the obsequious sea has addressed sovereigns since Xerxes' time. Or if the Imperial Governess were at Windsor, she might, at this very time, be walking on those mysterious Slopes on which it is a standing marvel that Royalty can preserve its equilibrium. When I speak of our gracious lady being awake and up at seven o'clock, I know that I am venturing into the realms of pure supposition; but remember I am Asmodeus, and can unroof palaces and hovels at will. Is it not, besides, a matter of public report that the Queen rises early? Does not the Court newsman (I wonder whether that occult functionary gets up early too) know it? Does not everybody know it—everybody say it? And what everybody says must be true. There are despatches to be read; private and confidential letters to foreign sovereigns to be written; the breakfasts, perchance, of the little princes and princesses to be superintended; the proofs, probably, of the last Royal etching or princely photograph to be inspected; a new pony to be tried in the riding-house; a new dog to be taught tricks: a host of things to do. Who shall say? What do we know about the daily life of royalty, save that it must be infinitely more laborious than that of a convict drudging through his penal servitude in Portland Prison? I met the carriage of H.R.H. the Prince Consort, with H.R.H. inside it, prowling about Pedlar's Acre very early the other morning, going to or coming from, I presume, the South-Western Railway Terminus. When I read of her Majesty's "arriving with her accustomed punctuality" at some rendezvous at nine o'clock in the morning, I can but think of and marvel at the amount of business she must have despatched before she entered her carriage. If there were to be (which heaven forfend!) a coronation to-morrow, the sovereign would be sure to arrive with his or her "accustomed punctuality;" yet how many hours it must take to try on the crown, to study the proper sweep of the imperial purple, to learn by heart that coronation oath which is never, never broken! For my part, I often wonder how kings and queens and emperors find time to go to bed at all.

So now, reader, not wholly, I trust, unedified by the cursory view we have taken of Babylon the Great in its seven-o'clock-in-the-morning phase, we have arrived at the end of our journey—to another stage thereof, at least. We have flown from Knightsbridge to Bermondsey, not exactly as the crow flies, nor yet as straight as an arrow from a Tartar's bow; but still we have gyrated and skimmed and wheeled along somehow, even as a sparrow seeking knowledge on the housetops and corn in the street kennels. And now we will go out of town.

Whithersoever you choose; but by what means of conveyance? By water? The penny steamboats have not commenced their journeys yet. The *Pride of the Thames* is snugly moored at Essex Pier, and *Waterman*, No. 2, still keeps her head under her wing—or under her funnel, if you will. The omnibuses have not yet begun to roll in any perceptible numbers, and the few stage coaches that are still left (how they linger, those cheerful institutions, bidding yet a blithe defiance to the monopolising and all-devouring rail!) have not put in an appearance at the White Horse Cellar in Piccadilly, the Flower Pot in Bishopsgate Street, or the Catherine Wheel in the Borough. So we must needs quit Babylon by railway. Toss up for a terminus with me. Shall it be London Bridge, Briarean station with arms stretching to Brighton the well-beloved, Gravesend the chalky and periwinkley, Rochester the martial, Chatham the naval, Hastings the saline, Dover the castellated, Tunbridge Wells the genteel, Margate the shrimpy, Ramsgate the asinine, Canterbury the ecclesiastical, or Herne Bay the desolate? Shall it be the Great Northern, hard by Battle Bridge and Pentonville's frowning bastille? No; the fens of Lincolnshire nor the moors of Yorkshire like me not. Shall it be the Great Western, with its vast, quiet station, its Palladio-Vitruvian hotel, and its promise of travel through the rich meadows of Berkshire and by the sparkling waters of Isis, into smiling Somerset and blooming Devon? No; cab fares to Paddington are ruinously expensive, and I have prejudices against the broad gauge. Shall it be the Eastern Counties? Avaunt! evil-smelling Shoreditch, bad neighbourhood of worse melodramas, and cheap grocers' shops where there is sand in the sugar and birch-brooms in the tea. No Eastern Counties carriage shall bear me to the pestiferous marshes of Essex or the dismal flats of Norfolk. There is the South-Western. Hum! The Hampton Court line is pleasant; the Staines, Slough, and Windsor delicious; but I fancy not the Waterloo Road on a fine morning. I am undecided. Toss up again. Heads for the Great Western; tails for the London and North-Western. Tails it is; and abandoning our aërial flight, let us cast ourselves into yonder Hansom, and bid the driver drive like mad to Euston Square, else we shall miss the seven o'clock train.

This Hansom is a most dissipated vehicle, and has evidently been up all night. One of its little silk window-curtains has been torn from its fastenings and flutters in irregular festoons on the inward wall. The cushions are powdered with cigar ashes; there is a theatrical pass-check, and the thumb of a white kid glove, very dirty, lying at the back. The long-legged horse with his ill-groomed coat, all hairs on end like the fretful porcupine his quills, and his tail whisking with derisive defiance in the face of the fare, carries his head on one side, foams at the mouth, and is evidently a dissipated quadruped, guilty, I am afraid, of every vice except hypocrisy. Of the last, certainly, he cannot be accused, for he makes not the slightest secret of his propensity for kicking, biting, gibbing, rearing, and plunging, a succession of which gymnastic operations brings us, in an astonishingly brief space of time, to George Street, Euston Square; where the cabman, who looks like a livery-stable edition of Don Cæsar de Bazan, with a horse-cloth instead of a mantle, tosses the coin given him into the air, catches it again, informs me contemptuously that money will grow warm in my pocket if I keep it there so long, and suddenly espying the remote possibility of a fare in the extreme distance of the Hampstead Road, drives off—"tools" off, as he calls it—as though the Powers of Darkness, with Lucifer and Damagorgon at their head, were after him.

I think the Euston Square Terminus is, for its purpose, the handsomest building I have ever seen, and I have seen a few railway stations. There is nothing to compare to it in Paris, where the termini are garish, stuccoed, flimsy-looking structures, half booths and half barracks. Not Brussels, not Berlin, not Vienna, can show so stately a structure, for a railway station, *bien entendu*; and it is only, perhaps, in St. Petersburg, which seems to have been built with a direct reference to the assumption of the Imperial crown at some future period by the King of Brobdignag, that a building can be found—the

Moscow Railway Terminus, in fact—to equal in grandeur of appearance our columniated palace of the iron road. But the Russian station, like all else in that "Empire of Façades," is deceptive: a magnificent delusion, a vast and splendid sham. Of seeming marble without it is; within, but bad bricks and lath and plaster.

PARLIAMENTARY TRAIN: PLATFORM OF THE LONDON AND NORTH-WESTERN RAILWAY.

Open sesame! Let us pass the crowds of railway porters, who have not much to do just now, and are inclined to lounge about with their hands in their pockets, and to lean—in attitudes reminding the spectator of the Grecian statues clad in green velveteen, and with white letters on their collars—on their luggage trucks, for the passengers by the seven o'clock train are not much addicted to arriving in cabs or carriages which require to be unloaded, and there are very few shilling or sixpenny gratuities to be earned by the porters, for the securing of a comfortable corner seat with your back to the engine, or that inestimable comfort, a place in a first-class carriage whose door the guard is good enough to keep locked, and in which you can make yourself quite at home with a bottle of sherry, some walnuts, and a quiet game at *écarté* or *vingt un*. The seven o'clock trainbands are not exactly of the class who drink sherry and play cards; they are more given to selling walnuts than to eating them. They are, for the most part, hard-faced, hard-handed, poorly-clad creatures; men in patched, time-worn garments; women in pinched bonnets and coarse shawls, carrying a plenitude of baskets and bundles, but very slightly troubled with trunks or portmanteaus. You might count a hundred heads and not one hat-box; of two hundred crowding round the pay-place to purchase their third-class tickets for Manchester, or Liverpool, or even further north, you would have to look and look again, and perhaps vainly after all, for the possessor of a railway rug, or even an extra overcoat. Umbrellas, indeed, are somewhat plentiful; but they are not the slim, aristocratic trifles with ivory handles and varnished covers—enchanter's wands to ward off the spells of St. Swithin, which moustached dandies daintily insert between the roof and the hat-straps of first-class carriages. Third-class umbrellas are dubious in colour, frequently patched, bulgy in the body, broken in the ribs, and much given to absence from the nozzle. Swarming about the pay-place, which their parents are anxiously investing, thirteen-and-fourpence or sixteen-and-ninepence in hand, are crowds of third-class children. I am constrained to acknowledge that the majority of these juvenile travellers cannot be called handsome children, well-dressed children, even tolerably good-looking children. Poor little wan faces you see here, overshadowed by mis-shapen caps, and bonnets nine bauble square; poor little thin hands, feebly clutching the scant gowns of their mothers; weazened little bodies, shrunken little limbs, distorted often by early hardship, by the penury which pounced on them—not in their cradles—they never had any—but in the baker's jacket in which they were wrapped when they were born, and which will keep by them, their only faithful friend, until they die, and are buried by the parish—poor ailing little children are these, and among them who shall tell how many hungry little bellies! Ah! judges of Amontillado sherry; crushers of walnuts with silver nut-crackers; connoisseurs who prefer French to Spanish olives, and are curious about the yellow seal; gay riders in padded chariots; proud cavaliers of blood-horses, you don't know how painfully and slowly, almost agonisingly, the poor have to scrape, and save, and deny themselves the necessaries of life, to gather together the penny-a-mile fare. It is a long way to Liverpool, a long way to Manchester; the only passengers by the seven o'clock train who can afford to treat the distance jauntily, are the Irish paupers, who are in process of being passed to their parish, and who will travel free. O! marvels of eleemosynary locomotion from Euston Square to Ballyragget or Carrighmadhioul!

But hark! the train bell rings; there is a rush, and a trampling of feet, and in a few seconds the vast hall is almost deserted. This spectacle has made me somewhat melancholy, and I think, after all, that I will patronise the nine o'clock express instead of the PARLIAMENTARY TRAIN.

Let us follow the crowd of third-class passengers on to the vast platform. There the train awaits them, puffing, and snorting, and champing its adamantine bit, like some great iron horse of Troy suddenly gifted with life and power of locomotion. By the way, I wonder how that same wooden horse we are supposed to read about in Homer, but study far more frequently in the pages of Lemprière, or in the agreeable metrical romance of Mr. Alexander Pope, really effected its entrance into Ilium. Was it propelled on castors, on rollers, or on those humble wooden wheels that quickened the march of the toy horse of our nonage—the ligneous charger from Mr. Farley's shop in Fleet Street, painted bright cream-colour, with spots resembling red wafers stuck all over him, a perpendicular mane, and a bushy tail? Very few first or even second-class carriages are attached to the great morning train. The rare exceptions seem to be placed there more as a graceful concession to the gentilities, or the respectabilities, or the "gigabilities," as Mr. Carlyle would call them, than with any reference to their real utility in a journey to the north. Who, indeed, among the bustling Anglo-Saxons, almost breathless in their eagerness to travel the longest possible distance in the shortest possible time, would care to pay first-class fare for a trip to Manchester, which consumes ten mortal hours, when, by the space-scorning express, the distance may be accomplished, at a not unreasonable augmentation of fare, in something like five hours? So the roomy six-seated chariots, with their arm-rests and head-rests, are well nigh abandoned; and the wooden boxes, which appear to have been specially designed by railway directors to teach second-class travellers, who can afford to pay more than third-class fare, that they had much better pay first-class, and go the entire animal (which, indeed, seeing how abominable are our second-class carriages in England, is a far preferable proceeding), are not much better tenanted. Some misanthropic men, in Welsh wigs and fur caps with flaps turned down over the ears, peer at us as we pass, pull up the window-frames captiously, as though they suspected us of a design to intrude on their solitude, and, watch in hand, call out in hoarse voices to the guard to warn him it is time the train had started. What is the use of being in a hurry, gentlemen? you will have plenty of breathing-time at Tring, and Watford, and Weedon, and some five-and-twenty other stations, besides opportunities for observing the beauties of nature at remote localities, where you will be quietly shunted off on to a siding to allow the express to pass you by.

But what a contrast to the quietude of the scarcely-patronised first and second-class *wagons* are the great hearse-like caravans in which travel the teeming hundreds who can afford to pay but a penny a mile! Enter one of these human menageries where the occupants are stowed away with little more courtesy or regard to their comfort than might be exemplified by the master of the ceremonies of one of Mr. Wombwell's vans. What a hurly-burly; what a seething mass; what a scrambling for places; what a shrill turmoil of women's voices and children's wailings, relieved, as in the *Gospodin Pomilaïou* (the Kyrie Eleison of the Russian churches), by the deep bass voices of gruff men! What a motley assemblage of men, women, and children, belonging to callings multifariously varied, yet all marked with the homogeneous penny-a-mile stamp of poverty! Sailors with bronzed faces and tarry hands, and those marvellous tarpaulin pancake hats, stuck, in defiance of all the laws of gravity, at the back of their heads; squat, squarely-built fellows, using strange and occasionally not very polite language, much given to "skylarking" with one another, but full of a simple, manly courtesy to all the females, and marvellously kind to the babies and little children; gaunt American sailors in red worsted shirts, with case-knives suspended to their belts, taciturn men expectorating freely, and when they do condescend to address themselves to speech, using the most astounding combination of adjective adjurations, relating chiefly to their limbs and their organs of vision; railway navvies going to work at some place down the line, and obligingly franked thither for that purpose by the company; pretty servant-maids going to see their relatives; Jew pedlars; Irish labourers in swarms; soldiers on furlough, with the breast of their scarlet coatees open, and disclosing beneath linen of an elaborate coarseness of texture—one might fancy so many military penitents wearing hair tunics; other soldiers in full uniform, with their knapsacks laid across their knees, and their muskets—prudently divested of the transfixing bayonets—which the old women in the carriage are marvellously afraid will "go off," disposed beside them, proceeding to Weedon barracks under the command of a staid Scotch corporal, who reads a tract, "Grace for Grenadiers" or "Powder and Piety," and takes snuff; journeymen mechanics with their tool-baskets; charwomen, servants out of place, stablemen, bricklayers' labourers, and shopboys.

PARLIAMENTARY TRAIN: INTERIOR OF A THIRD CLASS CARRIAGE.

Ay, and there are, I am afraid, not a few bad characters among the crowd: certain dubiously-attired, flash-looking, ragged dandies, with cheap pins in their foul cravats, and long greasy hair floating over their coat-collars, impress me most unfavourably, and dispose me to augur ill for the benefit which Manchester or Liverpool may derive from their visit; and of the moral status of yonder low-browed, bull-necked, villanous-looking gentleman, who has taken a seat in a remote corner, between two stern guardians, and who, strive as he may to pull his coat-cuffs over his wrists, cannot conceal the presence of a pair of neat shining handcuffs, there cannot, I perpend, exist any reasonable doubt. But we must take the evil with the good: and we cannot expect perfection, not even in a Parliamentary Train.

EIGHT O'CLOCK A.M.—ST. JAMES'S PARK—
THE MALL.

Of the great army of sightseers, there are few but have paid a visit to Portsmouth, and, under the guidance of a mahogany-faced man in a peajacket, who has invariably served in his youth as coxswain to Admiral Lord Nelson, K.C.B., have perambulated from stem to stern, from quarterdeck to kelson, that famous ship from whose signal halyards flew out, fifty-three years since, the immortal watchword "England expects every man to do his duty," in Trafalgar Bay. We are (or rather were, till the epoch of the late passport regulations and the war), an ambitious army of sightseers in this year of questionable grace, '59; and nothing less would serve us then for an autumn trip than a picnic in the Street of Tombs at Pompeii, a moonlight polka among the rank docks and charlocks and slimy reptiles of the Roman Colosseum, a yacht voyage up the gulf of Bothnia, or a four days' jolting in a *telega* from Moscow to the fair of Nishni-Novgorod. But in the days of yore, when this old hat was new, and Manlius was consul, and the eleven hours' route to the Continent existed not, we went a-gipsying in a less ostentatious manner. The Lions in the Tower, the Horns at Highgate, the Spaniards at Hampstead, the Wandering Minstrel at Beulah Spa; and on highdays and holidays a stage-coach and pleasure-boat journey to Portsmouth, Southampton, Netley Abbey, Carisbrook Castle, and the Undercliff; these filled up the simple measure of our pleasure-gadding. We are improved now-a-days, and go the grand tour like my lord; and are wiser, and better, and happier—of course.

When in the noble harbour of Portsmouth you have taken your wife, your sweetheart, or your friend the intelligent foreigner, to whom you wish to show the glories of England, and when the cicerone of the great war-ship has told his parrot-tale about admirals' quarter-galleries and officers' gun-rooms; when at last he has taken you into the cabin, and at the back shown you the sorrowful inscription painted on the stanchion, "HERE NELSON DIED!" did never a sudden desire come across you to be left alone—to have the army of sight-seers banished five hundred miles away—to be allowed to remain there in the silent cabin among the shadows, to muse on the memory of the great dead, to conjure up mind-pictures of that closing scene: the cannon booming overhead; the terrified surgeons with outspread bandages, and probes, and knives, knowing that their skill was of no avail; the burly shipmen crying like little children; and alone tranquil and serene among that sorrowful group, peaceful as an infant in its cradle, the Admiral, his stars and ribbons gleaming in the lantern's fitful rays, but never with so strong a light as the gory ghastliness of his death wound; the brave yellow-haired Admiral, with the puny limbs and giant's heart, waiting to die, ready to die, happy to die, thanking God that he had done his duty to his king, and meekly saying, "Kiss me, Hardy."

That inscription in the *Victory's* cabin has been to me the source of meditation frequent and infinitely pleasant. I love to think, walking in historical streets and houses, that my feet are treading over spots where men for ever famous have left an imprint of glory. I peer into the soil, the stones, the planks, to descry the shadowy mark of Hercules' foot, of the iron-plated sole of the warrior, the sandalled shoon of the saint, the dainty heel of the brocaded slipper of beauty. Every place that history or tradition has made her own is to me a field, not of forty, but of forty thousand footsteps; and I please myself sometimes with futile wishes that the boundaries of these footsteps might have been marked by plates of brass and adamant, as Nelson's death-place is marked on board his flagship. It were better, perhaps, to leave the exact spot to imagination; for though I would give something to know the very window of the Banqueting House from whence Charles Stuart came out to his death, and the precise spot where he turned to Juxon and uttered his mysterious injunction "Remember!" I would not care to know the particular branch of the tree to which Judas affixed his thrice-earned halter when he hanged himself: I could spare Mr. Dix the trouble of telling me the identical spot on the tavern table on which the coroner laid his three-cornered hat when he held his inquest on the worthless impostor Chatterton—a "marvellous boy" if you will, but one who perished in his miserable folly and forgery—and I could well exempt the legitimacy-bemused courtiers of Louis XVIII. from perpetuating, as they did in brass, the few inches of soil at Calais first pressed on his return to France by the foot of that gross fat man.

There are two cities in the world, London and Paris, so full of these footstep memories, so haunted by impalpable ghosts of the traces of famous deeds, that locomotion, to one of my temperament, becomes a task very slow, if not painfully difficult, of accomplishment. 'Tis a long way from the Luxor Obelisk to the Carrousel; but it's a week's journey when you feel inclined to stop at every half-dozen yards' distance, questioning yourself and the ministering spirits of your books, pointing your fingers to the paving-stones, and saying—Here the guillotine stood; here Louis died; here the daughter of Maria Theresa cast her last glance at the cupolas of the Tuileries; here Robespierre was hooted; here Théroigne de Méricourt was scourged; here Napoleon the Great showed the little king of Rome to the people; here, on the great Carrousel Place, he, arrayed in the undying gray coat and little hat, reviewed the veterans of his guard, many and many a time at EIGHT O'CLOCK IN THE MORNING.

EIGHT O'CLOCK A.M.: ST. JAMES'S PARK.

There! I have brought you round to the subject-matter of this article, and to the complexion of "Twice Round the Clock" again; and the stroke is, I flatter myself, felicitous—rivalling Escobar or Dom Calmet in Jesuitry, Metternich and Menschikoff in diplomacy. You thought doubtless that I was about to launch into an interminable digression; you may perhaps have said, scoffingly, that Admiral Lord Nelson, K.C.B., Maximillien Robespierre, Charles the First's head, and the Emperor Napoleon's cocked hat, could have nothing whatsoever to do with the Mall of Saint James's Park at eight o'clock in the morning. You are mistaken. The allusions to memorable footsteps were all cunningly devised with a reference to the great Field of Famous Footsteps—the Mall, which, were the imprint of those bygone pedal pressures marked out with landmarks, such as those in the *Victory's* cabin, would become a very Field of the Cloth of Brass. And what better time can there be to muse upon the traditional glories of the Mall and the fame of its frequenters, than eight a.m. in sweet summer time?

I grant the clown, the dunderheaded moneyspinner who votes that books are "rubbish," the cobweb-brained fop who languidly declares reading to be a "bore," will find in the broad smooth Mall, just a Mall, broad and smooth, and nought else—even as Peter Bell found in a primrose by the river's brim a yellow primrose, and nothing more. At eight o'clock in the morning, to clown, dunderhead, and cobweb-brain, the Mall is a short cut from Marylebone to Westminster; the water-carts are laying the dust; mechanics are going to work; there are some government offices in the distance; two

- 57 -

big guns on queer-looking carriages; some scattered children; a good many birds, making rather a disagreeable noise, in the green trees; and a few cows being milked in a corner. But come with me, dweller in the past, lover of ancient and pleasant memories, hand-and-glove friend of defunct worthies, shadowy acquaintances in ruffs and peaked beards and point lace. Let us deliver dunderhead and cobweb-brain to the tormentors, and, sitting on a rustic bench beneath a spreading tree, summon the Famous Footsteps; summon the dead-and-gone walkers to pace the Mall again. Here they come! a brave gathering, a courtly throng, a worshipful assemblage, but oft-times a motley horde and a fantastic crew. Here is Henry the Eighth's Mall, a park where that disreputable monarch indulged in "the games of hare and pheasant, partridge and heron, for his disport and pastime," and where he had a deer killed for the amusement of the "Embassador from Muscovie." Here is Saint James's Park in the reign of clever, shrewish, cruel Queen Bess—a park only used as an appendage to the tilt-yard and a nursery for deer: here is the "inward park" (now the inclosure and ornamental water), into which, so late as the commencement of Charles II.'s reign, access to the public was denied; and where, in 1660, Master Pepys saw a man "basted" by the keeper for carrying some people over on his back through the water. Here is Charles II.'s famous Mall, for the first time broad and smooth, the park planted and reformed by the celebrated French gardener, Le Nôtre, laid out with fish-ponds and a decoy for water-fowl; the Mall itself a vista of half a mile in length, on which the game of Pall Mall was played, and which, always according to curious Samuel Pepys, who "discoursed with the keeper of the Pall Mall as he was sweeping it," was floored with mixed earth, and over all that cockle-shells, powdered and spread to keep it fast; which, however, in dry weather, turned to dust and deadened the ball. In this park of Charles II. was the fantastic little territory of Duck Island, the ground contained within the channels of the decoy, and which London Barataria had revenues and laws and governors appointed by the king. The Duke of Saint Simon's friend, Saint Evremond, was one of these governors; Sir John Flock another. Close to Duck Island was Rosamond's Pond, a piece of water whose name bore a dim analogy to the *soubriquet* with which, in later years, Waterloo Bridge has been qualified; for it was in Rosamond's Pond that forsaken women came in preference, at even-song, to drown themselves. There was the Birdcage Walk, where Mr. Edward Storey kept his Majesty's aviary, and dwelt in the snug little hut recently demolished, known as Storey's Gate. There was the Mulberry Garden, into which the river Tyburn flows, and so into Tothill Fields and the Thames; and there was Spring Gardens, where the beaux went to look at the citizens' wives; and the citizens' wives, I hope, to drink chocolate, but I fear to look at the beaux.

But the famous footsteps? See, see in your mind's eye, Horatio, how the shadows of the old frequenters of the Mall come trooping along. Here is the founder of the feast himself, King Charles the Second, witty, worthless, and good-humoured, tramping along the broad expanse at *eight* o'clock in the morning, to the despair of his courtiers, who liked not walking so fast, nor getting up so early. You can't mistake the king's figure; 'tis that swarthy gentleman, with the harshly-marked countenance, the bushy eyebrows, the lively kindling gray eye, and the black suit and perriwig. He walks a little in advance of his suite with an easy, rapid gait, and at his heels follow a little barking multitude of dogs, black, black and white, or black and tan, with long silky ears and feathery tails. We may see him again, and on the Mall, but not at eight o'clock in the morning. It is the afternoon of a July day, and a court cavalcade comes flaunting in feathers forth from Whitehall. Here is King Charles, but in a laced and embroidered suit, and mounted on a gaily-caparisoned charger. He rides with his hand in that of a lady, in a white laced waistcoat and crimson petticoat, and who, the chroniclers say, with her hair dressed *à la negligence*, "looks mighty pretty," but she is very dark, and not very well favoured, and is a poor Portuguese lady who has the misfortune to be Queen of England, and to have the merriest and the worst husband in Europe. Here is La Belle Stuart, with her hat cocked, and a red plume, looking, with her sweet eye, little Roman nose, and excellent *taille*, the greatest beauty that the Clerk of the Acts ever did see in his life. Here is Lady Castlemaine, with a yellow plume, but in a terrible temper that the king does not take any notice of her, and in a rage when she finds that no gentleman presses to assist her down from her horse. Here is "our royal brother," James Duke of York, scowling and sulky, on his way through the Park to Hounslow, to enjoy his prime diversion of the chase, and escorted by a party of the guards in morions and steel corslets. Memory be good to us! how the shadows gather around! His Highness Oliver, Lord Protector of this realm, is being borne along the Mall in a sedan chair. He crouches uneasily in a corner of the gilded vehicle, as though he feared that Colonel Titus might be lying *perdu* under the linden trees, correcting the proof sheets of "Killing no Murder." Sir Fopling Flutter bids his coachman take the carriage to Whitehall, and walks over the park with Belinda. Now, years later, it is Jonathan Swift leaving his best gown and perriwig at Mrs. Vanhomrigh's, then walking up the Mall, by Buckingham House, and so to Chelsea. It is not a very well-conducted Mall just now, and Swift tells Stella that he is obliged to come home early through the park, to avoid the Mohocks. Now, back again, and to walk with decorous Mr. Evelyn, who is much shocked to see Nelly Gwynne leaning over her garden wall (overhanging the park),—she lived at 79, Pall Mall—and indulging in familiar discourse with "Old Rowley." Now we are in Horace Walpole's time, and the macaroni-cynic of Strawberry Hill is gallanting in the Mall with Lady Caroline Petersham, and pretty Miss Beauclerc, and foolish Mrs. Sparre. Now Lady Coventry and Walpole's niece, Lady Waldegrave, are mobbed in the park for being dressed in an "outlandish" fashion. Now, back and back again; and the Duchess of Cleveland is walking across the Mall on a dark night, pursued by three men in masks, who offer her no violence, but curse her as the cause of England's misery, and prophesy that she will one day die in a ditch, like Jane Shore. Forward, hark forward, and mad Margaret Nicholson attempts the life of George III., as he passes in his coach through the Mall to open Parliament. Backward, and James II. walks across the park from St. James's, where he had slept, to Whitehall, to be crowned. A very few years after his coronation, the Dutch Guards of William Prince of Orange marched across from St. James's to turn the unlucky Stuart out of Whitehall. And now, backwards and forwards, and forwards and backwards, the famous shadows mingle in a fantastic reel, a mad waltz of extinct footsteps. Sir Roger de Coverley and Mr. Spectator saunter under the limes; Beau Fielding minces by the side of Margaretta; Beau Tibbs airs his clean linen and lackered sword hilt; Mr. Pope meets Lady Mary's sedan, borne by Irish chair-men—the translator of the "Iliad" grins spitefully over his shoulder and makes faces at Lady Mary's black boy; Sir Plume instructs Sir John Burke in the nice conduct of a clouded cane; Goldsmith's good-natured man fraternises with Coleman's "brother who could eat beef;" Lord Fanny takes off his three-cornered hat to Mr. Moore, the inventor of the worm powders; Partridge, the almanack maker, discusses the motions of the heavenly bodies on the banks of Rosamond's Pond with Count Algarotti, and becomes so excited that he nearly adds "one more unfortunate" to the list of Ophelias in Rosamond's Pond, by tumbling into the water; Alfieri meets Lord Ligonier—tells him the measure of his sword, and makes a rendezvous with him for sunset in Hyde Park; Lord George Gordon passes Westminster to St. James's, followed by a mob of yelling, screaming Protestants. Real people dispute the passage of the Mall with imaginary personages. The encampment of 'Eighty, the Temple of Concord, and the Humane Society's drags, are inextricably mixed up with scenes from Wycherley and Etherege; and pet passages from the "Trivia" and the "Rape of the Lock." I must bring myself back to reason and St. James's Park, and eight o'clock in the morning. I must deal henceforth in realities. Here is one.

It is the morning of the 30th of January, 1649, and a King of England walks across the frozen park, from St. James's, where he has slept, to Whitehall, the palace of his fathers. Armed men walk before, armed men walk behind and around; but they are no guards of honour. They escort a prisoner to the scaffold. The High Court of Justice has adjudged Charles Stuart, King of England, a traitor, and has decreed that he shall be put to death by severing his head from his body. President Bradshaw has put off his red robe, the man without a name has put on his black mask; the axe is sharpened, the sawdust spread, the block prepared, the velvet-covered coffin yawns; on its lid is already the leaden plate with the inscription, "King Charles, 1649."

It is not my fault, dear reader, if the spot which your author and artist to command have selected for illustration of the eighth hour ante-meridian, be so rich in historical and literary recollections; that we may fancy every inch of its surface trodden and re-trodden till the very soil has sunk, by the feet of the departed great; that the student, and the lover of old lore, must arrest himself perforce at every tree, and evoke remembrance at every pace. And centuries hence the Mall of St. James's Park will be as famous to our descendants for our deeds as it is now to us for the presence of our ancestors. Is not the Mall yet one of the most favoured resorts of the British aristocracy? Do not the carriages of the nobility and gentry rattle over its broad bosom to dinner parties, to opera, to concerts, and to balls? We have seen their chariot lamps a hundred times—we humble pedestrians and plebeians— gleaming among the tufted trees, wills-o'-the-wisp of Belgravia and Tyburnia. Is not St. James's Park bounded now as then by high and mighty buildings: War Office, Admiralty, Stationery Office, Barracks? Do not the Duke of York's steps lead from the Duke of York's column, between two *corps de logis*, one occupied by wings—ethereal wings, though made of brick and stucco, of the House of Carlton, the abode of George the Great (the great Fritz was called "*der grosse*") of England? And the Mall itself? Is it not overlooked by Stafford House, the palatial; by Marlborough House, the vast and roomy, once sacred to the memory of the victor of Ramilies and of "Old Sarah!" but now given up to some people called artists, connected with something called the English school, and partially used as a livery and bait stable for the late Duke of Wellington's funeral car, with its sham trophies and sham horses? Does not a scion of royalty, no other than his Royal Highness the Duke of Cambridge, frequently condescend to walk from his lodgings in the Stable-yard, Saint James's, across the park to those Horse Guards, whose affairs he administers with so much ability and success? And, finally, at the western extremity of the Mall, and on the side where once was the Mulberry Garden, stands there not now a palace, huge in size, clumsy in its proportions, grotesque in decoration, mean in gross, frivolous in detail, infinitely hideous in its general appearance, but above whose ugly roof floats that grandest and noblest of all banners, the Royal Standard of England, and whose walls, half hospital, half barrack, as they remind us of, are hallowed as being part of Buckingham Palace, the abode of our good, and true, and dear Queen? She lives at the top of the Mall. She comes out by times on the Mall, in her golden coach, with the eight cream-coloured horses; her darling little daughter passed along the Mall to be married; let us hope, and heartily, to see more sons and daughters yet riding to their weddings through that field of famous footsteps. Let us hope that we may live to throw up our caps, and cry God bless them!

Great lords and ladies sweep the Mall no more with hoops and flowing trains of brocaded paduasoy, nor jingle on the gravel with silver spurs, nor crunch the minute pebbles with red heels. Broughams and chariots now convey the salt ones of the earth to their grand assemblies and solemn merry-makings; and the few aristocrats who may yet pedestrianise within the precincts, are so plainly attired that you would find it difficult to distinguish them from plain Brown or Jones walking from Pimlico to Charing Cross. His Royal Highness strides over from the Stable-yard to the Horse Guards in a shooting-jacket and tweed trousers, and in wet weather carries an umbrella. Nay, I have seen another Royal Highness—a bigger Royal Highness, so to speak, for he is consort to the Queen—riding under the trees of the Mall on a quiet bay, and dressed in anything but the first style of fashion. Were it not *scandalum magnatum* even to think such a thing, I should say that his Royal Highness's coat was seedy.

At this early eight o'clock in the morningtide, see—an exception to the rule, however—perambulating the Mall, a tremendous "swell." No fictitious aristocrat, no cheap dandy, no Whitechapel buck or Bermondsey exquisite, no apprentice who has been to a masquerade disguised as a gentleman, can this be. Aristocracy is imprinted on every lineament of his moustached face, in every crease of his superb clothes, in each particular horsehair of his flowing plume. He is a magnificent creature, over six feet in height, with a burnished helmet, burnished boots, burnished spurs, burnished sabre, burnished cuirass—burnished whiskers and moustache. He shines all over, like a meteor, or a lobster which has been kept a *little* too long, in a dark room. He is young, brave, handsome, and generous; he is the delight of Eaton Square, the cynosure of the Castor and Pollux Club, the idol of the corps de ballet of her Majesty's Theatre, the pet of several most exclusive Puseyite circles in Tyburnia, the mirror of Tattersall's, the pillar and patron of Jem Bundy's ratting, dog-showing, man-fighting, horse-racing, and general sporting house, in Cat and Fiddle Court, Dog and Duck Lane, Cripplegate. Cruel country, cruel fate, that compel Lieutenant Algernon Percy Plantagenet, of the Royal Life Guards, the handsomest man in his regiment, and heir to £9,000 a year, to be mounting guard at eight o'clock in the morning! He is mounting guard at present by smoking a cigar (one of Milo's best) on the Mall. By and by he will go into his barrack-room and draw caricatures in charcoal on the whitewashed wall. He will smoke a good deal, yawn a good deal, and whistle a good deal during the day, and will give a few words of command. For you see, my son, that we must all earn our bread by the sweat of our brow, and that the career even of a Plantagenet, with £9,000 a year, is not, throughout, a highway of rose-leaves!

From this gay and resplendent warrior, we fall, alas! to a very prosaic level. As eight o'clock chimes from the smoky-faced clock of the Horse Guards, I try in vain (I have dismissed my shadowy friends) to people the Mall with aristocratic visitants. Alas and indeed! the magnificent promenade of the park, on which look the stately mansions of the nobles, is pervaded by figures very mean, very poor and forlorn in appearance. Little troops of girls and young women are coming from the direction of Buckingham Palace and the Birdcage Walk, but all converging towards the Duke of York's column: that beacon to the great shores of Vanity Fair. These are sempstresses and milliners' workwomen, and are bound for the great Dress Factories of the West End. Pinched faces, pale faces, eager faces, sullen faces, peer from under the bonnets as they pass along and up the steps. There are faces with large mild eyes, that seem to wonder at the world and at its strange doings, and at the existence of a Necessity (it must be a Necessity, you know), for Jane or Ellen to work twelve hours a day; nay, in the full London season, work at her needle not unfrequently all night, in order that the Countess or the Marchioness may have her ball dress ready.

EIGHT O'CLOCK; OPENING SHOP.

There is another ceremony performed with much clattering solemnity of wooden panels, and iron bars, and stanchions, which occurs at eight o'clock in the morning. 'Tis then that the shop-shutters are taken down. The great "stores" and "magazines" of the principal thoroughfares gradually open their eyes; apprentices, light-porters, and where the staff of assistants is not very numerous, the shopmen, release the imprisoned wares, and bid the sun shine on good family "souchong," "fresh Epping sausages," "Beaufort collars," "guinea capes," "Eureka shirts," and "Alexandre harmoniums." In the smaller thoroughfares, the proprietor often dispenses with the aid of apprentice, light-porter, and shopman—for the simple reason that he never possessed the services of any assistants at all—and unostentatiously takes down the shutters of his own chandler's, green-grocer's, tripe, or small stationery shop. In the magnificent linendrapery establishments of Oxford and Regent Streets, the vast shop-fronts, museums of fashion in plate-glass cases, offer a series of animated *tableaux* of *poses plastiques* in the shape of young ladies in morning costume, and young gentlemen in whiskers and white neckcloths, faultlessly complete as to costume, with the exception that they are yet in their shirt sleeves, who are accomplishing the difficult and mysterious feat known as "dressing" the shop window. By their nimble and practised hands the rich piled velvet mantles are displayed, the *moire* and *glacé* silks arranged in artful folds, the laces and gauzes, the innumerable whim-whams and fribble-frabble of fashion, elaborately shown, and to their best advantage.

Now, all over London, the shops start into new life. Butchers and bakers, and candlestick makers, grocers and cheesemongers, and pastrycooks, tailors, linendrapers, and milliners, crop up with mushroom-like rapidity. But I must leave them, to revisit them in all their glory a few hours later. Leave, too, the Park and its Mall, with the cows giving milk of a decidedly metropolitan flavour, and the children and the nursemaids, and the dilapidated dramatic authors reading the manuscripts of their five-act tragedies to themselves, and occasionally reciting favourite passages in deep diapason on the benches under the trees. Leave, too, the London sparrows, and—would that we could leave it altogether—the London smoke, which already begins to curl over and cover up the city like a blanket, and which will not keep clear of the Mall, even at eight o'clock in the morning.

NINE O'CLOCK A.M.—THE CLERKS AT THE BANK, AND THE BOATS ON THE RIVER.

It is nine o'clock, and London has breakfasted. Some unconsidered tens of thousands have, it is true, already enjoyed with what appetite they might their præ-prandial meal; the upper fifty thousand, again, have not yet left their luxurious couches, and will not breakfast till ten, eleven o'clock, noon; nay, there shall be sundry listless, languid members of fast military clubs, dwellers among the tents of Jermyn Street, and the high-priced second floors of Little Ryder Street, St. James's, upon whom one, two, and three o'clock in the afternoon shall be but as dawn, and whose broiled bones and devilled kidneys shall scarcely be laid on the damask breakfast-cloth before Sol is red in the western horizon.

I wish that, in this age so enamoured of statistical information, when we must needs know how many loads of manure go to every acre of turnip-field, and how many jail-birds are thrust into the black hole *per mensem* for fracturing their pannikins, or tearing their convict jackets, that some M'Culloch or Caird would tabulate for me the amount of provisions, solid and liquid, consumed at the breakfasts of London every morning. I want to know how many thousand eggs are daily chipped, how many of those embryo chickens are poached, and how many fried; how many tons of quartern loaves are cut up to make bread-and-butter, thick and thin; how many porkers have been sacrificed to provide the bacon rashers, fat and streaky; what rivers have been drained, what fuel consumed, what mounds of salt employed, what volumes of smoke emitted, to catch and cure the finny haddocks and the Yarmouth bloaters, that grace our morning repast. Say, too, Crosse and Blackwell, what multitudinous demands are matutinally made on thee for pots of anchovy paste and preserved tongue, covered with that circular layer—abominable disc!—of oleaginous nastiness, apparently composed of rancid pomatum, but technically known as clarified butter, and yet not so nasty as that adipose horror that surrounds the truffle bedecked *pâté de foie gras*. Say, Elizabeth Lazenby, how many hundred bottles of thy sauce (none of which are genuine unless signed by thee) are in request to give a relish to cold meat, game, and fish. Mysteries upon mysteries are there connected with nine o'clock breakfasts. Queries upon queries suggest themselves to the inquisitive mind. Speculations upon speculations present themselves to him who is observant. Are those eggs we see in the coffee-shop windows, by the side of the lean chop with a curly tail, the teapot with the broken spout, and the boulder-looking kidneys, ever eaten, and if so, what secret do the coffee-shop proprietors possess of keeping them from entire decomposition? For I have watched these eggs for weeks together, and known them by bits of straw and flecks of dirt mucilaginously adhering to their shells, to be the selfsame eggs;

yet when I have entered the unpretending house of refreshment, and ordered "tea and an egg," I have seen the agile but dingy handmaiden swiftly approach the window, slide the glass panel back with nimble (though dusky) fingers, convey an egg to the mysterious kitchen in the background, and in a few minutes place the edible before me boiled, yet with sufficient marks of the straw upon it to enable me to discern my ancient friend. Who, again, invented muffins?—and what becomes of all the cold crossbuns after Good Friday? I never saw a crossbun on Holy Saturday, and I believe the boy most addicted to saccharine dainties would scorn one.

So hungry London breakfasts, but not uniformly well, at nine o'clock in the morning. In quietly grim squares, in the semi-aristocratic North-West End—I don't mean Russell and Bloomsbury, but Gordon, Tavistock, Queen, and Camden, on the one side, and Manchester and Portman on the other—the nine o'clock breakfast takes place in the vast comfortless dining-room, with the shining side-board (purchased at the sale of Sir Hector Ajacks, the great Indian general's, effects), and the portrait of the master of the house (Debenham Storr, R.A., pinxit), crimson curtain and column in foreground, dessert plate, cut orange, and—supposed—silver hand-bell in front ditto. This is the sort of room where there is a Turkey carpet that has been purchased at the East India Company's sale rooms, in Billiter Street, and which went cheap because there was a hole in one corner, carefully darned subsequently by the mistress of the house. The master comes down stairs gravely, with a bald head—the thin, gray hair carefully brushed over the temples, and a duffel dressing-gown. He spends five minutes in his "study," behind the breakfast dining-room; not, goodness knows, to consult the uncut books on the shelves—uncomfortable works, like Helps's "Friends in Council," that scrap of rusty BACON, and Mr. Harriet Martineau's "India," are among the number; but to break the seals of the letters ranged for him on the leather-covered table—he reads his correspondence at breakfast—to unlock, perchance, one drawer, take out his cheque-book, and give it one hasty flutter, one loving glance, and to catch up and snuggle beneath his arm the copy of the "Times" newspaper, erst damped, but since aired at the kitchen fire, which the newsvender's boy dropped an hour since down the area. It may be, too, that he goes into that uselessly (to him) book-furnished room, because he thinks it a good, a grand, a respectable thing to have a "study" at all. This is the sort of house where they keep a footman, single-handed—a dull knave, who no more resembles the resplendent flunkey of Eaton Square or Westbourne Terrace, than does the cotton-stockinged "greencoat" of the minor theatres; who is told that he must wear a morning jacket, and who accoutres himself in a striped jerkin, baggy in the back and soiled at the elbows, that makes him look like an hostler, related, on the mother's side, to a Merry Andrew. The mistress of the house comes down to nine o'clock breakfast, jingling the keys in her little basket, and with anxious pre-occupation mantling from her *guipure* collar to her false front, for those fatal crimson housekeeping books are to be audited this morning, and she is nervous. The girls come down in brown-holland jackets and smartly dowdy skirts, dubious as to the state of their back hair; the eldest daughter frowning after her last night's course of theology (intermingled with the last novel from Mr. Mudie's). As a rule, the young ladies are very ill-tempered; and, equally as a rule, there is always one luckless young maiden in a family of grown-up daughters who comes down to breakfast with her stockings down at heel, and is sternly reprimanded during breakfast because one of her shoes comes off under the table; he who denounces her being her younger brother, the lout in the jacket, with the surreptitious peg-top in his pocket, who attends the day-school of the London University, and cribs his sisters' Berlin-wool canvas to mend his Serpentine yacht sails with. The children too old to breakfast in the nursery come down gawky, awkward, tumbling, and discontented, for they are as yet considered too young to partake of the frizzled bits of bacon which are curling themselves in scorched agony on the iron footman before the grate, the muffins, which sodden in yellow butter-pools in the Minton plates on the severely-creased damask table-cloth, or the dry toast which, shrivelled and forbidding, grins from between the Sheffield-plated bars of the rack. The servants come in, not to morning breakfast, but to morning prayers. The housemaid has just concluded her morning flirtation with the baker; the cook has been crying over "Fatherless Fanny." The master of the house reads prayers in a harsh, grating voice, and Miss Charlotte, aged thirteen, is sent to her bed-room, with prospects of additional punishment, for eating her curl-papers during matins. The first organ-grinder arrives in the square during breakfast; and the master of the house grimly reproves the children who are beginning to execute involuntary polkas on their chairs, and glowers at the governess—she is such a meek young creature, marked with the small-pox, that I did not think it worth while to mention her before—who manifests symptoms of beating her sad head to the music. How happy, at least how relieved, everybody is when the master exchanges his duffel dressing-gown for a blue body-coat, takes his umbrella, and drives off in his brougham to the city or Somerset House! The children are glad to go to their lessons, though they hate *them* at most times, passably. Miss Meek, the governess, is glad to install herself in her school-room, and grind "Mangnall's Questions," and "Blair's Preceptor," till the children's dinner, at one o'clock; though she would, perhaps, prefer shutting herself up in her own room and having a good cry. The mistress finds consolation, too, in going downstairs and quarrelling with the cook, and then going upstairs and being quarrelled with by the nurse. Besides, there will be plenty of time for shopping before Mr. M. comes home. The girls are delighted that cross papa is away. Papa always wants to know what the letters are about which they write at the little walnut-tree tables with the twisted legs. Papa objects to the time wasted in working the application collars. Papa calls novel reading and pianoforte practice "stuff," with a very naughty adjective prefixed thereunto. This is the sort of house that is neatly, solidly furnished from top to toe, with every modern convenience and improvement: with bath-rooms, conservatories, ice cellars; with patent grates, patent door-handles, dish-lifts, asbestos stoves, gas cooking ranges, and excruciatingly complicated ventilatory contrivances; and this is also the sort of house where, with all the conveniences I have mentioned, every living soul who inhabits it is uncomfortable.

As the clock strikes nine, you see the last school-children flock in to the narrow alley behind St. Martin's Lane, hard by the Lowther Arcade, and leading to the national schools. They have been romping and playing in the street this half-hour; and it was but the iron tongue of St. Martin that interrupted that impending fight between the young brothers Puddicomb, from King Street, Long Acre, who are always fighting, and that famous clapper-clawing match between Polly Briggs and Susey Wright. At the last stroke of nine there hurries into the school corridor a comely female teacher in a green plaid shawl: and, woe be unto her! nine has struck full ten minutes, when the inevitable laggard of every school appears, half skurrying, half crawling, her terror combating with her sluggishness, from the direction of Leicester Square. She is a gaunt, awkward girl, in a "flibberty-flobberty" hat, a skimping gray cape, with thunder-and-lightning buttons, an absurdly short skirt, and lace-edged trousers, that trail over her sandaled shoes. Add to this her slate and satchel, and she is complete. When will parents cease, I wonder, to attire their children in this ridiculous and preposterous manner. Hannah (her name is Hannah, for certain!) left her home in Bear Street in excellent time for school; but she has dawdled, and loitered, and gloated over every sweetstuff and picture shop, and exchanged languid repartees with rude boys. She will be kept in to a certainty this afternoon, will Hannah!

Now is the matutinal occupation of the milkwoman nearly gone; her last cries of "Milk, ho!" die away in faint echoes, and she might reasonably be supposed to enjoy a holiday till the afternoon's milk for tea were required; but not so. To distant dairies she hies, and to all appearances occupies herself in scrubbing her milk pails till three o'clock. I have a great affection (platonic) for milkwomen. I should like to go down to Wales and see them when they are at home. What clean white cotton stockings they wear, on—no, not their legs—on the posts which support their robust torsos! How strong they are! There are many I should be happy to back, and for no inconsiderable trifle either, to thrash Ben Gaunt. Did you ever know any one who courted a milkwoman? Was there ever a milkwoman married, besides Madam Vestris, in the "Wonderful Woman?" Yes; I love them—their burly forms; their mahogany faces, handsomely veneered by wind and weather; their coarse straw bonnets flattened at the top; their manly lace-up boots, and those wonderful mantles on their shoulders, which are neither shawl, tippet, cape nor scarf, but a compound of all, and are of equally puzzling colour and patterns.

The postman is breakfasting in the interval between the eight and the ten o'clock delivery. Does he take his scarlet tunic off when he breakfasts? Does he beguile the short hour of refreshment by reading, between snaps of bread and butter and gulps of coffee, short extracts from "A Double Knock at the Postman's Conscience," by the Reverend Mr. Davis, Ordinary of Newgate? For if the postman reads not during breakfast-time, I am wholly at a loss to know, dog-tired as he must be when he comes home from his rounds at night, when he can find time for pursuing his literary studies. By the way, where does the postman lodge? I have occupied apartments in the same house with a policeman; I was once aware of the private residence of a man who served writs; and I have taken tea in the parlour of the Pandean pipes to a Punch-and-Judy; but I never knew personally the abode of a postman. Mr. Sculthorpe and Mr. Peacock know them but too frequently, to the postman's cost.

Nine o'clock, and the *grande armée* of "musicianers" debouches from Spitalfields, and Leather Lane, Holborn, and far-off Clerkenwell, and, in compact columns, move westward. Nine o'clock, and the sonorous cry of "Old clo'!" is heard in sequestered streets chiefly inhabited by bachelors. Nine o'clock, and another *grande armée* veers through Temple Bar, charges down Holborn Hill, escalades Finsbury, captures Cornhill by a dexterous flank movement, and sits down and invests the Bank of England in regular form. This is London going to business in the city.

NINE O'CLOCK A.M.: OMNIBUSES AT THE BANK.

NINE O'CLOCK A.M.: PENNY STEAMBOATS ALONGSIDE THE PIER AT LONDON BRIDGE.

If the morning be fine, the pavement of the Strand and Fleet Street looks quite radiant with the spruce clerks walking down to their offices, governmental, financial, and commercial. Marvellous young bucks some of them are. These are the customers, you see at a glance, whom the resplendent wares in the hosiers' shops attract, and in whom those wary industrials find avid customers. These are the dashing young parties who purchase the pea-green, the orange, and the rose-pink gloves; the crimson braces, the kaleidoscopic shirt-studs, the shirts embroidered with dahlias, deaths' heads, race-horses, sun-flowers, and ballet-girls; the horseshoe, fox-head, pewter-pot-and-crossed-pipes, willow-pattern-plate, and knife-and-fork pins. These are the glasses of city fashion, and the mould of city form, for whom the legions of fourteen, of fifteen, of sixteen, and of seventeen shilling trousers, all unrivalled, patented, and warranted, are made; for these ingenious youths coats with strange names are devised, scarves and shawls of wondrous pattern and texture despatched from distant Manchester and Paisley. For them the shiniest of hats, the knobbiest of sticks, gleam through shop-windows; for them the geniuses of "all-round collars" invent every week fresh yokes of starched linen, pleasant instruments of torture, reminding us equally of the English pillory, the Chinese cangue, the Spanish garotte, the French *lucarne* to the guillotine (that window from which the criminal looks out into eternity), and the homely and cosmopolitan dog-collar! There are some of these gay clerks who go down to their offices with roses at their button-holes, and with cigars in their mouths; there are some who wear peg-top trousers, chin-tufts, eye-glasses, and varnished boots. These mostly turn off in the Strand, and are in the Admiralty or Somerset House. As for the government clerks of the extreme West-end—the patricians of the Home and Foreign Offices—the bureaucrats of the Circumlocution Office, in a word—*they* ride down to Whitehall or Downing Street in broughams or on park hacks. Catch them in omnibuses, or walking on the vulgar pavement, forsooth! The flags of Regent Street they might indeed tread gingerly, at three o'clock in the afternoon; but the Strand, and at nine o'clock in the morning! Forbid it, gentility! I observe—to return to the clerks who are bending citywards—that the most luxuriant whiskers belong to the Bank of England. I believe that there are even whisker clubs in that great national institution, where prizes are given for the best pair of *favoris* grown without macassar. You may, as a general rule, distinguish government from commercial clerks by the stern repudiation of the razor, as applied to the beard and moustaches, by the former; and again I may remark, that the prize for the thinnest and most dandy-looking umbrellas must be awarded, as of right, to the clerks in the East India House—mostly themselves slim, natty gentlemen, of jaunty appearance, who are all supposed to have had tender affairs with the widows of East India colonels. You may know the cashiers in the private banking houses by their white hats and buff waistcoats; you may know the stock-brokers by their careering up Ludgate Hill in dog-carts, and occasionally tandems, and by the pervading sporting appearance of their costume; you may know the Jewish commission agents by their flashy broughams, with lapdogs and ladies in crinoline beside them; you may know the sugar-bakers and the soap-boilers by the comfortable double-bodied carriages with fat horses in which they roll along; you may know the Manchester warehousemen by their wearing gaiters, always carrying their hands in their pockets, and frequently slipping into recondite city taverns up darksome alleys, on their way to Cheapside, to make a quiet bet or so on the Chester Cup or the Liverpool Steeplechase; you may know, finally, the men with a million of money, or thereabouts, by their being ordinarily very shabby, and by their wearing shocking bad hats, which have seemingly never been brushed, on the backs of their heads.

"Every road," says the proverb, "leads to Rome;" every commercial ways leads to the Bank of England. And there, in the midst of that heterogeneous architectural jumble between the Bank of England itself, the Royal Exchange, the Poultry, Cornhill, and the Globe Insurance Office, the vast train of omnibuses, that have come from the West and that have come from the East—that have been rumbling along the Macadam while I was prosing on the pedestrians—with another great army of clerk martyrs outside and inside, their knees drawn up to their chins, and their chins resting on their umbrella handles, set down their loads of cash-book and ledger fillers. What an incalculable mass of figures must there be collected in those commercial heads! What legions of £. s. d.! What a chaos of cash debtor, contra creditor, bills payable, and bills receivable; waste-books, day-books, cash-books, and journals; insurance policies, brokerage, agio, tare and tret, dock warrants, and general commercial bedevilment! They file off to their several avocations, to spin money for others, often, poor fellows, while they themselves are blest with but meagre stipends. They plod away to their gloomy wharves and hard-hearted counting-houses, where the chains from great cranes wind round their bodies, and they dance hornpipes in bill-file and cash-box fetters, and the mahogany of the desks enters into their souls. Upon my word, I think if I were doomed to clerkdom, that I should run away and enlist; but that would avail me little, for I am equally certain that, were I a grenadier, and my commanding officer made me mount guard, that I should pop my musket into the sentry-box and run away too.

So the omnibuses meet at the Bank and disgorge the clerks by hundreds; repeating this operation scores of times between nine and ten o'clock. But you are not to delude yourself, that either by wheeled vehicle or by the humbler conveyances known as "Shanks's mare," and the "Marrowbone stage"—in more refined language, walking—have all those who have business in the city reached their destination. No; the Silent Highway has been their travelling route. On the broad—would that I could add the silvery and sparkling—bosom of Father Thames, they have been borne in swift, grimy little steamboats, crowded with living freights from Chelsea, and Pimlico, and Vauxhall piers, from Hungerford, Waterloo, Temple, Blackfriars, and Southwark—straight by the hay-boats, with their lateen sails discoloured in a manner that would delight a painter, straight by Thames police hulks, by four and six-oared cutters, by coal-barges, and great lighters laden with bricks and ashes and toiling towards Putney and Richmond; by oozy wharves and grim-chimneyed factories; by little, wheezy, tumbledown waterside public-houses; by breweries, and many-windowed warehouses; by the stately gardens of the Temple, and the sharp-pointed spires of city churches, and the great dome of Paul's looming blue in the morning, to the Old Shades Pier, hard by London Bridge. There is landing and scuffling and pushing; the quivering old barges, moored in the mud, are swaying and groaning beneath trampling feet. Then, for an instant, Thames Street, Upper and Lower, is invaded by an ant-hill swarm of spruce clerks, who mingle strangely with the fish-women and the dock-porters. But the insatiable counting-houses soon swallow them up: as though London's commercial maw were an hungered too, for breakfast, at nine o'clock in the morning.

TEN O'CLOCK A.M.—THE COURT OF QUEEN'S BENCH, AND THE "BENCH" ITSELF.

The author presents his compliments to the "neat-handed Phillis" who answers (when she is in a good temper, which is but seldom) the second-floor bell, takes in his letters, brings up his breakfast, stands in perpetual need of being warned not to light the fire with the proof-sheets of his last novel, pamphlet on the war, or essay on the Æolic digamma, or twist into cigar-lights the cheques for large amounts continually sent him by his munificent publishers, and exercises her right of search over his tea-caddy and the drawer containing his cravats, all-round collars, and billet-doux; the author and your servant presents his compliments to Phillis—ordinarily addressed by Mrs. Lillicrap, the landlady, as "Mariar, you 'ussey"—and begs her to procure for him immediately a skin of the creamiest parchment, free from grease, a bottle of record ink, a quill plucked from the wing of a hawk, vulture, or some kindred bird of prey, a box of pounce, a book of patterns of German text for engrossing, and a hank of red tape or green ferret, whichsoever, in her æsthetic judgment, she may prefer. He would be further obliged if she would step round to the author's solicitor, and ask, not for that little bill of costs, which has been ready for some time, but which he is not in the slightest hurry for—but for copies of Tidd's Practice, the Law List, and Lord St. Leonards' "Handy Book on Property Law." For I, the author, intend to be strictly legal at ten o'clock in the morning. I serve you with this copy of "Twice Round the Clock" as with a writ; and in the name of Victoria, by the grace, &c., send you greeting, and command—no, not command, but beg—that within eight days you enter an appearance, to purchase this volume. Else will I invoke the powers of the great *ca. sa.* and the terrible *fi. fa.* I will come against you, with sticks and staves, and the sheriff of Middlesex shall take you, to have and to hold, wheresoever you may be found running up and down in his bailiwick. *Son nutrito di latte legale.* I am fed with law's milk at this hour of the morning. Shear me the sheep for vellum, fill me with quips and quiddities; bind me apprentice to a law stationer in the Lane of Chancery, over-against Cursitor Street; and let me also send in a little bill of costs to my publishers, and charge them so much a "folio," instead of so much a "sheet."

This exercitation over, and the necessary stationery brought by Phillis, *alias* "Mariar," I approach my great, grim subject with diffident respect. What do I know of law, save that if I pay not, the Alguazils will lay me by the heels; that if I steal, I shall go to the hulks; that if I kill, I shall go hang? What do I know of *Sinderesis*, feoffors and feoffees, and the law of tailed lands? What of the Assize of *Mortdancestor*, tenants in dower, villein entry—of *Sylva cædua*, which is, I am sure you will be glad to hear, more familiarly known as the 45th of Edward the Third? These things are mysteries to me. I bought the *habeas corpus* once (the palladium of our liberties is an expensive luxury), but its custodian scarcely allowed me to look at it, and, hailing a cab, desired me to "look alive." I have been defendant in an action, but I never could make out why they should have done the things to me that they did, and why John Lord Campbell at Westminster should have been so bitter against me. I never was on a jury; but I have enjoyed the acquaintance of an Irish gentleman whose presence on the panel was considered invaluable at state trials, he having the reputation of an indomitable "boot-eater." Finally, I have, as most men have, a solicitor, a highly respectable party, who, of course, only charges me the "costs out of pocket." But what is the exact measure of "costs out of pocket?" I never knew.

Not wholly destitute of legal literature is your servant, however. In Pope and Arbuthnot's Reports (*vide* Miscellanies) I have read the great case of Stradlings *versus* Styles, respecting the piebald horses and the horses that were pied, and have pondered much over that notable conclusion (in Norman-French) by the reporter—"Je heard no more parceque j'etais asleep sur mong bench." I have followed the arguments in Bardell *versus* Pickwick: I have seen the "Avocat Patelin" and the "Lottery Ticket;" I have paced the Salle des Pas Perdus in Paris, and Westminster Hall, London; I knew a captain once who lived in the equally defunct "rules" of the Queen's Bench; and I have played racquets in the area of that establishment, as an amateur(?). So, then, though, in a very humble degree, I conceive myself qualified to discourse to you concerning legal London at ten o'clock in the morning.

The judges of the land—of Queen's Bench, Exchequer, and Common Pleas, Chief-Justices, Barons, and Puisne Judges, and Sages of the Court of Probate, Divorce, and Matrimonial Causes—are mostly jaunty, elderly gentlemen of cheerful appearance, given in private life to wearing light neckcloths, buff waistcoats, and pepper-and-salt trousers, and particularly addicted to trotting down to the Courts of Westminster mounted on stout hacks—'tis the bishops, *par excellence*, who ride the cobs—and followed by sober grooms. There are judges who, it is reported, make up considerable books for the Derby and Oaks—nay, for the double event. I have seen a judge in a white hat, and I have seen a vice-chancellor drinking iced fruit effervescent at Stainsbury's in the Strand.

Parliament Street and Palace Yard are fair to see, this pleasant morning in Term time. The cause list for all the courts is pretty full, and there is a prospect of nice legal pickings. The pavement is dotted with barristers' and solicitors' clerks carrying blue and crimson bags plethoric with papers. Smart attorneys, too, with shoe-ribbon, light vests, swinging watch-guards, and shiny hats (they have begun to wear moustaches even, the attorneys!), bustle past, papers beneath their arms, open documents in their hands, which they sort and peruse as they walk. The parti-coloured fastenings of these documents flutter, so that you would take these men of law for so many conjurors about to swallow red and green tape. And they do conjure, and to a tune, the attorneys. Lank office-boys, in hats too large, and corduroys and tweeds too short, and jackets, stained with ink, too short for them; cadaverous office-runners and process-servers, in greasy and patched habiliments, white at the seams; bruised and battered, ruby-nosed law-writers, skulking down to Westminster in quest of a chance copying job; managing clerks, staid men given to abdominal corpulence, who wear white neckcloths, plaited shirt-frills, black satin waistcoats, and heavy watch chains and seals, worn, in the good old fashion, underneath the vest, and pendulous from the base line thereof, file along the pavement to their common destination, the great Hall of Pleas at Westminster. The great solicitors and attorneys, men who may be termed the princes of law, who are at the head of vast establishments in Bedford Row and Lincoln's Inn Fields, and whose practice is hereditary, dash along in tearing cabs: you look through the windows, and see an anxious man, with bushy gray whiskers, sitting inside; the cushions beside and before him littered, piled, cumbered, with tape-tied papers. He has given Sir Fitzroy three hundred, Sir Richard five hundred, guineas, for an hour's advocacy. Thousands depend upon the decision of the twelve worthy men who will be in the jury-box in the course of an hour. See! one of them is cheapening apples at a stall at this very moment, and tells his companion (who has just alighted from a chaise-cart) that in that little shop yonder Marley murdered the watchmaker's shopman. Great lawyers such as these have as many noble fortunes in their hands as great doctors have noble lives. Of the secrets of noble reputations, doctors and lawyers are alike custodians; and, trustworthy.

The briefless barristers would like to patronise cabs, but they can't afford those luxuries. They walk down Parliament Street arm-in-arm, mostly men with bold noses of the approved Slawkenbergius pattern, and very large red or sandy whiskers. Whiskers cost nothing, noses are cheap—I had mine broken once for nothing, though it cost me several pounds sterling to get it mended again. Their briefless clothes are very worn and threadbare, their hats napless, their umbrellas—they always carry umbrellas—gape at the mouth, and distend at the nozzle. These barristers are second wranglers, fellows of their college, prizemen; they have pulled stroke-oar, and bibbed at wine parties given by marquises. They are very poor and briefless now. The chambers in the Temple are very high up; the carpet, ragged; the laundress is a tipsy shrew who pilfers; the boot-boy insists upon serving up small coal broiled with the mutton chops. It is but seldom, but very seldom, that they can order a steak at the "Rainbow," or demand a bottle of Port from the plump waiter the "Cock." No attorneys ascend their staircase; no briefs are frayed in being pushed through the aperture of their letter-boxes; editors are deaf, and the only magazine which receives their contributions don't pay. They cannot help asking themselves sometimes, sadly and querulously, poor fellows, of what avail is the grand classical education, tedious and expensive; the slaving for a degree or for honours; the long nights spent beneath the glare of the reading lamp, learning and re-learning the palimpsests of law; of what avail are the joints of mutton and bottles of heady wine consumed at the keeping-term dinners; of what avail the square of the hypothenuse, and the knowledge (in the best Latin) that strong men lived before Agamemnon; of what avail the wig (it is getting unpowdered), the gown (it is growing threadbare), and the big Greek prize-books with the College arms emblazoned on the covers? Lo! there is Tom Cadman, who has been an unsuccessful play-actor and an usher in a cheap boarding-school, writing leaders for a daily paper in the coffee-room of the "Albion," or returning thanks for the press at a champagne dinner; there is Roger Bullyon, of the Home Circuit, whose only talent is abuse, who knows no more of law than he does of the conduct to be expected from a gentleman, who will never, if he live till ninety, be more than a fluent, insolent donkey, and yet there he is, with more briefs than he can carry, or his clerk compute the fees on. But console yourselves, oh, ye briefless ones. Though the race be not to the swift, nor the battle to the strong, your chance is yet in the lucky-bag; the next dive may bring it forth splendid and triumphant.

"No one is so accursed by fate,

No one so utterly desolate,

But some heart, though unknown,

Responds unto his own."

Mr. Right, the attorney, is coming post-haste after you, his waistcoat pockets distended with retainers and refreshers. In that tremendous lottery of the law, as wise Mr. Thackeray terms it, who shall say that you may not be next the fortunate wretches who shall win the prize—the *gros lot*? To-day is poverty and heart-sickening hope deferred and the pawn-shop; but to-morrow may make you the thunderer before the judicial committee of the Privy Council on the great appeal from Bombay, Parsetjee-Jamsetjee-Ramsetjee Loll *versus* Boomajee-Krammajee-Howdajee Chow. It may make you standing counsel to the Feejee Islands Company, or defender of group 97 of Railway Bills. So, despair not, briefless man; but pause before you sell that sheet anchor of hope, of yours, for old iron.

Barristers in large practice drive over Westminster Bridge's crazy arches (the rogues have houses at Norwood and Tulse Hill, with conservatories and pineries) in small phætons or gleaming clarences, with sleek white horses. They have wives rustling in sheeny silks and glowing with artificial flowers, who, their lords being deposited in the temple of Theseus, are borne straight away to Stagg and Mantell's, or Waterloo House; or, perchance, to that glorious avenue of Covent Garden Market, where they price cucumbers at Mrs. Solomon's, and bouquets at Mrs. Buck's. For, note it as a rule, though it may seem a paradox, people who have kitchen-gardens and hot-houses are always buying fruit, flowers, and vegetables. The steady-going old Nisi Prius barristers, in good practice—sedate fogies—with their white neckcloths twisted like halters round their necks; pompous old fellows, who jingle keys and sovereigns in their pockets, as, their hands therein, they prop up the door-jambs of the robing-room, in converse with weasel-faced attorneys, are borne to Westminster in cabs. Very hard are they upon the cabman, paying him but the exact fare, and threatening him with the severest terrors of the law at the slightest attempt at overcharge; and much are they maledicted by the badged Jehus as they drive slowly away. These Nisi Prius worthies are great hands at a rubber of whist, and are as good judges of port-wine as they are of law.

Whence comes the Chief, the leader, the great advocate of the day, who carries attorney and solicitor general, chief-justice, chancellor, peer, written as legibly on his brow as Cain carried the brand?—how he reaches Westminster Hall, or how he gets away from it, no man can tell. He will make a four hours' speech to-day, drive eight witnesses to the verge of distraction, blight with sarcasm, and sear with denunciation, a semi-idiotic pig-jobber, the defendant in an action of breach of promise of marriage, in which the plaintiff is a stay-maker of the mature age of thirty-seven. What shrieks of laughter will ring through the court when in burning accents, in which irony is mingled with indignation, the Chief reads passages from the love-smitten but incautious pig-jobber's correspondence, and quotes from his poetical effusions (they *will* write poetry, these defendants) such passages as—

"When you tork

You are like roast pork."

Or,

"Say, luvley chine,

Will you be mine."

Two hours afterwards, and the Chief will be on the other side of Westminster Hall, in the Commons' House of Parliament, pounding away on the wrongs of a few people in Staffordshire who object to the odour of some neighbouring gas-works, and, to use an Americanism, "chawing up" the ministry at a tremendous rate. How is it that about the same time he manages to dine with the Merchant Cobblers at their grand old hall on St. Crispin's Hill; to take the chair at the festival of the Association for improving the moral condition of Mudlarks; to make a two hours' speech at the meeting for the suppression of street "catch-'em-alive-O's;" to look in at half-a-dozen west-end clubs; to hear Bosio—ah! poor Bosio, ah, poor swan, miasma'd to death in the horrid marshes of Ingria and Carelia—in the last act of the "Traviata;" and to be seen flitting out of the bar-parlour of Joe Muttonfist's hostelry in Mauley Court-yard, Whitechapel, where the whereabouts of the impending great fight between Dan Bludyer, surnamed the "Mugger," and Tim Sloggan, better known as "Copperscull," for two hundred pounds a-side, will be imparted to the patrons of the "fancy?" Tom Stoat, who knows everything and everybody, says he saw the Chief at the Crystal Palace Flower Show, and it is certain that he (the Chief) will be at the Queen's Ball to-night (he has a dinner party this evening), and that after the opera he will take a chop and kidney at Evans's. And after that? What a life! What frame can bear, what mind endure it! When does he study? when does he read those mammoth briefs? when does he note those cases, prepare those eloquent exordia and perorations? Whence comes the minute familiarity with every detail of the case before him which he seems to possess, the marvellous knowledge he displays of the birth, parentage, education, and antecedents of the trembling witnesses whom he cross-examines? What a career! and see, there is its Hero, shambling into Westminster Hall, a spare, shrunken, stooping, prematurely-aged man. He has not had a new wig these ten years, and his silk gown is shabby, almost to raggedness. He is no doubt arguing some abstruse point of law with that voluble gentleman, his companion, in the white waistcoat. Let us approach and listen, for I am Asmodeus and we are eaves-droppers. Point of law! Upon my word, he is talking about the Chester Cup.

TEN O'CLOCK A.M.: INTERIOR OF THE COURT OF QUEEN'S BENCH.

In with ye, then, my merry men all, to the hall of Westminster, for the Court of Queen's Bench is sitting. It is not a handsome court; it is not an imposing court. If I were to say that it was a very mean and ugly room, quite unworthy to figure as an audience-chamber for the judges of the land, I don't think that I should be in error. Where are the lictors and the fasces? Where the throned daïs on which the wise men of the Archeopagus should properly sit? The bench looks but an uncomfortable settle! the floor of the court is a ridiculous little quadrangle of oak, like a pie-board; the witness-box is so small that it seems capable of holding nothing but the shooting "Jack" of our toyshop experience; and the jury-box has a strong family likeness to one of the defunct Smithfield sheep-pens, where sit the intelligent jury, who have an invincible propensity, be the weather hot or cold, for wiping their foreheads with blue cotton pocket handkerchiefs. A weary martyrdom some of those poor jurymen pass; understanding a great deal more about the case on which they have to deliver at its commencement than at its termination; bemused, bewildered, and dazzled by the rhetorical flourishes and ingenious sophistry of the counsel on both sides, and utterly nonplussed by the elaborately obscure pleas that are put in. But the usher has sworn them in that they "shall will and truly try" the matter before them; and try it they must. To a man who has, perhaps, a matter of sixty or seventy thousand pounds at stake on the issue of a trial, the proceedings of most tribunals seem characterised by strange indifference, and an engaging, though, to the plaintiff and defendant, a somewhat irritating *laisser aller*. The attorneys take snuff with one another, and whisper jokes. The counsel chat and poke each other in the ribs; the briefless ones, in the high back rows, scribble caricatures on their blotting-pads, or pretend to pore over "faggot" briefs, or lounge from the Queen's Bench into the Exchequer, and from the Exchequer into the Bail Court, and so on and into the Common Pleas; the usher nods, and cries, "Silence," sleepily; the clerk reads in a droning monotonous voice documents of the most vital importance, letters that destroy and blast a life-long reputation of virtue and honour: letters that bring shame on noble women, and ridicule on distinguished men; vows of affection, slanderous accusations, outbursts of passion, anonymous denunciations, ebullitions of love, hatred, revenge. Some one is here, doubtless, to report the case for to-morrow's papers, but no active pens seem moving. The Chief has not assumed his legal harness yet; and the junior counsel employed in the case are bungling over their preliminaries. The faded moreen curtains; the shabby royal arms above the judge, with their tarnished gilding, subdued-looking lion, and cracked unicorn; the ink-stained, grease-worn desks and forms; the lack-lustre, threadbare auditory, with woe-be-gone garments and mien, who fill up the hinderpart of the auditory: though what they can want in the Court of Queen's Bench Heaven only knows; the bombazine-clad barristers, in their ill-powdered wigs—quite fail in impressing you with a sense of anything like grandeur or dignity. Yet you are in *Banco Reginâ*. Here our sovereign lady the Queen is supposed to sit herself in judgment; and from this court emanates the Great Writ of Right—the Habeas Corpus. To tell the truth, neither counsel, jury, nor audience seem to know or to care much about what is going on; but there are three persons who sit up aloft—not exactly sweet little cherubs, for they are very old, wrinkled men—who know the case like a book, and considerably better than many books; who have weighed the *pros* and *cons* to the minutest hair's breadth, to a feather's turn of the scale, who are awake and alive, alive O! to all the rhetorical flourishes and ingenious sophistry of the advocates, and who will tell the jury exactly what the case is made of in about a tithe of the time that the junior counsel would take in enumerating wrongs of which the plaintiff complains, or whose commission the defendant denies. It is an edifying sight to watch the presiding judge—that shrivelled man in petticoats—with his plain scratch wig all awry. Now he hugs his arms within his capacious sleeves; now he crosses his legs; now, yes, now he twiddles his judicial thumbs; now he nods his august head, allows it to recline over one shoulder, and seems on the point of falling off to sleep; now he leans wearily, his cheek in his hand, his elbow on the bench, first on one side, then on the other; then he rises, shakes his old head, yawns, and, with his hands in his pockets, surveys the outer bar through gold-rimmed spectacles. He seems the most bored, the most indifferent spectator there; but only wait till the chiefs on both sides have concluded their eloquent bamboozling of the jury; mark my Lord Owlett settle his wig and his petticoats then, sort and unfold the notes he has been lazily (so it seemed) scrawling from time to time, and in a piping, quavering voice, begin to read from them. You marvel at the force, the clarity, the perspicuity of the grand old man; you stand abashed before the intellect, clear as crystal, at an age when man's mind as well as his body is oft-times but labour and sorrow; you are astonished that so much vigour, so much shrewdness, so much eloquence, should exist in that worn and tottering casket. Goodness knows, I am not an optimist, and give but too much reason to be accused of *nil admirari* tendencies; yet I cannot help thinking that if on this earth there exists a body of men grandly wise, generously eloquent, nobly impartial, and sternly incorruptible, those men are the judges of England.

Come away though, now, Don Cleophas; we must go further afield. The case that is "on" just now is not of sufficient interest to detain us; though here is an episode sufficiently grotesque. An old lady is entitled to some damages, or to some verdict, or to some money or apology, or, at all events, something from somebody. My Lord Owlett suggests a compromise, and instructs counsel to ask her what she will take to settle matters.

"What will you take?" asks the gentleman in the bob-tailed wig of the old lady.

Now the old lady is very deaf, and merely shakes her head at the counsel, informing the jury, in confidence, that she is "very hard o' hearin'."

"His Lordship wants to know what you will take?" asks the counsel again; this time bawling as loud as ever he can in the old lady's ear.

"I thank his lordship kindly," the ancient dame answers stoutly, "and if it's no illconwenience to him, *I'll take a little warm ale!*"

And, amid a roar of laughter from the spectators, we quit the Court of Queen's Bench.

Nor must we linger, either, beneath William Rufus's carved roof-tree, so ingeniously heightened, and otherwise transmogrified, by Sir Charles Barry and his satellites. This is a different Westminster Hall to that which I knew in my childhood, just after the great fire of '34. There was no great stained glass window at the end then, no brazen Gothic candelabra, no golden House of Lords in the corridor beyond, where the eye is dazzled with the gilding, the frescoes, the scarlet benches and rich carpets, and where the Lord High Chancellor sits on the woolsack, like an allegory of Themis in the midst of a blaze of fireworks. In my time, the keeper of her Majesty's conscience and the Great Seal sat in a panelled room, like a dissenting chapel. Let us hasten forth from the Great Hall, for it is full of memories. I spoke of famous footsteps on the Mall, St. James's; how many thousand footsteps—

thousands?—millions rather, have been lost here in fruitless pacing up and down! Westminster Hall is always cool: well it may be so; the dust was laid and the air refrigerated centuries since by the tears and the sighs of ruined suitors. What a wondrous place the old hall is! what reminiscences it conjures up—they will *not* be laid in the Red Sea—of the gorgeous banquets of the Plantagenets, of the trials of Laud and Strafford, and of Laud and Strafford's master; of Mr. Jonathan Wild's ancestor walking the hall with a straw in his shoe; of poor little Lady Jane Grey and Guildford Dudley, her husband, standing their trial here on a velvet-covered platform in the midst of the hall, for treason to Bloody Mary. Did they ever cut a state prisoner's head off in Westminster Hall, I wonder, as they did Mary Stuart's in the hall at Fotheringay? The place is large enough.

TEN O'CLOCK A.M.: INTERIOR OF THE QUEEN'S BENCH PRISON.

Once again I stand within the precincts of the Queen's Bench; but where is my Lord Owlett, where the bewigged barristers and the jury-box with the "twelve honest men" within wiping their semperperspiring foreheads? I am standing in the centre of a vast gravelled area, bounded on the south side by a brick wall of tremendous height, and crowned by those curious arrangements of geometrical spikes known as *chevaux de frise*. To the north there is a range of ordinary-looking houses, the numbers of which are painted very conspicuously in white characters on a black ellipse above the doors, about which, moreover, there is this peculiarity, that they are always open. If you peep through the yawning portals, you will see that the staircases are of stone, and that the roofs of the rooms on the ground-floor are vaulted. There are no barred windows, no bolts, bars, or grim chains apparent, though from the back windows of these houses there is a pleasant prospect of another high wall, equally surmounted with *chevaux de frise*. When the spider has got the fly comfortably into his web, and has satisfied himself that he can't get out, I daresay that he does not take the trouble to handcuff him. In the midst of this gravelled area stands a pump, known as the "Dolphin;" to the right of this institution, and somewhat in the back-ground, is a great square building, called the "State House." The rooms here are double the size to those in the houses I have alluded to, and are accorded by the governor of the place as a matter of favour to those inmates of the—well, the college— who can afford to fill them with a sufficient quantity of furniture. Close to the State House is a strong iron gateway, through which the guardians of the college have a strong disinclination to allow the under-graduates to pass, unless they be furnished with a certain mysterious document called "a discharge." The guardians themselves are ruddy men with very big keys; but they seem on the very best terms with the gentlemen whose intended exercise outside the walls they feel compelled (doubtless through solicitude for their precious health) to debar, and are continually bidding them "good morning" in the most affable manner; it being also one of their idiosyncrasies to rub their noses with the handles of the big keys while going through the salutation. In days not very remote there were certain succursals, or chapels of ease, to the college, in the shape of dingy tenements in the borough of Southwark, extending as far as the Elephant and Castle; and in these tenements, which were called the "Rules," such collegians as were in a position to offer a fantastic guarantee entitled a "Bail Bond," were permitted to dwell, and thence they wrote letters to their friends and relations, stating that the iron was entering into their souls, and that they were languishing— well, never mind where—in college. These "rules" were abolished in the early years of her present Majesty's reign; and at the same time a stern Secretary of State prohibited the renewal of a notable saturnalia called "a Mock Election," of which no less celebrated an artist than Haydon painted a picture (he was himself a collegian at the time), which was bought, for considerably more than it was worth, by King George IV. The saturnalia was fast falling into desuetude by itself; but the Home Secretary also interfered to put a stop to the somewhat boisterous conviviality which had reigned among those collegians who had money, from time immemorial, and which had converted the Queen's Bench into a den of the most outrageous and disgraceful dissipation and revelry. Under the present not very stringent regulations (considering what a *carcere duro* is, the other *alma mater* of Whitecross Street, to say nothing of the hideous place called Horsemonger Lane), the collegians are restricted to the consumption of one quart of beer—which they may have just as strong as ever they like—or one imperial pint of wine, per diem, at their option; yet it is a very curious fact, that no collegian who was flush of cash was ever found to labour under any difficulty in providing sufficient refreshment for his friends when he gave a wine party in his room. The payment of rent is unknown in the college; and it is but rarely that the time-honoured system of "chummage," or quartering two or mere collegians in one room, and allowing the richest to pay his companions a stipulated sum to go out and find quarters elsewhere, is resorted to. As a rule, the collegian on his arrival, after spending one night in a vaulted apartment close to the entrance, and which bears a strong resemblance to the Gothic vault described in "Rookwood"—an apartment known as the "receiving ward"—has allotted to him, by solemnly-written ticket, a whitewashed chamber of tolerable size, moderately haunted by mice, and "passably" infested by fleas. Straightway there starts up, as it were from the bowels of the earth, a corpulent female rubicund in countenance, tumbled in garments, and profuse in compliments, assuring him that he is the very "Himage of the Markis of Scatterbrass, which his aunt let him out by composing with his creditors," or "Capting Spurbox, of the Hoss Guards, as 'ad champagne hevery mornin', and went through the court payin' nothink." She, for a small weekly stipend—say, five shillings—agrees to furnish your room; and in an astonishingly short space of time you find the bare cube transformed into a sufficiently comfortable bed-room and sitting-room. For eighteenpence a week extra you may have a double green baize door with brass nails, like a verdant coffin, and white dimity curtains to your windows, with real tassels. In the train of the stout tumbled female, there always follows a gaunt woman of no particular age, with ropy hair, a battered bonnet, and scanty garments apparently nailed to her angular form, who expresses, with many curtsies, her desire to "do for you." Don't be alarmed; she simply means that for three or four shillings a week she will clean your room, boil your kettle, and bring up the dinner, which has been cooked for you in the common kitchen of the college. She, too, has an acolyte, a weazened old man in a smock frock and knee shorts (though I think that he must be dead or have left college by this time[3]) who for a shilling a week will make your boots shine like mirrors; who resides here, and has resided here for many years, because he can't or won't pay thirty pounds, and who is reported to be worth a mint of money. So here the collegian lives, and makes as merry as he can under adverse circumstances. The same tender precautions adopted by the authorities of the college to prevent the unnecessary egress of those in *statu pupillari*, are enforced to preserve a due state of morality among them. There is a chapel, as there is an infirmary, within the walls; the lady collegians, of whom there is always a small number in hold, are kept in jealous seclusion. Dicing and card-playing are strictly prohibited, and contumacious contravention of the rules involves the probability of the recalcitrant student being immured in a *locus penitentiæ* called the "Strong Room." There he is kept for four and twenty hours, *without tobacco*. Horrible punishment! This is in the college attached to her Majesty's Bench. Pshaw! Why should I beat about the Bench, or the bush, any longer, or even endorse the quibble adopted by those collegians who wish to have their letters addressed to them genteelly, of "No. 1, Belvidere Place?" That which I have been describing is a debtors' jail—the Queen's Prison, in fact.

And what of the collegians—the prisoners—themselves? It is ten o'clock in the morning, and they are sauntering about in every variety of shabby deshabille, smoking pipes after their meagre breakfasts, walking arm in arm with one another, or with friends who have come to see them, and whose ingress is permitted from nine a.m. until seven p.m. None are allowed to enter after that hour; but those visitors already in are allowed to stop till nine in the evening. Some of the collegian prisoners, poor fellows, have women and little children with them, who are very silly and sentimental, in their illogical way; but you may depend on it that, in nine out of ten of these groups, the staple theme of conversation is the probability of the captive being "out next week." They are always going to be out next week, these caged birds; but they die sometimes in the Bench, for all that.

Don't you think, too, that it would be as graceful as expedient to draw a veil over these broken-down men? Even the felons in Pentonville are allowed to wear masks in the exercise-yard. Why should I, whose sternest, strongest aim it is to draw from Life, and from the life only, but who wish to pluck the mote from no man's eye, to cast a stone at no glass house built on the pattern of mine own, expatiate in word-pictures upon the dilapidated dandies, the whilom dashing bucks in dressing-gowns out at elbows, and Turkish caps with tassels, set, with a woe-begone attempt at jaunty bearing, on one side, the decayed tradesmen, the uncertificated bankrupts, the cankers of a calm world and a long peace, that prowl and shuffle through the yards of a debtors' prison? Why, every man of the world has acquaintances, if not friends, there. Why, poor old Jack, who gave the champagne dinners we were so glad to be invited to, has been in the Bench for months. Yonder broken-winged butterfly, relapsing, quite against the order of nature, into a state of grubhood again, may have gone through his Humanities with the best of us, and may say *Hodie mihi, cras tibi*. To-day he is in jail; but to-morrow I, you, my brother the millionaire, may be taken in execution; and who shall say that we shall have the two pounds twelve wherewith to purchase the *habeas corpus*?

ELEVEN O'CLOCK A.M.—TROOPING THE GUARD, AND A MARRIAGE IN HIGH LIFE.

I have the fortune, or misfortune, to live in a "quiet street," and am myself an essentially quiet man, loving to keep myself in the Queen's peace, and minding my own business, though devoutly wishing that people would not mind it for me in quite so irritating a degree. I sleep soundly when in health, and never question Mrs. Lillicrap's mystifying items in her weekly bill, of "mustard, vinegar, and mending," or "pepper, postage stamps, and mother-o'-pearl buttons." I never grumble at the crying of babies, remembering that a wise and good doctor once told me that those dear innocents pass the days of their nonage in a chronic state of stomach-ache and congestion of the brain, and console myself with that thought. I can even support, without much murmuring, the jangling of the pupils' piano at Miss Besom's establishment for young ladies, next door. Distance, and a party-wall, lend enchantment to the sound, and I set no more store by it than I do by the chirruping of the birds in the town-bred foliage at the extremity of Buckingham Street, or the puffing and snorting of the halfpenny steamboats at the "Fox-under-the-Hill." I am so quiet, that I can allow the family of a distant blood-relation to reside in the parlours for twelve months, without troubling myself about their health; and I never yet rebelled at the perverse orthography of the washerwoman, who persists in spelling my half-hose thus: "Won pare sox." When I die, I hope that they will lay me in a very quiet church-yard in Kent, that I know, where some one who cared for me has been mouldering away peacefully these four years, where the clergyman's blind white pony will browse upon the salad that I am eating by the roots; where the children will come and have famous games—their silver voices and pattering feet upon the velvet turf make out a pleasant noise, I wot; and where they will write "*Requiescat in pace*" upon my gravestone; if, indeed, I leave maravedis enough behind me for Mr. Farley to cut me an inscription withal.

Yet, quiet as I am, I become at Eleven o'Clock in the Morning on every day of the week save Sunday a raving, ranting maniac—a dangerous lunatic, panting with insane desires to do, not only myself but other people, a mischief, and possessed, less by hallucination than by rabies. For so sure as the clock of St. Martin's strikes eleven, so sure does my quiet street become a pandemonium of discordant sounds. My teeth are on edge to think of them. The "musicianers," whose advent from Clerkenwell and the East-end of London I darkly hinted in a preceding chapter, begin to penetrate through the vaster thoroughfares, and make their hated appearance at the head of my street. First Italian organ-grinder, hirsute, sunburnt, and saucy, who grinds airs from the "Trovatore" six times over, follows with a selection from the

"Traviata," repeated half a dozen times, finishes up with the "Old Hundredth" and the "Postman's Knock," and then begins again. Next, shivering Hindoo, his skin apparently just washed in walnut juice, with a voluminous turban, dirty white muslin caftan, worsted stockings and hobnailed shoes, who, followed by two diminutive brown imps in similar costume, sings a dismal ditty in the Hindostanee language, and beats the tom-tom with fiendish monotony. Next comes a brazen woman in a Scotch cap, to which is fastened a bunch of rusty black feathers, apparently culled from a mourning coach past service. She wears a faded tartan kilt, fleshings, short calico trews, a velveteen jacket, tin buckles in her shoes, and two patches of red brick-dust on her haggard cheeks, and is supposed to represent a Scottish highlander. She dances an absurd fling, interpolated occasionally with a shrill howl to the music of some etiolated bagpipes screeded by a shabby rogue of the male sex, her companion, arrayed in similar habiliments. Next come the acrobats—drum, clarionet, and all. You know what those nuisances are like, without any extended description on my part. Close on their heels follows the eloquent beggar, with his numerous destitute but scrupulously clean family, who has, of course, that morning parted with his last shirt. Then a lamentable woman with a baby begins to whimper "Old Dog Tray." Then swoop into the street an abominable band of ruffians, six in number. They are swarthy villains, dressed in the semblance of Italian goatherds, and are called, I believe, *pifferari*. They play upon a kind of bagpipes—a hideous pig-skin-and-walking-stick-looking affair, and accompany their droning by a succession of short yelps and a spasmodic pedal movement that would be a near approach to a sailor's hornpipe, if it did bear a much closer resemblance to the war-dance of a wild Indian. Add to these the Jews crying "Clo'!" the man who sells hearthstones, and the woman who buys rabbit-skins, the butcher, the baker, and the boys screaming shrill Nigger melodies, and rattling pieces of slate between their fingers in imitation of the "bones," and you will be able to form an idea of the quietude of our street. From the infliction of the soot-and-grease-bedaubed and tambourine-and-banjo-equipped Ethiopian serenaders, we are indeed mercifully spared; but enough remains to turn a respectable thoroughfare into a saturnalia.

I can do nothing with these people. I shout, I threaten, I shake my fist, I objurgate them from my window in indifferent Italian, but to no avail. They defy, scorn, disregard, make light of me. They are encouraged in their abominable devices, not merely by the idlers in the street, the servant-maids gossiping at the doors, the boys with the baskets, and the nurse children, but by the people at the windows, who seem to have nothing to do but to look from their casements all day long. There is an ancient party of the female persuasion opposite my humble dwelling, who was wont to take intense interest in the composition of my literary essays. She used to bring her work to the window at first; but she never did a stitch, and soon allowed that flimsy pretext to fall through, and devoted herself with unaffected enjoyment to staring at me. As I am modest and nervous, I felt compelled to put a stop to this somewhat too persevering scrutiny; but I disdained to adopt the pusillanimous and self-nose-amputating plan of pulling down the window blinds. I tried taking her portrait as she sat, like an elderly Jessica, at the casement, and drew horrifying caricatures of her in red chalk, holding them up, from time to time, for her inspection; but she rather seemed to like this last process than otherwise; and I was obliged to change my tactics. The constant use of a powerful double-barrelled Solomon's race-glass of gigantic dimensions was first successful in discomposing her, and ultimately routed her with great moral slaughter; and she now only approaches the window in a hurried and furtive manner. I daresay she thinks my conduct most unhandsome. She and the tall man in the long moustaches at number thirteen, all the pupils at the ladies' school next door, the two saucy little minxes in black merino and worked collars at number nine, and that man with the bald head shaped like a Dutch cheese, in the parlour at number nine, who is always in his shirt sleeves, drums with his fingers on the window panes, and grins and makes faces at the passers-by, and whom I conscientiously believe to be a confirmed idiot, are all in a league against me, and have an alliance, offensive and defensive, with the musical *canaille* below. They cry out "Shame" when I remonstrate with those nuisances: they shout and jeer at me when I sally forth from the door, and make rabid rushes at the man with the bagpipes: they inquire derisively whether I consider myself lord of the creation? I am tempted—desperately tempted—to avail myself of my rights as a Civis Romanus, to summon the aid of the police, and to give one of the grinders, howlers, or droners in charge. Mr. Babbage, the arithmetician, does it; why should not I? What progress can I make in "Twice Round the Clock" in the midst of this hideous din? But then I remember, with much inward trouble, that I have in public committed myself more than once in favour of street music—that I have laughed at the folly of putting down bagpipes and barrel-organs by act of Parliament. I remember, too—I hope in all its force and Truth—a certain axiom, that the few must always suffer for the enjoyment of the many—that we are not all sages in decimals and logarithms—or people writing in books and newspapers—that the sick, the nervous, the fastidious, and the hypochondriacal, are but drops of water in a huge ocean of hale, hearty, somewhat thick-skinned and thick-eared humanity, who like the noisy vagabonds who are my bane and terror in the quiet street, and admire their distressing performances. Some men cannot endure a gaping pig; to many persons the odour of all roots of the garlic family is intolerable. I hate cats. I had an aunt who said that she could not "abide" green as a colour. Yet we should not be justified, I think, in invoking the terrors of the legislature against roast pork, onions, cats, and green peas. Mr. Babbage must pursue his mathematical calculations in a study at the back of his house, and I must hie me to the Reading-room of the British Museum, or turn out for a stroll.

And in this stroll, which, if the weather be fine, almost invariably leads towards one or other of the parks, I am frequently permitted to witness the imposing ceremony of "trooping the guard" in the Palace-yard, St. James's. Why her Majesty's Foot Guards should be "trooped" at eleven o'clock in the morning, and in what precise evolutions the operation of "trooping" consists, I am unable to state. Eleven o'clock, too, does not seem always a rigidly adhered-to hour; for, on the mornings of the days consecrated to our "Isthmian games," to the cosmopolitan Derby, and the more aristocratic, but equally attractive Ascot Cup, the time taken is nine instead of eleven, doubtless for the convenience of the heavy guardsmen, who, with heavy cigars protruding from their heavy moustaches, and heavy opera-glasses slung by their sides, go solemnly down to the races in heavy drags.

To the uninitiated, "trooping the guard" appears to consist in some hundred and fifty grenadiers in full uniform, their drums and fifes and their brass band at their head, marching from the Horse Guards, across the parade ground, and along the Mall to the Palace-yard, where the Queen's colours are stuck into a hole in the centre, where the officer on guard salutes them, where the other officers chat in the middle of the quadrangle, and where officers and men, and a motley crowd of spectators, listen to the enlivening strains of the brass band playing selections from the popular operas of the day. No complicated manœuvres seem to be performed; the automaton-like inspection of the "troops" takes place on the other side of the park; and when the colours are firmly fixed, and left in charge of a sentry, the "troops" file off again, the officers repairing to their clubs, and the soldiers to their barracks, while the brass bandsmen at once subside into private life, and become civilians of decidedly Cockney tendencies.

Hungry men are said, sometimes, to lull the raging of their appetites by sniffing the hot, and, to some noses, fragrant breeze which is emitted from between the gratings of an eating-house. To some the contemplation of eel pies, smoking rounds of beef, rumpsteak pies, and pen'orths of pudding, shining in the glory of dripping, and radiant with raisins, is almost as satisfying as the absolute possession of those dainties. It is certain that contented spirits do yet exist, by whom the sight of the riches and the happiness of others is accepted as a compensation for the wealth and the felicity which they do not themselves enjoy. It is a very pleasant mental condition, this—to be able to stare a pastrycook's window out of countenance, and partake of, in imagination, the rich plum-cakes, the raspberry-tarts, and the lobster-patties, without coveting those dainties; to walk up Regent Street, and wear, mentally, the "ducks of bonnets," the Burnouse cloaks and the Llama shawls, which poverty forbids us to purchase;

to walk through the Vernon or Sheepshanks collections, and hang up the delightful Landseers, Websters, and Mulreadys in fantastic mind-chambers of our own; to call Hampton Court and Windsor our palaces, and St. James's and the Green our parks; to fancy that the good people who have horses and carriages, and jewels, and silks, and satins, have but a copyhold interest in them, and that the fee-simple of all these fine things is in us. Such imaginative optimists can sit down unmurmuringly to a Barmecide feast; the "Court Circular" pleases them as much as an invitation to the Queen's ball; a criticism on "Lucrezia Borgia" at the opera delights them as much as an actual stall at Covent Garden; and Mr. Albert Smith's Egyptian Hall ascent of Mont Blanc, and his more recent Chinese entertainment, are to them quite as full of interest and adventure as a real pilgrimage to Chamouni, a toilsome scramble up the "Grands Mulets," a sail in a sampan on the Canton river, or a "fightee pigeon" with the "Braves" in Hog Lane.

ELEVEN O'CLOCK A.M.: TROOPING THE GUARD AT ST. JAMES'S PALACE.

The immortal young ladies who have been occupied in their eternal crochet-work any time since the siege of Troy, and who are called the Fates, have decided that it is better for me to be Alone. I am condemned for life to soliloquise. None of the young women with whom I have (to adopt the term current in domestic service) "kept company," would, in the end, have anything to do with me. They were very punctual in sending me cards—one sent me cake, but that was long ago—when they were married. One said I squinted, another that I was ill-tempered, and a third wondered at my impudence. Joan went off to Australia to join her cousin the digger, who, having done well at Bendigo, had written home for a wife, as he would for a Deans' revolver. Sarah married the linendraper (I am happy to state that he manifested himself stupid and ferocious, and went, commercially, to the dogs within six months after marriage); as for Rachel, she positively fell in love with the tailor who came to measure me for my wedding suit, and married *him*. A nursemaid with a perambulator nearly tripped me up the other day, and sitting in that infantile chariot was Rachel's eldest. Even the young lady who sold sardines at Stettin, and who, while I was waiting three years since for the ice to break up in the Baltic, undertook to teach me the prettiest German I ever heard in Deutschland, evinced a decided partiality for a certain baker with a Vandyke beard, who was a member of the Philharmonic Society of that town on the Oder, and at length jilted me for a trumpeter in a dragoon regiment, a burly knave in a striped and fringed uniform, all red and yellow, like a flamingo. The heartless conduct of the grocer's daughter towards me has already been recorded in print. So I am alone. Not repining, however, but taking pleasure in other people's children, with the additional consolation of not having their little frocks and perambulators to pay for, and passably content to sit on a mile-stone by the great roadside, and smoke the calumet of peace, watching the wain of life, with youth on the box and pleasure in the dickey, tear by, till the dust thrown up by the wheels has whitened my hair, and it shall be time enough to think of a neat walking funeral for One.

Now, do you understand why I alluded to the pleasures of imagination in connection with the contemplation of cook-shops, pictures, and palaces? Now, do you comprehend how a hopelessly solitary man—if you put a single grain of philosophic *hachisch* into that pacific calumet of his—can derive so much pleasure and contentment from the sight of other folk's weddings? I say nothing of courtship, which, on the part of a third party, argues a certain amount of, perhaps, involuntary eavesdropping and espionage, but which, when the boys and girls love each other sincerely, is as delightful a sight as the sorest of eyes, the sorest of hearts, could desire to witness. What pretty ways they have, those simple young "lovyers!" what innocent prattlings and rompings, what charming quarrels and reconciliations! Edward would dance with Miss Totterdown last night; Clara flirted most shamefully with Wertha Bjornsjertnjöe, the Scandinavian poet, and Lady Walrus's last lion. What confiding billings and cooings! how supremely foolish they are! and what an abhorrent thing is common-sense in love at all! Wondrously like ostriches, too, are Jenny and Jemmy Jessamy. They hide their pretty heads in each other's bosoms, and fancy they are totally invisible. They have codes of masonic telegraphy, as legible as Long Primer to the meanest understanding. I reckon among my friends a professor of photography in fashionable practice, and marvellous are the stories he has to tell of the by-play of love that takes place sometimes in his glass studio. For you see, when, in order to "focus" a young couple before him, he throws the curtain of the camera over his head, Jenny and Jemmy Jessamy are apt, in the sweet ignorance of love, to fancy that the operator can't see a bit what is going on; so Jenny arranges Jemmy's hair, and gives the moustache a twist, and there is a sly kiss, and a squeeze, and a pressure of the foot or so, and a variety of harmless endearing blandishments, known to our American cousins (who are great adepts at sweet-hearting) under the generic name of "conoodling," and all of which are faithfully transmitted through the lens, and neatly displayed in an inverted position on the field of the camera, to the edification of the discreet operator. Oh, you enamoured young men and women, you don't know that the eyes of domestic Europe are always fixed on you, and that your pretty simperings and whimperings form a drama which becomes the source of infinite amusement and delight to the philosophic bystanders. And is it not much better so, and that our lads and lasses should court in the simple, kindly Anglo-Saxon way, than that we should adopt foreign manners, and marry our wives, as in France, starched and prim from the convent or the boarding-school? Away with your morose, sulky, icy, ceremonious courtships. The Shepherd in Virgil, the moralist said, grew acquainted with Love, and found him a native of the rocks. But he did not dwell there in sulky solitude, I will be bound. The rock was most probably the Rocher de Cancale, where he sat and ate *dinde truffée*, and quaffed Chambertin, with his Psyche, in a new bonnet and cream-coloured gloves, by his side. And they went to the play afterwards, and had merry times of it, you may be sure.

ELEVEN O'CLOCK A.M.: A WEDDING AT ST. JAMES'S CHURCH, PICCADILLY.

I am very fond of weddings, and, to abandon for a moment the egotism and engrossing self-sufficiency which so delightfully characterise my sex, I fancy that the sight of the solemnisation of matrimony has equal charms for that better part of creation, whose special vocation it is, under all circumstances, to be married and happy, but who are oft-times, alas! as hopelessly celibate as the Trappist. One can scarcely go to a wedding without seeing some of these brave knights-errant, these *preux chevalières* of womanhood, these uncloistered nuns, these hermits in a vale of wax lights and artificial flowers, clustering in the galleries, or furtively ensconced in pews near the altar. They are very liberal to the pew-openers, these kind old maids, and are always ready with smelling-bottles if there be any fainting going on. They take their part in the crying with praiseworthy perseverance, and echo the responses in heartrending sobs; they press close to the bride as she comes down the aisle on the arm of her spouse, and eye her approvingly and the bridesmaids criticisingly; then go home, the big Church Service tucked beneath their mantles—go home to the solitary mutton chop and bleak shining hearth, with the cut paper pattern grinning through the bars like a skeleton. There are some cynics who irreverently call old maids "prancers," and others who, with positive brutality, accuse them of leading monkeys in a place which I would much rather not hear of, far less mention. They are, to be sure, somewhat stiff and starched, have uncomfortable prejudices against even the moderate use of mild cigars, and persist in keeping hideous little dogs to snap at your ankles; but how often would the contemptuous term "old maid," were its reality known, mean heroic self-sacrifice and self-denial—patience, fortitude, unrepining resignation? No man, who is not a Caliban or Miserrimus, need remain, his life long, a bachelor. The Siamese twins married; the living skeleton was crossed in love, but afterwards consoled himself with a corpulent widow; the hunch-backed Scarron found a beautiful woman to love and nurse him; and General Tom Thumb turned benedict the other day. But how many women—young, fair, and accomplished, pure and good and wise—are doomed irrevocably to solitude and celibacy! Every man knows such premature old maids; sees among a family of blooming girls one who already wears the stigmata of old maidenhood. It chills the blood to see these hopeless cases, to see the women resign themselves to their fate with a sad meek smile—to come back, year after year, and find them still meek, smiling, but sad, confirmed old maids. It is ill for me, who dwell in quite a Crystal Palace of a glass house, to throw so much as a grain of sand at the windows opposite, but I cannot refrain from sermonising my fellows on their self-conceited bachelorhood. What dullards were those writers in the "Times" newspaper about marriage and three hundred a year! Did Adam and Eve have three halfpence a year when they married? Has the world grown smaller? Are there no Australias, Americas, Indies? Are there no such things as marrying on a pound a week in a top garret, and ending in a mansion in Belgrave Square? no such things as toil, energy, perseverance? husband and wife cheering one another on, and in wealth at last pleasantly talking of the old times, the struggles and difficulties? We hear a great deal now-a-days about people's "missions." The proper mission of men is to marry, and of women to bear children; and those who are deterred from marriage in their degree (for we ought neither to expect nor to desire Squire B. to wed Pamela every day) by the hypocritical cant about "society" and "keeping up appearances," had much better send society to the dogs and appearances to the devil, and have nothing more to do with such miserable sophistries.

This diatribe, which I sincerely hope will increase the sale of wedding-rings in the goldsmiths' shops forty-fold, brings me naturally to the subject of the second cartoon, by which the ingenious artist who transcribes my inky men and women into flesh and blood, has chosen to illustrate the hour of eleven o'clock in the morning. Here we are at a fashionable wedding at St. James's Church, Piccadilly.

If I had the tongue or pen of Mr. Penguin, the urbane and aristocratic correspondent of the "Morning Post," I should give you quite a vivid, and at the same time a refined, description of that edifying spectacle—a marriage in high life. How eloquent, and, by turn, pathetic and humorous, I could be on the bevy of youthful bridesmaids—all in white tulle over pink glacé silk, all in bonnets trimmed with white roses, and with bouquets of camelias and lilies of the valley! How I could expatiate, likewise, on the appearance of the beauteous and high-born bride, her Honiton lace veil, her innumerable flounces; and her noble parents, and the gallant and distinguished bridegroom, in fawn-coloured inexpressibles and a cream-coloured face; and his "best man," the burly colonel of the Fazimanagghur Irregulars; and the crowd of distinguished personages who alight from their carriages at the little wicket in Piccadilly, and pass along the great area amid the cheers of the little boys! They are all so noble and distinguished, that one clergyman can't perform the ceremony, and extra parsons are provided like extra oil-lamps on a gala night at Cremorne. The register becomes an autograph-book of noble and illustrious signatures; the vestry-room has sweet odours of Jocky Club and Frangipani lingering about it for hours afterwards; the pew-opener picks up white satin favours tied with silver twist. A white rose, broken short off at the stem, lies unregarded on the altar-steps; and just within the rails are some orange-blossoms from the bride's coronal. For they fall and die, the blossoms, as well as the brown October leaves. Spring has its death as well as autumn: a death followed often by no summer, but by cold and cruel winter. The blossoms fall and die, and the paths by the hawthorn hedges are strewn with their bright corses. The blossoms droop and die: the little children die, and the green velvet of the cemetery is dotted with tiny gravestones.

See, the bridal procession comes into garish Piccadilly, and, amid fresh cheers and the pealing of the joy-bells, steps into its carriages.

"Happy, happy, happy pair!

None but the brave,

None but the brave,

None but the brave, deserve the fair."

So sings Mr. John Dryden, whilom poet laureate. Let us hope that the brides of St. James's are all as fair as the bridegrooms are brave, and that they all commence a career of happiness by that momentous plunge into the waters of matrimony at eleven o'clock in the morning. With which sincere aspiration, I will clap an extinguisher on the Hymeneal torch, which I have temporarily lighted, and so to read the births, marriages, and deaths in the "Times."

NOON.—THE JUSTICE-ROOM AT THE MANSION-HOUSE, AND THE "BAY TREE."

The red-whiskered, quick-tempered gentleman, who carried the shiny leather bag and the bundle of sticks—umbrella and fishing-rods tied together like the fasces of a Roman lictor—and who wore a cloak gracefully over his forty-shilling suit of heather tweed, "thoroughly well shrunk," the gentleman who, at Morley's Hotel, Trafalgar Square, and at twenty minutes before twelve, engaged a Hansom cabman, No. 9,009, and bade him drive "like anything" (but he said like something which I decline to mention) to the London Bridge Terminus of the South-Eastern Railway, has thrust his bundle of sticks, &c., through the little trap-door in the cabriolet's roof, and has savagely ordered the driver to stop, or to drive him to Jericho, or to the deuce. But the high-towering Jehu of 9,009 cannot drive to the dominions of the deuce, even as did "Ben," that famous Jarvey of the olden time, immortalised in the ballad of "Tamaroo." He can drive neither to the right nor to the left, nor backwards nor forwards; for he is hemmed in, and blocked up, and jammed together in the middle of the Poultry; and just as a sarcastic saloon omnibus driver behind jeeringly bids him "keep moving," accompanying the behest by the aggressive taunt of "gardner;" and just as the charioteer of the mail-cart in front affectionately recommends him not to be in a hurry, lest he should injure his precious health, Twelve o'Clock is proclaimed by the clock of St. Mildred's, Poultry; and cabman 9,009 has lost his promised extra shilling for extra speed, and the red-whiskered gentleman has lost his temper, and the train into the bargain, and there will be weeping at Tunbridge Wells this afternoon, where a young lady, with long ringlets and a white muslin jacket, will mourn for her Theodore, and will not be comforted—till the next train arrives.

It is noon, high noon, in the City of London. Why did not the incautious cabman drive down Cannon Street, the broad and unimpeded? or why did he not seek his destination by crossing Waterloo Bridge—he of the red whiskers would have paid the toll cheerfully—and tread the mazes of Union Street, Borough? Perhaps he was an inexperienced cabman, new to its dædalian ways. Perhaps he was a prejudiced and conservative cabman, adhering to the old Poultry as the corporation adhered to the old Smithfield, and detesting newfangled thoroughfares. Perhaps he was a misanthropic cabman, whose chief delight was to make travellers lose trains. If such be the case, he has his wicked will now; and the red-whiskered gentleman, sulkily alighting, scowlingly pays him his legal fare, leaves him grumbling, and retires himself moodily muttering, conscious that he has nearly two hours before him through which to kick his heels, and not knowing what on earth to do with himself. Be of good cheer, red-whiskered, shipwrecked one. Comfort ye, for I am here, the wanderer of the clock-face, and the dweller on the threshold of time. I will show you brave sights, and make your heart dance with mulligatawny soup and Amontillado sherry at the "Cock," in Threadneedle Street. You are not hungry yet? Well, we will stroll into the Stereoscopic Company's magnificent emporium in Cheapside, and mock our seven senses with the delusions of that delightful toy, which, if Sir David Brewster didn't invent, he should properly have invented. You care not for the arts? Shall we cross by King Street, and have a stare at Guildhall, with Gog and Magog, and the monument that commemorates Beckford's stern resolve to "stand no nonsense" from George III.? Or we may stroll into Garraway's, and mark how the sale of sandwiches and sherry-cobblers may be combined with the transfer of land and the vending of freehold houses. There is the auction-mart, too, if you have a fancy to see Simony sales by auction, and advowsons of the cures of immortal souls knocked down for so many pounds sterling. There is the rotunda of the Bank of England, with its many-slamming, zinc-plated doors, and its steps and flags worn away by the boots of the ever-busy stockbrokers. We will not go into the Dividend Office, for I have no dividends to draw now, and the sight makes me sad; neither will we enter the Great Hall where William the Third's statue is (prettily noticed by Mr. Addison in a full-bottom-wigged allegory in the "Spectator"), and where the urbane clerks are for ever honouring the claims upon the old lady in Threadneedle Street; giving "notes for gold" and "gold for notes." We will not enter, because we don't want any change just now; and one of the Brothers Forrester, who is sure to be hovering about the court-yard, in conversation with yonder cock-hatted beadle in blazing scarlet, might think we came for gold or notes that didn't belong to us. The Bullion Office we cannot visit, for we haven't an order of admission; and there is one place especially, O rubicund-headed traveller, where we will be exceedingly cautious not to show our faces. That place is the interior of the Stock Exchange. I am not a "lame duck;" I never, to my knowledge, "waddled;" I never attempted to pry into the secrets of the "bulls" and the "bears;" my knowledge of stockjobbing is confined to the fact that I once became possessed, I scarcely know how, only that I paid for them, of fifty shares in a phantom gold-mining company; that I sold them, half an hour afterwards, at half-a-crown premium to a mysterious man in a dark room, up a court off Cornhill, who to every human being who entered his lair handed a long list covered with cabalistic figures, with the remark that it was "very warm," and which—the list, not the weather—I believe contained the current prices of stocks, though it might have related to the market value of elephants, for aught I knew; that I pocketed the fifty half-crowns, and that I have never heard anything of the phantom company from that day to this. Vice-Chancellor somebody will be down upon me some day as a "contributory," I suppose, and I shall be delivered over to the tormentors; but, meanwhile, I will tell you why I won't take my red-whiskered friend into the Stock Exchange—why I should like mine enemy to go there as soon as convenient. I have heard such horrible stories of the tortures inflicted by the members of the "House," upon unwary strangers who have strayed within its precincts; of the savage cries of "two hundred and one," the shrieks, the yells, the whistles, and the groans; the dancing round the captive, the covering him with flour, the treading on his miserable toes, the buffeting of his wretched ears, the uripping of his unhappy coat-collar, and chalking of his luckless back; the "bonneting," the "ballooning," and the generally fiendish cruelties which intruders upon the speculators for the "account" have to suffer, that I would sooner venture without permission behind the scenes of a well-regulated theatre, or attempt to beard the lion in his den, or walk up, unannounced, into the sanctum of the editor of the "Times" newspaper, or pay a morning call in a Choctaw wigwam, myself being a Pawnee or a Sioux, at war with my friends the C.'s, or pass through Portugal Street, Cursitor Street, or Chancery Lane, at any hour of the day or night, if my affairs should happen to embarrassed, than trust myself to the tender mercies of the members of the Stock Exchange. They are the staunchest and most consistent of Conservatives.

Whither, then, away! Why, bless me, how stupid I have been! The Mansion House police-court opens at noon precisely, and we may enjoy, gratuitously, the sight of the Corporation Cadi, the Cæsar of Charlotte Row, the great Lord Mayor of London himself, dispensing justice to all comers. By the way, I wish his Lordship would render unto us one little modicum of justice, combined with equity, by ridding us of the intolerable swarm of ragged, disgusting-looking juvenile beggars, who beset pedestrians at the doors of Messrs. Smith, Payne, and Smith's banking-house, and of the scarcely less intolerable importunities of the omnibus cads who are wrestling for old ladies and young children on the very threshold of the Mansion House. Here we are at the Municipal Hall of London's Ædiles; architecture grand but somewhat gloomily florid, like George the First, say, in a passion, his bulbous Hanoverian jaw flaming from his perturbed perriwig—glowering, half-angry, half-frightened, as he tears his embroidered coat-tail from the grasp of Lady Nithsdale, and obstinately refuses pardon for that poor Jacobite lord yonder cooped up in the gloomy Tower under sentence of death, but who, thanks to his wife's all-womanly devotion (well did Madame de Lavallete imitate her bright example to save *her* chivalrous husband just one hundred years afterwards), will cheat the headsman's axe and George's Hanoverian malice yet. The attic storey was evidently clapped on as an afterthought, and threatens to tumble over on to the portico; the whole is profusely ornamented, like everything civic, and reminds me generally of a freestone model of the Lord Mayor's state carriage, squared in the Corinthian manner, and the gilt gingerbread well covered with smoke and soot.

Not by that door in the basement will we enter, which is flanked by announcements relative to charity dinners, and youths who have absconded from their friends. Within that eternally-gaslit office is the place of business of the Eumenides of finance, whose grim duty it is to pursue forgers and bank-robbers through the world. There dwell, for thief-catching purposes, the terrible Forresters. Not by that door in Charlotte Row. Don't you see the handsome carriage, with the fat, brown, gaudily harnessed horses drawn up before it, and the superb powdered footmen sucking their bamboo-cane tops? How odd it is that you can always tell the difference between a footman appertaining to one of the high civic dignitaries, and the flunkey of a real patrician. The liveries, on a drawing-room day, for instance, are equally rich, equally extravagant in decoration, and absurd in fashion; both servitors sport equally large cocked-hats, equally long canes, and have an equal amount of powder dredged over their heads; yet, on either flunkey's brow are the stigmata "East" or "West" of Temple Bar, stamped as legibly as the brand of Cain. The door in Charlotte Row is his Lordship's private entrance; and her Ladyship is very probably at this moment preparing to go out for an airing. Not by that other lateral door in George Street—that low-browed, forbidding-looking portal. That is the prisoners' entrance. There the grim cellular van brings and waits for the victims of Themis. There it sets down and takes up, if not the chief actors, at least those who are most deeply interested in the moving drama which is every day enacted in the police tribunal of the Mansion House.

NOON: THE JUSTICE-ROOM AT THE MANSION HOUSE.

So—up this broad, roomy flight of granite steps on the Lombard Street side of the Mansion House frontage—on through a double barrier of swing-doors at the corresponding angle beneath the portico; and in less time than it would take to accept a bill (an operation in comparison to the celerity of which a pig's whisper is an age, and the pronunciation of the mystic words "Jack Robinson" a life-long task), we are within the sanctuary of municipal justice. The first thing that strikes the stranger, accustomed as he may be to frequenting other police-courts, is the unwonted courtesy of the officials, and their gorgeous costumes. About Bow Street, Lambeth, Westminster, there hangs an indefinable but pervading miasma of meanness and squalor. A settled mildew seems to infest the walls and ceiling, a chronic dust to mantle the furniture and flooring. No one connected with the court, officially or otherwise, with the single exception of the Magistrate—who, always smug and clean shaven, and in a checked morning neckerchief and a high shirt collar, looks like a judicial edition of Major Pendennis—seems to have had his clothes brushed for a week or his boots blacked for a month. A dreadful jail-bird odour ascends from the ill-favoured auditory. The policemen are shabby in attire and morose in manner. The buckles of their belts are dull, and their buttons tarnished. They hustle you hither and thither, and order you in or out in a manner most distressing to your nerves; and the gloomy usher thrusts a ragged Testament into your hands, and swears you as though he were swearing *at* you. But at the Mansion House there is a bluff, easy-going, turtle-and-venison-fed politeness generally manifest. You enter and you emerge from the court without being elbowed or shoved. The city policemen are more substantial-looking, well to do, and better natured men than their metropolitan *confrères*. Some of them have the appearance of small freeholders, and others, I am sure, have snug sums in the savings' banks. As to the jailers, ushers, court-keepers, warrant-officers, marshalmen, and other multifarious hangers-on of civic justice, they are mostly men of mature age, rosy, bald and white-headed sages, who remember Sir John Key and the great Sir Claudius Hunter, and mind the time when Mr. Alderman Wood rode on horseback at the side of Queen Caroline's hearse, on the occasion of the passage of that injured lady's funeral procession through the city. As to their attire, it is positively—if I may be allowed the use of a barbarism—"splendiferous." Stout broadcloth, bright gilt buttons, with elaborate chasings of civic heraldry, scarlet collars, with deep gold lace: none of your paltry blue blanketing, horn buttons, and worsted gloves. No doubt, when in full uniform, the "splendiferous" functionaries all wear cocked-hats. Maybe, feathers. There is one weazened creature who flits in and out of a side door, to the left of the Lord Mayor's chair, and is perpetually handing up printed forms to his Lordship or to the chief clerk. I don't know exactly what he is, whether the Lord Mayor's butler, or the sword-bearer's uncle, or the city-marshal's grandfather, or the water-bailiff's son-in-law; but the front of his coat is profusely ornamented with bars of gold braid, like pokers from Crœsus's kitchen, and on his shoulders he wears a pair of state epaulettes, the which give him somewhat of a military appearance, and, contrasting with his civilian spectacles and white neckcloth, would produce an effect positively sublime if it were not irresistibly ludicrous. The home of Beadledom—its last home, I am afraid, after the exhaustion of the Windsor uniform, and that of the Elder Brethren of the Trinity House—will be at the Mansion House.

The architect who has contrived the new Justice-room in this stately edifice must have been, if not a man of genius, at least one of original conceptions. The old police-court—sacred to the manes of Mr. Hobler—was simply a Cave of Trophonius and Den of Despair. There was no light in it—"only darkness visible;" and when you peered at the misty prisoner in the dock, you were always reminded of Captain Macheath in his cell, when the inhuman Mr. Lockit wouldn't allow him any more candles, and threatened to clap on extra fetters in default of an immediate supply on the captain's part of "garnish" or jail fees. But the Palladio who has arisen to remedy these defects has contrived to introduce a considerable amount of light—only it labours under the trifling disadvantage of being all in the wrong place. The Lord Mayor, with his back to the window, sits in a reflected light, just as does Wilkie's portrait of the Duke of York; and the fine effect of the city arms carved on his chair, to say nothing of his Lordship's gold chain and furred robe, is thereby totally lost. Mr. Goodman and the clerks, who are all very gentlemanly-looking individuals, much given to all-round collars and parting their hair down the middle, fill up commitments and make out summonses in a puzzling haze of chiaro oscuro; the reporters are compelled to pore over their "Times" with their noses close to the paper (for no one ever saw a police reporter do anything save read the newspaper, though we are sure to read a verbatim narrative of the case in which we are interested next day), and the general audience is lost in a Cimmerian gloom. To make amends, there is plenty of light on the ceiling, and some liberal patches of it on the walls, and a generous distribution of its bounty on the bald heads, golden epaulettes, and scarlet collars of the marshalmen. We can't have everything we want, not even in the way of Light. Let us be thankful that there is some of it about, even as it behoves us to be exceedingly grateful that there is such a vast amount of wealth in the world. Other people possess it—only, we don't.

This, then, is the justice-room of the Mansion House. I have not given you, *seriatim*, a George Robins's catalogue of its contents, but by bits and bits I trust you will have been enabled to form a tolerably correct mind-picture of its contents. My Lord Mayor in the chair, clerks before him, reporters to the right, marshalmen left; spectacled official at the desk in the left-hand corner—the summoning officer, I think—audience not too tightly packed into a neat pen at the back of the court; dock in the centre, and the prisoner—Ah! the prisoner!

Did it never strike you, in a criminal court of assize—"the judges all ranged, a terrible show," the solemn clerk of the arraigns gazing over the indictment, the spectators almost breathless with excited curiosity, rays from opera glasses refracted from the gallery, Regent Street bonnets and artificial flowers relieving the dark mass of the menfolk's dress, the bar bewigged, the eloquent advocate for the defence thundering forth genteel philippics against the eloquent counsel for the prosecution—did it never strike you, I say, what a terrible fuss and bother, and calling on Jupiter to lift a wagon wheel out of a rut, what a waste of words, and show, and ceremonial all this became, when its object, the End to all these imposing means, was one miserable creature in the dock, with spikes, and rue, and rosemary before him, accused of having purloined a quart pot? As for the prisoner who is this day arraigned before the mighty Lord Mayor—but first stand on tiptoe. There he is, God help him and us all! a miserable, weazened, ragged, unkempt child, whose head, the police reports will tell us to-morrow, "scarcely reached to the railing of the dock." He has been caught picking pockets. It is not his first, his second, his third offence. He is an incorrigible thief. The great Lord Mayor tells him so with a shake of his fine head of hair. He must go to jail. To jail with him. He has been there before. It is the only home he ever had. It is his preparatory school for the hulks. The jail nursing-mother to thousands, and not so stony-hearted a step-mother as the streets. He is nobody's child, nobody save the police knows anything about him, he lives nowhere; but in the eyes of the law he is somebody. He is a figure in a tabular statement, a neat item to finish a column in a report, withal. He is somebody to Colonel Jebb and Mr. Capper of the Home Office, and, in the end, the Ordinary of Newgate, the sheriffs, and, especially, somebody to CALCRAFT. He is somebody to whip, somebody to put to the crank, and into "punishment jackets," and to "deprive of his bed and gas," and gag, and drench with water, and choke with salt, and otherwise torture *à la mode de* Birmingham (Austin's improved method), somebody to build castellated jails for, somebody to transport, somebody to hang.

There are reformatories, you say, for such as these. Yes, those admirable institutions do exist; but do you know, O easily-satisfied optimist! that police magistrates every day deplore that reformatories, niggardly subsidised by a State grudging in every thing but jails, and gyves, and gibbets, are nine tenths of them full, and can receive no more inmates, even though recommended to them by "the proper authorities?" But the streets are fuller still of strayed lambs, and though wolves devour them by the score each day, the tainted flock of lost ones still increases and increases.

I must tell you, that before the "case of wipes," as an irreverent bystander called the *procès* of the pickpocket, was gone into (a good-for-nothing rascal that *filou*, deservedly punished, of course), what are called the night charges were disposed of. As I shall have something to say of the manners and customs of these night charges at another hour in the morning and in another place, I will content myself with informing you now, that a blue bonnet and black silk velvet mantle, charged with being drunk and disorderly in Cheapside the night before, were set at liberty without pecuniary mulct, it being her, or their, first offence; but a white hat with a black band, surmounting a rough coat, cord trousers, and Balbriggan boots, who had fought four omnibus conductors, broken eighteen panes of glass, demolished sundry waiters, and seriously damaged the beadle of the Royal Exchange (off duty, and enjoying the *dulce deripere in loco* in the shape of cold whiskey-and-water in a shady tavern somewhere up a court of the Poultry)— all in consequence of their (or his) refusal to pay for a bottle of soda-water, was fined in heavy sums—the aggregate cost of his whistle being about six pounds. The white hat was very penitent, and looked (the face under it likewise) very haggard and tired, and, in addition to his, or its, or their penalty, munificently contributed half a sovereign to the poor box. My Lord Mayor was severe but paternal, and hoped with benignant austerity that he might never see the white hat there again; in which hope, and on his part, I daresay the white hat most cordially joined.

I never could make out what they are always doing with paupers at the Mansion House. I never pay his Lordship a visit without finding a bevy of the poor things pottering about in a corner under the care of some workhouse official, and being ultimately called up to be exorcised or excommunicated, or, at all events, to have something done to them, under the New Poor Law Act. This morning there are at least a dozen of them, forlorn, decrepit, shame-faced, little old men, cowering and shivering, although the day is warm enough, in their uncomfortable-looking gray suits. Pauper females seem to be at a discount at the Mansion House, save when, brazen-faced, blear-eyed, and dishevelled, they are dragged in droves to the bar to be committed to Holloway prison, for a month's hard labour, for shivering innumerable panes of glass, throwing cataracts of gruel about, and expressing an earnest desire to lacerate with sharp cutlery the abdominal economy of the master of the City of London Union. Of incarnations of male impecuniosity, there is a lamentable plenty and to spare.

The pickpocket is succeeded by a distinguished burglar, well known in political—I beg pardon, in police—circles. There is no absolute charge of felony against him at present, and the only cause for his appearance to-day is his having been unfortunate enough to fall in with an acquaintance, who knew him by sight, in the shape of a city police-constable, who forthwith took him into custody for roaming about with intent to commit a felony. My Lord having heard a brief biographical sketch of his career, and being satisfied that he is a "man of mark" in a felonious point of view, sends him to Holloway for three months, which, considering that the fellow has committed, this time, at least, no absolute crime, seems, at the first blush, something very like a gross perversion of justice, and an unwarrantable interference with the liberty of the subject. When subsequently, however, I gather that a few inconsiderable trifles, such as a "jemmy," a bunch of skeleton keys, a "knuckle duster," and a piece of wax candle, all articles sufficiently indicative of the housebreaker's stock-in-trade, have been found in his possession, I cease to quarrel with the decision, and confess that my burglarious friend's incarceration, if not in strict accordance with law, is based on very sound principles of equity. After the housebreaker, there are two beggar women and a troop of ragged children—twenty-one days; and a most pitiable sight to see and hear—beggar woman, children, and sentence, and their state of life into which it has *not* pleased Heaven to call, but cruel and perverse man to send them. Then an Irish tailor who has had a slight dispute with his wife the night before, and has corporeally chastised her with a hot goose—a tailor's goose, be it understood—to the extent of all but fracturing her skull. He is sent for four months' hard labour, which is rather a pleasurable thing to hear, although I should derive infinitely more delectation from the sentence if it included a sound thrashing.

But, holloa! we have been here three-quarters of an hour, and it is close upon one o'clock. Come, my red-whiskered friend, I think we have had enough of the Mansion House Justice-room. Let us make a bow to his Lordship, and evaporate. You want some lunch, you say—you are hungry now; well, let us go and lunch accordingly; but where?

I mentioned Garraway's and the Cock. There is the Anti-Gallican, famous for soups. There is Birch's, with real turtle, fit for Olympian deities to regale upon. There is Joe's in Finch Lane, if you feel disposed for chop or steak, sausage or bacon, and like to see it cooked yourself on a Brobdignagian gridiron. No: you want something simple, something immediate; well, then, let us go to the Bay Tree.

I never knew exactly the name of the street in which the Bay Tree is situated. I know you go down a narrow lane, and that you will suddenly come upon it, as a jack-in-the-box suddenly comes upon you. The first time I was taken there was by a friend, who, just prior to our arrival at the house of refection, took me up a dark entry, showed me a small court-yard, and, at its extremity, a handsome-looking stone building. *That is Rothschild's*, he said, and I thought I should have fainted. I am not a City man, and when I come eastward, it is merely (of course) to make a morning call on my friend the Governor of the Bank of England, or the Secretary for India for the time being, at his palace in Leadenhall Street. When I travel in foreign parts, my brougham (of course) takes me to the London Bridge Terminus. Authors never come into the City now-a-days, save to visit their bankers or their publishers. Authors ride blood horses, dine with dukes, and earn ten thousand a year. Such, at least, is the amount of their income surmised to be by the Commissioners of Income Tax, when they assess them arbitrarily and at such a figure their opposing creditors declare their revenue should be estimated, when they petition the Court for the Relief of Insolvent Debtors.

I never sat down in the Bay Tree; though its premises include, I believe, vast apartments for smoking and punch-bibbing purposes. I never looked one of the innumerable assistants (are they barmen or barmaids?) in the face. I was always in such a hurry. All I know of the establishment is, that it is a capital place to lunch at, and that everything is very excellent and very cheap; and that the thousands who resort to it between eleven and three, always seem to be in as desperate a hurry as I am.

ONE P.M.—DOCK LONDON AND DINING LONDON.

This modest series of papers brought me, at the time of their composition, into great trouble, which was very nearly resulting in my complete discomfiture. Perhaps the severest of my trials was having to write the book at all, possessing, as is my misfortune, of course, a constitutional disinclination for the avocation to which I have devoted myself (as a *gagne pain*, or bread-winning mean). I didn't so much mind the ladies and gentlemen, who, since the commencement of the periodical in which these articles were originally published—ladies and gentlemen personally quite unknown to me—who overwhelmed me with correspondence; some denouncing, others upbraiding, many ridiculing, and a few—a very few— eulogising yours to command. I didn't so much object to the attentions of those professional begging-letter writers, who are good enough to include authors in their list of possible contributaries, and who were profuse lately in passionate appeals (in bold, clerkly hands) for pecuniary assistance; for though, like Bardolph, I have nothing, and cannot even coin my nose for guineas, or my blood for drachmas, it is not the less flattering to a man's minor vanities to receive a begging letter. I can imagine an old pauper out for a holiday, coming home to the workhouse, quite elated at having been accosted in the street by a mendicant, and asked for a halfpenny. I could bear with equanimity—nay, could afford to smile at—the people who went about saying things (who *are* the people who go about saying things, I wonder!) who ingeniously circulated reports that I was dead; that I wrote these papers under a pseudonym; that they were plagiarisms from some others written twenty years ago; and that I never wrote them at all. I disregarded such insinuations serenely; for who among us is exempt from such bald chat? The very stupidest have their Boswells—the very meanest have those to envy them, as well as the Great and Learned! There are people at this very moment, who are going about saying that Jones has pawned his plate, that the bailiffs are in Thompson's country house, that Robinson has written himself out, that Brown has run away with Jenkins's wife, that Muggins has taken to brandy-and-water, that Simpkins murdered Eliza Grimwood, that Larkins cut Thistlewood's head off, and that Podgers was tried at the Old Bailey, in the year 'thirty-five, for an attempt to set the Thames on fire. But I was infinitely harassed while the clock was ticking periodically—the efforts I had to make to keep it from running down altogether!—by the great plague of "Suggesters." From the metropolitan and suburban postal districts, from all parts of the United Kingdom—the United Kingdom, pshaw! from the Continent generally, and from across the broad Atlantic (fortunately, the return mail from Australia was not yet due)—suggestions poured in as thickly as letters of congratulation on one who has just inherited a vast fortune. If there had been five hundred in lieu of four-and-twenty hours in "Twice Round the Clock," the Great Suggestions I received had stomach for them all. The Suggesters would take no denial: I was bound under terrific penalties to adopt, endorse, carry out, their hints,—else would they play the dickens with me. I *must* have a sing-song meeting for nine p.m.; the committee of a burial club at ten; the dissecting-room of an hospital at eleven; a postal receiving-house, a lawyer's office, a rag, bones, and bottle shop, the tollgate of Waterloo Bridge, and the interior of a Hammersmith 'bus, at some hour or other of the day or night. The Suggestions were oral as well as written. Strange men darted up on me from by-streets, caught at my button with trembling fingers, told me in husky tones of their vast metropolitan experience, and impressed on me the necessity of a graphic tableau of Joe Perks, the sporting barber's, at one o'clock in the morning. Low-browed merchants popped from shady shell-fish shops, and, pointing to huge lobsters, asked where they could send the crustaceous delicacies with their compliments, and how excellent a thing it would be to give a view of the aristocracy supping at Whelks's celebrated oyster and kippered salmon warehouse after the play. And, finally, a shy acquaintance of mine, with a face like an over-ripe Stilton cheese, and remotely connected with the Corporation of London—he may be, for aught I know, a ticket-porter in Doctors' Commons, or a hanger-on to the water bailiff—favoured me with an occult inuendo that a word-picture of the Court of Common Council will be the very thing for four p.m., fluttering before my dazzled eyes a phantom ticket for the Guildhall banquet. In vain I endeavoured to convince these respectable Suggesters, that the papers in question were not commenced without a definite plan of action; that such plan, sketched forth years since, duly weighed, adjusted, and settled, after mature study and deliberation, not only so far as I am concerned, but by "parties" deeply learned in the mysteries of London Life, and versed in the recondite secret of pleasing the public taste, had at length been put into operation, and was no more capable of alteration than were the laws of the Medes and Persians. But all to no purpose did I make these representations. The Suggesters wouldn't be convinced; their letters continued to flow in. They found out my address at last (they have lost it now, ha, ha!), and knocked my door down; bringing me peremptory letters of introduction from people I didn't know, or didn't care five farthings about, or else introducing themselves boldly, in the "Bottle Imp" manner, with an implied "You must learn to love me;" they nosed me in the lobby, and saw me dancing in the hall, and my only refuge at last was to go away. Yes; the pulsations of time had to beat behind the dial of a clock in the rural districts; and these lines were written among the hay and the ripening corn, laughing a bitter laugh to think that the postman was toiling up the quiet street in London with piles of additional suggestions, and that the Suggesters themselves were waiting for me in my usual haunts, in the fond expectation of a button to hold, or an ear to gloze suggestions within.

I tried the sea-shore; but found London-super-Mare sweltering, stewing, broiling, frying, fizzing, panting, in the sun—like Marseilles, minus the evil odours—to such an extent, and so utterly destitute of shade, that I was compelled to leave it. The paint was blistering on the bright green doors; the shingly pavement seemed to cry out "Come and grill steaks on me!" the pitch oozed from the seams of the fishing-boats; the surf hissed as it came to kiss the pebbles on the beach; the dial on the pier-head blazed with concentric rays; the chains of the suspension bridge were red hot; the camera obscura glared white in the sunshine; the turf on the Steyne was brown and parched, like a forgotten oasis in a desert; the leaves on the trees in the pavilion gardens glittered and chinked in the summer breeze, like new bright guineas; the fly-horses hung their heads, their poor tongues protruding, their limbs flaccid, and their scanty tails almost powerless to flap away the swarms of flies, which alone were riotous and active of living creation, inebriating themselves with saccharine suction in the grocers' shops, and noisily buzzing their scanmag in private parlours; the flymen dozed on their boxes; the pushers of invalid perambulators slumbered peacefully beneath the hoods of their own Bath chairs; the ladies in the round hats found it too hot to promenade the cliff, and lolled instead at verandahed windows, arrayed in the most ravishing of muslin morning wrappers, and conversed languidly with exquisites, whose moustaches were dank with moisture, and who had scarcely energy enough to yawn. The captivating amazons abandoned for the day their plumed hats, their coquettish gauntlets, their wash-leather sub-fusk garments with the straps and patent-leather boots, and deferred their cavalcades on the skittish mares till the cool of the evening; the showy dragoon officers confined themselves, of their own free will, to the mess-room of their barracks on the Lewes road, where they sipped sangaree, smoked fragrancias, read "Bell's Life," and made bets on every imaginable topic. The hair of the little Skye terriers no longer curled, but hung supine in wiry hanks; the little children made piteous appeals to their parents and guardians to be permitted to run about without anything on; the two clerks at the branch bank, who are sleepy enough in the coldest weather, nodded at each other over the ledgers which had no entries in them. The only sound that disturbed the drowsy stillness of the streets was the popping of ginger-beer corks; and the very fleas in the lodging-houses lost all their agility and vivacity. No longer did they playfully leap—no longer archly gyrate; they crawled and crept, like their low relatives the bugs, and were caught and crushed without affording the slightest opportunity for sport. It was mortally hot at London-super-Mare, and I left it. Then I tried that English paradise of the west, Clifton; but woe is me! the Downs were so delightful; the prospect so exquisitely lovely; the Avon winding hundreds of feet beneath me, like a silver skein, yet bearing big three-masted ships on its bosom; the rocks and underwood so full of matter for pleasant, lazy cogitation, that I felt the only exertion of which I was capable, to be writing sonnets on the Avon and its sedgy banks, or making lame attempts at pre-Raphaelite sketches in water-colours; or thinking about doing either, which amounts to pretty nearly the same thing. So I came away from Clifton too, and hung out my sign HERE. (It is THERE now: swallows have come and gone, snows have gathered and melted, babies prattle now who were unborn and unthought of then.) Ye shall not know where Here was situated, oh, ye incorrigible Suggesters. No more particular indices of its whereabouts will I give, even to the general public, than that close to my study was a dry skittle-ground, where every day—the hotter the better—I exercised myself with the wooden "cheese" against the seven and a-half pins which were all that the dry skittle-ground could furnish forth towards the ordinary nine; that over-against this gymnastic course was an *étable*, a "shippon," as they call it in the north, where seven cows gravely ruminated; and that, at the end of a yard crowded with agricultural implements which old Pyne alone could draw, there was a Stye, from which, looking over its palings,

"All start, like boys who, unaware,

Ranging the woods to find a hare,

Come to the mouth of some dark lair:

Where, growling low, a fierce old bear

Lies amid bones and blood."

Not that any fierce or ancient member of the ursine tribe resided therein; but that it was the residence of a horrific-looking old sow, a dreadful creature, that farrowed unheard-of families of pigs, that lay on her broadside starboard the live-long day, winking her cruel eye, and grunting with a persistent sullenness. The chief swineherd proudly declared her to be "the viciousest beast as ever was," and hinted darkly that she had killed a Man. The chief swineherd and I were friends. He was my "putter-up" at skittles, and did me the honour to report among the neighbouring peasantry, that "barrin' the gent as cum here last autumn, and was off his head" (insane, I presume); I was "the very wust hand at knock-'em-downs he ever see." It is something to be popular in the rural districts; and yet I was not three miles distant from the Regent Circus.

My eyes are once again turned to the clock face. It is One o'Clock in the Afternoon, and I must think of London. Come back, ye memories: open Sesame, ye secret chambers of the brain, and let me transport myself away from the dry skittle-ground, the seven grave cows and the vicious sow, to plunge once more into the toil and trouble of the seething, eddying Mistress City of the world.

There are so many things going on at one o'clock in the day; the steam of life is by that time so thoroughly "up," that I am embarrassed somewhat to know which scenes would be the best to select from the plethora of tableaux I find among my stereoscopic slides. One o'clock is the great time for making business appointments. You meet your lawyer at one; you walk down to the office of the newspaper you may happen to write for, and settle the subject of your leading article, at one. One o'clock is a capital hour to step round to your stockbroker, in Pope's Head Alley, Cornhill, and do a little business in stocks or shares. At one o'clock the Prime Minister, or his colleagues, have resignation enough to listen (with tolerable patience) to some half dozen deputations who come to harangue them about nothing in particular; at one o'clock obliging noblemen take the chair at public meetings at the Freemasons', or the London Tavern. At one o'clock—from one to two rather—the aristocracy indulge in the sumptuous meal known as "lunch." At one o'clock that vast, yet to thousands unknown and unrecked of city, which I may call Dock London, is in full activity after some twenty minutes' suspension while the workmen take *their* lunch.

The ingenious and persevering artist who constructed that grand model of Liverpool, which we all remember in the Exhibition of 1851, and which is now in the Derby Museum of the city of the Liver, did very wisely in making the Docks the most prominent feature in his model, and treating the thoroughfares of the town merely as secondary adjuncts. For the Docks are in reality Liverpool, even as the poet has said that love is of man's life a part, but woman's whole existence. Our interest in the Queen of the Mersey commences at Birkenhead, and ends at Bramley Moore Dock, on the other side. I say Bramley Moore Dock, because that was the last constructed when I was in Liverpool. Some dozens more may have been built since I was there. Docks are like jealousy, and grow continually by what they feed on. We can ill afford to surrender so noble a public building as St. George's Hall, so thronged and interesting a thoroughfare as Dale Street; yet it must be confessed that the attention of the visitor to Liverpool is concentrated and absorbed by the unrivalled and magnificent docks. So he who visits Venice, ardent lover of art and architecture as he may be, gives on his first sojourn but a cursory glance at the churches and palaces; he is fascinated and engrossed by the canals and the gondolas. So the stranger in Petersburg and Moscow has at first but scant attention to bestow on the superb monuments, the picturesque costumes; his senses are riveted upon the golden domes of Tzaaks and the Kremlin. Liverpool is one huge dock; and from the landing-stage to West Derby island, everything is of the docks and docky. The only wonder seems to be that the ships do not sail up the streets, and discharge their cargoes at the doors of the merchants' counting-houses. But in London, in the suburbs, in the West-end, in the heart of the city oft-times, what do we know or care about the docks? There are scores of members of the Stock Exchange, I will be bound, who never entered the dock gates, and those few who have paid a visit to Dock London, may merely have gone there with a tasting-order for wine. When we consider that in certain aristocratic circles it is reckoned to be rather a breach of etiquette than otherwise to know anything about the manners and customs of the dwellers on the other side of Temple Bar, even as the by-gone snob-cynic of fashion and literature professed entire ignorance as to the locality of Russell Square, and wanted to know "where you changed horses" in a journey to Bloomsbury—unless, indeed, my Lord Duke or my Lady Marchioness happen to be a partner in a great brewing and banking firm, under which circumstances he or she may roll down in her chariot to the city to glance over the quarterly balance sheet of profit; when we consider that this world of a town has cities upon cities within its bosom, that in the course of a long life may never be visited; when we think of Bermondsey, Bethnal Green, Somers Town, Clerkenwell, Hoxton, Hackney, Stepney, Bow, Rotherhithe, Horsleydown—places of which the great and titled may read every day in a newspaper, and ask, languidly, where they are,—we need no longer be surprised if the Docks are ignored by thousands, and if old men die every day who have never beheld their marvels.

Coming home from abroad often, with an intelligent foreigner, I persuade him to renounce the Calais route and the South-Eastern Railway, and even to abjure the expeditious run from Newhaven. I decoy him on board one of the General Steam Navigation vessels at Boulogne, and when his agonies of sea-sickness have, in the course of half a dozen hours or so, subsided—when we have passed Margate, Gravesend, Erith, Woolwich, Greenwich even—when I have got him past the Isle of Dogs, and we are bearing swiftly on our way towards the Pool—I clap my intelligent foreigner on the back, and cry, "Now look around (Eugène or Alphonse, as the case may be); now look around, and see the glory of England. Not in huge armies, bristling with bayonets, and followed by monstrous guns; not in granite forts, grinning from the waters like ghoules from graves; not in lines of circumvallation, miles and miles in extent; not in earthworks, counter-scarps, bastions, ravelins, mamelons, casemates, and gunpowder magazines—shall be found our pride and our strength. Behold them, O intelligent person of foreign extraction! in yonder forest of masts, in the flags of every nation that fly from those tapering spars on the ships, in the great argosies of commerce that from every port in the world have congregated to do honour to the monarch of marts, London, and pour out the riches of the universe at her proud feet." After this flourishing exordium—the sense of which you may have heard on a former occasion, for it forms part of my peroration on the grandeur of

England, and, if my friends and acquaintances are to be believed, I bore them terribly with it sometimes—I enter into some rapid details concerning the tonnage and import dues of the port of London; and then permit the intelligent foreigner to dive down below again to his berth. Sometimes the foreign fellow turns out to be a cynic, and declares that he cannot see the forest of masts for the fog, if it be winter—for the smoke, if it be summer.

But the docks of London—by which, let me be perfectly understood, (I do not, by any means, intend to confine myself to the London Docks) I speak of Dock London in its entirety: of the London and St. Katherine's, of the East and West India, and the Victoria Docks—what huge reservoirs are they of wealth, and energy, and industry! See those bonding warehouses, apoplectic with the produce of three worlds, congested with bales of tobacco and barrels of spices; with serons of cochineal, and dusky, vapid-smelling chests of opium from Turkey or India; with casks of palm-oil, and packages of vile chemicals, ill-smelling oxides and alkalis, dug from the bowels of mountains thousands of miles away, and which, ere long, will be transformed into glowing pigments and exquisite perfumes; with shapeless masses of india rubber, looking inconceivably dirty and nasty, yet from which shall come delicate little cubes with which ladies shall eraze faulty pencil marks from their landscape copies after Rout and Harding—india rubber that shall be spread over our coats and moulded into shoes, yea, and drawn out in elastic ductility, to form little filaments in pink silk ligatures—I dare not mention their English appellation, but in Italian they are called "*legaccie*"—which shall encircle the bases of the femurs of the fairest creatures in creation; with bags of rice and pepper, with ingots of chocolate and nuggets and nibs of cocoa, and sacks of roasted chicory. The great hide warehouses, where are packed the skins of South American cattle, of which the horns, being left on the hides, distil anything but pleasant odours, and which lie, prone to each other, thirsting for the tan-pit. See the sugar warehouses, dripping, perspiring, crystallising with sugar in casks, and bags, and boxes.[4] How many million cups of tea will be sweetened with these cases when the sugar is refined! how many tomesful of gossiping scandal will be talked to the relish of those saccharine dainties! what stores of barley-sugar temples and Chantilly baskets for the rich, of brandyballs and hardbake for the poor, will come from those coarse canvas bags, those stained and sticky casks! And the huge tea warehouses, where the other element of scandal, the flowery Pekoe or the family Souchong, slumbers in tinfoiled chests. And the coffee warehouses, redolent of bags of Mocha and Mountain, Texan and Barbadian berries. And the multitudinous, almost uncataloguable, mass of other produce: shellac, sulphur, gum-benzoin, ardebs of beans and pulse from Egypt, yokes of copper from Asia Minor; sponge, gum-arabic, silk and muslin from Smyrna; flour from the United States; hides, hams, hemp, rags, and especially tallow in teeming casks, from Russia and the Baltic provinces; mountains of timber from Canada and Sweden; fruit, Florence oil, tinder, raw cotton (though the vast majority of that staple goes to Liverpool), indigo, saffron, magnesia, leeches, basket-work, and wash-leather! The ships vomit these on the dock quays, and the warehouses swallow them up again like ogres. But there is in one dock, the London, an underground store, that is the Aaron's rod of dock warehouses, and devours all the rest. For there, in a vast succession of vaults, roofed with cobwebs many years old, are stored in pipes and hogsheads the wines that thirsty London—thirsty England, Ireland, and Scotland—must needs drink. What throats they have, these consumers! what oceans of good liquor their Garagantuan appetites demand! Strange stories have been told about these docks, and the thirsty souls who visit them with tasting-orders; how the brawny coopers stride about with candles in cleft sticks, and, piercing casks with gimlets, pour out the rich contents, upon the sawdust that covers the floor, like water; how cases of champagne are treated as of as little account as though they were cases of small beer; how plates of cheese-crumbs are handed round to amateurs that they may chasten their palates and keep them in good tone of taste; how the coopers are well nigh infallible in detecting who are the tasters that visit these "wine vaults" with a genuine intention of buying, and who the epicureans, whose only object in visiting the London Docks is to drink, gratuitously on the premises, as much good wine as they can conveniently carry. Strange, very strange stories, too, are told of the occasional inconvenience into which the "convenient carriage" degenerates; of respectable fathers of families appearing in the open street, after they have run the tether of the tasting-order, staggering and dishevelled, and with bloodshot eyes, their cravats twisted round to the backs of their necks like bagwigs, and incoherently declaring that cheese always disagreed with them. I am candidly of opinion, however, that the majority of these legends are apocryphal, or, in the rare cases when they have a foundation in fact, belong to the history of the past, and that commercial sobriety, in the highest order, is the rule in the wine vaults of the London Docks.

ONE O'CLOCK P.M.: DOCK-LABOURERS RETURNING TO WORK.

But the Ships! Who shall describe those white-sailed camels? who shall tell in graphic words of the fantastic interlacing of their masts and rigging, of the pitchy burliness of their bulging sides; of the hives of human ants who in barges and lighters surround them, or swarm about their cargo-cumbered decks? Strange sight to see, these mariners from every quarter of the globe; of every variety of stature and complexion, from the swarthy Malay to the almost albino Finn; in every various phase of picturesque costume, from the Suliote of the fruitship, in his camise and capote, to the Yankee foremast-man in his red shirt, tarry trousers, and case-knife hung by a strand of lanyards to his girdle. But not alone of the maritime genus are the crowds who throng the docks. There are lightermen, stovedores, bargees, and "lumpers;" there are passengers flocking to their narrow berths on board emigrant ships; there are entering and wharfingers' clerks travelling about in ambulatory counting-houses mounted on wheels; there are land rats and water rats, ay, and some that may be called pirates of the long-shore, and over whom it behoves the dock policemen and the dock watchmen to exercise a somewhat rigid supervision—for they will pick and steal, these piratical ne'er-do-weels, any trifle, unconsidered or not, that comes handy to their knavish digits; and as they emerge from the dock-gates, it is considered by no means a breach of etiquette for an official to satisfy himself, by a personal inspection of their garments, that they don't happen to have concealed about them, of course by accident, such waifs and strays as a bottle of Jamaica rum, a lump of gutta percha, a roll of sheet copper, or a bundle of Havannah cigars.

But a clanging bell proclaims the hour of one, and the dock-labourers, from Tower Hill to the far-off Isle of Dogs, are summoned back to their toil. Goodness and their own deplenished pockets only know how they have been lunching, or on what coarse viands they have fed since noon. Many have not fed at all; for, of the motley herd of dock-labourers, hundreds, especially in the London Docks—where no recommendation save strength is needed, and they are taken on their good behaviour from day to day—are of the Irish way of thinking; and, wonderfully economical, provident, self-denying are those much maligned Hibernians when they are earning money. They are only spendthrifts and indolent when they have nothing. They will content themselves with a fragment of hard, dry bread, and the bibulous solace of the nearest pump, and go home cheerfully at dusk to the unsavoury den— be it in Whitechapel or in Bloomsbury or in far-off Kensington, for they prefer strangely to live at the farthest possible distance from their place of daily toil—where their ragged little robins of children dwell like so many little pigs under a bed. And there they will partake of a mess of potatoes, with one solitary red herring smashed up therein, to "give it a relish." They will half starve themselves, and go as naked as the police will permit them to go; but they will be very liberal to the priest, and will scrape money together to bring their aged and infirm parents over from the "ould country." That is folly and superstition, people will say. Of course, what people say must be right.

Some dock-labourers lunch on too much beer and too little bread; for they are held in thraldom by certain unrighteous publicans, who still pursue, with great contentment and delectation to themselves, but to the defrauding, ruin, and misery of their customers, the atrocious trade, now well nigh rooted from the manufacturing and mining districts, known as the "tommy-shop" system. I think I need scarcely explain what this system is, for, under its twin denomination of "truck," it has already formed a subject for Parliamentary inquiry. Let it suffice to say, that the chief feature in the amiable system consists in giving the labourer a fallacious and delusive credit to the amount of his weekly wages, and supplying him with victuals and drink (chiefly the latter) at an enormous rate of profit. The labourer is paid by his foreman in tickets instead of cash, and invariably finds himself at the end of the week victimised, or, to use a more expressive, though not so genteel a term, diddled, to a heart-rending extent. Dock-labourers who are in regular gangs and regularly employed, are the greatest sufferers by this unjust mode of payment. As to the casual toilers who crowd about the gates at early morning in the hope of being engaged for a working day, they are paid half a crown, and are free to squander or to hoard the thirty pence as they list. That industrious and peaceable body of men, the coalwhippers, groaned for a long period under the iniquities of the truck system; they are now protected by a special Act of Parliament, renewed from time to time; but the dock-labourers yet eat their bread leavened by a sense of injustice. There are none to help them; for they have no organisation, and very few friends. It is perfectly true that the dock-companies have nothing whatsoever to do with the social servitude under which their labourers groan; and that it is private speculators who work the system for their own aggrandisement; but the result to the labourer is the same. I don't think it matters to Quashie, the negro slave, when he is beaten, whether the cowhide be wielded by Mr. Simon Legree, the planter, or by Quimbo, the black driver.

Look at these labourers, and wonder. For it is matter for astonishment to know that among these meanly-clad, frequently ragged men, coarse, dirty, and repulsive in aspect, there are very many who have been tenderly bred and nurtured; who have been, save the mark, gentlemen! who have received University educations and borne the Queen's commission. And here also are the draff and husks of foreign immigration; Polish, German, and Italian exiles. They have come to this—down to this—up to this, if you choose; come to the old, old level, as old as Gardener Adam's time, of earning the daily bread by the sweat of the brow. It were better so than to starve; better so than to steal.

ONE O'CLOCK P.M.: DINING ROOMS IN BUCKLERSBURY.

What time the dock-labourers have finished lunch, another very meritorious class of human ants begin their prandial repasts. With just one thought at the vast number of merchants', brokers', shipping-agents', warehousemen's, wholesale dealers' counting-houses that exist in London city, you will be able to form an idea of the legions of clerks, juniors and seniors, who, invariably early-breakfasting men, must get seriously hungry at one p.m. Some I know are too proud to dine at this patriarchal hour. They dine, after office hours, at Simpson's, at the Albion, at the London, or, save us, at the Wellington. They go even further west, and patronise Feetum's, or the Scotch Stores in Regent Street, merely skating out, as it were, for a few minutes at noon, for a snack at that Bay Tree to which I have already alluded. Many, and they are the married clerks, bring neat parcels with them, containing sandwiches or bread-and-cheese, consuming those refreshments in the counting-house. In the very great houses, it is not considered etiquette to dine during office-hours, save on foreign-post nights. As to the extremely junior clerks, or office-boys, as they are irreverently termed, they eat whatever they can get, and whenever they can get it, very frequently getting nothing at all. But there are yet hundreds upon hundreds of clerks who consume an orthodox dinner of meat, vegetables, and cheese—and on high days and holidays pudding—at one p.m. Their numbers are sufficient to cram almost to suffocation the eating-houses of Cheapside, the Poultry, Mark Lane, Cornhill, and especially Bucklersbury. Of late years there has been an attempt to change the eating-houses of Cheapside into pseudo "restaurants." Seductive announcements, brilliantly emblazoned, and showily framed and glazed, have been hung up, relating to "turtle" and "venison;" salmon, with wide waddling mouths, have gasped in the windows; and insinuating mural inscriptions have hinted at the existence of "Private dining-rooms for ladies." Now, whatever can ladies—though I have the authority of Mr. Charles Dibdin and my own lips for declaring that there are fine ones in the city—want to come and dine in Cheapside for? At these restaurants they give you things with French names, charge you a stated sum for attendance, provide the pale ale in silver tankards, and take care of your hat and coat; but I like them not—neither, I believe, do my friends, the one-o'clock-dining clerks. Either let me go to Birch's or the Anti-Gallican, or let me take my modest cut of roast and boiled, my "one o' taters," my "cheese and sallary," at an eating-house in Bucklersbury—such a one as my *alter ego*, Mr. M'Connell, has here presented for your edification. And his pictured morals must eke out my written apophthegms—for this sheet is full.

TWO P.M.—FROM REGENT STREET TO HIGH CHANGE.

I breathe again. I see before me, broad-spread, a vista of gentility. I have done, for many hours to come, with shabby subjects. No more dams I'll make for fish—in Billingsgate; nor scrape trencher, nor wash dish, at second-rate eating-houses; nor fetch firing at requiring in Covent Garden or the Docks. Prospero must get a new man, for Caliban has got a new master: Fashion, in Regent Street.

I declare that when I approach this solemnly-genteel theme, my frame dilates, my eyes kindle, my heart dances. I experience an intense desire to array myself in purple and fine linen, knee shorts, lace ruffles, pink silk stockings, diamond buckles, and a silver-hilted sword; to have my hair powdered, and my jewelled *tabatière* filled with scented rappee; to sit with my feet on a Turkey carpet, before a table inlaid with *marqueterie*, wax candles in silver sconces (the candles all green, with fillagree *bobeches*) on either side; and then—while my Dulcinea in a hoop petticoat, a point lace apron, red-heeled *mules*, a *toupet* and a *mouche* on the left cheek, her feathered fan, painted by Fragonard on the finest chicken-skin, lying beside her—plays the minuet from "Ariadne" in an adjoining and gilded *salon*, decorated in the *Style Pompadour*, on the harpsichord; and on pink scented note-paper, with a diamond pointed pen and violet ink—the golden pounce-box at my elbow—then under these circumstances and with these luxurious appliances around me, I think I could manage to devote myself to the task of inditing matter concerning Regent Street in the smoothest dythrambics. This is rather a violent contrast to the dry skittle-ground, the cows, and the depraved sow which inspired me in the last chapter; but only take my subject into consideration: only permit me to inoculate you with one drop of the ethereal nectar which should be quaffed by every writer who would look upon Regent Street from a proper point of view. Ladies and gentlemen moving in the polite circles have—but that is long ago—accused me of being of Bohemia, and to that manner born; of writing a great deal too much about the Virginian weed in its manufactured state, and the fermented infusion of malt and hops; publishers have refused to purchase my novels because they contained too many descriptions of "low life;" because my heroes and heroines were too frequently ragged and forlorn creatures, who didn't go into "society," who didn't go to church, who were never seen at the May meetings in Exeter Hall, but who went to public-houses and penny-gaffs instead. Oh, lords and ladies! oh, brilliant butterflies of society! oh, respectable people of every degree! whose ear coarse language wounds, but who would have, believe me, to undergo much coarser deeds from the ragged ones you despise, were it not for the humble efforts of us poor pen-and-ink missionaries; O salt ones of the earth! think that you are but hundreds among the millions of the tattered and torn, who have never studied the "Handbook to Etiquette," nor heard of Burke and Debrett, and who would eat peas with their knives if they had any peas to eat—Heaven help them! They are around and about you always. I have no greed of gain in advocating their cause, for I am unknown to them, and am of your middle class, and am as liable to be stoned by the ragged ones for having a better coat than they any day. But woe be to you, respectables, if you shut your ears to their plaints and your eyes to their condition. For the stones may fly thick and fast some day; there may be none to help you, and it may be too late to cry for help.

I have heard Regent Street compared to the Boulevard des Italiens, to Unter-den-Linden at Berlin, to Broadway at New York, to the Montagne de la Cour at Brussels, to the Corso de' Servi at Milan, to the Toledo at Naples, to George Street, Sydney, and to the Nevskoi Perspective at Petersburg. In my opinion, Regent Street is an amalgamation of all these streets, and surpasses them all. Their elements are strained, filtered, refined, condensed, sublimated, to make up one glorious thoroughfare. Add to this, the unique and almost indescribable *cachet* which the presence of English aristocracy lends to every place it chooses for its frequentation, and the result is Regent Street. Of the many cities I have wandered into and about, there is but one possessing a street that can challenge comparison with—and that, I must confess, well nigh equals—the street that Nash, prince of architects, built for the fourth George. At a right angle from the pleasant waters of the river Liffey, there runs a street, wide in dimensions, magnificent in the proportions of its edifices, splendid in its temples and its palaces, though many of the latter, alas! are converted now into hotels, now into linen-drapers' shops; but on a golden summer's afternoon, when you see, speeding towards the column of Nelson in the distance, the glittering equipages of the rich and noble, who yet have their dwelling in Eblana; the clattering orderlies, on sleek-groomed horses, and with burnished accoutrements, spurring from the Castle towards the Post Office—and, beauty of beauties, the side walks on either hand converted into parterres of living flowers, the grand and glorious Irish girls, with their bright raiment and brighter eyes; you will acknowledge that Regent Street has a rival, that beyond St. George's Channel is a street that the triumphal procession of a Zenobia or a Semiramis might pass down, and that the queen of streets is Sackville Street, Dublin.

Do you know, youth of the present generation—for I fondly hope that I have good store of juveniles among my readers—that Regent Street has its antiquities, its archæologia, its topographical curiosities? Mr. Peter Cunningham knows them all by heart; I am not about to steal from the "Handbook of London" of our modern Camden; but will just tell you, in my desultory way, that, in the days when the Mews reared their head, an unsightly mass of brick buildings, in the area which is now Trafalgar Square; when Carlton House loomed at the eastern end of Pall Mall, instead of the ugly post erected as a monument of national gratitude to the Royal Duke who paid nobody; when the Golden Cross, Charing Cross, was hemmed in by a cobweb mass of dirty tenements, and Hungerford Market was yet a mass of fishy hovels ungraced by Hungerford Hall and Mr. Gatti's penny-ice shop; when the old "Courier" newspaper office stood (over-against Mr. Cross's older Exeter 'Change, with the elephant's tusks displayed outside, the shops beneath, and Chunee and the wild beasts all alive and roaring upstairs) in the space that now forms the approach to Waterloo Bridge; and when the vicinity of Temple Bar was blocked up by a brick-and-mortar *cloaca*, since swept away to form what is now termed Picket Place. Are you at all aware, neophytes in topographical lore, that the area of Regent Street the superb, was occupied by mean and shambling tenth-rate avenues, among which the chiefest was a large, dirty highway, called Great Swallow Street? Old Fuller (I don't know why he should be called "old" so persistently, for he did not attain anything like a venerable age) was in the habit of collecting information for the "Worthies of England" from the tottering crones who sat spinning by the ingle-nook, and from the white-headed grand-sires sunning themselves on the bench by the almshouse door. In like manner, I owe much of the information I possess on the aspect of London streets, at the time just previous to my nonage, to communing with nurses and nurses' female friends. The good folks who tend children, seldom deem that the little pitchers they say jestingly have long ears, will suck their lore in so greedily, or retain it so long.

My personal acquaintance with Regent Street dates from the year 'thirty-two, when I remember a great scrambling procession of operatives, with parti-coloured flags, emblazoned with devices I could not read, passing down it. Mrs. Esner, who was then attached to my person in a domestic capacity (she often calls upon me now, and, saying that she "nussed" me, expatiates on the benefits of a pound of green tea), told me that these operatives belonged to the "Trades Union." She said—though the good woman must have exaggerated—that they were half a million in number, and I recollect her portending, in a grave low voice, that there would be riots that night. I don't think that any occurred; but long after, whenever I saw a crowd I used to ask whether "there would be any riots" that night, just as I might have inquired whether there would be any bread-and-butter for tea. This was about the time that they used to call the great Duke of Wellington "Nosey," and "Sawbones," and to break his windows. I was too young to know then, that the Athenians grew tired of hearing Aristides called "The Just;" and that a nation once grumbled at having to pay for the palace it had bestowed upon that John Churchill, Duke of Marlborough, who won the battle of Blenheim. I think, too, there must have been something about the Cholera in my earliest recollections of Regent Street; yet, no: I lived in North Audley Street at that time, and opposite the mansion of the great Earl of Clarendon; for, as clearly as though it were yesterday, I see now in the eye to which the attention of Horatio, friend of Hamlet Prince of Denmark, was directed—a hot autumn afternoon. I am at the nursery-window in sad disgrace, and pouting because I have wrenched the sprightly wooden hussar from the horse which had the semi-circle of wire with the bullet at the end fixed in his stomach, and who used, with that impetus, to swing so deftly. There is much commotion in the great earl's mansion; for one of the servants partook too plentifully last night of gooseberry-fool after a rout his lordship gave—where are the "routs" and the "gooseberry-fools" now?—and she is dead this morning of cholera morbus. My female *entourage* are unanimously exacting in calling it cholera "morbus." The undertaker's men bring the body out; the shell gleams white in the afternoon's sunshine, and it is begirt with cords; "for," says the domestic oracles behind me, "it was so mortal swole that it would 'ave bust else." A horrible rumour runs about, that the coffin has been "pitched and sealed." What can "pitching and sealing" mean? There is a great crowd before the earl's door, who are violent and clamorous, because rumour—a servant's hall, an area gate, a coachman from-the-house-to-his-wife-in-the-mews rumour—bruits it about that the body has not been washed. My nurse says that they will have to send for the "padroll" with "cut-lashes." All these things sink into my little mind; and then the whole sequel, with a train of years behind it, fade away, leaving me with but one more recollection—that we had a twopenny cottage-loaf boiled in milk that day for dinner, which was consequently swollen to twice its natural size; and which the Eumenides of the nursery authoritatively assured me was, with brown sugar, the "best puddin' out." I know now that congested loaf to have been an insipid swindle.

I am again in Regent Street, but at another window, and in another house. There is no nurse now, but a genteel young woman, aged about thirty—she asked me once, for fun, how old she was, and I guessed, in all youthful seriousness, fifty, whereupon she slapped me—to take care of me. Her name is Sprackmore, she has long corkscrew ringlets, and is very pious, and beneath her auspices I first study the "Loss of the *Kent* East Indiaman," and the "Dairyman's Daughter." She has fits, too, occasionally. I am just of that age to be a hollow-eyed little boy in a tunic, with a frill and a belt, and to be dreadfully afraid of the parent I used a year before to love and caress with such fearless confidence. They say I am a clever child, and my cleverness is encouraged by being told that I am not to ask questions, and that I had much better go and play with my toys than mope over that big volume of Lyttelton's "History of England," lent to me by Mr. Somebody, the lawyer—

I see him now, very stout and gray, at the funeral whenever any of us dies: of which volume—it is in very shabby condition—I break the top-cover off by letting it fall from the chair, which is my reading-desk. I suffer agonies of terror and remorse for months, lest the fracture should be discovered, though I have temporarily repaired it by means of a gimlet and a piece of twine. Then, one bright day, my cousin Sarah gives me a bright five-shilling piece—I take her to the opera now, but she always remembers my childish dependence upon her, and insists upon paying the cab home—and take Lyttelton's "History," still with great fear and trembling, to a bookbinder's in Broad Street, Golden Square, who tells me that the "hends is jagged," and that there must be a new back, lettering, and gilding to the book. He works his will with it, and charges me four shillings and sixpence out of the five shilling-piece for working it; but to tell of the joyful relief I feel when I bring Lyttelton's "History" back safe and sound! I do not get rid of my perturbation entirely, however, till I have rubbed the back against the carpet a little to soil it, in order that it may not look too new. Oh! the agonies, the Laocoon-like conscience windings, the Promethean tortures, that children suffer through these accidental breakages! Oh! the unreasoning cruelty of parents, who punish children for such mischances! So I am the little boy in a tunic; and I daresay that, with my inquisitiveness, and my moping over books, I am an intolerable little nuisance. I am at the Regent Street window, and much speculation is rife as to whether the King, who is lying mortally sick at Windsor, is dead. For it is within a few minutes of eleven, and at that time the well-known troop of Horse Guards pass on their way to St. James's; and it is reasonably inferred that, if King William be gathered to his fathers, the standard will be furled. The Guards pass; they wore helmets, with plumes above them shaped like black mutton chops—not the casques with the flowing horse-hair they wear now; and to be sure the standard is furled, in a species of drab umbrella case. The King is dead for sure; nay, he does not die for a full week afterwards; the flag was merely furled because the day was dark and lowering, presaging rain.

TWO O'CLOCK P.M.: REGENT STREET.

I told you hours since that I lived in the house in Regent Street in which the Marquis de Bourbel forged his letters of credit.[5] I think that I am qualified to speak of the place, for, walking down it the other day, I counted no less than eleven houses, between the two circuses, in which I had at one time dwelt. But they were all early, those remembrances, and connected with the time when the colonnade of the Quadrant existed—"*La ville de Londres*," as the foreign engravers of pictorial note-paper used grandiloquently to call it. Whatever could have possessed our Commissioner of Woods and Forests to allow those unrivalled arcades to be demolished! The stupid tradesmen, whose purblind, shop-till avarice led them to petition for the removal of the columns, gained nothing by the change, for the Quadrant, as a lounge in wet weather, was at once destroyed; and I see now many of the houses, once let out in superior apartments, occupied as billiard-rooms and photographic studios, and many of the shops invaded and conquered by cheap tailors. The Quadrant colonnade afforded not only a convenient shelter beneath, but it was a capital promenade for the dwellers in the first-floors above. The *entresols* certainly were slightly gloomy; and moustached foreigners, together with some gaily-dressed company still naughtier, could with difficulty be restrained from prowling backwards and forwards between Glasshouse Street and the County Fire Office. But, perambulating Regent Street at all hours of the day and night, as I do now frequently, I see no diminution in the number of moustached, or rouged, or naughty faces, whose prototypes were familiar to me, years agone, in the brilliant Quadrant. As to the purlieus of the County Fire Office, they are confusion, and a scandal to London and its police. The first-floor balconies above were in my childhood most glorious playgrounds. There I kept preserves of broken bottles and flowerpots; on those leads I inscribed fantastic devices in chalk and with penknives, drawing silver diagrams through the cake of dust and dried refrain that covered the metal; and often have I come to domestic grief through an irresistible propensity for poaching on the balconies of the neighbours on either side. Still in a state of tunic-hood, I remember a very tall, handsome gentleman, with a crimson velvet under-waistcoat—I saw his grave in Perè la Chaise last winter—who was my great aider and abettor in these juvenile escapades. He had a wondrous weapon of offence called a "sabar-cane," a delightful thing (to me then), half walking-stick, half pea-shooter, from which he used to discharge clay pellets at the vagrant cats on the adjoining balconies. He it was who was wont to lean over the balcony, and fish for people's hats with a salmon-hook affixed to the extremity of a tandem-whip; he it was who came home from the Derby (quite in a friendly manner) to see us one evening, all white—white hat, white coat, white trousers, white waistcoat, white neckerchief, white boots, to say nothing of the dust and the flour with which he had been plentifully besprinkled at Kennington Gate. He had won heavily on some horse long since gone to grass for ever, was very merry, and insisted upon winding-up our new French clock with the snuffers. He it was who made nocturnal excursions from parapet to parapet along the leads, returning with bewildering accounts of bearded men who were gambling with dice at No. 92; of the tenor of the Italian Opera, who, knife in hand, was pursuing his wife (in her nightdress) about the balcony, at No. 74; and of Mademoiselle Follejambes, the *premier sujet* of the same establishment, who was practising *pirouettes* before a cheval glass at the open window of No. 86, while Mademoiselle Follejambe's mamma, with a red cotton pocket-handkerchief tied round her old head, was drinking *anisette* out of a tea-cup. You must be forbearing with me, if, while I speak of Regent Street, I interlard my speech with foreign languages a little. For, from its first erection, the Quadrant end of Regent Street has been the home of the artistic foreigners who are attracted to London during the musical and operatic season, less by inclination for the climate and respect for the institutions of England, than by a profound admiration for the circular effigies, in gold, (with neatly milled edges) of her Majesty the Queen, which John Bull so liberally bestows on those who squall or fiddle for him, provided they be of foreign extraction. Let me not be too unjust, however, to Bull. Find him but a real English tenor, and J. B. will smother him in bank-notes, and deafen him with plaudits. From the balconies of Regent Street, I have seen the greatest *cantatrici* and *ballerine* of this age. The Grand Cham of tenors, who has *never* been replaced—no signor Mario, no Signor Giuglini, no Signor Mongini, no Signor Tamberlik, no Mr. Sims Reeves, no Mr. George Perren—

the incomparable Rubini, had lodgings opposite, once, to where we dwelt, at a shawl shop. I have watched the sedulous care which that eminent man took of his health, marvelled at the multitudinous folds of silk or woollen stuff, like the turban of an Asiatic, with which he encircled his invaluable throat when he took out-door exercise. I have seen, through his open window, the basso of basso's, Papa Lablache, the man with the lion's head, the Falstaffian abdomen, and the ten times stentorian lungs, eat maccaroni for twenty-seven consecutive minutes, till he seemed determined to outdo all the ribbon-swallowing conjurors who had ever lived. We used to say that he was practising for Leporello. He had a kindly heart, Papa Lablache, and preserved a kindly remembrance of the hearty English people, among whom he made his fortune. Though he would sometimes facetiously declare, that when his voice was no longer fit to be heard in a Continental city, he would come to England to settle, and sing *"Fra questi sordi"* among these deaf ones—for whom he would still be quite good enough—his heart never cooled towards the old country; and, moribund at Naples, when the supreme Hour was fast arriving, he raised himself on his couch, and essayed to sing a song he loved very well—"Home! sweet Home!" But, as the silver cord loosened, he murmured, *"Mi manca la voce"*—"My voice fails me;" and so died.

To say nothing of a dreadful German basso, one of the regular line-of-battle ship voices, with 56-pounders on the first deck, who was once a next-door neighbour in the Quadrant, and when he used to call for his servant thus,"PAOOLO!" shook the flower-pots on our own balcony; or of an egregious fiddler, with long hair, who, in imitation of his predecessor, Paganini, gave out that he had sold himself to the devil, but who was, I believe, an arrant humbug with a mania for practising in the open air—it may have been as a medium of advertisement—and used to attract large crowds in the street beneath listening to his complicated fiddlements. Yet I must spare a word for Madame—I really forget whom, but it ended with "heim," I think—who had the six-and-thirty Austro-Sclavonic children who used to perform the mirror dance and other terpsichorean feats at her Majesty's Theatre and whom she used to drill on the balcony like soldiers. They made a tremendous noise, these tiny *figurantes*, and in the hours of recreation were not unaccustomed to fight among themselves. Then Madame Somethingheim would sally forth on the balcony and cut savagely into their poor young bodies with a switch, and after much howling on their part, and chasing to and fro on hers, restore peace.

The colonnades are as fruitful to me in recollections as the balconies. How many miles of daily walks have I gone over, the hand of a toddling little sister in mine, and with strict injunctions not to stray beyond the shadow of the columns, and with prohibitions, under dreadful menaces, of venturing in Air Street on the one side or Vigo Lane on the other! I wore, I remember, then, an absurd blue cloak, too short for me, and lined with red, and with a brass clasp somewhat resembling the ornament on a cartouch box. This cloak chafed and fretted me, and was the bane and terror of my existence; for I knew, or fancied I knew, that every passer-by must know that it had never been made for me, which, indeed, it never had, having formerly been of far larger dimensions and the property of an officer in his Majesty's light infantry. I believe that there was a domestic ukase promulgated for our benefit against crossing the road; but we did cross it nevertheless, with many looks to the right and the left, not only to secure ourselves against threatening carriage wheels, but with reference to the possible appearance of parents and guardians. There was a delightful bird-stuffer's shop at the corner of a court, with birds of paradise, parrots, and hummingbirds of gorgeous plumage, and strange creatures with white bodies and long yellow beaks and legs that terrified while they pleasured us. Then there was the funeral monument shop, with the mural tablets, the obelisks, the broken columns, the extinguished torches, and the draped urns in the window, and some with the inscriptions into the bargain, all ready engraved in black and white, puzzling us as to whether the tender husbands, devoted wives, and affectionate sons, to whom they referred, were buried in that grisly shop—it had a pleasant, fascinating terror about it, like an undertaker's, too. There was Swan and Edgar's, splendid and radiant, then as now, with brave apparel (how many times have I listened to the enthusiastic cheers of Swan and Edgar's young men, on the occasion of the proprietors giving their annual banquet to their *employés*?), and even then replete with legends of dishonest fares, who caused a cab to halt at the Regent Street entrance, got out, said they would be back in a moment, and then darting through the crowded shop, knavishly escaped at the Piccadilly end. There was the Italian statuary shop, with Canova's Graces, the crouching Venus, and the birds round a vase in alabaster; and, above all, there was Mrs. Lipscombe's shop—I don't mean the staymaker's, but the one next to that, the filter shop, with the astonishing machines for converting foul and muddy water, like gruel, thick and slab, into a sparkling, crystal stream. What a miracle it seemed to me that the goblet, filled to the brim, and yet into which, from the filter above, drops continually fell, never overflowed! How I used to watch the little cork ball, kept in a continually bounding state of agitation by the perpendicular jet of water—watch it with almost breathless agitation, when, every now and then, the centre of gravity would be lost, and the little ball would tumble in the basin beneath—the whole was covered by a glass shade—till, caught up once more, it would be sent in eddying whirls higher than ever! I have seen the same experiment tried since with bigger balls—and of marble—very like twenty-four pounders—at the *Grandes Eaux* of Versailles, and in the gardens of Peterhoff. Stone Neptunes and Tritons surrounded the basin, and the jets of water, forty feet high, sent the spray flying in the faces of the spectators; but none of these hydraulic displays ever came up, in my opinion, to the tiny squirt, with the little cork ball, underneath the glass shade, in Mrs. Lipscombe's window. Does she make stays and sell filters yet, I wonder! What a curious mixture of avocations! I know of none stranger since the names of M. Fenwick de Porquet and Mrs. Mary Wedlake were amalgamated, and inquiries as to whether we "bruised our oats yet," were alternated with pressing questions of *"Parlez vous Français?"*

When I thus walked the Regent Quadrant, twenty years since, it was haunted by a class of men, now, I am happy to believe, almost entirely extinct. We have plenty of rogues in our body corporate yet. The turf has its blacklegs and touts; the nightside of London is fruitful in "macemen," "mouchers," and "go-alongs." You must not be angry with me for using slang terms; for did not a clergyman, at a highly-respectable institution, deliver a lecture on slang the other day, and did not the "Times" quote him? We are not free from skittle-sharps, card-cheats, "duffers," and ring-droppers; nay, even at remote country race-courses, you may find remnants of the whilom swarming tribe of "charley-pitchers," the knavish gentry who pursue the games of "under seven or over seven," "red, black, leather and star," or inveigle the unwary with "three little thimbles and one small pea." But a stern and righteous legislation has put down nine-tenths of the infamous dens where any fool who chose to knock was fleeced to the last lock of wool. If a man wants to be vicious (in the gambling way) now, he must have the *entrée* to the abodes of vice, and a nodding acquaintance with the demon. A neophyte is not allowed to ruin himself how and where he likes. In the days of which I make mention, Regent Street and its purlieus abounded in open gambling houses, and to the skirts of these necessarily hung on a deboshed regiment of rogues, who made their miserable livings as runners, and decoy-ducks, and bravos to these abominable nests. They were called "Greeks," and two o'clock in the afternoon was their great time for turning out. From what infected holes or pestiferous garrets in Sherrard, or Brewer, or Rupert Street, they came, I know not; but there they were at the appointed hour, skulking with a half sheepish, half defiant stride up and down Regent Street. Miserable dogs mostly, for all their fine clothes—always resplendently, though dirtily, attired. They wore great white coats, shiny hats, and mosaic jewellery, which was just then coming into fashion. There was another fashion, in which they very nearly succeeded, by adopting, to drive out, and make permanently disreputable: that of wearing moustaches. They used to swagger about, all lacquered, pomatumed, bejewelled, and begrimed, till I knew them all by sight and many of them by name and repute. There was Jack Cheetham, the lord's son, he who was thrown out of the window at Frascati's, and killed the Frenchman in the Bois de Vincennes. There was Captain Dollamore, who married the rich widow, and was arrested for her milliner's bill the week afterwards. There was Charley Skewball; he was called

Charley, but he was a baronet, had once been a gentleman, and was the greatest rogue unhung. Mr. Thackeray knows these men well. They are his Count Punters, Major Loders, M. de Caramboles, Hon. Algernon Deuceaces; but they are extinct among us as a class, O Titmarsh; and simple people, who read your admirable novels, wonder whom the monsters are that you draw. They are dead; they are at the hulks; they are feebly punting at the few remaining gambling places on the Rhine: they flaunted in the bad prime of their manhood when I was a child. I have outgrown them; and only now and then, when I am out very late, collecting materials for "Twice Round the Clock," I come upon a stray Jack or Charley—ragged and drivelling, his fine feathers all moulted or smirched, his occupation quite gone—who sidles up to me and calls me "Your honour," and with salt-rheumy lips, whimpers forth a supplication for "A penny towards a night's lodging."

When our dear Queen Victoria was crowned, I began to lose sight of Regent Street—lost sight of it by degrees altogether, and came not back to it, as an observer, for many years. I rather avoided the place, for I had a bitter baptism of physical misery in the beginning of my working life: wanting food and raiment, not through prodigality (that came afterwards), but through sheer penury and friendlessness. And Regent Street, for all my querulous childhood, was associated with too many memories of happier days gone for ever. You know what the Italian rhymester says—

"Nessun maggior dolore

Che ricordarsi del tempo felice

Nella Miseria."

An Englishman has stolen the thought in some lines about "a sorrow's crown of sorrow," whose summing up I forget; but the sense of the passage is that the times are exceedingly hard, when, destitute and footsore, you pass by a house, and glance at the windows once lighted up by feasting in which you participated; when you think of the rooms, once swept by the robe of the woman whom you loved, but that now, house, windows, rooms, are the portion of strangers. I say I went away from Regent Street, and came not back. There were reasons. I became of the Strand and Fleet Street a denizen, and Temple Bar entered into my soul. For I was affiliated to a great mystery of Masonry, called Literature, and had to follow the behests of my mother lodge. You don't see much of Regent Street, during your apprenticeship, if you begin at the lowermost degree, I can assure you. Now I am a master-mason, free and accepted, and can hold my own; albeit I shall never be an

Office-bearer, or "Grand," of my lodge, or rise to the superlatives of the Royal Arch or the Thirty-third.

Behold Regent Street at two p.m., in the accompanying cartoon. Not without reason do I declare it the most fashionable street in the world. I call it not so for the aristocratic mansions it might possess; for the lower parts of the houses are occupied as shops, and the furnished apartments are let, either to music or operatic celebrities or to unostentatious old bachelors. But the shops themselves are innately fashionable. There was a dash of utilitarianism mingled with the slightly Bohemian tinge of my Regent Street of twenty years ago; there were bakers' shops, stationers, and opticians, who had models of steam engines in their windows. There was a grocer not above selling orange marmalade, brown sugar, and Durham mustard. I remember buying a penny cake of chocolate of him one morning; but I find the shop now expanded into a magnificent emporium, where are sold wines, and spirits, sweetmeats and preserves, liqueurs and condiments, Bayonne ham, Narbonne honey, Bologna sausages, Russian caviare, Iceland moss, clotted cream, and *terrines* of *pâté de foie gras*. Indeed, Regent Street is an avenue of superfluities—a great trunk-road in Vanity Fair. Fancy watchmakers, haberdashers, and photographers; fancy stationers, fancy hosiers, and fancy staymakers; music shops, shawl shops, jewellers, French glove shops, perfumery, and point lace shops, confectioners and milliners: creamily, these are the merchants whose wares are exhibited in this Bezesteen of the world.

TWO O'CLOCK P.M.: HIGH CHANGE.

Now, whatever can her ladyship, who has been shopping in Regent Street, have ordered the stalwart footman, who shut the carriage door with a resounding bang, to instruct the coachman to drive her to the Bank for? Her ladyship's own private bank is in a shiningly aristocratic street, by Cavendish Square, embosomed among green trees. She does not want to buy ribbons or lace on Ludgate Hill, artificial flowers in St. Paul's Churchyard, or fine linen in Cheapside. No; she has a very simple reason for going into the city: Sir John, her liege lord, is on 'Change. He will be there from half-past two to three, at which hour High 'Change, as it may be called, closes, and she intends to call for him, and drive him to the West-end again. By your leave, we will jump up behind the carriage, heedless of the stalwart footman; for we are in the receipt of fern-seed, and invisible.

Going on 'Change seems to be but a mechanical and mercantile occupation, and one that might with safety be entrusted to some confidential clerk; yet it is not so; and the greatest magnates of commerce and finance, the Rothschilds, the Barings, the Huths, the legions of London's merchant-princes, are to be found chaffering in the quadrangle every day. In the old Exchange, they used to point out the particular column against which the elder Rothschild was wont to lean. They called the old man, too—marvellous diplomatist in financial combinations as he was—the Pillar of the Exchange. You know that the colonnades—whose ceilings are painted in such elaborate encaustic, and with such a signal result in ruin from damp and smoke—are divided into different promenades, variously designated, according to the nations of the merchants who frequent them. Thus—there are the Italian Walk, the Spanish Walk, the Portuguese Walk, the Danish Walk, and—a very notable walk it is too—the Greek Walk. Here you may see, jabbering and gesticulating, the crafty, keen-eyed, sallow-faced Smyrnians, Suliotes, Zantrites, and Fanariotes, individuals much given to speculations in corn, in which, if report does them no injustice, they gamble most egregiously.

Three o'clock strikes—or rather chimes—from the bell-tower of Mr. Tite's new building. The quadrangle of the Exchange is converted into an accurate model of the Tower of Babel. The mass of black-hatted heads—with here and there a white one, like a fleck of foam on the crest of a wave—eddies with violence to and fro. Men shout, and push, and struggle, and jostle, and shriek bargains into one another's ears. A stranger might imagine that these money and merchandise dealers had fallen out, and were about to fight; but the beadle of the Exchange looks on calmly; he knows that no breach of the peace will be committed, and that the merchants and financiers are merely singing their ordinary pæan of praise to the great god Mammon. Surely—if there be not high treason in the thought—they ought to pull down Mr. Lough's statue of Queen Victoria, which stands in the centre of the quadrangle, and replace it by a neat effigy of the Golden Calf.

THREE P.M.—DEBENHAM AND STORR'S AUCTION-ROOMS, AND THE PANTHEON BAZAAR.

The travelled reader has visited that astonishing *atelier* of mosaics and *pietra dura* in Florence maintained at the charges of the late Grand Duke of Tuscany, (he has been signally kicked off thronedom, since the first writing of these presents), and has watched with admiring amazement the patient ingenuity with which the artisans adjust the tiny little vitreous and metallic fragments, that, firmly imbedded in paste, make the fruits and flowers, the birds and angels of the mosaic. What an impossible task it is, apparently, to form the microscopic bits into comely shapeliness, symmetrical in form and glowing with rich colours! yet how deftly the artists accomplish their task! how the work grows beneath their nimble hands! What astonishing memories these *maître* mosaicists must have, remembering to a pin's point where the high lights on the petals of a rose will fall, and storing up in their minds archives of the eyelashes of the Madonna, precedents for every scintillation of the rays in the golden nimbus round His head! The mosaicists of Rome, and Florence, and Venice—though the glorious art has well-nigh died out in the Adriatic city—are the real administrative reformers, after all. The right thing in the right place is their unvarying motto, and they are never found putting the round men in the square holes, or *vice versâ*.

I have been led into this train of thought by the contemplation of the exigencies of "Twice Round the Clock." Time, my slave for once, though he has been my stern and cruel master for years and years, and at whom I mean to throw a dart when this series shall be completed—Time, who is my bond servant, to fetch and carry, to hew wood and draw water for yet a span, has culled from the wild garden of Eternity, and thrown at my feet, a heterogeneous mass of hours, minutes, and seconds, and has said with a mocking subserviency—"There, my master, there are the hours of the day and night, and their minutest subdivisions; try and paste them on your printed calendar; try and reconcile your men and women to them; try and apportion in its proper measure of time each grain of sand to the futile rivings and strivings of your conceited humanity. You have stumbled on from hour to hour since the sun was young, telling, with indifferent success, the good and bad deeds that are done in London as the relentless needle pushes round and round the dial. Here, then, is Three o'Clock in the Afternoon. Take it; see what you can make of it, and much good may it do you!" And as Time, or the vagrant thought I have embodied for the nonce, says this, he sticks his tongue into his cheek, as though he thought that three o'clock in the afternoon were rather a poser to me.

Old man with the scythe and hour-glass, I defy thee! I will admit that three o'clock post meridian, requires much deliberation and cogitation, in order to give the millions of human marionettes, of whom I hold, temporarily, the strings, their suitable employment; but it is rather from a profusion than a paucity of scenes and things germane to the hour that I am embarrassed. At three, 'Change is still going on, though its busy time, the acmè of its excitement, is over. As the clock strikes four, the city of London is in full pant; the clerks rush up Cheapside, and dive down the wealthy narrow lanes, their bursting bill-books (secured by leather-covered chains tied round their bodies) charged with "three months after date, please pay to the order," which they cram into letter-boxes for acceptance. The private banking houses in Lombard Street are in an orderly uproar of finance. The rattling of shovels is incessant; office-boys cast thousands of pounds, in notes, bills, and money, to the cashier, carelessly, across the counter, paying vast sums in to their masters' accounts; and the mighty partners—in checked neckerchiefs, buff waistcoats, and creaking boots: tremendous bank-partners, who are baronets, and members of Parliament, lords even—stalk back from 'Change, pay a farewell visit to the bank parlour, have a short but solemn confab with confidential subordinates, relative to coming transactions at the clearing-house, and then enter their carriages, and are borne to clubs, to the House of Commons, to Greenwich dinners, or, perchance, if they have a dinner-party at home, to their magnificent villas at Putney and Roehampton. What a colony of bankers dwell there! the *sommités* of the *haute finance* seem to entertain as decided a partiality for the banks of the Thames, as the stockbrokers do for Brixton and Tulse Hill. Rare lives these money keepers lead—scattering in the West that which they gather in the East. Graperies, pineries, conservatories, ice-houses, dinner-parties, balls, picnics; all these do they enjoy: they, their comely wives and handsome daughters. They marry into the aristocracy! they have countesses and marchionesses in their list of partners. It is not so many centuries ago since the bankers were humble sellers of gold plate, dwelling in Lombard Street and the Chepe, and following the great courtiers round the quadrangle of the Exchange, intreating their lordships' honours to be allowed to keep their cash. Worthy individuals, however, are the majority of these bankers, and it is but very rarely indeed that they make ducks and drakes of their customers' moneys. They are not so very proud either, for all their splendid carriages and horses; and here, upon my word, is Baron Lionel de Rothschild tearing up Ludgate Hill in a common Hansom cab; but he, like the bad man whom Martial in an epigram declares not to be so much vicious as vice itself, is less a Banker than a Bank.

As three o'clock grows old, and the tide of business shows unmistakeable indices of an ebb at no very remote period, so far as the city is concerned, that same business is at the West-end in its extremest activity. The shops of the West Strand, Piccadilly, Oxford and Regent Streets, are thronged with customers, chiefly ladies; the roadway is encumbered with carts and carriages; and street avocations—the minor commerce of the mighty mart—are in full swing. Thick-necked and beetle-browed individuals, by courtesy called dog-fanciers, but who in many cases might with as much propriety answer to the name of dog-stealers—forbidding-looking gentry, in coats of velveteen, with large mother-o'-pearl buttons, and waistcoats of the neat and unpretending moleskin—lurk about the kerbs of the purlieus of Regent Street and Waterloo Place (the police drive them away from the main thoroughfares), with the little "dawgs" they have to sell tucked beneath their arms, made doubly attractive by much washing with scented soap, and the further decoration of their necks with pink or blue ribbons. Here is the little snub-nosed King Charles—I hope the *retroussé* appearance of his nasal organ is not due to the unkind agency of a noose of whipcord—his feathery feet and tail, and his long silky ears, sweeping the clean summer pavement. Here is the Newfoundland pup, with his bullet head and clubbed caudal-appendage, winking his stupid little eyes, and needing, seemingly, an enormous amount of licking into shape. Here is the bull-dog, in his full growth, with his legs bowed, his tail inclining to the spiral, his broad chest, thin flanks, defined ribs, moist nozzle, hare lip, bloodshot eyes, protruding fang, and symmetrical patch over one eye; or else, in a state of puppyhood, peeping from his proprietor's side-pocket, all pink and white like a morose sucking-pig become a hermit. Here is the delightful little toy English terrier, with his jet-black coat, erect neck, and tan paws; and here the genuine Skye, gray or brown, like an unravelled ball of worsted. See, too, grimacing at all who come to view, like a mulatto at a slave auction, who fancies himself good-looking, the accomplished French poodle, with his peaked nose, woolly wig, leggings, and tail band, and his horrible shaved, salmon-coloured body. He can dance; he can perform gun-drill; he can fall motionless, as though dead, at the word of command; he can climb up a lamp-post, jump over a stick, hop on one leg, carry a basket in his mouth, and run away when he is told that a policeman is coming. You can teach him to do anything but love you. These, and good store of mongrels and half-breeds that the dealer would fain palm upon us as dogs of blood and price, frisk and fawn about his cord-trouser covered legs; but where is the toy-dog *par excellence*, the playful, snappish, fractious, facetious, charming, utterly useless little dog, that, a quarter of a century since, was the treasure of our dowagers and our old maids? Where is the Dutch pug? Where is that Narcissus of canine Calibanism, with his coffee-coloured coat, his tail in a ring like the blue-nosed baboon's, his crisped morsels of ears, his black muzzle, his sharp, gleaming little teeth, his intensely red lips and tongue? Is he extinct, like the lion-dog from Malta, the property of her Majesty the Queen, and the "last of his race," whom courtly Sir Edwin Landseer drew? Are there no more Dutch pugs? They must exist somewhere.

Cunning dealers owning *recherché* kennels in the New Road or at Battle Bridge, or attending recondite "show clubs," held at mysterious hostelries in the vicinity of Clerkenwell, must yet have some undoubted specimens of the pug for sale. There must be burghers yet, in the fat comfortable houses at Loo by the Hague, or in the plethoric, oozy vicinage of Amsterdam—there must be Tietjens, and Tenbroecks, and van Ramms, and van Bummels, whose pride it is, amidst their store of tulip bulbs, china vases, cabinet pictures by Breughel and Ostade, lacquer-work from Japan, and spice-boxes from Java, to possess Dutch pugs in the flesh. But the creature is seen no more in London streets, and we must be content with him on Hogarth's canvases, in Linacre's engravings, or modelled in china, as we see him in the curiosity shops. I have indeed seen the elephant—I mean the Dutch pug—alive and snarling, once in my life. He was led by a bright scarlet ribbon—scarlet, mind, not pink or blue—attached to his silver collar; and there must have been something in the appearance of my youthful legs (I was but five, and they were bare, plump, and mottled) that excited his carnivorous propensities, for, long as is the lapse of time, I remember that he rushed at me like a coffee-coloured tiger. His mistress was a Duchess, the grandest, handsomest Duchess that had ever lived (of course, I except Georgina of Devonshire) since the days of that Grace of Queensberry of whom Mr. Thackeray was good enough to tell us in the "Virginians." She, my Duchess, wore a hat and feathers, diamonds, and a *moustache*—a downy nimbus round her mouth, like that which Mr. Philip insinuates rather than paints in his delightful Spanish girls' faces. I see her now, parading the cliff at Brighton, with her black velvet train—yes, madam, her train—held up by a page. She was the last duchess who drove down to Brighton in a coach and six. She was the last duchess who at Twelfth-night parties had a diamond ring baked in the cake which was to be distributed by lots. Before she came to her coronet, she had been a singing woman at a playhouse, had married a very foolish rich old banker, and, at his death, remarried a more foolish and very poor duke. But she was an excellent woman, and the relative to whom she left the bulk of her wealth, is one of the most charitable, as I am also afraid she is one of the most *ennuyée,* ladies in England. I am proud of my reminiscence. It is not every one that has seen a Dutch pug and the Duchess of St. Albans alive.

Body of me! here am I wasting my time among the dog-fanciers—(when the name of the man in the iron mask, the authorship of "Junius," the murderer of Caspar Hauser, and the date of the laws of Menu, shall be known, it shall also be patent to all men why trafficking in dogs and horses seem necessarily connected with roguery)—here am I descanting on poodles and pug-dogs, when, with quick observant eyes, I should be noting the hundred little trades that are being driven at three o'clock in the afternoon. The feverish industry—the untiring perseverance—the bitter struggle, and all for yon scanty morsel of bread, and a few inches of space for repose at night in a fourpenny lodging-house! Follow the kerb-stone from the County Fire Office to St. Martin's Lane. See the itinerant venders of catch-'em-alive-o's, of cheap toys, of quires of writing-paper, sealing-wax and envelopes, all for the small charge of one penny; see the industrials who have walking-sticks, umbrellas, gutta-percha whips, aërated balls, locomotive engines and statuettes of Napoleon in glass phials, that make us wonder, as with flies in amber, however they, the engines and statuettes, got there; the women who have bouquets to dispose of—how many times have they been refreshed beneath the pump, this droughty day?—the boys and girls in looped and windowed raggedness striving to sell fruit, flowers, almanacks, pencils, fusees—anything, to keep the wolf from the door. He is always at the door, that wolf—always at that yawning portal, and his name is Famine. The worst of the brute is, that he comes not alone—that he has a friend, a brother wolf with him, who hankers round the corner, and is always ready to pop in at the door at the slightest suspicion of a summons. This wolf is a full-paunched rogue, and liberal, too, of succulent, but *poisoned* food to his friends. This is the thief wolf, the gallows wolf, the Calcraft wolf. *Lupus carnifex*. He keeps up an incessant whining baying, which, being interpreted, means, "Work no more. See how hard the life is. What's the good of working? Come and Steal." Look here, my lords and gentlemen—look here, my right honourable friends—look here, my noble captains—look here, your honours' worships—come out of your carriages, come out of your clubs, come out of your shooting-boxes in the Highlands, and your *petites maisons* in the Regent's Park, and look at these faded and patched creatures. I tell you that they have to rise early and go to bed late—that they have to work hours and hours before they can turn one penny. They have never been taught; they are seldom fed, and more seldom washed; but *they don't steal*. I declare that it is a wonder they do not—a marvel and a miracle they do not. They remain steadfastly honest; for, in the troubled sea of their lives, Almighty Mercy has planted a Pharos, or light-house. The night is pitchy black oft enough; the light revolves—is for a time invisible—and the poor forlorn, tempest-torn man watches the blank horizon in all but mute despair; but the blessed gladdening gleam comes round again, as we have all seen it many a time on the ocean, and, sighing, the honest man resolutely keeps on his course.

Following the kerb-stone myself from the before-mentioned County Fire Office to St. Martin's Lane, and passing through Leicester Square—which, what with the Alhambra "Palace" and its hideous American posters, the Great Globe, and the monster *cafés chantants*, I begin to be rather uncertain about recognising—passing, not without some inward trembling, the stick shop at the corner of the lane, while on either side of the portal those peculiarly ugly carved clubs—the very Gog and Magog of walking-stickery—keep watch and ward, I cut dexterously through the living torrent that is flowing from Charing Cross toward St. Giles's (they were villages once,

Charynge and Saint Gyles's—ha! ha!) and commence the ascent of New Street, a feat well nigh as disagreeable, if not as perilous, as that of Mont Blanc. I hate this incorrigible little thoroughfare; this New Street. It is full of bad smells, mangy little shops, obstructions, and bad characters. There is a yawning gin-palace at its south-western extremity. The odours of its eating-houses—especially of a seedy little French *pension bourgeoise* about half way up—are displeasing to my nostrils. The cigars vended in New Street are the worst in London, and the sweetstuff shops are mobbed—yes, mobbed—by children in torn pinafores who *never* have any pocket handkerchiefs. Of late days, photographers have hung out their signs and set up their lenses in New Street; and if, passing through the street, you escape being run over by a wagon or upset by an inebriated market-gardener, you run great risks of being forcibly dragged into the hole tenanted by a photographic "artist," and "focussed," willy nilly. Thoroughfares, almost inconceivably tortuous, crapulous, and infamous, debouch upon New Street. There is that Rose Street, or Rose Alley, where, if I be not wrong in my topography, John Dryden, the poet, was waylaid and cudgelled; and there is a wretched little haunt called Bedfordbury, a devious, slimy little reptile of a place, whose tumble-down tenements and reeking courts spume forth plumps of animated rags, such as can be equalled in no London thoroughfare save Church Lane, St. Giles's. I don't think there are five windows in Bedfordbury with a whole pain of glass in them. Rags and filthy *loques* are hung from poles, like banners from the outward walls. There is an insolent burgher of Bedfordbury, who says I owe him certain stivers. Confound the place! its rags, its children, its red herrings, and tobacco-pipes crossed in the windows, its boulders of whitening, and its turpentine-infected bundles of firewood!

The pursuit of New Street, thus maledicted, brings me to King Street, Covent Garden, a broad, fair, well-conducted public way, against which I have no particular prejudice; for it leads up to Covent Garden Market, which I love; and it contains within its limits the Garrick Club.

Before, however, you come to the Garrick, before you come to the coffee-shop where there is that strange collection of alarming-looking portraits; before you come to Mr. Kilpack's cigar divan and bowling-alley, you arrive at the door of an unpretending, though roomy mansion, the jambs of whose portals are furnished with flattering catalogues relative to "this day's sale," and the pavement before whose frontage is strewn with fragments of straw and shreds of carpeting. It is strange, too, if you do not see half a dozen or so burly-looking porters lounging about the premises, and a corresponding number of porter's knots, the straw stuffing bulging occasionally from rents in their sides, decorating the railings, as the pint pots do the iron barriers of the licensed victuallers. This mansion contains the great auction-room of Messrs. Debenham and Storr. Let us enter without fear. There is scarcely, I think, so interesting an exhibition in London; yet, in contradistinction to the majority of London exhibitions, there is nothing to pay.

In this monstrous amalgam of microcosms, London, a man may, if he will only take the trouble, find that certain places, streets, rooms, peculiar spots and set apart localities, are haunted by classes of people as peculiar as the localities they affect, and who are seldom to be found anywhere else. In the early forenoon, long before business hours commence, the benches of the piazza of the Royal Exchange have their peculiar occupants—lank, mystic-looking men, mostly advanced in years, and shiny in threadbare blackclothdom. They converse with one another seldom, and when they do so, it is but in furtive whispers, the cavernous mouth screened by the rugose hand, with its knotted cordage of veins and its chalkstoned knuckles, as though the whisper were of such commercial moment that the locutor feared its instantaneous transport to the ears of Rothschild or Baring, and the consequent uprising or downfalling of stocks or corn, silk or tallow. Who are these men, these Exchange ghosts, who haunt the site of Sir Thomas Gresham's old "Burse?" Are they commission agents come to decay, bankrupt metal brokers, burnt-out, uninsured wharfingers, lame ducks of the Stock Exchange, forced even to "waddle" from the purlieus of Capel Court? There they sit day after day—their feet (lamentably covered with boots of fastidious bigness, for, alas! the soles are warped, the sides crack, the heels are irrevocably lopsided) beating the devil's tattoo on the stone pavement, their big cotton umbrellas distilling a mouldy moisture, or a pair of faded Berlin gloves, quite gone and ruined at the fingers, lying on the bench beside them. Their battered hats oscillate on their heads through overloading with tape-tied papers, and oft-times, from the breast-pocket of their tightly-buttoned coats, they drag leathern pocketbooks, white and frayed at the edges like the seams of their own poor garments, from which pocketbooks they draw greasy documents, faded envelopes, sleezy letters, which have been folded and refolded so often that they seem in imminent danger of dropping to pieces like an over-used passport at the next display. With what an owl-like, an oracular, look of wisdom they consult these papers! What are they all about? The bankruptcy of their owners thirty years ago, and the infamous behaviour of the official assignees (dead and buried years since)? their early love correspondence? their title-deeds to the estates in Ayrshire, and the large pasture lands in the Isle of Skye? Who knows? But you never see these ghostly time-waiters anywhere but on 'Change, and out of 'Change hours. Directly the legitimate business of that place of commercial re-union commences, they melt away imperceptibly, like the ghost of Hamlet's father at cock-crow, coming like shadows and so departing.

The dreadful night dens and low revelling houses of past midnight London, the only remnants left among us of the innumerable "finishes" and saloons and night-cellars of a former age, have also their peculiar male population, stamped indelibly with the mint-mark of the place, and not to be found out of it, save in the dock of the adjacent police-court. Where these *ruffiani*, these copper captains and cozening buz-gloaks, are to be found during the day, or even up to midnight—for in the gallery even of any decent theatre they would not be admitted—must remain a secret; perhaps, like the ghoules and afrits, the bats and dragons of fable, they haunt ruinous tombs, deserted sepulchres, church-yards sealed up long since by the Board of Health; but so soon as two or three o'clock in the morning arrives, they are to be found wherever there are fools to be fleeced or knaves to plot with. You study their lank hair and stained splendid stocks, their rumpled jay's finery and rascal talk, their cheap canes and sham rings; but they, too, fade away with the dawn—how, no man can say, for the meanest cabman would scorn to convey them in his vehicle—and are not beheld any more till vagabondising time begins again.

"Supers," too—or theatrical supernumeraries, to give them their full title—are a decidedly distinctive and peculiar race; and though reported, and ordinarily believed, to exercise certain trades and handicrafts in the daytime, such as shoemaking, tailoring, bookbinding, and the like, my private belief is that no "super" could exist long in any atmosphere remote from behind the scenes or the vicinity of the stage-door of a theatre. Look, too, at the audience of a police court: look at the pinched men who persist in attending the sittings of the Insolvent Debtors' Court in Portugal Street, or hang about the dingy tavern opposite, and who consume with furtive bites Abernethy biscuits and saveloys, half hidden in the folds of blue cotton pocket-handkerchiefs. Yes, the proverb reads aright—as many men, so many minds; and each man's mind, his idiosyncrasy, leads him to frequent a certain place till he becomes habituated to it, and cannot separate himself therefrom. There are your men who delight in witnessing surgical operations, and those who never miss going to a hanging. There is a class of people who have a morbid predilection for attending coroners' inquests, and another who insist upon going to the Derby, be the weather wet or dry, cold or hot, though they scarcely know a horse's fore from his hind legs, and have never a sixpenny bet on the field. There is a class who hang about artists' studios, knowing no more of painting than Mr. Wakley does of poetry; there are the men you meet at charity dinners, the women you meet at marriages and christenings. Again, there is a class of eccentrics, who, like the crazy Earl of Portsmouth, have an invincible *penchant* for funerals—"black jobs," as the mad lord used to call them; and finally, there are the people who haunt SALES BY AUCTION.

THREE O'CLOCK P.M.: DEBENHAM AND STORR'S AUCTION-ROOMS.

Walk into Debenham and Storr's long room, and with the exercise of a little judgment and keenness of observation, you will be enabled to recognise these amateurs of auctions in a very short space of time, and to preserve them in your memory. They very rarely bid, they yet more rarely have anything knocked down to them; indeed, to all appearances, the world does not seem to have used them well enough to allow them to buy many superfluities, yet there they stand patiently, hour after hour, catalogue in hand—they are always possessed of catalogues—ticking off the amount of the bids, against the numbers of the articles which they never buy; you should remark, too, and admire, the shrewd, knowing, anxious scrutiny which they extend to the articles which are hung up round the room, or which are held up for inspection by the porter, as the sale proceeds. They seem actually interested in the cut of a Macintosh, in the slides of a telescope, in the triggers of a double-barrelled gun; they are the first to arrive at, the last to leave the Sale; and then, in the close of the afternoon, they retire, with long-lingering footsteps, as though—like the gentleman for whom a judge of the land and twelve honest men had settled that a little hanging was about the best thing that could be done, and who so often fitted the halter, took leave, and traversed the cart—they were "loath to depart," which I am willing to believe they are. I imagine to myself, sometimes, that these men are cynical philosophers, who delight in the contemplation of the mutabilities of property; who smile grimly—within their own cynical selves—and hug themselves at the thought, not only that flesh is grass, that sceptre and crown must tumble down, and kings eat humble pie, but that the richest and the rarest gems and gew-gaws, the costliest garments, the bravest panoplies, must come at last to the auctioneer's hammer.

Perhaps you would like to know what they are selling by auction at Debenham and Storr's this sultry July afternoon. I should very much like to know what they are not selling. Stay, to be just, I do not hear any landed estates or advowsons disposed of: you must go to the Auction Mart in Bartholomew Lane if you wish to be present at such Simoniacal ceremonies; and, furthermore, horses, as you know, are in general sold at Tattersall's, and carriages at Aldridge's repository in St. Martin's Lane. There are even auctioneers, I am told, in the neighbourhood of Wapping and Ratcliffe Highway, who bring lions and tigers, elephants and ourangoutangs, to the hammer; and, finally, I must acquit the respectable firm, whose thronged sale-room I have edged myself into, of selling by auction such trifling matters as human flesh and blood.

But from a chest of drawers to a box of dominoes, from a fur coat to a silver-mounted horsewhip, from a carpenter's plane to a case of lancets, from a coil of rope to a silk neck-tie, from a dragoon's helmet to a lady's thimble, there seems scarcely an article of furniture or wearing apparel, of use or superfluity, that is not to be found here. Glance behind that counter running down the room, and somewhat similar to the narrow platform in a French *douane*, where the luggage is deposited to be searched. The porters move about among a heterogeneous assemblage of conflicting articles of merchandise; the clerk who holds aloft the gun or the clock, or the sheaf of umbrellas, or whatever other article is purchased, hands it to the purchaser, when it is knocked down to him, with a confidential wink, if he knows and trusts that customer, with a brief reminder of "money" and an out-stretched palm, signifying that a deposit in cash must be forthwith paid in case such customer be not known to him, or, what will sometimes happen, better known than trusted. And high above all is the auctioneer in his pulpit, with his poised hammer, the Jupiter Tonans of the sale.

And such a sale! Before I have been in the room a quarter of an hour, I witness the knocking down of at least twenty dress coats, and as many waistcoats and pairs of trousers, several dozen shirts, a box of silk handkerchiefs, two ditto of gloves, a roll of best Saxony broadcloth, a piece of Genoa velvet, six satin dresses, twelve boxes of artificial flowers, a couple of opera glasses, a set of ivory chessmen, eighteen pairs of patent leather boots—not made up—several complete sets of carpenters' tools, nine church services, richly bound, a carved oak cabinet, a French bedstead, a pair of china vases, a set of harness, three boxes of water colours, eight pairs of stays, a telescope, a box of cigars, an enamel miniature of Napoleon, a theodolite, a bronze candelabrum, a pocket compass, twenty-four double-barrelled fowling-pieces (I quote *verbatim* and *seriatim* from the catalogue), a parrot cage, three dozen knives and forks, two plated toast-racks, a Turkey carpet, a fishing-rod, winch, and eelspear, by Cheek, a tent by Benjamin Edgington, two dozen sheepskin coats, warranted from the Crimea, a silver-mounted dressing-case, one of eau-de-Cologne, an uncut copy of Macaulay's "History of England," a cornet-à-piston, a buhl inkstand, an eight-day clock, two pairs of silver grape-scissors, a poonah-painted screen, a papier-maché work-box, an assortment of variegated floss-silk, seven German flutes, an ivory casket, two girandoles for wax candles, an ebony fan, five flat-irons, and an accordion.

There! I am fairly out of breath. The mere perusal of the catalogue is sufficient to give one vertigo. But whence, you will ask, the extraordinary incongruity of the articles sold? We know when a gentleman "going abroad" or "relinquishing housekeeping," and who is never—Oh dear, no!—in any manner of pecuniary difficulty, honours Messrs. So-and-So with instructions to sell his effects, what we may look forward to when the carpets are hung from the windows with the sale-bills pinned thereon, and the auctioneer establishes a temporary rostrum on the dining-room table. We know that after the "elegant modern furniture" will come the "choice collection of pictures, statuary, and *virtù*," then the "carefully-selected library of handsomely-bound books," and then the "judiciously assorted stock of first-class wines." But what gentleman, what tradesman, what collector of curiosities and odds and ends even, could have brought together such an astounding jumble of conflicting wares as are gathered round us to-day! The solution of the enigma lies in a nutshell, and shall forthwith be made manifest to you. The articles sold this afternoon are all *pawnbrokers' pledges unredeemed*, and this is one of Messrs. Debenham and Storr's quarterly sales, which the law hath given, and which the court awards. Your watch, which your temporary pecuniary embarrassments may have led you to deposit with a confiding relative thirteen months since, which your renewed pecuniary embarrassments have precluded you from redeeming, and which your own unpardonable carelessness has made you even forget to pay the interest upon, may be among that angling bundle of time-pieces which the clerk holds up, and on which the auctioneer is, at this very moment, descanting.

The eloquence of the quarterly sale does not by any means resemble the flowery Demosthenic style first brought into fashion among auctioneers by the distinguished George Robins. Here are no ponds to be magnified by rhetoric into fairy lakes, no little hills to be amplified into towering crags, no shaven lawns to be described as "boundless expanses of verdure." The auctioneer is calm, equable, concise, but firm, and the sums realised by the sale of the articles are reasonable—so reasonable, in fact, that they frequently barely cover loan and interest due to the pawnbroker. But that is his risk; and such is the power of competition in trade, that a London pawnbroker will often lend more upon an article than it will sell for. In the provinces the brethren of the three golden balls are more cautious; and in Dublin they are shamefully mean in their advances to their impoverished clients; but it is in Paris *par excellence*, that the great national pawning establishment, the Mont de Piété, manifests the most decided intention, by the microscopic nature of its loans, of taking care of itself.

Much noise, much dust, and an appreciable amount of confusion, must necessarily, my patient friend and companion, exist at every auction, though it must be admitted, to the credit of Messrs. Debenham and Storr, that their proceedings are always marked by as much regularity and decorum as the nature of their transactions will admit of. For auctioneering is the Bohemianism of commerce; and whether it be the purser of a man-of-war selling the effects of a deceased Jack Tar before the mainmast; an impromptu George Robins, with a very large beard, knocking down red flannel shirts, jack-boots, and gold rocking-cradles at the Ballarat diggings; my former friends, the fish salesmen, brandishing their account-books over their piscine merchandise in Billingsgate; or the courtly Robins, *in propriâ personâ*, eloquently bepuffing the Right Hon. the Earl of Cockletops's broad acres, which he has been honoured with instructions to sell, in consequence of the insolvency of his Lordship, there always enters into the deed of selling something wild, something picturesque, and something exciting. It is strange, too, how soon the virtues of auctioneering are apt to degenerate into vices; and how thin a barrier exists between its legitimate commercial business and an imbroglio of roguish chaffering.

So is it on the turf. There, on the velvet verdant lawn before the Grand Stand at Epsom, sits, or stands, or reclines, my Lord the immaculate owner of Podasokus or Cynosure. Betting-book in hand, he condescends to take the odds from Mr. Jones, who may have been a journeyman carpenter ten years since, but whose bare word is good now for a hundred thousand pounds. The peer and the plebeian bet together amicably; they respect their parole agreements; they would disdain to admit the suspicion of a fraud in their transactions; they are honourable men both, though they might, I acknowledge, do something better for a livelihood than gamble on the speed of a racehorse; yet, all honourable men as they are on the turf, within two feet of them, *outside* the Grand Stand railing, are some hundreds of turfites depending for their existence upon exactly the same means—betting, but who cheat, and lie, and cozen, and defraud, and swagger about in an impudent boastfulness of roguery, till the most liberal-minded member of the non-cheating community must regret, almost, that the old despotic punishments are gone out of vogue, and that a few of these rogues' ears cannot be nailed to the winning post, a few of them tied up to the railings of the Grand Stand and soundly swinged, and a few more placed in neat pillories, or commodious pairs of stocks beneath the judge's chair. Like the honourable betters inside, and the thievish touts outside, electioneering is apt to suffer by the same disreputable companionships; and within a few stones' throw of Garraway's, there may be pullulating an infamous little watch-box of dishonesty, where a thick-lipped, sham Caucasian auctioneer, is endeavouring, with the aid of confederates as knavish as he, to palm off worthless lamps, lacquered tea-trays, teapots of tin sophisticated to the semblance of silver, and rubbishing dressing-cases, upon unwary country visitors, or even upon Cockneys, who, were they to live to the age of Methuselah, would never be thoroughly initiated into the ways of the town.

And now stand on one side: the auction company—it is nearly four o'clock—stream forth from Debenham's. I spoke of the amateurs of auctions—the people who persist in attending them, but who rarely appear to become purchasers of anything. There is not much difficulty, however, in discerning who the people are who are really bidding and really buying. Here they come, bagged and bundled, and gesticulating and jabbering. They are Jews, my dear. They are the hook-nosed, ripe-lipped, bright-eyed, cork-screw ringleted, and generally oleaginous-looking children of Israel. They cluster, while in the sale-room, round the auctioneer and his clerk, who (the last) seems to have an intimate acquaintance with them all. They nod and chuckle, and utter Hebrew ejaculations, and seem, all the while that the sale is proceeding, to be in an overboiling state of tremour and nervous excitement. A sale by auction is to them as good—better—than a play; so is everything on this earth, in, about, or in the remotest connection with which, there is something that can be bought, or something that can be sold, or something that can be higgled for. If ever you attend auctions, my friend and reader, I should advise you not to bid against the Jews. If it seem to you that any one of the Caucasian Arabs has set his mind upon the acquisition of an article, let him bid for it and buy it, a'goodness name; for if you meddle with the matter, even by the augmentation of a sixpence, he will so bid and bid against you, that he will bid you, at last, out of your hat, and out of your coat, and out of your skin, and out of your bones; even as the cunning man of Pyquag, that Diedrich Knickerbocker tells of, questioned Anthony van Corlear, the trumpeter, out of his fast-trotting nag, and sent him home mounted on a vile calico mare.

There are some here, who are dissatisfied with the bargains they have made, and are squabbling in a lively manner on the foot pavement. Mark, I entreat you, among them, those dusky-faced females, mostly given to the loose and flabby order of corpulency, who are shabbily dressed, yet with a certain tendency to the wearing of lace bonnets, and faded cashmeres, and who have moreover a decided penchant for golden bangles and earrings, and rings with large stones that do not shine. You cannot make up your mind at once that they are Jewesses, because they have a conflicting facial resemblance to Gipsies. During the sale they have been reclining, not to say squatting, on the broad goods counter in shabby state, like second-hand sultanas, making bids in deep contralto voices, or mysteriously transmitting them through the intermediary of glib Jew boys with curly heads. These commercial females must be reckoned among the million and one mysteries of London. I imagine them to be the ladies dwelling in remote suburbs or genteel neighbourhoods gone to decay, who, in the columns of the "Times," are always expressing a desire to purchase second-hand wearing apparel, lace, jewellery, and books, for the purpose of exportation to Australia, and for which they are always willing to pay ready money, even to the extent of remitting post-office orders in immediate return for parcels from the country. They, too, I think, must keep the mysterious "ladies' wardrobe shops" known to the Abigails in aristocratic families, and which are, a little bird has told me, not altogether unknown to the patrician occupants of the noblest mansions of the realm. Thus, there seems to be a perpetual round of mutation and transmutation going on among clothes. The natural theory of reproduction here seems carried to its most elaborate condition of practice; and, bidding adieu to Debenham and Storr's, the chaffering Jews, and the dusky ladies' wardrobe women, my mind wanders to Rag Fair, thence to the emporium of Messrs. Moses and Son, and thence, again, to Stultze, Nugee, and Buckmaster, and I end in a maze of cogitation upon the "Sartor Resartus" of Thomas Carlyle.

Come, let us struggle into the open, and inhale the flower-laden breeze that is wafted from Covent Garden market. There, we are in King Street; and, I declare, there is my aunt Sophy's brougham, with my identical aunt and my cousin Polly in the interior of the vehicle. They are bound, I will go bail, either to the Soho Bazaar or to the Pantheon, in Oxford Street. Jump up behind; fear no warning cry of "whip behind" addressed to the coachman by malevolent street boy, disappointed in his expectations of an eleemosynary ride. Remember, we are invisible; and as for the dignity of the thing, the starched, buckramed, and watchspringed-hooped skirts of my female relatives take up at least three and a half out of the four seats in the brougham: the remaining moiety of a place being occupied, as of right, by my aunt's terrier, Jip, who threatens vengeance with all his teeth on any one who should venture to dispossess him.

I told you so. They have passed Charles Street, Soho, whisked by the Princess's Theatre, and alighted beneath the portico of the Pantheon. The affable beadle (whose whiskers, gold-laced hat-band, livery buttons, and general deportment, are as superior to those the property of the beadle of the Burlington Arcade, as General Washington to General Walker) receives the ladies with a bow. He is equalled, not surpassed, in polished courtesy, by his brother beadle at the conservatory entrance in Great Marlborough Street, who bows ladies out with a dignified politeness worthy of the best days of Richelieu and Lauzun.

So into the Pantheon, turning and turning about in that Hampton-Court-like maze of stalls, laden with pretty gimcracks, toys, and *papier maché* trifles for the table, dolls and children's dresses, wax flowers and Berlin and crotchet work, prints, and polkas, and women's ware of all sorts. Up into the gallery, where you may look down upon a perfect little ant-hill of lively industry. And, if you choose, into that queer picture-gallery, where works by twentieth-rate masters have been quietly accumulating smoke and dust for some score years, and where the only conspicuous work is poor shiftless Haydon's big nightmare picture of "Lazarus." They have lately added, I believe, a photographic establishment to the picture-gallery of the Pantheon; but I am doubtful as to its success. It requires a considerable amount of moral courage to ascend the stairs, or to enter the picture department at all. The place seems haunted by the ghosts of bygone pictorial mediocrities. It is the lazar-house of painting—an hospital of incurables in art.

THREE O'CLOCK P.M.: THE PANTHEON BAZAAR.

I am not aware whether any of my present generation of readers—people are born, and live and die, so fast now-a-days—remember a friend of mine who dwelt in an out-of-the-way place called Tatty-boy's Rents, and whom I introduced to the public by the name of Fripanelli. He was a music-master—very old, and poor, and ugly; almost a dwarf in stature, wrinkled, decrepit; he wore a short cloak, and the boys called him "Jocko;" indeed, he was not at all unlike a baboon in general appearance. But Fripanelli in his time—a very long time ago—though now brought to living in a back slum, and teaching the daughters of chandlers' shopkeepers, had been a famous professor of the tuneful art. He knew old Gaddi—Queen Caroline's Gaddi—well: he had been judged worthy to preside at the pianoforte at Velluti's musical classes; and he had even written the music to a ballet, which was performed with great *éclat* at the King's Theatre, and in which the celebrated Gambalonga had danced. To me, Frip. had an additional claim to be regarded with something like curiosity mingled with reverence; for he had positively been, in the halcyon days of youth, the manager of an Italian opera company, the place of whose performance was—wherever do you think?—the Pantheon, in Oxford Street. Now, as I stand in the lively bazaar, with the prattling little children, and the fine flounced ladies, I try to conjure back the days when Fripanelli was young, and when the Pantheon was a theatre. From here in the vestibule—where the ornamented flower-pots, and the garden-chairs of complicated construction, and the busts with smoky cheeks and noses, and marvellously clubbed heads of hair, have their *locus standi*—from here sprang the grand staircase. There was no Haydon's picture of Lazarus for our grandfathers and grandmothers in hoops and powder—you must remember that Fripanelli looks at least two hundred and fifty years of age, and is currently reported to be ninety—to stare at as they trotted up the degrees. Yonder, in the haven of bygone mediocrities in the picture-gallery, may have been the crush-room; the rotunda at the back of the bazaar, where now the vases of wax-flowers glimmer in a perpetual twilight, must have been the green-room; the conservatories were dressing-rooms, and the stage door was undoubtedly in Great Marlborough Street. How I should have liked to witness the old pigtail operas and ballets performed at the Pantheon, when Fripanelli and the century were young. "Iphigenia in Aulis," "Ariadne in Naxos," "Orestes and Pylades," "Daphnis and Chloë," "Bellerophon," "Eurydice," the "Clemency of Titus," the "Misfortunes of Darius," and the "Cruelty of Nero"—these were the lively subjects which our grandfathers and grandmothers delighted to have set to Italian music. Plenty of good heavy choruses, tinkle-tankling instrumental music, plaintive ditties, with accompaniments on the fife and the fiddle, and lengthy screeds of droning recitatives, like the Latin accidence arranged for the bagpipes. Those were the days of the unhappy beings of whom Velluti and Ambrogetti were among the last whom a refined barbarity converted into *soprani*. The Italians have not many things to thank the first Napoleon for; yet to his sway in Italy humanity owes the abolition of *that* atrocity. They dig up some of the worthy old pigtail operas now, and perform them on our modern lyric stage. A select audience of fogies, whose sympathies are all with the past, comes to listen, and goes to sleep; and "Iphigenia in Aulis," or "Ariadne in Naxos," is consigned to a Capuletian tomb of limbo. Days of good taste are these, my masters, when aristocratic ears are tickled by the melodious naughtinesses of the great Casino-and-Codliver-oil opera, the "Traviata;" by the Coburg melodrama, mingled with Mrs. Ratcliffe's novel, and finished with extracts from Guicciardini's "Annals"—called the "Trovatore," [who was it fried that child, or broiled him, or ate him: Azucena, Leonora, the Conde di Luna, Mrs. Harris, all or any of them?] or by the sparkling improbabilities of "Rigoletto," with its charming Greenacre episode of the murdered lady in the sack. We manage those things so much better now-a-days. And the ballets, too; do you know positively that in the pig-tail opera times, the lady dancers wore skirts of decent length? do you know that Guimard danced in a hoop that reached nearly to her ankles, and that Noblet wore a corsage that ended just below her armpits, and a skirt that descended far below her knees? Do you know, even, that Taglioni, and Ellsler, and Duvernay, the great terpsichorean marvels of twenty years since, disdained the meretricious allurements of this refined and polished age, that calls garters "elastic bands," and winces at a grant of twenty pounds a year for providing living models for the students of the Dublin Academy?—that strains at these gnats, and swallows the camel of a ballet at the opera! Oh, stupid old pig-tail days, when we could take our wives and sisters to hear operas and see ballets, without burning with shame to think that we should take, or they suffer themselves to be taken, to witness a shameless exhibition, fit only for the *blasé* patricians of the Lower Empire!

In the memoirs of old Nollekens, the sculptor, you will find that he was an assiduous frequenter of the Italian Opera at the Pantheon, to which he had a life admission—it did not last *his* life though, I am afraid—and that he sat in the pit with his sword by his side, and a worsted comforter round his neck. This must surely, however, have been before the days of Fripanelli's management. It is hard to say, indeed, for the Pantheon has been so many things by turns and nothing long. Once, if I mistake not, there was wont to be an exhibition of wax-work here; once, too, it was famous as a place for masquerades of the most fashionable, or, at least, of the costliest description. Here Charles Fox and Lord Maldon, with dominoes thrown over their laced clothes, and masks pressed upon their powdered perukes, reeled in from the chocolate houses and the E. O. tables; here, so the legends say, the bad young prince, who afterwards became a worse old king, the worthless and witless wearer of the Prince of Wales's three ostrich plumes—here George III.'s eldest born met the beautiful Perdita. He ill-treated her, of course, afterwards, as he ill-treated his wives (I say wives, in the plural number, do you understand?) and his mistresses, his father, his friends, and the people he was called upon to govern. He lied to, and betrayed, them all; and he was *Dei gratiâ*, and died in the odour of civil list sanctity, and they have erected a statue to his disreputable memory in Trafalgar Square.

Soft, whisper low, tread softly: the Pantheon was once a church! Yes, there were pews in the area of the pit, and free-sittings in the galleries. There is a singing, buffooning place in Paradise Street, Liverpool, where they dance the Lancashire clog-hornpipe, yell comic songs on donkeys' backs, perform acrobatic feats, juggle, strum the banjo, clank the bones, belabour the tambourine, stand on their heads, and walk on the ceiling. This place is called the Colosseum, *but it was once a chapel*. The pews, with very slight alteration, yet exist, and on the ledges where the hymn-books were wont to lie, stand now the bottles of Dublin stout and ginger-pop. I do not like these violent revolutions, these galvanic contrasts. They are hideous, they are unnatural, they are appalling. To return to the Pantheon—I still follow the legends—after it had been a masquerading temple and a wax-work show, and then a church, it was changed once more into a theatre; but *mark what followed*. One Saturday night the company were playing "Don Giovanni," and midnight had struck before the awful tramp of the Commendatore was heard re-echoing through the marble corridors of the libertine's palace, and the last tube of maccaroni stuck in Leporello's throat; but when, the finale being at its approach, and to cap the climax of the catastrophe, twelve demons in flame-coloured garments, and bearing torches flaming with resin, rose from trap-doors to seize the guilty Don, the manager, who had been watching the scene from the wing, rushed on the stage with a screech of horror, crying out, *"There are thirteen! There are thirteen!"* And so there were! A solitary demon, with flaming eyes, a tail of incredible length, and bearing *two* torches, appeared, no man knew whence—*he* hadn't come up a trap to the foot-lights (the audience screaming and fainting by scores), danced a ghastly *pas seul*, cut six, and disappeared in a blaze of livid-coloured fire, which had *not* been provided in the usual iron pans by the property man.[6] Whether he took Don Giovanni or the manager away with him the legend does not state; but it is certain that the latter went bankrupt a month afterwards, of course as a punishment for his sins; whereupon the lease of the Pantheon was purchased by a sober-minded speculator, who forthwith converted it into a bazaar, as which it has greatly thriven ever since.

I am very fond of buying toys for children; but I don't take them to the Pantheon for that purpose. I fear the price of the merchandise which the pretty and well-conducted female assistants at the stalls have to sell. I have been given to understand that incredible prices are charged for India-rubber balls, and that the quotations for drums, hares-and-tabors, and Noah's arks, are ruinously high. I have yet another reason for not patronising the

Pantheon as a toy mart. It frequently happens that I feel slightly misanthropic and vicious in my toy-dealing excursions, and that my juvenile friends have sudden fits of naughtiness, and turn out to be anything but agreeable companions. Woe betide the ill-conditioned youngsters who cause me to assume the function of a vicarious "Bogey!" But I serve them out, I promise you. To use a transpontine colloquialism, ungenteel but expressive, I "warm them." Not by blows or pinches—I disdain that; not by taking them into shops where they sell unwholesome pastry or deleterious sweetstuff—I have no wish to impair their infantile powers of digestion; though both processes, I have been given to understand, are sometimes resorted to by child-quellers; but I "warm" them by taking them into toy shops and buying them *ugly toys*. Aha! my young friends! who bought you the old gentleman impaled on the area railing while in the act of knocking at his own street door, and who emitted a dismal groan when the pedestal on which he stood was compressed? Who purchased the monkey with the horrible visage, that ran up the stick? who the dreadful crawling serpent, made of the sluggishly elastic substance—a compound of glue and treacle, I believe—of which printers' rollers are made, and that unwound himself in a shudderingly, reptile, life-like manner on the parlour carpet? Who brought you the cold, flabby toad, and the centipede at the end of the India-rubber string, with his heavy chalk body and quivering limbs, the great-grandfather of all the irreverent daddy-long-legs who wouldn't say their prayers, and were taken, in consequence, by those elongated appendages, and thrown, with more or less violence, downstairs? This is about the best method I know for punishing a refractory child. There is another, an almost infallible and Rarey-like process of taming juvenile termagants in the absence of their parents; but it entails a slight modicum of physical cruelty. Say that you are left alone with a child, too young to reason with, and who *won't* behave himself. Don't slap him: it is brutal and cowardly on your part; besides, it *leaves marks*, and you don't want to make an enemy of his mother. Don't make faces at him: it may spoil the beauty of your own countenance, and may frighten him out of his little wits. *Shake him.* Shake him till he becomes an animated whirligig. He isn't appalled; he is only bewildered. He doesn't know what on earth the unaccustomed motion means: then wink at him, and tell him that you will do it again if he doesn't behave himself; and it is perfectly wonderful to see to what complete submission you can reduce him. It is true that a grown person must be a callous brute to try such measures with a defenceless infant; but let that pass—we can't get on in the world without a little ruffianism. I have heard, even, that in the matrimonial state a good shaking will from time to time—but soft!

The young ladies who serve behind the counters at the Pantheon, are much given to working the spiky cobweb collars in which our present belles delight, and which are worked in guipure, or crotchet, or application, or by some other process with an astounding name of which I am profoundly ignorant. To their lady customers they behave with great affability. The gentlemen, I am pleased, though mortified to say, they treat with condescension mingled with a reserved dignity that awes the boldest spirit. It is somewhat irritating, too, to know that they can be as merry as grigs among themselves when they so choose; and it is a bending of the brows, a clinching of the fists, and a biting of the lips matter, to see them flitting from stall to stall, romping with one another in a pastoral manner, and retailing merry anecdotes, which may possibly be remarks on your personal appearance. Yet I have known a man with large whiskers (he went to the bad, and to Australia, and is now either high in the government or in the police over there) to whom a young lady assistant in the Pantheon, on a very wet day, once lent a silk umbrella. But he was always a bold man, and had a winning way with the sex.

It is time, if you will excuse my mentioning it, that we should quit this labyrinth of avenues between triple-laden stalls, all crowded with ladies and children, whose voluminous *jupons*—the very babes and sucklings wear crinoline now—render locomotion inconvenient, not to say perilous. Pass the refreshment counter, where they sell the arrowroot cakes, which I never saw anywhere else, and let us enter the conservatory—a winter garden built long ere Crystal Palaces or Jardins d'Hiver were dreamt of, and which to me is as pleasant a lounge as any that exists in London: a murmuring fountain, spangled with gold and silver fish, and the usual number of "winking bubbles beading at the brim;" and good store of beautiful exotic plants and myriad-hued flowers. The place is but a niche, a narrow passage, with a glass roof and a circle at the end, where the fountain is, like the bulb of a thermometer; but to me it is very delightful. It is good to see fair young faces, fair young forms, in rainbow, rustling garments, flitting in and about the plants and flowers, the fountain and the gold fish. It is good to reflect how much happiness and innocence there must be among these pretty creatures. The world for them is yet a place for flirting, and shopping, and dancing, and making themselves as fair to view as they and the looking-glass and the milliner can manage. The world is as yet a delightful Pantheon, full of flowers—real, wax, and artificial, and all pleasant—sandal-wood fans, petticoats with worked edges, silk stockings, satin shoes, white kid gloves, varnished broughams, pet dogs, vanille ices, boxes at the opera, tickets for the Crystal Palace, tortoise-shell card-cases, enamelled visiting-cards, and scented pink invitation notes, with "*On dansera*" in the left-hand bottom corners, muslin slips, bandoline, perfumes, ballads and polkas with chromo-lithographed frontispieces, and the dear delightful new novels from Mudie's with uncut leaves, and mother-o'-pearl paper knives with coral spring handles to cut them withal. They have kind mammas and indulgent port-wine papas, who bring them home such nice things from the city. They sit under such darling clergymen, with curls in the centre of their dear white foreheads; they have soft beds, succulent dinners, and softly-pacing hacks, on which to ride in coquettish-looking habits and cavalier hats. John the footman is always anxious to run errands for them; and their additional male acquaintance is composed of charming creatures with white neckcloths, patent leather boots, irreproachable whiskers, and mellow tenor voices. Oh! the delightful world; sure, it is the *meilleur des mondes possible,* as Voltaire's Doctor Pangloss maintained. It is true that they were at school once, and suffered all the tyranny of the "calisthenic exercises" and the French mark, or were, at home, mewed up under the supervision of a stern governess, who set them excruciating tasks; but, oh! that was such a long time since, they were so young then—it was ever such a long time ago. You silly little creatures! it was only the day before yesterday, and the day after to-morrow———. But "gather ye rosebuds while ye may," and regard not old Time as he is a-flying. For my part, I will mingle no drop of cynicism in the jewelled cup of your young enjoyment; and I hope that the day after to-morrow, with unkind husbands and ungrateful children, with physic-bottles and aches and pains, and debts and duns, may never come to you, and that your pretty shadows may never be less.

You see that I am in an unusual state of mansuetude, and feel for the nonce inclined to say, "Bless everybody"—the Pope, the Pretender, the Pantheon, the pretty girls, and the sailors' pig-tails, though they're now cut off. Every sufferer from moral *podagra* has such fits of benevolence between the twinges of his gout. But the fit, alas! is evanescent; and I have not been ten minutes in the conservatory of the Pantheon before I begin to grumble again. I really must shut my ears in self-defence against the atrocious, the intolerable screeching of the parrots, the parroquettes, the cockatoos, and the macaws, who are permitted to hang on by their wicked claws and the skin of their malicious beaks to the perches round the fountain. The twittering of the smaller birds is irritating enough to the nervously afflicted; but the parrots! ugh! that piercing, long-continued, hoarse shriek—it is like a signal of insane communication given by a patient at Hanwell to a brother lunatic at Colney Hatch. The worst of these abominable birds is, that they cannot or will not talk, and confine themselves to an inarticulate gabble. However, I suppose the fairest rose must have its thorns, and the milkiest white hind its patch of darker colour; so it is incumbent on us, in all charity, to condone the ornithological nuisance which is the main drawback to a very pretty and cheerful place of resort. Only, I should like to know the people who buy the parrots, in order that I might avoid them.

As we entered by Oxford Street, with its embeadled colonnade, it becomes our bounden duty to quit the building by means of that portal which I assumed to have been in days gone-by the stage-door of the pig-tail opera-house, and which gives egress into Great Marlborough Street. I can't stand the parrots; so, leaving my aunt (I wish she would lend me a hundred pounds), and my cousin (I wish she would lend me a kiss, and more sincerely do I wish that either of them existed in the flesh, or elsewhere but in my turbid imagination); leaving these shadowy relatives genteelly bargaining (they have already purchased a *papier maché* inkstand and a coral wafer-stamp), I slip through the conservatory's crystal precincts, inhale a farewell gust of flower-breeze, pass through a waiting-room, where some tired ladies are resting till their carriages draw up, and am genteelly bowed out by affable beadle No. 2.

And now, whither away? Shall I cross the road, and commence the first of a series of six lessons in dancing from Miss Leonora Geary? Shall I visit the harp and pianoforte establishment of Messrs. Erard, and try the tone of an "upright grand?" Shall I hie me to Marlborough Street police-court, and see how Mr. Bingham or Mr. Hardwick may be getting on? No: I think I will take a walk down Regent Street (one cannot too frequently perambulate that delightful thoroughfare at the height of the season), turn off by Vigo Lane, and take a stroll—a five minutes' stroll, mind, for I have an appointment close to St. George's Hospital, and Mr. Decimus Burton's triumphal arch, as soon after four as possible—down the Burlington Arcade.

I remember once refecting myself at a public dinner—the Tenth Anniversary Festival of the Hospital for Elephantiasis, I think it was—when my next neighbour to the right (to the left was a rural dean) was a gentleman in a white waistcoat that loomed large like the lateen sail of a Palermian felucca, and whose convivial countenance was of the exact hue and texture of the inside of an over-ripe fig. He took remarkably good care of himself during dinner time, had twice spring soup, and twice salmon and cucumber, led the waiters a terrible life, and gathered quite a little grove of bottles of choice wine round him. I am bound to say that he was not selfish or solitary in his enjoyment, for he pressed a peculiar Sautern upon me, and an especial Chateau Lafitte (the landlord must have known and respected him), with a silver label hanging to its bottle neck, like the badge of a Hansom cabman. He also recommended gosling to me, as being the very thing to take after lamb, in a rich husky voice, that did one good to hear. At the conclusion of the repast, after we had dabbled with the rosewater in the silver-gilt shield, which it is the custom to send round, and which nobody knows exactly what to do with—I always feel inclined to upset it, for the purpose of eliciting an expression of public feeling, and clearing the atmosphere generally; and when the business of the evening, as the absurd system of indiscriminate toast-giving is termed, had commenced, and the professional ladies and gentlemen were singing something about the "brave and bearded barley" in execrable time and tune, of course in the most preposterously irrelevant connection with the health just drank—either the Army and Navy, or the two Houses of

Parliament—my neighbour with the ripe fig countenance turned to me, and wiping his moist lips with his *serviette*, whispered these remarkable words: "Sir, a public dinner is the sublimation of an assemblage of superfluities." He said no more during the evening, filled up his name, however, for a handsome amount in the subscription-list (his name was announced amid thunders of applause by the secretary, but I really forget whether he was a general or a wholesale grocer), and went away in anything but a superfluous state of sobriety. But his words sank deep into my mind, and they bring me at once to the Burlington Arcade.

Which is to me another sublimate of superfluities: a booth transplanted bodily from Vanity Fair. I don't think there is a shop in its *enceinte* where they sell anything that we could not do without. Boots and shoes are sold there, to be sure, but what boots and shoes? varnished and embroidered and be-ribboned figments, fitter for a fancy ball or a lady's chamber, there to caper to the jingling melody of a lute, than for serious pedestrianism. Paintings and lithographs for gilded boudoirs, collars for puppy dogs, and silver-mounted whips for spaniels, pocket handkerchiefs, in which an islet of cambric is surrounded by an ocean of lace, embroidered garters and braces, fillagree flounces, firework-looking bonnets, scent bottles, sword-knots, brocaded sashes, worked dressing-gowns, inlaid snuff-boxes, and falbalas of all descriptions; these form the stock-in-trade of the merchants who have here their tiny *boutiques*. There are hair-dressers' shops too; but I will be bound that their proprietors would not be content with trimming a too luxuriant head of hair. They would insist upon curling, oiling, scenting, and generally tittivating you. They would want you to buy amandine for your hands, kalydor for your hair, dentifrice, odonto, *vinaigre de toilette*, hair-brushes with ivory backs, and tortoiseshell pocket-combs with mirrors appended to them. They would insist that you could not live without *pommade Hongroise* and *fixatures* for the moustaches, or Frangipani for the pocket-handkerchief. I have very few ambitions, but one is to become the proprietor of a house in the Burlington Arcade, and forthwith to open a chandler's shop in the very midst of its vanities and its whim-whams. The reproof, I trust, would be as stern, though I am afraid it would have as little effect, as that of the uncompromising patriots of the reign of terror, who planted the parterres of the Tuileries gardens with potatoes. To the end of time, I perpend, we shall have this hankering after superfluities, and little princesses will ask their governesses why the people need starve for want of bread, when there are such nice Bath buns in the confectioners' shop windows.

But the clock of St. James's warns me that I am due at Hyde Park Corner, and passing by yet another beadle, I emerge into Piccadilly.

FOUR P.M.—TATTERSALL'S, AND THE PARK.

Was there not a time when Hyde Park Corner was the Ultima Thule of London, and Kensington was in the country?—when Hammersmith was far away—a district known only to washerwomen and nursery gardeners—and Turnham Green and Kew were places where citizens took their wives to enjoy the perfection of ruralisation? Was it not to the Hercules' Pillars at Hyde Park Corner that Squire Western sent his chaplain to recover the snuff-box, which the worthy landed-gentleman and justice of the peace had left there when he halted to bait? Was not Hyde Park Corner a rendezvous for highwaymen, where they listened with eagerness for "the sound of coaches;" and parted, some towards Fulham, some towards Hounslow, some towards the Uxbridge road, where they might meet full-pouched travellers, and bid them "stand and deliver?" I remember, myself, old Padlock House at Knightsbride, standing in the midst of the roadway, like Middle Row in Holborn, or the southern block of Holywell Street in the Strand, with the padlock itself fixed in the grimy wall, which, according to the legendary wishes of a mythical testator, was never to be pulled down till the lock rotted away from its chain, and the chain from the brick and mortar in which it was imbedded. The cavalry barracks at Knightsbride seemed to have been built in the year One, and we boys whispered that the little iron knobs on the wall of the line of stables, which are, it is to be presumed, intended for purposes of ventilation (though I am not at all certain about the matter yet) were miniature portholes, at which fierce troopers, with carbines loaded to the muzzle, and ready pointed, kept guard every day, in order to repel the attacks of the "Radicals." Alack-a-day! but the "Radicals" seem to be getting somewhat the better of it at this present time of writing. Kensington High Street seemed to belong to a hamlet of immense age; the old church was a very cathedral—built, of course, by William of Wykeham; and as for Holland House, there could not be any doubt about that. It came in naturally with the Conqueror, and the first Lord Holland.

Hyde Park Corner before the battle of Waterloo must have been a strange, old-fashioned-looking place. No Apsley House: the site was occupied by the old woman who kept the apple-stall, or the bun-house, or the curds and whey shop, and who wouldn't be bought out, save at enormous prices, by his late Grace, Field-Marshal Arthur Duke of Wellington. No triumphal arch; and, thank good taste, no equestrian statue of the late F. M. Arthur Dux, &c., on the summit thereof. No entablatured colonnade, with nothing to support, towards the Park. No Achilles statue. A mean, unpicturesque, common-place spot, I take it. What could you expect of an epoch in which the Life Guards wore cocked hats and pig-tails, the police-officers red waistcoats and top boots, when the king *de jure* was mad, and the king *de facto* wore a wig and padded himself? A bad time. We have a lady on the throne now who behaves as a sovereign should behave, and London grows handsomer every day.

I declare that it does; and I don't care a fig for the cynics—most of them ignorant cynics, too—who, because they have accomplished a cheap tour to Paris, or have gone half-way up the Rhine, think themselves qualified to under-rate and to decry the finest metropolis in the world. I grant the smoke—in the city—and I confess that the Thames is anything but odoriferous in sultry weather, and is neither so blue nor so clear as the Neva; but I say that London has dozens and scores of splendid streets and mansions, such as I defy Paris, Vienna, Berlin, or St. Petersburg—I know their architectural glories by heart—to produce. I say that Pall Mall beats the Grand Canal at Venice; that Regent Street, with a little more altitude in its buildings, would put the Boulevard des Italiens to shame; and that Cannon Street makes the Nevskoi Perspective hide its diminished head. Some of these days, when I can get that balance at the banker's I have been waiting for so long, I shall sit down and indite a book entitled, "A Defence of London, Architecturally Considered," the which I shall publish at my own expense, as I am certain no publisher would purchase the copyright.

Take Hyde Park Corner. Between the Brandenburg Thor at Berlin and the Puerta del Sol at Madrid, you will not find a gayer, more picturesque, more sparkling scene. Ugly and preposterous as is the man in the cocked hat, who holds the rolling-pin and is wrapped in the counterpane, on the top of the arch, we are not for ever giving ourselves wry necks in the attempt to look up at him; and the arch itself is noble and grandiose. Then, opposite, through the *a giorno* of Mr. "Anastasius" Hope's colonnade, that supports nothing, you catch a glimpse of the leafy glories of Hyde Park—carriages, horses, horsewomen, Achilles' statue, and all. And again, to the right of the arch, is St. George's Hospital, looking more like a gentleman's mansion than an abode of pain; and to the left the ever-beautiful, ever-fresh, and ever-charming Green Park. And then far away east stretches the hill of Piccadilly, a dry Rialto (only watch it at night, and see the magical effects of its double line of gas-lamps); and westward the new city that the Londoners have built after their city was finished, beyond the Ultima Thule. Magnificent lines of stately mansions, towering park gates, bring us to the two gigantic many-storeyed edifices at Albert Gate, which were for a long time christened "Gibraltar," because they were supposed to be impregnable, no tenant having been found rich or bold enough to "take them." Taken they both were at last, however. The further one, or at least its lower portion, has been for a considerable period occupied by a banking company; while the near one—ah! that near Gibraltar, has had two strange tenants—the representatives of two strange fortunes. There dwelt the Railway King, a gross, common, mean man, who could not spell very well, Rumour said: but to him—being king of iron roads and stuffed with shares even to repletion, such shares being gold in those days, not dross—came the nobles of the land, humbling themselves on their gartered knees, and pressing the earth with their coroneted brows, and calling him King of Men, that he might give them shares, which he gave them. So this gross man was "hail fellow well met" with the nobles, and was drunk at their feasts and they at his, and he sat in the Parliament House, and made laws for us; and when he sent out cards of invitation, the wives and daughters of the nobles rose gladly in the night season, and having painted their faces and bared their necks, and put tresses of dead men's hair on their heads, they drove in swift chariots to Albert Gate, and all went merry as a marriage bell.

"But, hush! hark! a deep sound strikes like a rising knell!"

It was indeed the great knell of universal railway smashdom, the St. Sepulchre's boom of found-out humbug. So down went the Railway King, and down into the kennel toppled the iron crown—not so much of Lombardy, this time, as of those Lombards whose arms are three golden spheres. An iron crown to moralise over, that; and of which, as of a red-hot halfpenny, the motto reads appositely—"*Guai a chi la tocca*," "Woe be to him who touches it."

Albert Gate, the near house, yet saw lighted rooms, and great revelry and feasting, and a brave tenant; no other than Master Fialin Persigny, Ambassador of France. Courtly, witty, *rusé* Persigny Fialin! the nobles and princes were as glad to come to his merry-makings as in the old time, when the now broken-down Railway Stag held high court there. Crafty Fialin! he must have rubbed his hands sometimes, with a sly chuckle, as, from the upper chambers of his splendid house, he tried to descry, far off at Kensington, a now waste spot where once stood GORE HOUSE. And, oh! he must have sung—"What a very fine thing it is to be Ambassador-in-law to a very magnificent three-tailed Bashaw of an Emperor, and to live at Albert Gate." Not so many years since, though, master and man were glad to take tea at Gore House, with the beautiful Woman who wrote books, and the handsome Count who painted portraits; when the Bashaw's bills were somewhat a drug in the discount market, and his ambassador did not precisely know how to make both ends meet. All of which proves that the world is full of changes, and that fortune is capricious, and that master and man have made an uncommonly good thing of it.

Don't be afraid of a sudden raid on my part towards the lands that lie beyond Brentford. My present business lies close to Hyde Park Corner, close to St. George's Hospital. We have but to turn down Lower Grosvenor Place, and lo and behold, we are at our destination—TATTERSALL'S.

I suppose the British Empire could not progress prosperously without Tattersall's; so, I suppose, we must cry Tattersall's and the Constitution! Tattersall's and our Ancient Institutions! Tattersall's and Liberty! And, indeed, of the last there seems in reality to be much liberty, and equality, and fraternity in all connected with horse-racing; and at Tattersall's, though the resort of the most patrician turfites, the democratic element is appreciably strong. So long as both parties pay their bets, dukes and dustmen, Jews and jockeys, seem to meet upon a cheerful footing of "man to man" at this peculiarly national establishment.

The astute prophets who vaticinate in the Sunday newspapers, and who never can, by the remotest chance of possibility, be wrong in their calculations, are in the habit of speaking of the sporting transactions at Tattersall's as "Doings at the Corner." I think it would be slightly more appropriate if they were to characterise them as "Doings at the Corners," for of corners, and a multiplicity of them, Tattersall's seems made up. It is easy enough to distinguish the whereabouts of the great temple of horse-racing, for from Hyde Park Corner far down Grosvenor Place, you will find at FOUR O'CLOCK (business has been going on throughout the afternoon), a serried line of vehicles, with the horses' heads towards Pimlico. Equipages there are here of every description and grade. Lordly mail phætons, the mettlesome steeds impatiently champing at the bit, and shaking their varnished, silver-mounted, crest-decorated harness; slim, trim, dainty gentlemen's cabriolets (I am sorry to see that those most elegant of private vehicles are becoming, year after year, fewer in number), with high wheels and tall gray horses, and diminutive, topbooted tigers, squaring their little arms over the aprons; open carriages and pairs, with parasolled ladies within (for even rank and beauty do not disdain to wait at Tattersall's while my Lord or Sir John goes inside to bet, and perhaps also to put something on the favourite for Lady Clementina or the Honourable Agnes); gigs and dog-carts, sly little broughams with rose-coloured blinds and terriers peeping from beneath them, and whose demure horses look as though they could tell a good many queer stories if they chose; taxed carts, chaise carts, and plain carts, that are carts and nothing else. I should not be at all surprised indeed to see, some fine afternoon, a costermonger's "shallow," donkey, greenstuff-baskets and all, drawn up before Tattersall's, while its red 'kerchiefed, corduroyed, and ankle-jacked proprietor stepped down the yard to inquire after the state of the odds. There is, you may be sure, a plentiful sprinkling of Hansom cabs among the wheeled things drawn up. The Piccadilly cabmen are exceedingly partial to fares whose destination is Tattersall's. Such fares are always pressed for time, and always liberal; and they say that there are few Jehus on the stand between the White Horse Cellar and Hyde Park Corner who do not stand to win or lose large sums by every important racing event.

When you arrive at a building called St. George's School of Medicine, and at the door of which, at most times of the day, you will find lounging a knot of medical students, who should properly, I take it, in this sporting locality, have a racing and "down-the-road" look, but who, on the contrary, have the garb and demeanour of ordinary gentlemen—(What has become of the old medical student whom Mr. Albert Smith used to caricature for our amusement, with his shaggy overcoat, white hat, lank hair, short thick stick, staring shawl, short pipe, and slangy manners and conversation? Is he extinct as a type, or did he never exist, save in the lively imagination of that popular writer, and whom I hope all good luck will attend?)—When you have passed this edifice, sacred to Galen, Celsus, Hippocrates, and the rest of the Faculty of Antiquity, it will be time for you to turn down a narrow lane, very like one leading to an ordinary livery-stable, and to find yourself suddenly in a conglomeration of "corners." At one corner stands a building with a varnished oak door, that does not ill resemble a dissenting chapel with a genteel congregation, and fronting this, screened from the *profanum vulgus* by a stout railing, sweeps round a gravelled walk, surrounding a shaven grass-plat of circular form. This is the famous "Ring," of which you have heard so much; and the building that resembles a dissenting chapel is none other than Messrs. Tattersall's subscription rooms. Within those to ordinary mortals unapproachable precincts, the privacy of which is kept with as much severity as the interior of the Stock Exchange, the great guns of the turf discharge their broadsides of bets. They do not always confine themselves to the interior, however; but, when the weather is fine and betting hot, particularly on settling days, when there is an immense hubbub and excitement possessing every one connected with the turf, from the smallest stable-boy up to Lords Derby and Zetland, they come forth into the open, and bet round the grass plat. Now cast your eyes to the right (you are standing with your back to Grosvenor Place), and you will see a low archway, passing through which a hand points to you the spot where Mr. Rarey, the horse-tamer, had his office; while on the other side is a counting-house, somewhat dark and mysterious in aspect, where the names and prices of more racers and hunters than you or I ever heard of are entered in Tattersall's bulky ledgers. Beyond the archway stretches a spacious court-yard, the centre occupied by a species of temple, circular in form, with painted wooden pillars and a cupola, surmounted by a bust of George IV. Beneath the cupola is the figure of a fox sedent and regardant, something like the dog of Alcibiades, and looking, in troth, very cunning and foxy indeed. To the right, looking from the archway, are stables, with a covered penthouse in front; to the left, another archway, with more stables and coach-houses.

FOUR O'CLOCK P.M.: TATTERSALL'S.

Tattersall's is a curious sight at all times, and has something pervading it quite *sui generis*. Even when the ring is deserted by the gentleman turfites, and when no sales by auction of race-horses, hunters, carriage-horses, carriages, or fox-hounds, are proceeding in the court-yard (the auctioneer's rostrum is close to the king-crowned, fox-decorated temple), there is ample food for observation and amusement in the contemplation of the extraordinary array of hangers-on, who, at all times and seasons, summer and winter, are to be found about the purlieus of the Corner. I do not so much speak of the mere grooms, stable-boys, coachmen, and helpers, who have horses to mind or carriages to look after. You may find their prototypes down every mews, and in every livery-stable. The originals to whom I allude are to be seen only here, and on race-courses, hanging about the grand-stand and the weighing-house. They are entirely different to the nonchalant individuals who, in short coats, and a straw in their mouths, haunt the avenues of Aldridge's Repository, in St. Martin's Lane. They would appertain, seemingly, to a superior class; but from top to toe—laterally, horizontally, vertically, and diagonally—they are unmistakeably horse-flesh loving, and by horse-flesh living, men. It is not but you will find white neckcloths and black broadcloth in their attire, but there is a cut to the coat, a tie to the neckcloth, that prevents the possibility of error as to their vocation. They are sporting men all over. Hard-featured, serious-looking, spare-limbed men mostly, much given to burying their hands in their coat-pockets (never in their trousers), and peaceably addicted to the wearing of broad-brimmed hats. Now, the general acceptation of a "sporting" man would give him a tall, shiny hat, with a narrow brim, and considerably cocked on one side; yet I do verily believe that, were these men attired in buttonless drab, brown beavers, striped worsted hose, and buckles, that they would preserve the same sporting identity. They are the wet Quakers of the turf. What the exact nature of their multifarious functions about horses may be, I am not rightly informed. I conjecture them to be trainers, country horse-dealers, licensed victuallers with a turn for sporting, gentlemen farmers who "breed a colt" occasionally, or, maybe, perfectly private individuals led by an irresistible penchant to devote themselves to the study and observation of horses, and led by an uncontrollable destiny to hang, their lives-long through, about the Corner. Hangers-on of a lower grade there are in plenty. Striped-sleeved waistcoats, corduroy or drab cloth smalls and leggings; nay, even the mighty plush galligaskins of coachmanhood, top boots, fur and moleskin caps, sticks with crutches and a thong at the end, to serve, if needful, as whips; horseshoe scarf pins, and cord trousers made tight at the knees, and ending in laced-up boots. These—the ordinary paraphernalia of racing attire—are to be met with at every step; while the bottommost round of the sporting ladder is to be found in a forlorn creature in a stained ragged jerkin, that once was scarlet, matted hair, and naked feet. *He* hangs about the entrance, calls everybody "captain," and solicits halfpence with a piteous whine. I suppose he is a chartered beggar, licensed to pursue his harmless mendicancy here. Perhaps he may have kept hounds and harriers, carriages and horses—may have spent ten thousand a year, gone to the dogs, and turned up again at Tattersall's. Who knows? You had better give him the benefit of the doubt, and, commiserating his ragged-robin appearance, bestow sixpence on him.

Now let us take a peep at the magnates who are jotting down the current state of the odds in betting-books. Look at them well, and wonder. Why, all the world's a ring, and all the men and women in it merely betters. To come more nearly towards exactitude, it seems as though a good portion of at least the male part of the community had sent representatives to Tattersall's, while the genuine sporting element does not seem by any means so strong as you might reasonably expect. The genus "swell," with his long surtout, double-breasted waistcoat, accurately-folded scarf, peg-top trousers, eyeglass, umbrella, and drooping moustache, is perhaps predominant. And our friend the "swell" is indeed a "welcome guest," in the "ring," for he has, in the majority of instances, plenty of money, is rather inclined to bet foolishly—not to say with consummate imbecility—so long as his money lasts he pays with alacrity, and it takes a long time to drain him dry even at betting, which is a forcing engine that would empty another Lake of Haarlem of its contents in far less time than was employed to drain the first.

Your anxious sporting man, with lines like mathematical problems in his shrewd face, is not of course wanting in the assemblage. Here, too, you shall see the City dandy, shining with new clothes and jewellery, who has just driven down from the Stock Exchange to see what is going on at "Tat's," and who is a member of the "Ring" as well as of the "House." But those, perhaps, who seem the most ardent in their pursuit of the fickle goddess, as bearing on the Doncaster St. Leger, are certain florid elderly gentlemen, in bright blue body coats, with brass buttons and resplendent shirt-frills, and hats of the antique elegant or orthodox Beau Brummel form and cock.

Such is the outward aspect of the Ring. Into its penetralia, into the mysteries of its combinations, I, rash neophyte, do not presume to inquire. They are too awful for me. I am ignorant of them, nor, if I knew, should I dare to tell them. I should expect the curtain of the temple to fall down and overwhelm me, as befell the rash stranger who ventured to watch from, as he thought, a secure point of espial, the celebration of the mysteries of Isis at Thebes. Besides, I never could make either head or tail of a betting-book. *Poeta nascitur non fit*, say the Latins. *On devient cuisinier mais on naît rôtisseur*—"One may become a cook, but one is born a roaster," say the French; and I verily believe that the betting-man is to the manner born, and that if he does not feel an innate vocation for the odds, he had much better jump into a cauldron of boiling pitch than touch a betting-book—which theory I offer with confident generosity for the benefit of those young gentlemen who think it a proper thing and a fast thing to make up a book for the Derby or the Oaks, whether they understand anything about the matter or not.

To all appearances, the Ring and the Subscription-room, with the adjacent avenues for the outsiders (you should see the place on the Sunday afternoon before the Derby) are quite sufficient to take up all the accommodation which the "Corner" can afford; but there are many other things done within Messrs. Tattersall's somewhat crowded premises. There is the auctioneering business; the sales, when whole studs are brought to the hammer, and thousands of pounds' worth of horseflesh are disposed of in the course of a few minutes. There are the days for the sale of all manner of genteel wheeled vehicles, which have been inspected on the previous day by a committee *de haut goût*, of which ladies belonging to the *élite* of fashion are not unfrequently members. For the cream of nobility is, oft-times, not too proud to ride in second-hand carriages.

One more episode of "Corner" life, and I must quit the queer, motley scene. Down below the Subscription-room is another corner occupied by an old-fashioned hostelry, called the "Turf Tap," and here the commonalty of Tattersall's frequenters are to be found at any hour of the day, occupied with the process of sustentation by liquid refreshment. And yet, though the place is almost entirely "used" by sporting men, it has very little the appearance of a "sporting" public-house. No portraits of "coaching incidents," or famous prize-fighters, decorate its walls; no glass-cases containing the stuffed anatomies of dogs of preternaturally small size, and that have killed unheard-of numbers of rats in a minimum of minutes, ornament its bar-parlour; no loudly-boisterous talk about the last fight, or the next race coming off, echoes through its bar; and the landlord hasn't a broken nose. The behaviour of the company is grave and decorous, almost melancholy; and on the bench outside, wary-looking stablemen, and sober grooms, converse in discreet undertone on "parties" and "events," not by them, or by any means, to be communicated to the general public. Tattersall's is a business-like place altogether, and even its conviviality is serious and methodical.

I think I should like to ride a horse and take a turn in Rotten Row, if I only knew how to accomplish the equestrian feat; but I am really afraid to adventure it. There are some people who do things capitally which they have never been taught; and who ride and drive, as it were, by intuition. Irishmen are remarkable for this faculty, and I do not regard as by any means a specimen of boastfulness, the reply of the young Milesian gentlemen to the person who asked him if he could play the fiddle, that he did not know, but that he dared say he could, *if he tried*. But I am afraid that the mounting of the easiest-going park hack would be too much for your obedient servant, and that the only way of insuring security, would be to get inside the animal and pull the blinds down; or, that being zoologically impossible, to have my coat skirts nailed to the saddle; or to be tied to the body of my gallant steed with cords, in the manner practised in the remotest antiquity by the young men of Scythia on their first introduction to a live horse, and their commencement of the study of equitation. I passed three days once at the hospitable mansion of a friend in Staffordshire, who, the morning after my arrival, wanted me to do something he called "riding to hounds." I said, "Well out of it," respectfully declined the invitation, and retired to the library, where I read Roger de Wendover's "Flowers of History" till dinner time. I daresay the ladies, who all rode like Amazons, thought me a milk-sop; but I went to bed that night without any broken bones. I have an acquaintance, too, a fashionable riding-master at Brighton, a tremendous creature, who wears jack-boots, and has a pair of whiskers like the phlanges of a screw-propeller. He has been obliging enough to say that he will "mount" me any time I come his way, but I would as soon mount the topmost peak of Chimborazo.

FOUR O'CLOCK P.M.: THE PARK.

I beg to state that this short essay on horsemanship is *àpropos* of Hyde Park and notably of Rotten Row, into which I wander after quitting Tattersall's, and where, leaning over the wooden rails, I contemplate the horsemen and horsewomen caracoling along the spongy road with admiration, not unmixed with a little envy. What a much better, honester world it would be if people would confess a little more frequently to that feeling of envy? For Envy is not always, believe me, grovelling in a cavern, red-eyed and pale-faced, and gnawing a steak sliced off her own liver. Envy can be at times noble, generous, heroic. If I see a gay, gallant, happy, ingenious boy of eighteen, and for a moment envy him his youth, his health, his strength, his innocence, the golden prospect of a sunshiny futurity, that stretches out before him, does it follow that I wish to deprive him of one of those gifts, or that I bear him malice for possessing them? I declare it does not follow. I say to him—*I, curre!* "Good luck have thou, with thine honour—ride on;" and as I go home to my garret, if I envy the bird as he sings, need I shoot him? or the dog as he lies winking and basking in the sun, need I kick him? or the golden beetle trudging along the gravel, need I trample on him? But people cry fie upon the envy that is harmless, and must needs assume a virtue if they have it not; and concerning that latter quality my private belief is, that if Virtue were to die, Hypocrisy would have to go into the deepest mourning immediately.

I am glad to say that I am not by any means alone as I lean over the rails. Whether it is that they can't or won't ride, I know not; but I find myself surrounded by groups of exquisites, who, to judge by their outward appearance, must be the greatest dandies in London. For once in a day, I see gentlemen dressed in the exact similitude of the emblazoned cartoons in the "Monthly Magazine of Fashion." I had always, previously, understood those pictorial prodigies to be gross caricatures of, and libels on, at least the male portion of the fashionable world. But I find that I am mistaken. Such peg-top trousers! such astounding waistcoat patterns! such lofty heels to the varnished boots! such Brobdignagian moustaches and whiskers! such ponderous watch-chains, bearing masses of coins and trinkets! such bewildering varieties of starched, choking all-round collars! such breezy neckties and alarming scarves! Ladies, too—real ladies—promenade in an amplitude of crinoline difficult to imagine and impossible to describe; some of them with stalwart footmen following them, whose looks beam forth conscious pride at the superlative toilettes of their distinguished proprietresses; some escorted by their bedizened beaux. Little foot-pages; swells walking three, sometimes four, abreast; gambolling children; severe duennas; wicked old bucks, splendidly attired, leering furtively under the bonnets—what a scene of more than "Arabian Nights" delight and gaiety! And the green trees wave around, around, around; and the birds are on the boughs; and the blessed sun is in the heavens, and rains gold upon the beauteous Danaës, who prance and amble, canter and career, on their graceful steeds throughout the length of Rotten Row.

The Danaës! the Amazons! the lady cavaliers! the horsewomen! can any scene in the world equal Rotten Row at four in the afternoon, and in the full tide of the season? Bois de Boulogne, Course at Calcutta, Cascine at Florence, Prado at Madrid, Atmeidan at Constantinople—I defy ye all. Rotten Row is a very Peri's garden for beautiful women on horseback. The Cliff at Brighton offers, to be sure, just as entrancing a sight towards the end of December; but what is Brighton, after all, but London-super-Mare? The sage Titmarsh has so christened it; and the beauties of Rotten Row are transplanted annually to the vicinity of the Chain Pier and Brill's baths. Watch the sylphides as they fly or float past in their ravishing riding-habits and intoxicatingly delightful hats: some with the orthodox cylindrical beaver, with the flowing veil; others with roguish little wide-awakes, or pertly cocked cavaliers' hats and green plumes. And as the joyous cavalcade streams past, (I count the male riders absolutely for nothing, and do not deem them worthy of mention, though there may be marquises among them) from time to time the naughty wind will flutter the skirt of a habit, and display a tiny, coquettish, brilliant little boot, with a military heel, and tightly strapped over it the Amazonian riding trouser.

Only, from time to time, while you gaze upon these fair young daughters of the aristocracy disporting themselves on their fleet coursers, you may chance to have with you a grim town Diogenes, who has left his tub for an airing in the park; and who, pointing with the finger of a hard buckskin glove towards the graceful *écuyères*, will say: "Those are not all countesses' or earls' daughters, my son. She on the bay, yonder, is Laïs. Yonder goes Aspasia, with Jack Alcibiades on his black mare Timon: see, they have stopped at the end of the ride to talk to Phryne in her brougham. Some of those dashing delightful creatures have covered themselves with shame, and their mothers with grief, and have brought their fathers' gray hair with sorrow to the grave. All is not gold that glitters, my son."

FIVE O'CLOCK P.M.—THE FASHIONABLE CLUB, AND THE PRISONERS' VAN.

The English are the only "Clubable" people on the face of the earth. Considering the vast number of clubs which are more or less understood to flourish all over the Continent, and in the other hemisphere, it is within possibility that I shall be accused of having uttered something like a paradox; but I adhere to my dictum, and will approve it Truth. Not but that, concerning paradoxes themselves, I may be of the opinion of Don Basilio in the "Barber of Seville," expressed with regard to calumny. "Calumniate, calumniate," says that learned casuist; "calumniate, and still calumniate, *something will always come of it.*" So, in a long course of paradoxes, it is hard but that you shall find a refreshing admixture of veracity.

Do you think you can call the French a "clubable" nation, because in their revolutions of '89 and '48 they burst into a mushroom crop of clubs? Do you think that the gentleman whom a late complication of political events brought into connection with a committee of Taste, consisting of twelve honest men assembled in a jury-box, and whom, the penny-a-liners were kind enough to inform us, was in his own country known as "Bernard le Clubbiste," could be by any means considered as what we called a "club-man?" Could he be compared with Jawkins or Borekins, Sir Thomas de Boots, Major Pendennis, or any of the Pall Mall and St. James's Street bow-window loungers, whom the great master of club life has so inimitably delineated? No more than we could parallelise the dingy, garlic-reeking, revolutionary club-room on a three-pair back at the bottom of a Paris court-yard, with its "tribune," and its quarrelsome patriots, to the palatial Polyanthus, the Podasokus or the Poluphlosboion. French clubs ever have been—and will be again, I suppose, when the next political smash affords an opportunity for the re-establishment of such institutions—mere screeching, yelling, vapouring "pig-and-whistle" symposia; full of rodomontading stump orators, splitting the silly groundlings' ears with denunciations of the infamous oppressors of society—the society that wears pantaloons without patches, and has one-and-ninepence in its pockets; yelping for communism, equal division of property, and toothpicks, solidarity, nationalities, and similar moonshine-and-water ices; "demanding heads," with fierce imprecations about universal fraternity, till their own troublesome bodies—for society's mere peace and quietness' sake—are securely shackled and straight-waistcoated up, and carted away in police-vans to deep-holded ships, whence, after much salutary sea-sickness, they are shot out on the shores of conveniently pestilential Cayennes and Nouka-Hivas. A plague on such clubs and clubbists, say I, with their long hair, flapped waistcoats, and coffee-shop treasonable practices. They have done more harm to the cause of Liberty than all the wicked kings and kaisers, from Dionysius to the late Bomba—now gone to his reward, and who is enjoying it, I should say, hot and hot by this time—have done to the true and heaven-ordained principle of royalty.

In Imperial Paris there are yet clubs of another sort existing, though jealously watched by a police that would be Argus-eyed if its members were not endowed with a centuple power of squinting. There are clubs—the "Jockey," the "Chemin de Fer," and establishments with great gilded saloons, and many servitors in plush and silk stockings; but they are no more like our frank English clubs than I am like Antinous. Mere gambling shops and arenas for foolish wagers; mere lounging-places for spendthrifts, sham gentlemen, gilt-fustian senators, and Imperialist patricians, with dubious titles, who haunt club-rooms, sit up late, and intoxicate themselves with alcoholic mixtures—so aping the hardy sons of Britain, when they would be ten times more at home in their own pleasant, frivolous Boulevard *cafés*, with a box of dominoes, a glass of sugar-and-water, and Alphonso the *garçon* to bring it to them. Such pseudo-aristocratic clubs you may find, too, at Berlin and Vienna, scattered up and down north Italy, and in Russia, even, at Petersburg and Moscow, where they have "English" clubs, into which Englishmen are seldom, if ever, admitted. Some English secretaries of legation and long-legged *attachés*, have indeed an *ex-officio* entry to these continental clubs, or "*cercles*," where they come to lounge and yawn in the true Pall Mall fashion; but they soon grow tired of the hybrid places; and the foreigners who come to stare and wonder at them, go away more tired still, and, with droll shrugs, say, "*Que c'est triste!*" The proper club for a Frenchman is his *café*; for, without a woman to admire him or to admire, your Monsieur cannot exist; and in the slowest provincial town in France there is a *dame de comptoir* to ogle or be ogled. The Russian has more of the clubable element in him; but clubs will never flourish in Muscovy till a man can be morally certain that the anecdote he is telling his neighbour will not be carried, with notes and emendations, in half an hour, to the Grand Master of Police. As for the German, put him in a beer-shop, and give him a long pipe with his mawkish draught, and—be he prince, professor, or peasant—he will desire no better club; save, indeed, on high convivial occasions, when you had best prepare him a cellar, where he and his blond-bearded, spectacled fellows may sit round a wine-cask, and play cards on the top thereof.

I don't exactly know how far the English club-shoot has been grafted on the trunk of American society, but I can't believe that the club-proper flourishes there to any great extent. I like the Americans much, recognising in them many noble, generous, upright, manly qualities; but I am afraid they are too fond of asking questions—too ignorant or unmindful of the great art of sitting half an hour in the company of a man whom you know intimately, without saying a word to him, to be completely clubable. Moreover, they are a people who drink *standing*, delighting much to "liquor up" in crowded bar-rooms, and seldom sitting down to their potations—a most unclubable characteristic. All sorts of convivial and political *réunions* exist, I am aware, in the United States, to a high degree of organisation; and I have heard glowing accounts of the comfortable, club-like guard-rooms and stations of the New York volunteers and firemen; but I can't exactly consider these in the light of clubs. They are not exclusive enough—not concrete enough—not subject to the rigid but salutary discipline of that *Imperium in Imperio*, or rather, *Rempublicam in Republicâ*, the committee of a club.

In England, the Ancient Order of Druids were undeniably the first clubmen, keeping things remarkably snug, and delighting much in house-dinners at the sign of the Misletoe, where a roasted Ancient Briton was no rare dish. It might aid, too, to clear up the puzzling enigma of Stonehenge—who built it, and how, and why?—if we were to look upon Druidism in a purely club-light. I should like to know whence the money came which the Megatherium or the Mastodon Clubs in Pall Mall cost to build. We know that Captain Threadbare, late of the Rifles, that the Hon. Jemmy O'Nuffin, respectively members of those grand *cénacles*, didn't find the money; that they never paid anything towards their clubs, save the entrance fee and the subscription; and that they dine there, nine months out of the year, for eighteen-pence. Other members did, do, will do the same; yet there the club stands, stately and superb, with its columns of multi-coloured marbles, its stately halls, its sumptuous furniture, its army of liveried lacqueys. A belted earl might ruin himself in building such a mansion; yet Captain Threadbare and Jemmy O'Nuffin call it their club, and it is theirs to all intents and purposes. Cunning men, when you express excusable wonder at the thing, whisper, "Debentures!" and debentures seem in truth to have been the seven hundred times seven gifted servants, who have hoisted this Fortunio of a place to its proud position. Why should not Stonehenge have been built by debentures?

The old Saxon Wittenagemotte must have been strongly impregnated with the club element; and the resemblance of clubs to parliaments has come down to this day. What, after all, is our much-vaunted British House of Commons but a club of the first water, somewhat more exclusive than its brethren of St. James's, and black-balling its scores of candidates every general election? It has its reading-rooms, coffee-rooms, and smoking-rooms; the members lounge in and out, and loll on forms and benches, just as they would do in Pall Mall; and while some five hundred members indulge in the real *dolce far niente* of club life, smoking, and reading, and dawdling, and dozing, and refreshing themselves, and never troubling themselves about club matters, save when they are called upon to vote, the affairs of the club (and of the nation too, by the way) are managed by a snug little committee, who do all the work and all the talking, and are continually popping themselves into snug little berths connected with the management of that other great club which lies beyond the walls of St. Stephen's, and is called the Country.

And the middle ages, sunk as the unthinking believe them to have been in barbarism, had their clubs, and brave ones too. Thorough clubmen were the old Freemasons; secret and sturdy, and swift in action; and it's O! to see the club-houses they erected in the fanes that are yet the pride and glory of our cathedral towns. When you look at their crenelated towers, and at the strange sculptures in the rich spandrils of their arches, in their groins and corbels, in their buttresses and great rose windows, and cunningly-traced roodscreens and carved bench-ends, you shall find copious store of club-marks, and secret signs, and passes only known to themselves, and, grotesque and frivolous as to the uninitiated they seem, truly drawn from the innermost arcana of the great mystery of masonry. The old Vehmgericht, too, with its grim symbols, and warnings of the cord and dagger—may not that be considered as a club? The Flagellants and the Rosicrucians, were not those queer sects clubs? and what were the Council of Trent, and the Diet of Worms, but select clubs, frequented by ecclesiastical and political "swells?"

I am not about to confound the convivial club—with its one room and its quaint rules, ancient or modern—with its latest perfection, all Portland stone and plate-glass, gas chandeliers, and luxurious ottomans. Before, however, I come to the fashionable club of 1859, I may be permitted, I hope, to discourse for awhile on the jovial clubs, high, low, and middle class, which have made this metropolis cosy and picturesque for at least two centuries.

There can be little doubt that the Restoration gave a marvellous incentive to club-life in London. On the one hand, the sour Puritans and fierce Independents, driven into holes and corners by the advent of Charles II., had other places of meeting than the conventicles where they offered their surreptitious worship; and at these stray places of re-union, they comforted and refected themselves in their own grim, uncomfortable fashion. On the other hand, the Cavaliers had their riotous assemblages, where they met to sing "Down among the dead men," and drink their king's health on their knees; the revival of humorous and theatrical literature filled the taverns and coffee-houses with wits and dramatists, instead of pedants and theologians; table companions formed into knots, and knots into throngs, and these at length formed themselves into clubs, where they could jest and criticise, argue and carouse, at their ease, without the fear of interlopers; and though, so late as the days of Foote and Chatterton, a stranger of good address and brilliant conversation could form a rallying coffee-house acquaintance with the most famous wits of the town, it was difficult for him to be admitted into their inner circle; even as, in our own time, a man may find plenty of conversation in a railway carriage or an hotel coffee-room, at a German Spa or a charity dinner, but must not feel surprised if his voluble acquaintance of the previous evening cut him dead the next time he meets him. The change of succession at the Revolution gave an impetus both to the establishment and to the exclusiveness of the clubs. While William, the Dutchman, held his uneasy, hooked-nose pre-eminence in this country, innumerable were the dim taverns in whose securest rooms stealthy clubs, with cabalistic names, were held; where, when the club-room doors were tightly closed, Captain Henchman, late of Roper's horse, turned out to be Father Slyboots, high up in the order of Jesus, where sympathy was openly avowed for Sir John Fenwick, and the exiles of St. Germains were yet spoken of as the possessors of the Crown; and where, after William's death, the health of "the little gentleman in black velvet," meaning the molehill over which, according to the Jacobites, the king's horse had stumbled, when William fell and dislocated his collar-bone, was enthusiastically drunk. It would have been hard, too, if the days of Queen Anne—the Augustan era in which Swift, Gay, Pope, Addison, Prior, Bolingbroke, Somers, and Dorset, held their glorious sway of intellect—had not been fruitful in the production of clubs; and it is to the first quarter of the eighteenth century that we may trace the birth of our most famous clubs. The accession of George the First, embittering as it did a new question of the succession to the throne, gave a fresh lease of popularity to the Jacobite clubs, which had languished somewhat during the reign of Anne, for sheer want of something to conspire about. They were held all over London: in taverns and mug-houses, in the purlieus of Westminster and the Mint in Southwark, and in the multitudinous courts and alleys about Cornhill and the Exchange. How I should like to have seen one of these old honest, wrong-headed Jacobite club meetings! There was our old friend Captain Henchman, *alias* Father Slyboots, grown gray in conspiring; always in active correspondence with Rome and St. Germains, Douai and St. Omer, and, as of yore, fiercely hunted by Mr. Secretary's messengers, from his Majesty's Cockpit, at Whitehall. There were old Roman Catholic baronets and squires, from Lancashire and Cheshire, who would as soon have thought of surrendering their ancestral faith in the false and fickle Stuarts, as of abandoning their old shields of arms and trees of descent; there were hot-headed young counsellers from the Temple; and otherwise steady-going Jacobite mercers, and goldsmiths, and vintners, whose loyalty to the dethroned house had somewhat of a commercial tinge in it, as you see now radical hatters and grocers proud to blazon the Royal arms above their doors, and the Lord Chamberlain's warrant in their windows, as "purveyors, by appointment, to her most Gracious Majesty." The landlord was a staunch Jacobite, of course; how, indeed, should he be otherwise? His grandfather had fought at Naseby field; and his father had furnished one of King Charles the Second's madams with clove-gillyflower water, and had never been paid for it. The drawer was Jacobite to the backbone (he turned traitor afterwards, it is true; was the means of hanging half the club, and retired with a handsome competence to the plantations, where he was exceedingly prosperous in the export of tobacco and the import of kidnapped children, and died elder and deacon)—but who but he brought in the great China bowl filled with a clear fluid, across which the company drank, with clasped hands, the toast of "The king over the water." Ah, days of furious party and faction differences, but of self-sacrificing honour and loyalty, ye shall return no more! It was lucky for the Jacobite club-men when their convivialities were not interrupted by the irruption through the window of a party of the Foot Guards, who had climbed over the adjoining tiles. Traitors were always in their camp: spies always watching them. The English ambassador in Paris knew of their goings on, and revealed their bacchanalian machinations to wary Mr. Secretary at the Cockpit; and every now and then would come a tide of evil days, and the venue of the club would be changed; Father Slyboots would go into closer hiding, baffling pursuit as a verger of Westminster Abbey, compounding with skippers of smuggling luggers for conveyance to Dunkirk or Fecamp, crouching in the "priest's hole" of some old Roman Catholic mansion of the North country, or indeed, good man, as the times were very bad, purchasing a stout horse and betaking himself to the road with Captain Macheath and Cornet O'Gibbet, and Duvalising travellers,—of course confining himself to those who were of the Hanoverian way of thinking. Not the first honest man who has turned highwayman: besides, was it not for the greater glory of Church and King? When the club had its next meeting, it might be in '16 or in '46 (for the century was quite gray-headed before the Jacobite clubs quite died out), there would be a lamentable hiatus here and there in the list of members. Where was Sir William Flowerdeluce?—Shot at Sheriffmuir. Where Colonel Belmain?—Hanged at Carlisle. Where young Christopher Layer, the barrister, gallant, devoted, enthusiastic?—His head was rotting on a spike, over Temple Bar, within sight of his old chambers. Where Jemmy Dawson, the pride, the pet, the pearl of the Jacobites, the dashing swordsman of Townley's ill-fated Manchester Regiment?—Go ask the judge and jury, go ask the hangman, go ask the veiled lady in the black coach, who follows the fatal hurdle to Kennington Common, and sits out the hideous drama, and when she sees the heart of him she loves cast into the flames, and his fair limbs dismembered by the executioner, swoons and dies.

I have been reading a little old book, bearing the date of 1725, which professes to give a "Complete Account" of the principal clubs of London and Westminster. Its authorship is anonymous; yet I think I can discern traces of a certain fine Roman hand, well-known to me, in its composition, and I don't think I am in error in ascribing it to Mr. Ned Ward, the scurrilous though amusing author of the "London Spy." Its contents must be taken, of course, *cum grano salis*, with the other lucubrations of that diverting vagabond; yet I am ready to believe that many of his clubs were then existent. Some of them, indeed, have come down to our own times. According to the writer of the "Complete Account," there was the "Virtuous Club," established as a succursal to the Royal Society (which, indeed, was little more than a club at its commencement), at the Golden Fleece, a tavern in Cornhill, whence they moved to the Three Tuns, in Southwark: a queer locality, indeed, for the white-neckclothed savants, who now have their habitat in Burlington House. The chronicler treats them somewhat contemptuously, as collectors of "pickled maggots and mummies' toenails," and seems considerably to prefer the "Surly Club," held at some out-of-the-way place near Billingsgate Dock, whose members had "a stoker to attend their fire"—I did not know the appellation "stoker" was so old—a skinker to ignify their pipes, and a chalk accountant to keep a trencher register of the club reckoning, lest the landlord below should be tempted to augment the scot by means of a double-notched chalk. The principal feature of the "Surly Club" appeared to lie in the members being all surly, ill-tempered, wrangling chuffs, who were bound to abuse each other and the world generally, at their every time of meeting. I believe that there are London clubs, not yet extinct, which carry out the principles of the "Surly Club" in a remarkably undeviating manner. Then there was the "Split-Farthing Club," instituted by a society of usurers and money-spinners, who met together in the dark, in order to avoid the expense of candle or lamp-light, and of which the Hopkins immortalised by Pope was a distinguished member. The "Ugly Club" (which yet flourishes, I believe,) owed its foundation to a superlatively ugly fellow by the name of Hatchet (whence the term "hatchet-faced"), who had a nose of such immense size, that he was one day in the street charged by a butcher-boy with overturning a tray full of meat, when his head was at least a foot distant therefrom. A violent attempt was made to break up the "Ugly Club" by a committee of spinsters, who made unheard-of attempts to marry the members *en masse*, but in vain. Jack Wilkes was elected perpetual president of the "Ugly Club," early in the reign of George III., and Honorè Gabriel Riquetti, Count de Mirabeau, who had some slight connection with the first French Revolution, was unanimously chosen an honorary member on his visit to England. I must not forget to mention the "Unfortunate Club," held at the sign of the "Tumbledown Dick," in the Mint. To have been at least once bankrupt (a fraudulent failure was preferred), or to have come in some way in collision with the laws of the country, was a *sine quâ non* in the qualification for a member of the "Unfortunates." The Market Women's, or "Flat-cap Club," was at one time quite a fashionable place of meeting, being frequented by many of the wild gallants from the Rose, and Tom King's coffee-house, who treated the lady company to burnt brandy and flowing "Winchesters" (*i. e.*, Winchester measures) of "powerful three thread"—our modern porter. Then there was the "Lying Club," among whose voluminous rules were these, that the chairman was to wear a blue cap and a red feather, and that if any member, in the course of an evening, told a lie more impudent and egregious than he, the chairman, could manage to cap, he was at once to vacate the chair in favour of the superior Mendax. There was a very stringent rule, inflicting a severe fine upon any member who should presume, between the hours of nine and eleven of the clock, to tell one word of truth, unless, indeed, he prefaced it with the rider of "By your leave, Sir Harry"—Sir Harry Gulliver being the name of the original chairman of the club. There was the "No-Nose Club," the "Beggars' Club," the "Thieves' Club," and the "Northern or Yorkshire Tyke's Club;" and, to sum up, there was a horrific assembly, founded in the reign of Charles II., and called the "Man-killing Club." The members of this savage corporation were debased Life-guardsmen, broken-down bullies, and old scarified prize-fighters. The prime qualification for membership was the commission of homicide. The "Mohocks," "Scourers," and "Sweaters" of Queen Anne's time, were, as may readily be imagined, highly prominent members of this murderous fraternity, which might have flourished much longer but for the interference of the Sheriff's hangman in ordinary, who disposed of the members with such amazing despatch and persistence, that the club could not at last form a quorum, and was so dissolved.

The "Irish Fortune-hunters' Club" I am somewhat chary of recognising, for I am afraid that it existed only in the lively fancy of Mr. Ned Ward or his imitator. There is, indeed, a copy of some resolutions of the club appended to the "Complete Account," but I am inclined to consider them apocryphal. Leave, by these resolutions, is given to Captain Donahoo to change his name to Talbot Howard Somerset; Captain Macgarret is empowered to change the place of his nativity from Connemara to Cornwall; and Lieutenant Dunshunner is presented with a suit of laced camlet at the club expense, in order to his successfully prosecuting his suit with Miss Bridget Tallboys, "with ten thousand pounds fortune; in the event of which happy consummation, he is to repay the price of the suit with interest, and moreover to release from his captivity at the Gate-house the club secretary, therein confined on suspicion of debt."

Very different is the bran-new modern club whose interior my faithful artist has depicted, and whose appearance at five o'clock in the afternoon I am now called upon to describe. Gentlemen members of clubs, these gorgeous palaces are but the growth of one generation. Your fathers had, it is true, their Wattier's, the Cocoa-Tree, White's, and Boodle's, but those were considerably more like gambling-houses than clubs. To obtain admission was exceedingly difficult, and to remain a member was, save to men of immense fortune, absolutely ruinous. Hundreds of the superior middle-classes, nay, even of the aristocracy, who would consider themselves social Pariahs now-a-days, if they did not belong to one or more clubs, were perfectly content, a score of years since, to frequent the coffee-rooms of hotels and taverns. A modern London club is the very looking-glass of the time; of the gay, glittering, polished, improved utilitarian, material age. Nothing more can be done for a palace than the fitters-up of a modern club have done for it. The march of upholstering intellect is there in its entirety. It must be almost bewildering to the modest half-pay captain or the raw young ensign, to the country gentleman, the book-worm fellow of his college, or the son of the country squire, fresh from dog-breaking and superintending the drains on his father's estate, to find themselves suddenly transferred from the quiet lodgings in St. Alban's Place, the whitewashed barrack-room, the ivy-grown parsonage, the tranquil oak-sporting rooms of "Keys" or "Maudlin," the dull comfort of the country mansion-house, to this great hectoring palace, of which he is the twelve-hundreth part proprietor, and where he may live on the fatness of the land, and like a lord of the creation, for twenty guineas entrance fee, and a subscription of ten guineas a year. He has a joint-stock proprietorship in all this splendour; in the lofty halls and vestibules; in the library, coffee-rooms, newspaper and card-rooms; in the secretary's office in the basement, and in the urbane secretary himself; in the kitchen, fitted with every means and appliance, every refinement of culinary splendour, and from whence are supplied to him at cost prices dishes that would make Lucullus wild with envy, and that are cooked for him, besides, by the great *chef* from Paris, Monsieur Nini Casserole, who has a piano and a picture-gallery in the kitchen—belongs, himself, to a club, little less aristocratic than his masters', and writes his bills of fare upon laced-edged note-paper. From the gorgeous footmen in plush and silk-covered calves, which the flunkeys of duchesses could scarcely rival, to the little foot-page in buttons; from the letter-racks to the French-polished peg on which he hangs his hat in the hall; from the books in the library to the silver spoons in the plate-basket; from the encaustic mosaic on the pavement of the hall to the topmost turreted chimney-pot—he has a vested interest in all. He cannot waste, he cannot alienate, it is true; he can but enjoy. Debentures have taken care of that; yet the fee-simple is in part his; he is the possessor of an entailed estate; yet, for all purposes of present enjoyment, he sits under his own roof on his own ground, and eats his own mutton off his own plate, with his own knife and fork. Oh! the wonderful workings of debentures, and the inestimable benefits they confer on genteel persons with expensive tastes and small incomes! Do you know that a man may drink wines at his club, such as, were he to order them at an hotel, the head waiter would hold up his hands at the extravagance of the order, or else imagine that he had Rothschild or Mr. Roupell dining in No. 4 box; nay, might perchance run round to the chambermaid to ask how much luggage the gentleman had. Rare ports, "worn-out ports," grown colourless from age and strength, that cannot be looked at without winking—wondrous bitter Sherries—strange yellow Rhine wines, that gurgle in the glass when poured out—Claret that has made bankrupt the proprietors of the *vignobles* who grew them, or else sent them mad to think their stock was out—indescribable Cognacs—Maraschinos and Curaçoas that filtrate like rich oil: all these are stored by special wine-merchants in the cellars of the club. The chief butler himself, a prince among the winepots, goes forth jauntily to crack sales, and purchases, standing, the collections of cunning amateurs in wines. You shall smoke such cigars at a club as would make Senor Cabana himself wonder where they were purchased. Everything is of the best, and everything is cheap; only the terms are, as the cheap tailors say, "for ready money." Tick is the exception, not the rule, at a club; though there have been Irish members who have run goodly scores in their time with the cook and the waiter.

A man may, if he be so minded, make his club his home; living and lounging luxuriously, and grazing to his heart's content on the abundant club-house literature, and enjoying the conversation of club friends. Soap and towels, combs and hair-brushes, are provided in the lavatories; and there are even some clubs that have bed-rooms in their upper storeys, for the use of members. In those that are deficient in such sleeping accommodation, it is only necessary to have a tooth-brush and an attic in an adjacent bye-street; all the rest can be provided at the club. Thus it is that, in the present generation, has been created a type peculiar thereunto—the club-man. He is all of the club, and clubby. He is full of club matters, club gossip. He dabbles in club intrigues, belongs to certain club cliques, and takes part in club quarrels. No dinners are so good to him as the club dinners; he can read no journals but those he finds in the club news-paper-room; he writes his letters on the club paper, pops them into club envelopes, seals them with the club seal, and despatches them, if they are not intended for postage, by the club messengers. He is rather sorry that there is no club uniform. He would like, when he dies, to be buried in a club coffin, in the club cemetery, and to be followed to the grave by the club, with members of the committee as pall-bearers. As it is, when he has shuffled off this mortal coil, his name appears on a board among the list of "members deceased." That is his epitaph, his hatchment, his *oraison funêbre*.

FIVE O'CLOCK P.M.: THE FASHIONABLE CLUB.

The great complaint against clubs is, that they tend towards the germination of selfishness, exclusiveness, and isolation; that they are productive of neglect of home duties in married men, and of irrevocable celibacy in bachelors. Reserving my own private opinion on this knotty point, I may say that it is a subject for sincere congratulation that there are no ladies' clubs. We have been threatened with them sometimes, but they have always been nipped in the bud. It is curious to see how fiercely this tolerant, liberal, large-headed creature, Man, has waged war against the slightest attempt to establish a club on the part of the gentler sex. From the Parisian malecontents of the first revolution, who broke into the lady assemblies of the *Jacobines* and *Tricoteuses*, and broke up the clubs in question by the very expeditious process of turning the fair members into the street, after subjecting them to a castigation whose use is ordinarily confined to the nursery; from those ungallant anti-clubbists (they all belonged to clubs themselves, you may be sure) to Mr. Mark Lemon, who, in a *petite comédie*, brought the guns of satire to bear with terrible effect on an incipient agitation for lady clubbism, such institutions, on the part of the ladies, have always been put down, either by violence or by ridicule. The Tyrant Man is even, I am informed, disposed to look with jealousy on the "committees of ladies" which exist in connection with some deserving charities, and on the "Dorcas societies" and "sewing circles" of provincial towns; and all meetings to advocate the rights of woman, he utterly abhors.

I daresay that you would very much like to know the name of the particular club, the tableau of which adorns this sheet, and would feel obliged if I would point out the portraits of individual members: you would be very much pleased to be told whether it is the Carlton, the Reform, the Travellers', the Athenæum, the Union, the United Service Senior or Junior, the Guards, the Oriental, the Oxford and Cambridge, the Parthenon, the Erectheum, the Wyndham, Whyte's, Boodle's, or the Army and Navy. No, Fatima; no, Sister Anne. You shall not be told. Clubbism is a great mystery, and its adepts must be cautious how they explain its shibboleth to the outer barbarians. Men have been expelled from clubs ere now for talking or writing about another member's whiskers, about the cut of his coat, and the manner in which he eats asparagus. I have no desire for such club-ostracism; for though, Heaven help me, I am not of Pall Mall or St. James's, I, too, have a club whose institutes I revere. *"Non me tua fervida terrent, dicta, Ferox."* I fear not Jawkins, nor all the Borekins in Borekindom; but *"Dii me terrent, et Jupiter hostis."* I fear the awful committee that, with a dread complacency, can unclub a man for a few idle words inadvertently spoken, and blast his social position for an act of harmless indiscretion.

Clubs, after all, are rather pleasant institutions than otherwise, yet they have not escaped the lash of the moralist. Turning over, as I dismiss the subject, the leaves of my little old book, I come on the following passage: "Though the Promotion of Trade, and the Benefits that arise from Conversation, are the Specious Pretences that every Club or Society are apt to assign as a Reasonable Plea for their Unprofitable Meetings, yet more Considerate Men have found by Experience that the End thereof is a Promiscuous Encouragement of Vice, Faction, and Folly, and the Unnecessary Expense of that Time and Money which might much better be Employed in their own Business, or spent with much more Comfort in their Several Families." I don't say what the ladies' verdict will be on this opinion, though I can divine it; but I take off my hat to the moralist, capital letters and all, and, leaving him to grumble, will be off to the club.

Stay, stay, *siste viator*. I have an appointment. When have I not? I begin to think that I am the Wandering Jew, and there is decidedly no rest for the soles of my feet. Still the cry is "onward." Wherever that club of mine may be situated, it is clear that I must bend my course towards Bow Street, Covent Garden.

And why to Bow Street, an't please you? To gaze upon the resuscitated glories of the Royal Italian Opera? To dine at Nokes's succulent restaurant, where erst was the "Garrick's Head?" To obtain an order for admission to the workhouse from the relieving officer of the Strand Union Office? To hire theatrical costumes at Mr. May's? or to bail a friend out of the station-house? Not so. And yet my business has something to do with the metropolitan police. I wish to witness the departure of the PRISONERS' VAN.

About five p.m. the ladies and gentlemen who, through the arbitration of Mr. Hall, Mr. Jardine, or Mr. Henry, stipendiary magistrates, have settled their little differences with Justice, are conveyed to those suburban residences, in which, for the benefit of their health, and in the interests of society, it is judged necessary, *par qui de droit*, they shall for a stated term abide. The vehicle which bears them to their temporary seclusion enjoys different names; some technical, others simply humorous. By some it is called "Her Majesty's Carriage," from the fact that the crown and the initials "V. R." are painted on the panels. More far-fetched wags call it "Long Tom's Coffin." The police and the reporters, for shortness, call it "The Van." In this vehicle the malefactors who have in the course of the day been arraigned before the tribunal of the Bow Street Police-court, are conveyed to the various jails and houses of correction in and about the metropolis, there to undergo the several terms of imprisonment and hard labour, as the case may be, to which they have been sentenced. Sometimes the court sits late, and the van does not take its departure before half-past five; but five is the ordinary time when the great black, shining, cellular omnibus, drawn by two strong horses, with its policeman driver, and policeman conductor in a snug little watch-box, rolls away from Bow Street. It is a prison on wheels, a peripatetic penitentiary, a locomotive hulk. Criminals both in and out of prison regard it with a species of terror, not unmixed with admiration, and, as is their wont, they have celebrated it in that peculiar strain of ballad poetry for which London roguery has been so long distinguished. In that celebrated collection of dishonest epics, the "Drury Lane Garland," in fit companionship with "Sam Hall," "County Jail," "Seven years I got for priggin'," and the "Leary Man," I find a ballad on the subject of the Bow Street chariot of disgrace, of which the refrain is—

"Sing Wentilator, separate cell,

Its long, and dark, and hot as well.

Sing locked-up doors—git out if you can,

There's a crusher outside the prisoners' wan!"

A "crusher," or policeman, there is indeed, not only in the little watch-box on the exterior, to which I have alluded, but in the narrow corridor between the cells into which the carriage is divided in the interior. It is the former functionary's duty to keep the outer door securely locked; the latter to take care that no communication takes place between the passengers confined in this penal omnibus, either through the ventilators on the roof, or by talismanic tappings at the panels which divide them.

FIVE O'CLOCK P.M.: THE PRISONERS' VAN.

When the hour of departure arrives, you see the pavement and carriage-way of Bow Street studded with a choice assemblage of the raggedry, ruffianry, felonry, misery, drunkardry, and drabbery, whom the infamous hundred of Drury, and the scarcely less infamous tithing of Covent, have cast out into a thoroughfare which, two hours hence, will be re-echoing to the wheels of carriages bearing noble lords and ladies to listen to the delicious Bosio (alas!) in the "Traviata," or the enchanting notes of Tamberlik in "Otello." London is full of violent contrasts; but this is the grimmest in the whole strange catalogue. See, the warder in the watch-box has descended from his perch, and with a patent key opened the portal of the van, revealing a second janitor inside. And now the passengers destined for the lugubrious journey come tumbling out of the court door, and down the steps towards the van. Some handcuffed, some with their arms folded, or their hands thrust in their pockets in sullen defiance; some hiding their faces in their grimy palms for very shame. There are women as well as men, starved sempstresses, and brazen courtezans in tawdry finery. There are wicked graybeards, and children on whose angel faces the devil has already set his indelible brand. There are ragged losels rejoicing to go to jail as to a place where they shall at least have bread to eat and a bed to lie on; there are dashing pickpockets in shiny hats and pegtop trousers braided down the seams. There are some going to prison for the first, and some for the fiftieth time. One by one they are thrust rather than handed into the van. The shabby crowd gives a faint, derisive cheer, the door bangs, the policeman-conductor ensconces himself in his watch-box, and the Prisoners' Van drives off.

The Pharisee thanked Heaven that he was not "as that Publican." Down on your knees, well-nurtured, well-instructed youth, and thank Heaven for the parents and friends, for the pastors and masters, to whose unremitting care and tenderness, from your cradle upwards, you owe it that you are not like one of these miserable Publicans just gone away in the prisoners' van. But thank Heaven humbly, not pharisaically. A change at nurse, the death of a parent—one out of the fifty thousand accidents that beset life—might have thrown you into the sink of misery and want, foulness and crime, in which these creatures were reared, and you might have been here to-day, not gazing on the spectacle with a complacent pity, but trundled with manacles on your wrists into this moving pest-house, whose half-way house is the jail, and whose bourne is the gallows.

SIX P.M.—A CHARITY DINNER, AND THE NEWSPAPER WINDOW AT THE GENERAL POST-OFFICE.

Some years ago, at the cozy little dining club held in my friend Madame Basque's back-parlour, in the Rue de la Michodière, and the city of Paris, I had the advantage of the friendship of one of the most intelligent and humorous of the American gentlemen. There is such a personage—the vulgar, drawling, swearing, black-satin-vested, stove-pipe-hatted, whittling, smoking, expectorating, and dram-drinking Yankee loafers, who infest the Continent, notwithstanding; and a very excellent sample of the accomplished and unpretending gentleman was the American in question. He had paid a visit to England, in which country his sojourn had been of about three months' duration; but he frankly confessed to me that having come purposely unprovided with those usually tiresome and worthless figments, letters of introduction—the very Dead-Sea apples of hospitality, goodly on the exterior, and all dust and ashes within—he had not, with the exception of his banker, who asked him to dinner once as a courteous acknowledgment of the ponderosity of his letter of credit, possessed one single acquaintance, male or female, during his stay in the metropolis of the world. I asked him whether he had not felt very lonely and miserable, and sufficiently inclined, at the end of the first week, to cast himself over any given bridge into the river Thames. Not in the slightest degree, he replied. I politely hinted that perhaps, as an American, he possessed the genial facility, common to his countrymen, of making himself at home wheresoever he went, and of forming agreeable travelling acquaintances, occasionally ripening into fast friends, by the simple process of saying "Fine day, stranger." Not at all, he replied. He kept himself to himself, and indeed he was of a disposition, save in casual moments of unbending, quite surprising for its saturnine taciturnity. At all events, I urged, he could not have amused himself much by prowling about the streets, sleeping at hotels, dining in coffee-rooms, frequenting theatres and singing-rooms, and wandering in and out of museums; but I was wrong again, he said. He had seldom been so jolly in his life. I began to think either that he was quizzing me—"gumming" is the proper Transatlantic colloquialism, I think—or else that he was the Happy Man described in the Eastern apologue. But then, the Happy Man had, as it turned out, no shirt; and my American was remarkable for displaying a vast amount of fine linen, both at breast and wristbands, profusely decorated with studs, chains, and sleeve-buttons. How was it, then, I asked, giving the enigma up in sheer bewilderment. "Wall," answered my friend with his own peculiar dry chuckle, "I used to ride about all day on the tops of the omnibuses; and very fine institutions for seeing life in a philosophical spirit, those omnibuses of yours are, sir." He said Sir—not "Sirree," as Anglo-Americans are ordinarily assumed to pronounce that title of courtesy. I understood him at once; saw through him; had done the same thing myself; and admired his penetrative and observant aptitude.

Never ride inside an omnibus—I apostrophise, of course, the men folks; for till arrangements are made (and why should they *not* be made?) for hoisting ladies in an easy-chair to the breezy roof—they can manage such things on board a man-of-war—the vehicular ascent is incommodious, not to say indecorous, for the fair sex. But Ho, ye men, don't ride inside. A friend of mine had once his tibia fractured by the diagonal brass rod that crosses the door; the door itself being violently slammed to, as is the usual custom, by the conductor. Another of my acquaintance was pitched head foremost from the interior, on the mockingly fallacious cry of "all right" being given—was thrown on his head, and killed. Inside an omnibus you are subjected to innumerable vexations and annoyances. Sticks or parasols are poked in your chest and in the back of your neck, as a polite reminder that somebody wants to get out, and that you must seize the conductor by the skirt of his coat, or pinch him in the calf of the leg, as an equally polite request for him to stop; you are half suffocated by the steam of damp umbrellas; your toes are crushed to atoms as the passengers alight or ascend; you are very probably the next neighbour to persons suffering under vexatious ailments, such as asthma, simple cold in the head, or St. Vitus's dance; it is ten to one but that you suffer under the plague of babies; and, five days out of the seven, you will have a pickpocket, male or female, for a fellow-passenger. The rumbling, the jumbling, the jolting, and the concussions—the lurking ague in the straw when it is wet, and the peculiar omnibus fleas that lurk in it when it is dry, make the interior of one of these vehicles a place of terror and discomfort; whereas outside all is peace. You have room for your legs; you have the fresh air; you have the lively if not improving conversation of the driver and the conductor, and especially of the right-hand box-seat, who is invariably in some way mysteriously connected with dogs and horses, and a great authority thereupon. Finally, you have the inestimable advantage of surveying the world in its workings as you pass along: of being your own Asmodeus, and unroofing London in a ride from the White Horse Cellar to Hammersmith Gate. The things I have seen from the top of an omnibus!—more markedly in the narrow streets through which, from the main thoroughfare being blocked up by the incessant paving, lighting, sewerage, or electric telegraph communications of underground London, one is compelled to pass. Now a married couple enjoying an animated wrangle in a first-floor front; now a servant-maid entertaining a policeman, or a Life Guardsman, with a heart's devotion and cold shoulder of mutton, in a far-down area; now a demure maiden lacing her virgin bodice before a cracked triangle of a looking-glass, at an attic window; now lords and ladies walking with parasols and lapdogs, and children in the private gardens of noble mansions, screened from the inquisitive pedestrians by sullen brick walls; now domestics hanging out the clothes in back-yards (seen over the roofs of one-storey houses), malicious birds of prey waiting, doubtless, round the corner for the fell purpose of pecking off their noses, while the astute King is in his counting-house on the second floor counting out his money, and the Queen, with the true gentleness of womanhood, is in the front kitchen, eating bread and honey in confident security, recking little of the four-and-twenty blackbirds baked in a pie, or of the song of sixpence—or rather of five shillings—which I am this day singing about them all, in consideration of an adequate pocketful of rye. So shall you look down and see those things; but chiefly shall you enjoy delectation and gather experience from the sight of the men and women who are continually passing beneath you in carriages and in cabs; yea, and in carts and barrows. Varied life, troubled life, busy, restless, chameleon life. The philosopher may learn much by reading the tradesmen's names over the shop-fronts, which—he will never read them as he passes along the pavement—will give him quite a new insight into nomenclature. But only let him consider the carriages and the cabs, and he may learn wisdom in the ways of mankind in every rood of ground he traverses.

Sweethearting in cabs and carriages; passionate appeals for mercy; men brawling and fighting; lunatics being borne away to captivity; felons, shackled and manacled to the chin, being taken to jail, and perhaps to death, by stern policemen and jailers; frantic women kneeling on carriage-floors, women with dishevelled hair, streaming eyes, clasped hands raised to a Heaven which is never deaf but is sometimes stern, a weeping child clinging to their disordered dress, and money and jewels cast carelessly on the carriage cushions; gamblers carding and dicing; knaves drugging fools; debtors in the charge of sheriff's officers; roysterers gone in drink; the "fatal accident" on its way to the hospital, lying all bruised and bloody across the policeman's knee; the octogenarian in his last paralytic fit, and the mother suckling her first infant. All these dramas on four wheels may be seen by him on the top of the omnibus, who may, if of a caustic turn, rub his hands, and cry, "Aha! little do you reck that a chiel is above you taking notes, and, faith, that he'll print them!"

You see, there are some elements of sadness, nay, of deep and terrible tragedy, in these vehicular panoramas—the unconscious show-vans; but at Six o'Clock in the Evening the cabs and carriages on which you look down offer, mostly, a far pleasanter spectacle. They are full of people going out to dinner. Some in broughams, coupés, double-bodied carriages, and the occupants of these are ladies and gentlemen, attired in the full panoply of evening costume, and whom, at the first blush, you might take for members of the highest aristocracy. But they are not so. They simply belong to the first-class genteel circles, the very superior middle ranks; the dwellers in Lower Belgravia—Brompton, Kensington, and Pimlico; or in Lesser Tyburnia—Bayswater and Notting Hill. They have all the airs and graces, all the allurements, of the titled and the exclusive; but they have not the genuine Hall-mark of nobility and fashion; they are but Britannia metal, electro-gilt in a very superior manner. The undeniable Patricians, the satraps of our modern Persian splendour, do not dine (would not supper be a more appropriate term?) till half-past seven, or even eight, post meridian. They can have, I should imagine, but scant appetites for their dinner at that advanced period of the evening, unless, indeed, they partake of it in the ancient Roman manner, lolling on the *triclinium*, crowning themselves with flowers, and following, between the courses, the swinish examples of Apicius and Lucullus. Better, I take it, a mutton chop at the Cock, or the Cheshire Cheese, than these nasty Ancient Roman repasts. It is true our moderns stay their aristocratic stomachs early in the afternoon with a copious lunch of hot meats and generous wines; and they say that her blessed Majesty herself, like a good, sensible woman, makes her real dinner at two o'clock, with her little children, in the nursery, and takes but a mere bite and sup at the grand stall-fed feast of gold plate in the evening.

But there are plenty of good dinners going on at six o'clock in the evening, and plenty of good diners-out to attend them. Masters in Chancery, who are renowned judges of port-wine, dine at six. Six, for half-past, is the dinner-hour for East India Directors. Let us hope that their dinners will continue to be as good as of yore, though the new India Bill leaves them nothing to direct. Members of Parliament, during the session, dine whenever they can, and sometimes not at all; but on "no House" days, six o'clock—always taken with a reservation for the half-past, for "six o'clock sharp" is entirely gone out of fashion, save with Muswell Hill stock-brokers, Manchester Square proctors, Bedford Row solicitors, and people who live in Bloomsburia—is the great time for them to drop into their clubs, sneer over the evening papers, gnash their teeth because there may happen to be no leading articles eulogistic or abusive of them therein, and *prendre des informations*, as the French say (though why I could not just as well say it in English, save that the cook at the club is a Frenchman, puzzles me), about what there may be good for dinner. But I must not forget that I am on the top of an omnibus, looking down on the people in the broughams and the cabs. Admire that youthful exquisite, curled, and oiled, and scented into a sufficient semblance of the "Nineveh Bull," with whom Mr. Tennyson was so angry in "Maud." His glossy hair is faultlessly parted down the occiput and down the cranium behind. White as the fleece of Clarimunda's sheep is his body linen. Stiff as the necks of the present generation is his collar. Black as Erebus is his evening suit. Shining like mirrors are the little varnished tips of his jean-boots. Severe as the late General Picton is the tie of his cravat. This *gracilis puer* is going to dine in Thurlow Square, Brompton. That gold-rimmed lorgnon you see screwed into his face, to the damaging distortion of his muscles, will not be removed therefrom—nor during dinner, nor during wine-taking, nor during the evening party which will follow the dinner, nor during the "little music," the dancing, the supper, the shawling, the departure, and the drive home to his chambers. He will eat in his eyeglass, and drink in his eyeglass, and flirt and polk in his eyeglass. I am almost persuaded that he will sleep in his eyeglass (I knew a married lady who used to sleep in her spectacles, which led to a divorce: *she* alleged the cause to be systematic cruelty, but what will not an enraged woman say?); and I should not be in the least surprised if he were to die in his eyeglass, and be buried in his eyeglass, and if the epitaph on his gravestone were to be *"veluti in speculum."*

Down and down again, glance from the omnibus summit, and see in that snug, circular-fronted brougham, a comfortable couple, trotting out to dinner in the Alpha Road, St. John's Wood. Plenty of lobster sauce they will have with their salmon, I wager; twice of boiled chicken and white sauce they will not refuse, and oyster patties will they freely partake of. A jovial couple, rosy, chubby, middle-aged, childless, I opine, which makes them a *little* too partial to table enjoyments. They should be well to do in the world, fond of giving merry, corpulent little dinners of their own, with carpet dances afterwards, and living, I will be bound (our omnibus is ubiquitous, remember) at Maida Hill, or Pine Apple Gate. There is another couple, stiff, starched, angular, acrimonious-looking. Husband with a stern, Lincoln's Inn conveyancing face, and pilloried in starch, with white kid gloves much too large for him. Wife, with all manner of tags, and tags, and odds and ends of finery fluttering about her: one of those women who, if she had all the rich toilettes of all King Solomon's wives on her, would never look well dressed. I shouldn't like to dine where they are going. I know what the dinner will be like. Prim, pretentious, dismal, and eminently uncomfortable. There will be a saddle of mutton not sufficiently hung, the fish will be cold, the wines hot, and the carving-knives will be blunt. After dinner the men will talk dreary politics, redolent of stupid Retrogression, and the women will talk about physic and the hooping-cough. Yet another couple—husband and wife? A severe swell, with drooping moustaches of immense length, but which are half whiskers. Transparent deceit! A pretty lady—gauzy bonnet and artificial flowers, muslin jacket, skirts and flounces oozing out at the sides of the carriage; hair *à la* Eugénie, and a Skye terrier with a pink ribbon. I know what *this* means. Greenwich, seven o'clock dinner (they are rather late, by the way, but they pass us on London Bridge, and the coachman will drive rapidly), water souché, whitebait, brown bread and butter, and iced punch; cigar on balcony, and contemplation of the moon. Ride on, and be happy. Rejoice in your youth—and never mind the rest. It will come, O young man, whether you mind it or not.

Hallo! there he is. I thought so. With a red face, shaven to the superlative degree of shininess, with gills white and tremendous, with a noble white waistcoat, and from time to time nervously consulting his watch, lest he should be half a minute behind time with the spring soup, rides by in a swift Hansom, the old gentleman who is going to a Charity Dinner. Blessings on his benevolent, gastronomic old head, he never misses one. He is going as quick as double fare will convey him to the London Tavern. Quick! oh thou conductor, let me descend, for I must take a Hansom too, and follow my venerable friend to the London Tavern; and, by cock and pye, I will go dine there too.

I think my readers must be by this time sufficiently acquainted with the fact that I am endowed with a very nervous temperament. Indeed, were I to say that I start at my own shadow, that I do fear each bush an officer, that I am continually in terror of Sudden Death, that I would rather not go upstairs in the dark, and that (which is not at all incompatible with a nervous organisation) in circumstances of real moment, in imminent life-peril, in a storm, in a balloon, in a tumult, and in a pestilence, I am perfectly master of myself, and, with a complete Trust and Reliance, am quite contented and happy in my mind: when I state this, I don't think I need blush to own that I am as mortally afraid now of the boys in the street as in the old days when they pelted me with sharp stones because I preferred going to school quietly instead of playing fly-the-garter in the gutter. I am afraid of my last schoolmaster (he is quite bankrupt and broken, and pays me visits to borrow small silver occasionally), and yet call him reverentially, "Sir." I am afraid of ladies—not of the married ones, in whom I take great delight, talking Buchan's "Medicine," Acton's "Cookery," and Mrs. Ellis with them, very gravely, till they think me a harmless fogey, hopelessly celibate, but sensible; not of the innocent young girls, with their charming *naïveté* and pretty sauciness; but of the "young ladies," who are "out," and play the piano, and sing Italian songs—of which, Lord bless them! they know no more than I do of crochet-work—and who fling themselves, their accomplishments, and their low-necked dresses, at men's heads. I am afraid of policemen, lest in an evanescent fit of ill temper they should take me up, and with their facile notions of the obligations of an oath, swear that I was lurking about with intent to commit a felon; and, transcendentally, I am afraid of waiters. I watch them—him—the Waiter, with great awe and trembling. Does he know, I ask myself, as he fills my tumbler with iced champagne, that half-and-half is a liquid to which I am more accustomed? Does he know that, sumptuously as I dine to-day, I didn't dine at all yesterday? Is he aware that Mr. Threadpaper is dunning me for that dress-coat with the watered-silk facings? Can he see under the table that the soles of my boots are no better than they should be? Is it within his cognizance that I have not come to the Albion, or the London Tavern, or the Freemasons', as a guest, but simply to report the dinner for the "Morning Meteor?" Does he consider the shilling I give him as insufficient? Shilling! He has many more shillings than I have, I trow. He pulls four pounds in silver from his pocket to change one a crown-piece. To-day he is Charles or James; but to-morrow he will be the proprietor of a magnificent West-end restaurant, rivalling Messrs. Simpson and Dawes at the Divan, or Mr. Sawyer at the London. So I am respectful to the waiter, and fee him largely but fearfully; and, were it not that he might take me for a waiter in disguise, I would also call him "Sir."

I no sooner arrive at the London Tavern, *pari passu* with the old gentleman with the gills and the white neckcloth, than I feel myself delivered over to the thraldom of waiterdom. An urbane creature, who might pass for a Puseyite curate, were not the waitorial stigmata unmistakeably imprinted on him, meets me, and tells me in an oleaginous undertone, which is like clear turtle-soup, that the Anniversary Festival of the Asylum for Fatuous Monomaniacs is on the second floor to the right. A second waiter meets me at the foot of the stair-case, and whispers discreetly behind the back of his hand, "Two storeys higher, sir." A third waylays me benevolently on the first-floor landing, and mildly ravishes from me my hat and stick, in return for which he gives me a cheque much larger than my dinner ticket; which last is taken from me on the second floor by a beaming spirit, the bows of whose cravat are like wings, and who hands me to a Dread Presence—a stout, severe man with a gray head, who is in truth the head-waiter at this Anniversary Festival, and who with a solemn ceremony inducts me into the reception-room.

Here, in a somewhat faded, but intensely respectable-looking apartment, I find about fifty people I don't know from Adam, and who are yet all brothers or uncles or cousins-german, at the least, of my rubicund white-waistcoated friend. And, to tell the truth, I don't know him personally, though his face, from meeting him at innumerable festivals, is perfectly familiar to me. So are those of the other fifty strangers. I have heard all their names, and all about them; but one is not expected to remember these things at public dinners. You take wine with your next neighbour; sometimes converse with him about eating and drinking, the merits of the charity, the late political tergiversation of the chairman, the heat of the weather, the fine voice of Mr. Lockey, and the pretty face of Miss Ransford, and there an end. Your interlocutor may be to-morrow the lawyer who sues you, the author whose book you will slaughter in a review, the Commissioner of Insolvency who may send you back for eighteen months. To have met a man at a public dinner is about as valid a claim to the possession of his acquaintance, as to have met him in the Kursaal at Hombourg, or on the steps of the St. Nicholas Hotel at New York. After some twenty years of public dining together, it is not, I believe, considered a gross breach of etiquette to make the gentleman who has been so frequently your fellow *convive* a very distant bow should you meet him in the street; but even this is thought to be a freedom by some rigid sticklers for decorum.

In genteel society, the half hour before dinner is generally accepted as a time of unlimited boredom and social frigidity, but there you have the relief, if not relaxation, of staring the guests out of countenance, making out a mental list of the people you would not like to take wine with, and turning over the leaves of the melancholy old albums, every page of which you have conned a hundred times before. But in the half hour (and it frequently is a whole one) before a public dinner, you have no albums or scrapbooks to dog's-ear. There is no use in staring at your neighbours: the types of character are so similar—big and crimsoned sensuous faces looming over white waistcoats, with a plentiful sprinkling among them of the clerical element. You can't smoke, you can't (that is, I daren't) order sherry and bitters. If you look out of the window, you see nothing but chimney pots, leads, and skylights, with a stray vagrant cat outrunning the constable over them; and the best thing you can do is to bring an amusing duodecimo with you, or betake yourself to one of the settles, and twiddle your thumbs till dinner-time. But, joy, joy, here are quails in the conversational famine; here is a welling spring in the wilderness. The door opens, and the sonorous voice of the head-waiter announces THE CHAIRMAN.

Very probably he is a lord. A philanthropic peer, always ready and willing to do a kind turn for anybody, and to the fore with his chairmanship, his set speeches, and his fifty-pound note for "fatuous monomaniacs," "intellectual good-for-nothings," or "decayed bailiffs." He may be a regular dining-out lord, a not very rich nobleman, who has grown gray in taking the chair at charity dinners, and who is not expected to give anything to the institution save the powerful weight of his presence and influence. He may be a young lord, fresh caught, generously eager (as are, I am rejoiced to say, the majority of our young lords now-a-days) to vindicate the power and willingness for usefulness of his order; striving to show that there is not so much difference between his coronet and the Phrygian cap, save that one is made of velvet and the other of red worsted (ah! that irreconcileable red worsted), very impulsive, very imprudent, sometimes slightly imbecile, but full of good intentions and honest aspirations; or he may be a member of Parliament, a veteran of the back benches, burning to make up for his silence in the House by his eloquence in the forum of a tavern dinner. He may be a worthy banker or merchant, who gets through the speech-making before him in a business-like manner, and does not allow it in the least to interfere with the consumption of his proper quantum of wine; or he may be, as is very frequently the case, a lion—the "great gun"—the last blast of Fame's trumpet for the hour: a lawyer, a traveller, a philosopher, or an author, whom the managing committee have secured, just as the manager of a theatre would secure a dwarf, a giant, a wild beast tamer, a blind piper, or a sword swallower, to enhance the receipts of the exhibition.

About thirty of the fifty people I don't know from Adam gather immediately in a circle round the chairman. The few who have the honour to be on speaking terms with him jostle him sociably, and shake hands with him with a rueful expression of contentment. Those who don't know him rub their hands violently, breathe hard, stare fixedly at him, and whisper to one another that he is very like his portrait, or that he isn't at all like his portrait, or that he is getting old, or that he looks remarkably young, or some equally relevant banalities. The remaining twenty guests gather in the window-bays, and stare at nothing particular, or else read the printed prospectus of the Asylum for Fatuous Monomaniacs, and wonder how many of the fine list of stewards announced may be present on the occasion. As for the chairman, he takes up a position with his back safely glued (so it seems) to the mantelpiece, and preserves a dignified equanimity, working his head from side to side in his white neckcloth like that waxen effigy of Mr. Cobbett, late M.P. for Oldham, which terrifies country cousins by its vitality of appearance (those drab smallclothes and gaiters were a great stroke of genius) at Madame Tussaud's.

By this time a crowd of more people you don't know from Adam, and often outnumbering the fifty in the waiting-room, have gathered on the staircase, the landing, and have even invaded the precincts of the dining saloon, where they potter about the tables, peeping for the napkins which may contain the special cards bearing their name and denoting their place at the banquet. These are the people who *do* know one another; these are the stewards, patrons of the charity, or gentlemen connected with its administration. They are all in a very excellent temper, as men need be who are about to partake of a capital dinner and a skinful of wine, and they crack those special jokes, and tell those special funny stories, which you hear nowhere save at a public dinner. Then, at the door, you see a detachment of waiters, bearing fasces of long, blue staves, tipped with brass, which they distribute to sundry inoffensive gentlemen, whose real attributes are at once discovered, and who are patent to the dining-out world as Stewards. They take the staves, looking very much ashamed of them; and, bearing besides a quaint resemblance to undertakers out for a holiday, and in a procession, which would be solemn if it wasn't funny, precede the chairman to his place of honour.

The tables form three sides of an oblong quadrangle: sometimes the horse-shoe form is adopted. In the midst, in a line with the chairman, and as close to his august presence as is practicable, is a table of some ten or a dozen *couverts*, devoted to some modestly-attired gentlemen (some of them not in evening costume at all), whose particular places are all assigned to them; who for a wonder seem on most intimate terms mutually, and take wine frequently with one another; who are waited upon with the most sedulous attention, and have the very best on the table, both in the way of liquids and solids, at their disposal. They apply themselves to the consumption of these delicacies with great diligence and cheerfulness; but they do not seem *quite* sufficiently impressed with the commanding merits of the Royal Asylum for Fatuous Monomaniacs. I wonder what special business brings these gentlemen hither. At some distance from this table, towards the door, but still in a line with the chairman, you see a pianoforte, and a couple of music-stands; partially concealed behind a crimson baize screen, beneath the gallery at the end, sit some stalwart individuals, of martial appearance, and superbly attired in scarlet and gold lace, whom you might easily, at first, mistake for staff officers, but whom their brass trombones and ophicleides speedily proclaim to be members of the band of one of the regiments of Guards. And high above all, supported on the sham scagliola Corinthian columns, with the gilt capitals, is a trellised balcony, full of ladies in full evening dress. What on earth those dear creatures want at such gatherings,—what pleasure they can derive from the spectacle of their husbands and friends over-eating and sometimes over-drinking themselves, or from the audition of stupid speeches, passes my comprehension. There they are, however, giggling, fluttering, waving tiny pocket-handkerchiefs, and striving to mitigate the meaty miasma of the place by nasal applications to their bouquets or their essence bottles; and there they will be, I presume, till public dinners go out of fashion altogether.[7]

SIX O'CLOCK P.M.: A CHARITY DINNER.

I do not think I am called upon to give the bill of fare of a public dinner. I have no desire to edit the next republication of Ude, or Doctor Kitchener, Soyer, or Francatelli; besides, I could only make your and my mouth water by expatiating on the rich viands and wines which "mine host" (he is always mine host) of the Albion, the London Tavern, or the Freemasons', provides for a guinea a-head. You remember what I told you the friend with the face like an over-ripe fig said of public dinners—that they were the sublimation of superfluities; and, indeed, if such a repast be not one of those in which a man is called upon to eat Italian trout, Dutch dory, Glo'ster salmon, quails and madeira, Cherbourg pea-chicks, Russian artichokes, Macedonian jellies, Charlottes of a thousand fruits, Richelieu puddings, vanilla creams, Toulouse leverets, iced punch, hock, champagne, claret, moselle and burgundy, port, sherry, kirschwasser, and pale brandy, I don't know the meaning of the word superfluity at all.

Some three hours after the company have sate down to dinner; after the "usual loyal and constitutional toasts," with the usual musical honours; after the toast of the evening—"Prosperity to the Royal Asylum for Fatuous Monomaniacs"—with its accompanying (more or less) eloquent speech from the noble or distinguished chairman, beseeching liberal pecuniary support for so deserving an institution; after the prompt and generous response, in the way of cheques and guineas, from the guests; after a tedious programme of glees and ballads has been got through, and the chairman has discreetly vanished to his carriage; after the inveterate diners-out, who *will* tarry long at the wine, have received one or two gentle hints that coffee awaits their acceptance in an adjoining apartment; and about the time that the feast begins to wear a somewhat bleared and faded aspect (the lights cannot grow pale till they are turned off, for these are of the Gas Company's providing), the waiters slouch about with wooden trays, full of ruined dessert-plates, cracked nuts, muddy decanters, and half-emptied glasses; cherry stalks, strawberry stems, squeezed oranges, the expressed skins of grapes, litter the tables; chairs are standing at all sorts of eccentric angles; and crumpled and twisted napkins are thrown pell-mell about. There is an end to the fine feast: the cates are eaten, the wine drunk. Lazarus the beggar might have taken his rags out of pawn (had he indeed any such rags to mortgage), and his thin-limbed little brats might have grown plump and rosy on a tithe of the money that has been wasted this night in guttling and guzzling. Wasted? Oh! say not wasted, Cynic; take the mote from thine own eye. Grumbler, for shame! I have done ill, I think, to caricature the name even of any public charity. Let the "Fatuous Monomaniacs" be numbered with the rest of my exploded fantastic conceits. Let this rather be remembered: that the tavern feast of superfluities is prolific in generous and glorious results; that from this seemingly gross and sensual gathering spring charity, love, mercy, and benevolence. Pardon the rich dinners and rare wines; look over the excess in animal enjoyments; forgive even the prosy speeches; for *the plate has gone round*. To-morrow Lazarus shall rejoice in his rags, and blind Tobias shall lift up his hands for gratitude; the voice in Rama shall be hushed and Rachel shall weep no more; and all because these good gentlemen with the rosy faces and the white waistcoats have dined so well. For these dinners are for the benefit of the sick and the infirm, the lunatic and the imbecile, the widow and the orphan, the decayed artist and the reduced gentlewoman, the lame, the halt, the blind, the poor harlot and the penitent thief, and they shall have their part in these abundant loaves and fishes; and the sublimation of superfluities must be condoned for the sake of those *voluntary contributions* which are the noblest support of the noble charities in England. Remember the story of the Pot of Ointment. These superfluities yield a better surplus than though the spikenard was sold for an hundred-pence and given to the poor.

A very cream of waiters has taken good care of me during the evening. He now fetches me my walking gear, and as he pockets my modest "largesse," whispers confidentially that he has had the honour of "seeing me afore;" and, blushing, I remember that I have met him at private parties. It is well for me if I can slip downstairs quietly, hail a cab, and drive to one of the operas; for an act of the "Trovatore" or "Lucrezia Borgia" are, in my opinion, far better than Seltzer water in restoring the balance of one's mind after an arduous public dinner. But it oft-times happens that a man in your memorialist's position has to pass a *quart d'heure de Rabelais*, worse than paying the bill, after one of these festive meetings. For, in a roomy apartment downstairs, lighted by waxen tapers, such things as pens, ink, and paper, coffee, cognac, and cigars, are, by the forethought of the liberal proprietors of the establishment, laid out for the benefit of those merry gentlemen you saw upstairs at the small table in a line with the chairman, where they were so well taken care of; and if circumstances compel me to be in a merry mood to-night, I must hie me into this roomy chamber, and scribble a column or so of "copy" about the dinner, which will appear to-morrow morning in the "Meteor." Rubbing my eyes as I glance over the damp sheet between my own warm ones in bed, I wonder who ever could have written the report of all those elegant speeches. It seems at least a year since I dined with the "Fatuous Monomaniacs."

This is again six o'clock p.m., but not by any means on the same evening. The occasion could have no possible connection with going out to dinner, for it happens to be six o'clock "sharp:" and, moreover, it is on Friday, a day on which it is supposed to be as unlucky to go out to dinner as to go to sea, to marry, to put on a new coat, to commence a new novel, to cut your nails, or buy tripe. Now, what can I be doing in the city on this Friday evening?

Certainly not to perform any of the operations alluded to above. Scarcely on business. Bank, Exchange, wharfs, Custom-house, money-market, merchants' counting-houses, are all closed, and the inner city, the narrow winding lanes, that almost smell of money, are deserted. What am I doing so close to St. Paul's Cathedral, and why do I turn off by St. Martin's-le-Grand? For the simple reason, that Friday evening is the very best one in the seven to witness the spectacle I am going to see—Newspaper Fair at the General Post Office.

In the vast vestibule, or hall, of the establishment so admirably presided over by Mr. Rowland Hill (for I do not reckon the aristocratic placeman who is, turn and turn about, Whig or Tory, its nominal chief, for much), and whose fostering care has made it (with some slight occasional shortcomings) the best-managed and most efficient national institution in Europe, you may observe, in the left-hand corner from the peristyle, and opposite the secretary's office (tremendous "counts" are the clerks in the secretary's office, jaunty bureaucrats, who ride upon park hacks, and are "come for" by ringlets in broughams at closing time, but who get through their work in about half the time it would take the ordinary slaves of the desk, simply because their shrewdness and knowledge of the world enables them to "see through a case" before the average man of tape and quill can make up his mind to docket a letter) a huge longitudinal slit in the panelling above, on which is the inscription "For newspapers only." And all day long, newspapers only, stringed or labelled, are thrust into this incision; and the typographed lucubrations of the some five hundred men who, for salaries ranging from twenty shillings to twenty pounds per week, have to think, and sometimes almost feel, in the Anglo-Saxon tongue, for some sixty millions of people (I say nothing of the re-actionary influence upon foreign nations), go forth to the uttermost ends of the earth. But as six o'clock approaches (and six o'clock sharp is the irrevocable closing time for the departure of newspapers by the current night's mail), they open a tall window above, and the newspapers are no more thrust, but flung in.

SIX O'CLOCK P.M.: THE NEWSPAPER WINDOW AT THE GENERAL POST-OFFICE.

It is on this congenial ground that I meet those juvenile friends to whom I introduced a large circle of acquaintances, even in the second hour of "Twice Round the Clock"—I mean the newspaper boys. In another page I said, jestingly, that I was afraid of boys. I must except from the category the newspaper boys. I have been sadly harassed and teazed by them in their out-of-door or bagful state, when they go round to purchase newspapers: for I once happened to be editor of a cheap journal, at whose office there was no editor's room. I was compelled, occasionally, to read my proofs behind the counter, in the presence of the publisher and his assistant, and I have endured much mental pain and suffering from the somewhat too demonstrative *facetiæ* of the young gentlemen engaged in the "trade." Verbal satire of the most acutely personal nature was their ordinary mode of procedure; but, occasionally, when the publication (as sometimes happened) was late in its appearance, their playfulness was aggravated to the extent of casting an old shoe at me, and on one signal occasion a bag of flour. Still the newspaper boy is the twin-brother of the printer's devil; and, much as I have seen of those patient, willing little urchins, I should be a brute if I were hard to them, here.

The newspaper boys are, of course, in immense array at the six o'clock fair on Friday evening. They are varied, as currants are by sultanas in a dumpling, by newspaper men, who, where the boys struggle up to the window and drop in their load, boldly fling bags full, sacks full, of journals into the yawning casement. There is a legend that they once threw a boy into the window, newspapers and all. But at six o'clock everything is over—the window is closed—and newspaper fair is adjourned to the next Friday.

SEVEN O'CLOCK P.M.—A THEATRICAL GREEN-ROOM, AND "BEHIND THE SCENES."

Dear friends and readers, we are approaching the sere and yellow leaf of our peregrinations "round the clock." As the year wanes, as golden August points to the culminating glories of the year, but with oft-times a dark and impetuous storm presaging the evil days of winter that are to come, so I feel, hour after hour, that our (to me) pleasant intercommunications are destined to cease. You have been very forbearing with me, have suppressed a justifiable petulance at my short-comings, my digressions, my wayward fancies and prejudices, because you know (I hope and trust) that I am always your faithful servant and willing scribe, that (errors excepted, as the lawyers say) I have but one aim and end in these papers—to tell you the truth about London, its life and manners; to describe what I have seen, to tell you what I know; and to place before you, very timidly and under all correction, certain things which, in my opinion, it behoves you, and all who have a faith in the better part of humanity, to think about. Indeed, it is a very great privilege for a writer to be placed face to face with a hundred thousand critics every week, in lieu of half a hundred every half-year or so. He is flouted, and jeered, and scouted, and scolded, and remonstrated with, every time the penny post comes in; but he makes friends every week. He knows that his words are winged; he knows that he appeals to men who will understand his views, and to women who will sympathise with him; and though he may be as a pedlar, carrying about petty wares—ribbons, and tags, and small jewellery, and soap, and sweetstuff—he is vain enough to imagine that he can carry cheerfulness and content into many households; and that in speaking our common language of hopes and fears, likes and dislikes, he does not belie his cognomen of a "Welcome Guest." If he—if I—thought otherwise, I would tear this sheet, sell my reversion, buy an annuity of £20 a year, and join the convent of La Trappe, to wear a cowl, sing matins and complins, eat black radishes, and dig my own grave, to-morrow.

Seven o'clock post meridian has brought us at least the artificial abnegation of daylight, and has subjected us to the *régime* of gaslight. You had a twinkle of that unwholesome vapour, under the head of public dinners; but henceforth Sol will shine no longer on our labours. It is seven o'clock in the evening, and we are going to the play.

When I state that the subjects of this article are a Theatrical Green-Room, and "Behind the Scenes," I anticipate some amount of intellectual commotion among the younger, and especially the "fast" portion, of my readers. Jaunty young clerks, and incipient men about town, dwelling in decorous country boroughs, will be apt to fancy that I am about to launch into a deliriously exciting account of those charmed regions which lie beyond the stage-door; that my talk will be altogether of spangles, muslin, skirts, and pink tights. Nay, even my young lady readers may deceive themselves with the idea that I shall draw a glowing picture of the dangerous, delightful creatures who flutter every night before theatrical audiences, and of the dear, naughty, wicked, darling marquises, earls, and baronets who lounge behind the scenes. *Helas! il n'en est rien.* I know all about green-rooms, wings, and prompt-boxes. I have been in the artistes' *foyer* of the Grand Opera, in the flies of her Majesty's, and in the mezzanine floor of the Princess's. I am not about to be cynical, but I must be prosaic, and mean to tell you, in a matter-of-fact way, what the green-room and behind the scenes of a London theatre are like at seven o'clock.

It is strange, though, what a fascination these forbidden regions exercise over the uninitiated. I never knew any one yet who was actuated by an inordinate desire to visit the vestry-room of a church, or to see the cupboard where the rector and curate's surplices are suspended on pegs, or where the sacramental wine is kept. It is but seldom that I have seen anybody who evinced a particular curiosity to see a pawnbroker's ware-room, at the top of the spout, or to become acquainted with the arcana of a butcher's slaughter-house (though I must confess, myself, to having once, as a schoolboy, subscribed fourpence, in company with about ten others, to see a bullock killed)—yet everybody wants to go "behind the scenes." Some twenty months since, I had business to settle with a firm of solicitors, haughty, precise, distant, and sternly business-like, who dwelt in Bedford Row. I think that some one who was a client of the firm had a judgment against me, to which was witness one Frederick Pollock, at Westminster; but let that pass. I settled the matter, and thought myself well out of the firm and its clutches, when the penultimate junior partner, a middle-aged, respectable man, with a prematurely-bald head, asked me to dinner at Verrey's. He was good enough to allow me to order the repast, and politely deferred to my preference for *Macon vieux* over hot sherry; but, towards the cheese, he hinted that a man of the world, such as I seemed to be, ought never to be in difficulties (I have been hopelessly insolvent since the year '27, in which I was born), and that he would esteem it a very great favour if I would take him "behind the scenes" some night. Yes; this man of tape and quill, of green ferret and pounce, of sheepskins and abominable processes, positively wanted to see the Eleusinian mysteries of the interior of a London theatre. I showed them to him, and he is grateful still. I meet him occasionally at places of public resort. He is next to senior partner now, but he never hints at six-and-eightpence when I ask a legal question; and his most valuable act of friendship is this, that whenever the Sheriff of Middlesex is moved to run up and down in his bailiwick, with a special reference to my disparagement, I receive a mysterious message, generally conveyed by a battered individual, who wipes his face on the sleeve of his coat, and is not averse to taking "something short," that there is "something out" against me, and that I had better look sharp. Whereupon I look out as sharp as I can for the most convenient tenth milestone out of Babylon.

Now, friend and fellow-traveller of mine, do you mind transforming yourself for the nonce into the friendly solicitor, and coming with me "behind the scenes?" I know that with these continual metamorphoses I am making a very golden ass of Apuleius of you; but it is all, believe me, for your benefit. I don't want you to stand a dinner at Verrey's. I only want you to put on the slippers of patience and the spectacles of observation, and to follow me.

There is, the moralist hath said, a time for all things, and that much libelled institution, a theatre, has among its Bohemian faults of recklessness and improvidence, the somewhat rare virtue of punctuality. Even those events of its daily life which depend for the extent of their duration upon adventitious circumstances, are marked by a remarkably well-kept average. Theatrical rehearsals generally commence at ten o'clock in the morning; and though it will sometimes happen, in the case of new pieces about to be produced—especially pantomimes and *spectacles*, that the rehearsal is prolonged to within a few minutes of the rising of the curtain for the evening performance, the usual turning of an ordinary rehearsal's, or series of rehearsals' lane, is four o'clock p.m. Then the *répétitêur* in the orchestra shuts up his fiddle in its case, and goes home to his tea. Then the young ladies of the *corps de ballet*, who have been indulging in saltatory movements for the last few hours, lay aside their "practising dresses"—generally frocks of ordinary material, cut short in the manner immortalised by that notable pedlar, Mr. Stout, in his felonious transaction with the little old woman who fell asleep by the king's highway—and subside into the long-flounced garments of common life, which are to be again replaced so soon as seven o'clock comes, by the abridged muslin skirts and flesh-coloured continuations of ballet-girlhood. The principal actresses and actors betake themselves to dinner, or to a walk in the park, or give themselves a finishing touch of study in the parts they are not yet quite perfect in, or, it may be, mount the steep theatrical stairs to the mountainous regions where dwell the theatrical tailor and tailoress—I entreat them to excuse me, the *costumier* and the mistress of the robes—with whom they confer on the weighty subject of the dresses which they are to wear that evening. The carpenters abandon work; the scene-shifters, whose generic name in technical theatrical parlance is "labourers," moon about the back part of the stage, seeing that the stock of scenery for the evening is all provided, the grooves duly blackleaded and the traps greased, and all the "sinks" and "flies," ropes and pulleys, and other theatrical gear and tackle, in due working order. For, you see, if these little matters be not rigidly and minutely attended to, if a rope be out of its place or a screw not rightly home, such trifling accidents as mutilation and loss of life are not unlikely to happen.

That the occurrence of such casualties is of so extreme a rarity may be ascribed, I think, to the microscopic care and attention which these maligned theatrical people bestow on every inch of their domain behind the scenes. They have to work in semi-darkness, and under many other circumstances of equal disadvantage; but, next to a fire-engine station and the 'tween decks of a man-o'-war, I do not think that I can call to mind a more orderly, better-disciplined, better-tended place than that part of a theatre which lies behind the foot-lights.

Now, mouse-like, from undiscovered holes, patter softly mysterious females in tumbled mob-caps and battered bonnets, who, by the way, have been pottering stealthily with brooms and brushes about the pit and boxes in the morning, disappearing towards noon. They proceed to disencumber the front of the house of the winding-sheets of brown holland in which it has been swathed since last midnight. These are the "cleaners," and when they have made the house-clean and tidy for the audience of the evening, dusted the fauteuils, and swept the lobbies, they hie them behind the scenes, see that the proper provision of soap and towels exists in the dressing-rooms, perhaps lend a hand to the scene-shifters, who are completing *their* afternoon's labour by scientifically irrigating the stage with watering-pots; or, if a tragedy is to be performed, spreading the green baize extending to the foot-lights—that incomprehensible green baize—that field *vert* on which Paris dies combatant, and Hamlet lies rampant, and without whose presence it is considered by many dramatic sages no tragedy could possibly be enacted.[8] Meanwhile, the property-man has brought to the verge of the wings, or laid out in trays and hampers, ready to be conveyed below by his assistants, the necessary paraphernalia and appurtenances for the pieces in that night's bill. Shylock's knife and scales, Ophelia's coffin, Claude Melnott's easel and maulstick, Long Tom Coffin's mob-cap; the sham money, sham words, sham eatables and drinkables of this unreal and fantastic world, are all prepared. Presently the myrmidons of the wardrobe will take the required costumes from their frowning presses, and convey them to the dressing-rooms, ready for the histrionics who are to wear them. High up above all, above ceiling, and flies, and chandelier, in his lofty skylighted studio, the scene-painter throws down his "double-tie" brush, bids his colour-grinder clean his boots, indulges in a mighty wash, and dresses himself for the outward world. He improves marvellously by the change. But ten minutes since he was an almost indescribable scarecrow, in a tattered suit of canvas and list slippers, and bespattered from head to foot with dabs of colour. And now he turns out a trim gentleman, with a watch-chain, a moustache, an eye-glass, and kid gloves, and he walks off as gingerly to the artistic or literary club to which he may belong, as though he had never heard of size or whitewash in his life.

By five o'clock the little industries that have prevailed since the rehearsal ended are mostly completed; and the theatre becomes quite still. It is a complete, a solemn, almost an awful stillness. All the busy life and cheerful murmur of this human ant-hill are hushed. The rows of seats are as deserted as the degrees of some old ruined amphitheatre in Rome. The stage is a desert. The "flies" and "borders" loom overhead in cobweb indistinctness. Afar off the dusky, feeble chandelier, looks like a moon on which no sun condescends to shine; and were it not for one ray of golden afternoon sunlight, that from a topmost window shines obliquely through the vast dimness, and rescues the kettle-drums in the orchestra from tenebrose oblivion, you might fancy this place, which two hours hence will be brilliantly lighted up, full of gorgeous decorations and blithesome music, and a gay audience shouting applause to mimes and jesters and painted bayadères, chasing the golden hours with frolic feet—you might fancy the deserted theatre to be a Valley of Dry Bones.

Only two functionaries are ever watchful, and do not entertain the slightest thought, either of suspending their vigilance, or of leaving the theatre. At the entrance, in his crabbed little watch-box by the stage-door, the grim man in the fur cap, who acts as Cerberus to the establishment, sits among keys and letters for delivery. Of a multifarious nature is the correspondence at a stage-door. There are County Court summonses, seductive offers from rival managers to the popular tragedian of the day, pressing entreaties for orders, pink three-cornered notes scented and sealed with crests for the *première danseuse*, frequently accompanied by pinned-up *cornets* of tissue-paper containing choice bouquets from Covent Garden. There are five-act tragedies, and farces, written on official paper for the manager; solicitations for engagements, cards, bills, and applications for benefit tickets. But the grim man at the stage-door takes no heed of them, save to deliver them to their proper addresses. He takes no heed either (apparently) of the crowds of people, male and female, who pass and repass him by night and by day, from Monday till Saturday. But he knows them all well, be assured; knows them as well as Charon, knows them as well as Cerberus, knows them as well as the turnkey of the "lock" in a debtor's prison. Scene-shifter or popular tragedian, it is all one to him. He has but to obey his *consigne* to let no one pass his keyed and lettered den who is not connected with the theatre, or who has not the *entrée* behind the scenes by special managerial permission; and in adhering to that, he is as inflexible as Death. And while he guards the portal, Manager Doldrum sits in his easy-chair in his manuscript-littered private room upstairs. The rehearsal may be over, but still he has work to do.

He has always work to do. Perhaps he anticipates a thin house to-night, and is busy scribbling orders which his messenger will take care shall permeate through channels which shall do the house no harm. Or he may be glancing over a new farce which one of the accredited authors of the theatre has just sent in, and with black-lead pencil suggesting excisions, additions, or alterations. Or perhaps he tears his hair and gnashes his teeth in dignified privacy, thinking with despair upon the blank receipts of the foregone week, murmuring to himself, "Shall I close! shall I close?" as a badgered and belated Minister of State might ask himself, "Shall I resign?"

I wonder how many people there are who see the manager airing his white waistcoat in his especial stage-box, or envy him as he drives away from the theatre in his brougham, or joyfully takes his cheque on Ransom's for that last "stunning" and "screaming" new farce that forty pounds were given for, and that ran four nights; I wonder how many of these outsiders of the theatrical arcana know what a persecuted, hunted dog, a genteel galley-slave, a well-dressed Russian serf, is the theatrical manager. He may well be coarse and *brusque* in his manners, captious and pettish in conversation, remiss in answering letters, averse to parting with ready money for manuscripts which are often never acted, and more often never read. Do you know the life he leads? Mr. Pope's existence at Twickenham (or Twitnam), about the period when he instructed "good John," his man, to say that he was sick, or dead, was a combination of halcyon days compared to the life of a theatrical manager. Are there sons "destined their fathers' souls to cross," who "pen a stanza when they should engross?" are there men with harum-scarum lunatic projects, with tomfool notions that they are tragedians, with tragedies and farces, to estimate whose real value one should make a handsome deduction for the injury done to the paper on which they are written? are there madcap young ladies, newly-whipped at boarding-school, who fancy that they have the vocal powers of Grisi or Bosio, or the tragic acquirements of Ellen Tree or Helen Faucit (excuse the Kean and Martin marital prefixes: the old names are *so* pleasant)? are there mad mothers who vehemently insist that their skimping daughters can dance like Rosati or Pocchini? are there "guardians," in other words the proprietary slaveholders of dwarfs and contorsionists, precocious pianists, and female violoncellists? are there schemers, knaves, Yankee speculators, foreign farmers of singers with cracked voices, bores or insipid idlers—they all besiege the theatrical manager, supplicate, cajole, annoy, or threaten him. If he doesn't at once accede to their exorbitant terms, they forthwith abuse him scurrilously out of doors. He is a robber, an impostor, a miser, a Jew. He has been transported. He is insolvent. He came out ten years since in the provinces, and in light comedy, and failed. He beats his wife. He was the ruin of Miss Vanderplank, and sent men into the house to hiss and cry out "pickles" when Toobey the tragedian was performing his starring engagements, because, forsooth, Toobey did not draw. He owes ten thousand pounds to Miss Larke, the *soprano*. He buys his wardrobe in Petticoat Lane. He drinks fearfully. He will be hung. I have been an editor, and know the amenities that are showered on *those* slaves of the lamp; the people who accuse you of having set the Thames on fire, and murdered Eliza Grimwood, if you won't accept their interminable romances, and darkly insinuate that they will have your heart's blood if you decline to pay for poems copied from the annuals of eighteen hundred and thirty-six; but to find the acme of persecution and badgering commend me to a theatrical manager.

Return we to our muttons. The theatre sleeps a sound, tranquil sleep for some hundred minutes; but about six it begins to wake again to fresh life and activity. At half-past six it is wide awake and staring. The "dressers," male and female, have arrived, and are being objurgated by incensed performers in their several *cabinets de toilette*, because they are slow in finding Mr. Lamplugh's bagwig, or Mademoiselle Follejambe's white satin shoes. The call-boy—that diminutive, weazened specimen of humanity, who has never, so it seems, been a boy, and never will be a man—has entered upon his functions, and already meditates a savage onslaught on the dressing-room doors, accompanied by a shrill intimation that the overture is "on." Let us leave the ladies and gentlemen engaged in the theatre to complete the bedizenment of their apparel, and, pending their entrance into the green-room, see what that apartment itself is made of.

Of course it is on a level with the stage, and within a convenient distance of that prompt-box which forms the head-quarters of the call-boy, and where he receives instructions from his adjutant-general, the prompter. In country theatres, the green-room door is often within a foot or so from the wing; and there is a facetious story told of a whilom great tragedian, who, now retired and enjoying lettered and dignified ease as a country gentleman, was, in his day, somewhat remarkable for violent ebullitions of temper. He was playing Hamlet; and in the closet scene with Gertrude, where he kills the old chamberlain, who lies in ambuscade, and just at the moment he draws his rapier, it occurred to his heated imagination that an inoffensive light comedian, ready dressed for the part of Osric, who was standing at the green-room door within reasonable sword range, was the veritable Polonius himself. Whereupon the tragedian, shrieking out, "A rat! a rat! dead, for a ducat—dead!" made a furious lunge at the unhappy Osric, who only escaped instant death by a timely hop, skip, and jump, and fled with appalling yells to a sofa, under which he buried himself. Tradition says that the tragedian's rapier went right through the wood-work of the half-opened door; but I know that tradition is not always to be trusted, and I decline to endorse this particular one now.

Our present green-room is a sufficiently commodious apartment, spacious and lofty, and fitted up in a style of decoration in which the Louis Quinze contends with the Arabesque, and that again with the Cockney Corinthian. The walls are of a pale sea-green, of the famous Almack's pattern; and the floor is covered with a carpet of remarkably curious design and texture, offering some noteworthy specimens of worsted vegetation run to seed, and rents and fissures of extraordinary polygonal form. In one corner there is a pianoforte—a grand pianoforte; at least it may have been at one time deserving of that high-sounding appellation; but it is now a deplorable old music-box, with a long tail that would be much better between its legs, and keys that are yellow and worn down, like the teeth of an old horse. There is a cheval glass, too, in tolerably good repair, for the *danseuses* to arrange their skirts withal; and over the chimney-piece there is another great glass, with a tarnished frame and longitudinal crack extending over it, in the sides of which—the interstices of the frame, I mean, not the crack—are stuck notices having reference to the rehearsals to be held on the morrow. "All the ladies of the ballet at ten;" "All the company for reading of new piece at twelve." So may run the wafered announcements signed in the fine Roman hand of the prompter or stage-manager. There are varied pilasters, in imitation of scagliola, supporting the ceiling; the doors are handsomely panelled with gilt headings. There are four tall windows in a row, with cornices wofully dingy, and draped with curtains of shabby moreen. There is good store of settees and ottomans covered with faded chintz. Everything about the place bears that "stagey," unreal, garish, dream-like aspect, that seems inherent to things theatrical, and makes us, directly we pass the stage-door, look upon everything, from the delusive banquet on the imitation marble table, to the paint on the singing chambermaid's cheeks, as a mockery and a delusion—as the baseless fabric of a vision, that will soon fade and leave not a wrack behind. And yet I have said (*vide ante et supra*) that "behind the scenes is common-place." And so it is; but it is the common-place of dreamland, the every-day life of the realms of Prester John, the work-a-day existence of the kingdom of Cockaigne, or of that shadowy land where dwell the Anthropophagi, and men "whose heads do grow beneath their shoulders."

SEVEN O'CLOCK P.M.: A THEATRICAL GREEN-ROOM.

What shall I assume the first piece that is to be performed this night to be? Will you have the "Flowers of the Forest," the "Poor Strollers," "Sweethearts and Wives," "Pizarro," the "Padlock," or a "Game at Romps?" What do you say to a fine old English comedy, such as "John Bull," or the "School of Reform," with a dissipated young squire, a gouty, ill-tempered, and overbearing old lord of the manor, an intensely-virtuous tenant-farmer, a comic ploughman, a milkmaid with a chintz gown tucked through the placket-holes, and a song, and a spotless but a persecuted maiden? No; you will have none of these! Suppose, then, we take our dear old genial friend, the "Green Bushes"—long life and good luck to Mr. Buckstone, and may he write many more pieces as good for our imaginary theatre. See; the green-room clock points to ten minutes to seven—I left that out in my inventory of the furniture. The call-boy has already warned the ladies and gentlemen who are engaged for the first scene, that their immediate presence is required, and the erst-deserted green-room fills rapidly.

See, here they came—the kindly old friends of the "Green Bushes"—Miami and Jack Gong, and Master Grinnidge; and yet, dear me, what are these strange, wild costumes mingled with them? Oh! there is a burlesque after the drama. It is somewhat early in the evening for those who are to play in the second piece to come down dressed; but then you are to consider this as a special green-room, a specimen green-room, an amalgam of the green-room element generally. This model *foyer* is to have something of the Haymarket and something of the Adelphi—the old by-gone, defunct Adelphi, I mean—

a spice of the Olympic, a tinge of the Lyceum, and a dash of the Princess's, about it. I except the green-room of Drury Lane, which never resembled anything half so much as a family vault, and the green-rooms of the two Operas, which, though splendidly furnished and appointed, are almost deserted during the performances, the great *tenori* and *soprani* preferring to retire to their dressing-rooms when any long intervals of rest occur.

"Things"—to use a bit of "Green Bushes" *facetiæ*, invented, I am willing to believe, by that incorrigible humourist, Mr. Wright, and which has grown proverbial—"things isn't as they used to was;" and the attractions of green-rooms have deteriorated, even within my time. When I say "my time," I mean a quarter of a century; for as I happened to be almost born in a prompt-box and weaned in a scene-painter's size-kettle, and have been employed in very nearly every capacity in and about a theatre—save that of an actor, which profession invincible modesty and incurable incompetency prevented me from assuming—I feel myself qualified to speak about the green-rooms with some degree of authority. To have read a three-act melodrama to a (scarcely) admiring audience, and to have called "everybody for the last scene" in a green-room, gives a man, I take it, a right to be heard.

But, to tell the truth, green-rooms now-a-days are sadly dull, slow, humdrum places of resort. In a minor theatre they are somewhat more lively, as there is there no second green-room, and the young sylphides of the *corps de ballet* are allowed to join the company. The conversation of these young ladies, if not interesting, is amusing, and if not brilliant, is cheerful. They generally bring their needle-work with them if they have to wait long between the scenes (frequently to the extent of an entire act) in which they have to dance, and they discourse with much *naïveté* upon the warmth or coldness of the audience with reference to the applause bestowed, the bad temper of the stage-manager, and their own temporary indisposition from corns, which, with pickled salmon, unripe pears, the proper number of lengths for a silk dress, and the comparative merits of the whiskers and moustaches of the musicians in the band (with some of whose members they are sure to be in love, and whom they very frequently marry, leaving off dancing and having enormous families), form the almost invariable staple of a ballet-girl's conversation. Poor simple-minded, good-natured, hard-working little creatures, theirs is but a rude and stern lot. To cut capers and wear paint, to find one's own shoes and stockings, and be strictly virtuous, on a salary varying from nine to eighteen shillings a week—this is the pabulum of a ballet-girl. And hark in thine ear, my friend. If any man talks to you about the syrens of the ballet, the dangerous enchantresses and cockatrices of the ballet, the pets of the ballet, whose only thoughts are about broughams and diamond *aigrettes*, dinners at Richmond, and villas at St. John's Wood—if anybody tells you that the majority, or even a large proportion, of our English *danseuses* are inclined this perilous way, just inform him, with my compliments, that he is a dolt and a teller of untruths. I can't say much of ballet morality abroad; of the poor *rats de l'opera* in Paris, who are bred to wickedness from their very cradle upwards; of the Neapolitan *ballerine*, who are obliged to wear green *calzoni*, and to be civil to the priests, lest they should be put down altogether; or of the poor Russian ballet-girls, who live altogether in barracks, are conveyed to and from the theatre in omnibuses, and are birched if they do not behave themselves, and yet manage somehow to make a bad end of it; but as regards our own sylphides, I say that naughtiness among them is the exception, and cheerful, industrious, self-denying perseverance in a hard, ungrateful life, the honourable rule.

There are yet a few green-rooms where the genus "swell" still finds a rare admittance. See here a couple in full evening costume, talking to the pretty young lady in the low-necked dress on the settee; but the swell is quite a fish out of water in the green-room of these latter days. Managers don't care quite so much for his patronage, preferring to place their chief reliance and dependence on the public. The actors don't care about him, for the swell is not so generous as of yore in taking tickets for the benefits of popular favourites. Actresses mistrust him, for the swell has given up raising actresses to the peerage. The ballet-girls are half afraid of him; and when they don't fear him, they laugh at him. So the swell wanders in and out of the green-room, and stares at people uneasily, and at last escapes to his brougham or his cabriolet at the stage-door. Now and then a wicked old lord of the unrighteous evil-living school of British peers, now happily becoming rarer and rarer every day, will come sniggering and chuckling into a green-room, hanging on the arm of the manager, with whom he is on the most intimate terms, and who "My Lords" him most obsequiously. He rolls his scandalous old eyes in his disreputable, puckered face, seeking some pretty, timid, blushing little flower, whom he may blight with his Upas gaze, and then totters away to his stage-box, where he does duty for the rest of the evening with a huge double-barrelled opera-glass.

Such is the green-room of to-day, quiet, occasionally chatty (for actresses and actors can be pleasant enough among themselves, in a cosy, sensible manner, talking about butcher's meat, and poor's-rates, and Brompton omnibuses); but not by any means the glittering Temple of Radiant Delight that some might feel inclined to imagine it. There have been days—and I remember them—when green-rooms were very different places. There were women on the stage then who were Queens as well as actresses, and had trains of admirers round their flowing robes. There was a slight nervous man in those days—a famous writer of plays and books that yet live, and will live while our English language is spoken—a strange-looking, high-cheek-boned man, with long hair carelessly thrown away from his forehead, and a piercing eye, that seemed to laugh to scorn the *lorgnon* dangling from its ribbon. I have seen him so, his spare form leaning against the mantel, and he showering— yes, showering is the word—arrowy *bon mots* and corruscating repartees around him. He is dead: they all seem to be dead, those brilliant green-room men—Jerrold, Talfourd, Kenney, Haynes Bayley, Hook, A'Beckett. They have left no successors. The modern play-wrights skulk in and out of the manager's room, and are mistaken at rehearsal for the property-men. They forsake green-rooms at night for drawing-rooms, where they can hear themselves praised, or smoking-rooms of clubs, where they can abuse one another; and if A. says a good thing, B. books it for his next *petite comédie*, which does not hurt A. much, seeing that he stole it from C., who translated it hot-and-hot from Monsieur de D., that great plagiarist from Lope de Vega.

Come, let us leave the green-room to its simple devices, and see what they are doing "Behind the Scenes." You and I, we know, are in the receipt of fern-seed, and can walk invisible without incommoding ourself or anybody else, be the pressure ever so great; but I should strongly advise all swells and other intruders, if any such remain, either to withdraw into the shadiest recesses of the green-room, or to "get out of that"—to use an Irishism, without the least possible delay. For "Behind the Scenes" is clearly no place for them. If I were the manager of a theatre, I would not admit one single person into the *coulisses* save those connected with the night's performance, nay, nor allow even the *employés* of the theatre, till the call-boy summoned them to approach the wing. Madame Vestris established this Spartan rule of discipline, and found it answer in making her theatre the best-managed in Europe; but it will be observed that no such *ordre du jour* has been promulgated in the theatre behind whose scenes we find ourselves to-night. What a confusion, what a hubbub, what a throng and bustle! The *dramatis personæ*, you will perceive, no longer contemplate the performance of the "Green Bushes." Hoops, powder, brocade, black-patches, high-heeled shoes, bag-wigs, flapped waistcoats, and laced-hats prevail. This must be some Pompadour or Beau Tibbs piece—"Court Favour," or "Love's Telegraph," or some last century dramatic conceit by Mr. Planché or Mr. Dance. How the carpenters scuffle and stamp, entreating the bystanders, not always in the politest terms, to get out of the way! Now and again the prompter rushes from his box, and in a hoarse *sotto voce*, that would be a shriek if it were not a whisper, commands silence.

SEVEN O'CLOCK P.M.: BEHIND THE SCENES.

Upon my word, there is that unlucky old Flathers, the heavy man, who *never* knows his part; there he is again, evidently imperfect, and taking a last desperate gulp of study, sitting in the property arm-chair, on the very brink of the stage. And see there—don't blush, don't stammer, but make as polite a bow as you can—there is Mrs. Woffington Pegley, in full Pompadour costume, and such a hoop! She is only twenty-three years of age; has had two husbands; Count Schrechny-synesky, the Moldo-Wallachian ambassador, is reported to be madly in love with her; she rides in the park, she hunts, she drives, she owns a yacht, she has more diamonds and Mechlin lace than a duchess, and she is the most charming actress of the day. To be sure, she can't read very fluently, and can scarcely write her own name, but *que voulez vous?*

Don't you know that queer, quaint passage in good old Dr. Johnson's life, where, soon after the production of his tragedy of "Irene," and when the lexicographer had even gone to the extent of appearing behind the scenes of the playhouse in a scarlet coat and laced-hat fiercely cocked, he suddenly told David Garrick that he could visit him behind the scenes no more, assigning his own honest sufficient reason? The pretty actresses were too much for Samuel. He was but mortal man—mortal man. Their rosy cheeks—never mind whether the roses were artificial or not—their white necks, and dainty hands and feet, their rustling brocades and laced tuckers, disturbed the equanimity of our great moralist and scholar. He fled from the temptation wisely. Who can wonder at it? Who, that is not a misogynist, can sufficiently case himself in brass to withstand the Parthian glances of those pretty dangerous creatures? Surely they dress better, look better, walk better, sit better, stand better, have clearer voices, cheerier laughs, more graceful curtsies, than any other women in the world. But they are not for the likes of you or me, Thomas. See, there is fat, handsome Captain Fitzblazer of the "Heavies," the Duke of Alma's aide-de-camp, pretending to flirt with little Fanny Merrylegs, the *coryphée*, and the rogue has one eye on Mrs. Woffington Pegley. I wish some robust scene-shifter would tread on his varnished toes. The Pegley is aware of the Fitzblazerian *œillade*, I wager, though she makes-believe to be listening to young Martinmas, the walking gentleman's, nonsense. Come away, Thomas, come away, my friend. Let us strive to be as wise in our generation as Sam Johnson was in his, and write to Davy Garrick that we will come "behind the scenes" no more.

EIGHT O'CLOCK P.M.—HER MAJESTY'S THEATRE, AND A PAWNBROKER'S SHOP.

I think that I have held out something like a guarantee, in the course of these papers, that my readers shall be introduced to a fair amount of fashionable life. How far I have performed my promise it is for them to judge; but I am not, myself, without misgivings. True it is that, under my guidance, they have perambulated Regent Street; have dined off the fat of the land at a Public Dinner; have betted at Tattersall's; ridden in the Park; heard the band play at St. James's; strolled through the Pantheon Bazaar; and lounged in a theatrical green-room: but then, have not I, discourteous *cicerone*, cajoled them into visiting strange unlovely places, dismal to look upon; persuaded them to hang up their harps by the willows of the Custom-house quay, and listen to the slang of oyster-boatmen and bargees, at Billingsgate; forced them to haunt the purlieus of police-courts, and witness the departure of prison-vans and their felonious cargoes; to keep bad hours, and associate with newspaper boys, market-gardeners, paupers, and common people who travel by parliamentary train; to become acquainted, in fact, with scenes and people distressingly low and unfashionable? It is true that I have not taken them to the lanes of Petticoat and Field; to Duke, his Place; or St. Mary, her Axe; or Bevis, his Marks; or Rag, its Fair; or Whitechapel, its Butcher Row; or Ratcliff, its Highway; or Lock, his Fields; or Somers Town, its Brill; or Rats, their Castle; or Whetstone, its Park; or Jacob, his Island; or Southwark, its Mint; or Lambeth, its New Cut; or St. Giles, its Church Lane and Hampshire Hog Lane. If I have not moved them so to travel with me, it is not, I fear, through any *laches* of intention or deficiency of will, but simply because I have at different seasons travelled over every inch of the road I have named with other readers, and that I have a decent horror of repeating myself, and respect for the maxim of *non bis in idem*.

Be my demerits granted or disallowed, I have still some time left to me wherein to make amends. Though it may be my duty, ere we have finished, to lead you again into dismal and wretched places, you shall have at least an instalment of fashionable life now; and—follow honest Sancho's advice as to not looking the gift-horse in the mouth; be satisfied with my assurance that this present one is of the pure Godolphin Arabian lineage, elegant in form, unquestionable in mettle, electrical in swiftness. The next may be but a sorry nag, spavined, blown, wind-galled, and sprung. You must take the bad with the good, in this world, and in all things.

Ladies and gentlemen, we are going to the Opera—to her Majesty's Theatre in the Haymarket; and by eight o'clock it behoves us all to be in our seats, if we wish to hear the first bars of the overture. It is true that if we are so fortunate as to possess, or to hire, or to have opera-boxes given to us, we do not, frequently, make our appearance in the theatre till past nine o'clock; and that, if we are lessees or renters of stalls, the ballet has frequently commenced before we condescend to occupy our seats; but if the pit or the amphitheatre be our destination, we had much better present ourselves at the entrance immediately the doors open, and secure seats with what speed we may. It is a peculiarity of her Majesty's Theatre that whether the "house" be a good one or a bad one, there are always, before the termination of the first act of the opera, some occupants of the pit who are compelled to content themselves with standing-room.

Opinions are divided as to the place in the *enceinte* of the magnificent theatre where the greatest enjoyment of the performance can be obtained. To some, a box on the grand tier—vast, roomy, with space for six to sit abreast—is considered the superlative of operatic felicity. Others hold out stoutly for the artistic fourth tier, where, they declare, they can hear and see better than their lowly-placed neighbours. There are many who abide by the stalls, despite of those who declare that in the front rows thereof the voices of the singers are drowned by the contiguity of the braying band. The pit has its defenders, who allege that distance not only "lends enchantment to the view," but chastens the instrumental exuberances of the orchestra; but perhaps the most energetic advocates of the merits of their own particular seats are the dwellers in the high-up amphitheatre or gallery, who boldly declare that it is in that elevated position alone, that you can enjoy, in the full extent of their beauty, the gems of the opera, and that the sole place fit for the presence of the genuine amateur is the operatic paradise, ascent to which is permitted for the sum of three-and-sixpence or half-a-crown.

Be our election, however, the stalls. From those comfortable *fauteuils* let us explore the ample field—see what the open, what the covert yield; and, as we expatiate over this scene of Man, own that, though "a mighty maze," it is "not without a plan." For there is a plan of her Majesty's Theatre in the box-office.

Am I treading on any one's toes, disturbing any one's prejudices, predilections, or pre-formed opinions, in asseverating that the interior of Mr. Lumley's establishment offers, with one exception, the most magnificent *coup-d'-œil* of any Opera in Europe that I have seen? Mark the cunning qualification! I say, *that I have seen*; for they tell me that there is an Opera at Barcelona (which nutty sea-port I have never visited), a theatre surpassing in grandeur, and richness of decoration, all the lyric temples of the continent or of these isles; and so far as mere *size* is concerned, the palm must, I believe, be yielded to Parma, in which caseous Italian city there exists—yet unexplored by me—a huge tumble-down, ruinous, leaky, mildewed *salle*, which is as the Tower of Babel of Opera-houses the Great Bonassus of theatres. I speak of the houses which these weak eyes, in the course of many years' wandering, have surveyed, through powerful-lensed lorgnettes. Give me her Majesty's. Above the dreary Scala, with its naked tiers above tiers, its *sediti chuisi*, and the three reserved front rows of the pit, where the authorities were compelled to put the white-blanketed Austrian officers, lest they should come to blows (they often squabbled in the lobbies even) with the spiteful Milanese; the ghastly, dingy, ill-lighted Scala—(it is bigger by far than her Majesty's, though)—with its rabbit-hutch-like private boxes, whose doors are scrawled over with the penny plain and twopence coloured-like coats of arms of the effete and decadent Lombardian nobility. Above the boasted Grand Opera at Paris, tawdry, inconvenient, and chopped up into unreasonable sections. Above the Burg Theater, at Vienna; the Theatre de la Monnaie, at Brussels. Above, even, the superb little Opernhaus, at Berlin, which, though a gem in its way, is but as a diamond *aigrette* to the Koh-i-noor. Above the late Royal Italian Opera House, in Bow Street, Covent Garden, London, which was simply a big theatre, ill-built, and undecorated. For the solitary exception I have hinted at you must go north, very far north into Europe, and in the city of Moscow, in the empire of Holy Russia, you shall find an Italian Opera House unprecedented, I verily believe, for size, for splendour, for comfort, for elegance, and for taste. It was not my fortune to be present in Moscow on the occasion of the coronation *fêtes*, when the theatre I speak of was opened to the public preparatory to the regular winter season; but for a description of its glories I must refer those curious in operatic matters to my friend Mr. Henry Sutherland Edwards, who was resident many months in the city of the Kremlin, and whom I sincerely wish I could persuade to do, in better part, for Moscow the holy that which I have myself endeavoured, according to my lights, to do for St. Petersburg the mundane.

Look around you, in the vast arena of her Majesty's. Wonder and admire, for such a sight it is not permitted to you often to behold. Look around, and around again, the enormous horseshoe; look from base to summit, at this magnificent theatre, glorious with beauties and with riches. Here are gathered the mighty, and noble, and wealthy, the venerable and wise, the young and beauteous of the realm. The prime minister seeks at the opera a few hours' relaxation from the toils of office; the newly-married peeress there displays the dazzling diamonds custom now, for the first time, permits her to wear; the blushing maiden of seventeen, "just out"—that very day, perhaps, presented at Court—smiles and simpers in a shrine of gauze and artificial flowers. Mark yonder, that roomy box on the grand tier, which a quiet, plainly-dressed party has just entered. There is a matronly lady in black, with a few bugle ornaments in her *coiffure*. She ensconces herself in a corner, her back towards the audience, screens herself with a curtain, and then calmly proceeds to take a review of the front rows of the stalls, and the occupants of the proscenium boxes. It is not considered etiquette to take more than a cursory glimpse of the matronly lady in black through *your* opera-glass.

Presently there sits down by the matronly lady's side, a handsome, portly, middle-aged gentleman, in plain sober evening dress, and with a very high forehead—so high, indeed, that I don't think that the assumption that the middle-aged gentleman's head inclined to baldness would be unreasonable. In the opposite angle of the box sits a demure young lady—sometimes a couple of demure ones—who doesn't move much or speak much; and at the back of the *loge* are two gentlemen in white waistcoats, who never sit down, and, from the exquisitely uncomfortable expression of their countenances, would appear to be standing on one leg. Now, take the hat of your heart off, for your head, according to operatic sumptuary laws, must be already uncovered, and with your spirit salaam thrice three times, for the matronly lady is Victoria Queen of England, and the middle-aged gentleman, inclined to corpulence and baldness, is his Royal Highness the Prince Consort. The demure ones are maids of honour or ladies in waiting; and as for the white-waistcoated uncomfortables (seemingly) on one leg, one may be the tremendous Gold Stick himself, and the other—who shall say I—the ineffable Phipps, pride of chivalry and pearl of privy purses.

On the same tier, but nearer the stage, there is a narrow box, holding only two persons *de face*, at whose occupants you may gaze without any glaring dereliction of the proprieties. See, a lady who screens herself behind the amber satin drapery, even more completely than her Majesty, and by her side an elderly gentleman, with a large mouth, a very stiff white neckcloth, and a very severe aspect, and about whose tendency to baldness there cannot exist any doubt, inasmuch as his cranium is as bare and polished as a billiard-ball. It would be a pardonable guess to presume this individual to be a member of the College of Preceptors, or a proctor, fresh from Doctors' Commons; but if you eye him narrowly through the many-lensed lorgnette, you will perceive that he wears a little badge of parti-coloured ribands at his button-holes, and on some evenings you may even discern a brilliant star tacked on the left breast of his coat. Who is this distinguished bald one? I must not be personal with less distinguished people than royalty, and so I will content myself with calling him his Excellency. His Excellency dwells in an enormous mansion in Belgravia, where he gives grand parties. His own little cabinet is, I am told, decorated with charming-coloured lithographs, representing scenes Oriental and operatic; and, indeed, his Excellency has been throughout his long and ornamental life a consistent and liberal patron of Terpsichore. He never misses a new ballet night now. Occasionally, his Excellency has some business to transact with the Baron Fitzharris, Earl of Malmesbury; but the old fogies of the clubs, and the chronic alarmists of the newspapers, are haunted by the notion that his Excellency is perpetually weaving plots, and entangling British statesmen in the mazes of his dark diplomacy. For my part, I think that very often, when his Excellency is supposed to be busily occupied in concocting his Machiavelian plots, the good man is quietly at home snipping away the outlines of his favourite coloured lithographs, and pasting them in albums or on screens. You know what the Chancellor Oxenstiern said to his son anent the small amount of wisdom with which this world is governed; and I think as much might be said concerning diplomacy. But his Excellency has a terrible reputation for undermining, plotting, and counter-plotting, and is supposed to be, intellectually, a compound of the dark and crooked astuteness of Talleyrand, Metternich, ex-Inspector Field, and the late Joseph Ady.

I might tire you out, and exhaust a space already growing limited, by drawing portraits of the denizens of opera-boxes. Our glances at them must be, perforce, rapid, for I dare not linger. See, there (he comes late, does not seem to enjoy the music much, and stays but for an hour) seventy-three years worth of learning, of genius, of wit, of eloquence, and patriotism—that glorious edifice of humanity, of which the first stone was laid by a young north-country advocate, who was a friend of Jeffrey and Sydney Smith, and wrote stinging articles in the "Edinburgh Review." No man so famous as that whilom chancellor has her Majesty's Theatre reckoned among its audience, since the days when, in spotless white waistcoat, and creaseless cravat, with a silver buckle behind, the great duke was wont to make his bow at the court of Euterpe, not because, honest man, he cared much for operas, Italian or English, but because he considered it to be a matter of duty towards that aristocracy of which, though a premier duke, he was the prince, to show himself in their places of resort. He went everywhere, the brave old boy, to balls and concerts, to routs and banquets. In the house of feasting, when the goblets were wreathed with flowers, and the cymbals clashed, there was Duke Arthur, long after his gums were toothless, his eyes dim, his joints stiffened, and the drums of his ears muffled. And, next morning, at eight o'clock, you would still see him on duty, at early service, in St. James's Church, reading out the responses to the Psalms as though they were words of command.

EIGHT O'CLOCK P.M.: THE OPERA.

There, in her family box, is the still beautiful marchioness, with that crop of ringlets unequalled in luxuriance. There, in the stalls, is Captain Fitzblazer, the Duke of Alma's aide-de-camp, whom we met "behind the scenes" an hour since. "Jemmy" Fitzblazer—he is always known as "Jemmy," though there are not half-a-dozen men of his acquaintance who would presume thus familiarly to address him to his face—is getting very middle-aged and gray-headed now. He is not slim enough in the waist. Adonis is growing fat. Narcissus has the gout. Lesbia's sparrow is moulting. A sad reflection, but so runs the world.

I should be wilfully deceiving you, and unworthy the name I have been always striving to gain—that of a faithful chronicler—if I were to lead you to imagine that the brilliant theatre is full only of rank, fashion, wealth, and happiness. Are any of the terms I have used synonymous, I wonder. There are many aching hearts, doubtless, beneath all this jewellery and embroidery; many titled folks who are thinking of pawning their plate on the morrow, many dashing young scions of aristocracy, who, between the bars of the overture, are racking their brains as to how on earth they are to meet Mephibosheth's bill, and whether a passage through the Insolvent Court would not be, after all, the best way out of their difficulties. And in the great equality that dress-coats, bare shoulders, white neckcloths, and opera-cloaks make among men and women, how much dross and alloy might we not find among the gold and silver! In the very next box to the mother of the Gracchi, resplendent among her offspring, in her severe beauty, is poor pretty lost

Mrs. Demmymond, late Miss Vanderplank, of the Theatres Royal. The chaste Volumnia, who only comes to the opera once in the season, and always goes away before the commencement of the ballet, is elbowed in the crush-room by Miss Golightly, who has one of the best boxes that Mr. Sams can let, and who comes with a head of flaxen hair one night, and with raven black tresses the next. Captain Spavin, of the 3rd Jibbers, shudders when he finds his next-stall neighbour to be his long-suffering tailor; and Sir Hugh Hempenridge, baronet, is covered with confusion when he feels the hawk-glance of little Casay, the sheriff's officer (and none so bravely attired as he) darted full at him from Fops' Alley.

Fops' Alley! The word reminds me of bygone operatic days, and I sigh when, looking round the house, I remember how Time, the destroyer, has left a mark, too, upon these *cari luoghi*. It is true that many of those reminiscences may not be worth sighing for; but is there not always something melancholy in the fading away of old associations? Where is the Omnibus Box? The longitudinal den answering to the *Loge Infernale* at Paris, and the *Fosse aux Lions* at Madrid, yet has its customary locality over the orchestra, on the Queen's side of the proscenium; but where are its brilliant, witty, worthless occupants? But one, the gay young prince, who, if report says true, kicked, with his own royal foot, through the panels of the door of communication leading from the Omnibus Box to the stage, and for that night—the night of the famous Tamburini and Coletti disturbance—locked by special order of M. Laporte, has become a Respectable, holds high office, does his work well, and occupies himself far more with the subjects of soldiers' kit and barrack accommodation, than with squabbles between Tweedledum and Tweedledee. But where are the rest? Where the dashing spirits and impetuous madcaps of twenty years since? One is in a lunatic asylum, and another is paralytic, and a third is prowling about the gambling-places on the Rhine, and the last I saw of a fourth, was once, in 1852, descending the stairs of the Hotel des Bains, at Dieppe, when a companion, drawing me on one side as a broken, bowed, decrepit, sunken-eyed, gray-headed, prematurely-aged man passed us tottering on a stick, whispered to me, "See! there goes D'Orsay;" who died a fortnight afterwards.

A Liberal, I hope—a Democrat, if you will—on some not unimportant public topics, I cannot help a species of meek wailing Conservatism upon the decadence of some of our social institutions. This is the age of abolition—of doing away with and putting down. They have robbed our grenadiers of their worsted epaulettes. The beefeaters in the Tower have been deprived of those scarlet and embroidered tunics, that contrasted so quaintly with the pantaloons and highlows of everyday life, and thrust into buttoned-up coats and brass buttons. The barristers' wigs will go next, I suppose, and the cocked-hat of the parish beadle—his red plush shorts and buckled shoon are already departed. I have fears for the opera; I tremble for the days when there will be bonnets in the upper tiers and paletots in the pit. When I mind the opera first, it was a subaltern's, and not a sergeant's, guard that kept watch and ward under the portico. The officer on duty had a right of entrance *ex officio* into the pit, and it was splendid to see him swinging his bearskin and flashing his epaulettes in Fops' Alley. The very name of Fops' Alley is becoming obsolete now. The next generation will forget its locality. In those days, on drawing-room nights, the men used to come in their court suits and uniforms, their stars and badges, the ladies in their ostrich plumes and diamond necklaces, only taking off their trains. There were opera-hats in those days—half moon cocked-hats; now the men carry Gibuses like pancakes. The link boys are disappearing—the leather-lunged, silver-badged fellows, who shouted so sonorously that Lady Sardanapalias' carriage stopped the way. And the glories of the operatic stage; are not those inconstant singing birds fled now? Can all the Arditis in the world compensate for Costa, with his coat thrown back, and those immortal, tight-fitting white kid gloves? He was the first man who ever succeeded in parting his hair down the back; and now, he too is growing bald, and he has cajoled Grisi the mellifluous, and Mario the heroic, to pipe their nightingale notes among the coach-builders of Long Acre, and the fried-fish shopmen of Drury Lane. Of the glorious unequalled, unapproachable Four—Grisi, Rubini, Tamburini, and Lablache—who once electrified the world in the "Puritani," three are dead: the first is in Covent Garden provoking malevolent criticism. Where are the other Four, the Terpsichorean quartett, the immortals who danced the *pas de quatre*! Ah! Mademoiselle Piccolomini, you are very arch and pretty; ah! Mademoiselle Marie Taglioni, you are a *spirituelle* and graceful dancer; but you are not the giants and giantesses of the old Dead Days.

"You little people of the skies,

What are you when the sun shall rise!"

But the sun is set, and there is darkness, and I am afraid that I am prosing *in re* her Majesty's Theatre, as old playgoers will prose about Jack Bannister, sir, and Dowton, and Munden, and Fawcett.

There is lately come to town, at least within these latter years, an Italian gentleman by the name of Verdi, to whose brassy screeds, and tinkling cymbalics, it is expected that all *habitués* of the opera must listen, to the utter exclusion and oblivion of the old musical worthies who delighted the world with their immortal works before Signor Verdi was born. I have brought you to her Majesty's Theatre, and this is unfortunately a Verdi night. You may listen to him, but I won't. Thersites Theorbo, the editor of the "Spinet" (with which is incorporated that famous musical journal the "Jew's Harp"), may accuse me of being "perfunctory," or of being an ass—no one minds Thersites Theorbo, knowing him to be a good fellow, much bemused in Cavendish tobacco and counterpoint; but I will shut my eyes, and muse upon the bygone glories of the opera. The place is a mass of memories. Things and books, and scenes and men, and stories, come teeming on my brain as I sit in my stall, heedless of Signor Verdi and his musical machinations. From that shelf, well known to me, where nestle my dog's-eared Rabelais, my Montaigne, my annotated edition of Captain Grose's Dictionary of the Vulgar Tongue, my Shakspeare, and my beloved Jeremy Taylor, I take down garrulous old Pepys, and read—"Jan. 12, 1667. With my Lord Brouncker to his house, there to hear some Italian Musique, and here we met Tom Killigrew, Sir Robert Murray, and the Italian Signor Baptista, who had prepared a play for the Opera, which Sir T. Killigrew do intend to have up; and here he did sing one of the acts. He is himself the poet as well as the musician, and did sing the whole from the words without any musique prick'd, and played all along on a harpiscon most admirably, and the composition most excellent." And then I mind me of an advertisement in the "London Gazette," in 1692, setting forth how "the Italian lady that is lately come over, that is so famous for singing, will sing at the concerts at York Buildings during the season." The season! There was a "season" in William the Deliverer's time, then. So I call to mind Dick Steele's serio-comic announcement in the fourth number of the "Tattler," of how "Letters from the Haymarket inform us that on Saturday night last the opera of 'Pyrrhus and Demetrius' was performed with great applause." Then from the beginning of Italian opera in England, a grand trunk line extending to our days, I shunt off on to innumerable little branches and loop-lines. I see the Faustina and the Cuzzoni coming to blows—Sir Robert Walpole backing the first, his lady the second. I am, for the nonce, an ardent partisan of Mrs. Tofts. Then I have a vision of Mrs. Fox Lane, in a hoop of preternatural size, bidding General Crewe get out of her house, because he professed his ignorance as to whom Signora Mingotti was—the Mingotti who told Dr. Burney that she had "been frequently hissed by the English for having a toothache, a cold, or a fever, to which the good people of England will readily allow every human being to be liable except an actress or a singer." And then I bow down in awe before the radiant shadow of Farinelli, great and good, unmoved by misfortune, unspoilt by fame—Farinelli, whose dulcet notes cured a Spanish king of madness, who was thought worthy to receive the decorations of the orders of St. Jago and of Calatrava—Farinelli, of whom honest Will Hogarth could not help falling a little foul in the "Rake's Progress," but who was, nevertheless, as singularly modest and upright as he was unprecedentedly gifted in his art. Unprecedentedly! recall the word. I bow before a greater shadow, though of one who wrote, and sang not, save to his pretty wife.[9] I see a little boy, in a grave court suit, and his young locks curling like the tendrils of the vine, sitting before the harpsichord in the orchestra of the great theatre of Milan. It is the first night of a new opera, and the opera is his—this almost suckling. Upstairs, in a box near the chandelier, is the little man's father, sobbing, and smiling, and vowing candles to the Virgin, if his dear child's opera succeeds. And it does succeed, and all Milan is full of that small maestro's, that maestrino's fame, the next day. I see him again, years afterwards, grown to be a slight, vivacious little personage, in a scarlet pelisse and a cocked-hat. He is standing behind the scenes at the wing of the Imperial Theatre at Vienna, and it is again the first night of the performance of a new opera—his own. There is a singer in a Spanish costume, and who must be, I take it, a species of barber. When he sings a song, commencing "*Non più andrai farfallone amoroso*," the little man in the scarlet pelisse and cocked-hat begins to beat his palms together in applause, and murmurs "*Bravo! Bravo!* Benucci!" But when the singer winds up in that magnificent exercitation to Cherubino, "*Alla vittoria! Alla gloria militar!*" the house comes down with applause. The people shout out; the fat-headed musicians in the orchestra beat their violin bows violently against their desks, and (quite in defiance of operatic discipline) cry "*Bravo! Bravo! Viva! viva! grande maestro!*" I see the same little man lying sick and pining on his bed at Salzburg. The intrigues of Salieri, the ingratitude of courts, the quick forgetfulness of the public, are nothing to him now. Little does it matter if he have been indeed poisoned with *aqua tofana*, or if he be dying of that common, but denied disease, a broken heart. *He has written the Requiem* (recreant Sussmayer will strive to rob him even of *that* fame after death), and his last hour is approaching. The poor Swan dies; and then the sluice-gates of my eyes are opened, and I remember that this was Johann Wolfgang von Mozart.

Upon my word and honour there is Van Poggi, the chorus-singer, on the stage. I am recalled at once from dreamland to actualities. There is an old operatic saying that her Majesty's Theatre, in the Haymarket, could not be complete without Van Poggi, and now behold that lyrical Widdicomb. According to the same tradition—not always trustworthy—Van Poggi was the identical chorus-singer who assisted Velluti to alight from his barge the night the last of those male *soprani* made his first appearance (in the opera of the "Crociato in Egitto") before an audience who had almost forgotten the fame of the Pacchierottis, the Rubinellis, and the Marchesis. Van Poggi wears wonderfully well. Nobody knows his exact nationality: whether he is a Dutchman, a Dane, or an Italian. His residence has never been precisely ascertained. The management have no occasion to rout him up, for he is always punctual at rehearsal. During the vacation he retires to Paris, where he tells his friends that he is to be found between ten and four every day in the Long Gallery of the Louvre. During the London season you may contemplate Van Poggi between the same hours in Mr. Zerubbabel's cigar-shop in the Quadrant, at whose door he generally stands in a Spanish cloak faced with velvet. He never sang any better or any worse than he sings now; he was never promoted to play the smallest separate part, such as is from time to time assigned to the gentleman who appears in the bills as Signor N. N., or *non nominato*. It is believed that Van Poggi would faint if he had to deliver a line of recitative. Yet there is a very general opinion in operatic circles that her Majesty's Theatre would come to hopeless grief if Van Poggi were not among the chorus. At the commencement of the season there are always anxious inquiries at the box-office as to whether Van Poggi is secured; and a reply being given in the affirmative, the lovers of the lyrical drama breathe freely, and the subscription progresses. No one knows what became of Van Poggi in the dark and dismal interregnum during which Mr. Lumley was compelled to close his doors. Mysterious offers of better parts, and better salaries, had, it is reported, been made to Van Poggi, emanating from a quarter not a hundred miles from Bow Street, Covent Garden; but the patriotic chorister scornfully refused them. He was still seen to haunt Mr. Zerubbabel's cigar-shop at the commencement of the musical season; then he suddenly disappeared; and whether he went abroad, or wrapped himself in the Spanish cloak and so lay torpid for two years like a dormouse, must for ever remain a matter for speculation. But it is certain that when the Haymarket Phœnix arose from its ashes, and light once more shone on its amber satin curtains, there was Van Poggi, at the first chorus rehearsal, as fresh as paint, and looking better than ever. And it is moreover reported, that when his Excellency, whom a combination of political difficulties (which began about the time some English grenadiers were sent out to Gallipoli) had forced to leave this country, and who did not return for upwards of three years, when his Excellency Baron —— made his first visit to his beloved opera-house, the piece of the evening being "Lucia di Lammermoor," he swept the ranks of those preposterous sham Highlanders, who are discovered singing a sham hunting chorus, anxiously with his lorgnette, and at last cried out with a satisfied accent: "*Bon, voilà* Van Poggi." He had recognised that chorus-singer in his kilt, and was thenceforth persuaded that the opera season was safe.

There is a new ballet to-night, in which the enchanting little Pocchini, most modest and most graceful of modern *danseuses*, is to appear; and Signor Verdi's opera is very long, and I am aweary of his figments, and cannot sit them out. Besides, I want your presence, trusty friend and companion, always in the interest of "Twice Round the Clock." We have a little business to transact; and as it is getting towards nine o'clock, we had better transact it at once. Leave we then the dazzling temple, let us hie to an obscure retreat, to your servant known, where we can leave our opera-glasses, divest ourselves of our white cravats, and throw paletots over our evening dress. There, a few touches, and the similitude of swells is taken away from us. Now let us plunge into a labyrinth of narrow streets to attain our unfashionable goal, for, upon my word, our destination is a pawnbroker's shop.

EIGHT O'CLOCK P.M.: INTERIOR OF A PAWNBROKER'S SHOP.

Where the long lane from St. Giles's to the Strand divides the many-branching slums; where flares the gas over coarse scraps of meat in cheap butchers' shops; where brokers pile up motley heaps of second-hand wares—from fishing-rods and bird-cages to flat-irons and blankets; from cornet-à-pistons and "Family Encyclopædias" to corkscrews and fowling-pieces; where linen-drapers are invaded by poorly-clad women and girls, demanding penn'orths of needles, ha'porths of buttons, and farthingworths of thread; where jean stays flap against the door jambs, and "men's stout hose" gleam gaunt in the shop-windows; where grimy dames sit in coal and potato-sheds, and Jew clothesmen wrestle for the custom of passengers who don't want to buy anything; where little dens, reeking with the odours of fried fish, sausages, and baked potatoes, or steaming with reminders of à-la-mode beef and hot eel soup, offer suppers, cheap and nasty, to the poor in pocket; where, in low coffee-shops, newspapers a fortnight old, with coffee-cup rings on them, suggest an intellectual pabulum, combined with bodily refreshment; where gaping public-houses receive or disgorge their crowds of tattered topers; where "general shops" are packed to overflowing with heterogeneous odds and ends—soap, candles, Bath brick, tobacco, Dutch cheese, red herrings, firewood, black lead, streaky bacon, brown sugar, birch brooms, lucifer matches, tops, marbles, hoops, brandy balls, packets of cocoa, steel pens, cheap periodicals, Everton toffy, and penny canes; where on each side, peeping down each narrow thoroughfare, you see a repetition only of these scenes of poverty and misery; where you have to elbow and jostle your way through a teeming, ragged, ill-favoured, shrieking, fighting population—by oyster-stalls and costermongers' barrows—by orange-women and organ-grinders—by flower-girls and match-sellers—by hulking labourers and brandy-faced viragos, squabbling at tavern doors—by innumerable children in every phase of weazened, hungry, semi-nakedness, who pullulate at every corner, and seem cast up on the pavement like pebbles on the sea-shore. Here, at last, we find the hostelry of the three golden balls, where the capitalist, whom men familiarly term "my uncle," lends money on the security of plate, jewellery, linen, wearing apparel, furniture, bedding, books—upon everything, in fact, that is not in itself of so perishable a nature as to warrant the probability of its rotting upon my uncle's shelves.

The pawnbroker's shop window—the *étalage*, as our Parisian neighbours would term it—presents a medley of merchandise for sale; for I suppose the host of the three balls buys-in sundry articles at the quarterly sales of unredeemed pledges, of whose aspect you have already had an inkling in these pages, which he thinks are likely to sell in his particular neighbourhood. Of course, the nature and quality of the articles exhibited vary according to the locality. In fashionable districts (for even Fashion cannot dispense with its pawnbrokers) you may see enamels and miniatures, copies of the Italian masters, porcelain vases, bronze statuettes, buhl clocks, diamond rings, bracelets, watches, cashmere shawls, elegantly-bound books, and cases of mathematical instruments; but we are now in an emphatically low neighbourhood, and such articles as I have alluded to are likely to attract but few purchasers. Rather would there seem a chance of a ready sale for the bundles of shirts, and women's gear, and cheap printed shawls; for the saws, and planes, adzes, gimlets, and chisels; for the cotton umbrellas; for the heavy silver watches that working men wear (though they, even, are not plentiful); for the infinity of small cheap wares, for sale at an alarming reduction of prices.

Let us enter. Behold the Bezesteen of borrowed money. This, too, might be compared, with a grim mockery, to the theatre; for hath it not private boxes and a capacious stage, on which is continually being performed the drama of the "Rent Day," and the tragi-comedy of "Lend me Five Shillings?"

See the pawners, so numerous that the boxes can no longer remain private, and two or three parties, total strangers to one another, are all crowded into the same aperture. It is Saturday night, and they are deliriously anxious to redeem their poor little remnants of wearing apparel for that blessed Sunday that comes to-morrow, to be followed, however, by a Black Monday, when father's coat, and Polly's merino frock, nay the extra petticoat, nay the Lilliputian boots of the toddling child, will have to be pawned again. Certain wise men, political economists and pseudo-philanthropists, point at the plethora of pawnbrokers' shops as melancholy proofs of the poor's improvidence. But the poor are *so* poor, they have at the best of times so very little money, that pawning with them is an absolute necessity; and the pawnbroker's shop, that equitable mortgage on a small scale, is to them rather a blessing than a curse. Without that fourpence on the flat-iron, there would be very frequently no bread in the cupboard.

It is Saturday night, and my uncle, who on other days of the week shuts at six o'clock in winter and eight in summer time, does not close his doors, and drives a roaring trade till midnight. The half-pence rattle, shillings are tested, huge bundles rumble down the spout, and the little black calico bags, containing the tickets having reference to the goods desired to be redeemed, and which the assistant will look out in the warehouse, fly rapidly upwards. It is time now for us to redeem that trifling little matter which we pawned last Tuesday, on purpose to have an excuse for visiting the pawnbroker's shop to-night; and, casting glances in which curiosity is not unmixed with compassion, go back to Signor Verdi and her Majesty's Theatre. Thou, at least, my friend, may do this—I will leave thee in the vestibule for awhile; for, between the hours of nine and ten, I have other clock matters to which I must attend.

NINE O'CLOCK P.M.—HALF-PRICE IN THE NEW CUT, AND A DANCING ACADEMY.

An inedited anecdote of Samuel Johnson, LL.D.,—an anecdote passed over or ignored by Boswell, Croker, Piozzi, and Hawkins,—an anecdote to allude to which, perhaps, Lord Macaulay might disdain, while Mr. Carlyle might stigmatise it as an "unutterable sham of mud-volcano gigability," but in which I have, nevertheless, under correction, the most implicit faith, relates that the Sage's opinion was once asked by Oliver Goldsmith (Mr. Boswell of Auchinlech being present, of course) as to whether he approved, or did not approve, of the theatrical institution known as "half-price?" The Doctor was against it. "Sir," he reasoned, or rather decided, "a man has no right to see half an entertainment. He should either enjoy all or none." "But, sir," objected Goldsmith deferentially, "supposing the entertainment to be divided into equal halves, both complete in themselves, has not a man a right to suit his pocket and his convenience, and see only one half?" "Sir, you are frivolous," thundered the Doctor; "the man has but Hobson's choice: the second moiety of the entertainment. If he go at first price, he must pay whole price." "But, sir," suggested Bozzy with a simper, "how would it stand, if the man coming at half-price promised the doorkeeper to go away punctually at nine o'clock, when the second price commenced?" "Hold *your* tongue, sir," said Doctor Johnson, whereat Mr. Boswell of Auchinlech was abashed, and spake no more till the kindly old Doctor invited him to tea, with blind Miss Williams and Mr. Levett the apothecary.

I am sure that it must be a matter of lamentation for any man with a well-regulated mind to be under the necessity of disagreeing with so eminent an authority as Doctor Johnson—with the rough, genial, old bear, who had had so many sorrows of his own when young; had danced upon so many hot plates, and to the very ungenteelest of tunes; had been so pitilessly muzzled and baited by mangy curs, that he yet made it his delight in age and comparative affluence to take the young bears under his protection, to assuage their ursine sorrows, and lick them with a lumbering pity into shape. I am equally certain that few would even *dare* to differ from the scholar, critic, poet, dramatist, essayist, moralist, philosopher, and Christian gentleman, whose pure life and death in an unbelieving age are an answer for all time to the ephemeral brilliance of the fribble Chesterfield, the icicle Hume, the stalactite Gibbon, and the flashy Bristol-diamond Voltaire. Still, in the interests of the British drama (and assuming my anecdote to be otherwise than apocryphal), I must, perforce, dissent from the Doctor, and pin my faith to half-price. The absence of a second price is suitable enough for such exotic exhibitions as the Italian operas and the French plays; but I deplored the suspension of that dramatic *habeas corpus* in the palmy Lyceum days of

Madame Vestris's management. There is something supercilious, pragmatical, maccaronyish, un-English, in the announcement, "No half-price." How immeasurably superior is the fine old British placard, now, alas! so seldom seen, "Pit full: standing-room only in the upper boxes!"

There is a transpontine theatre, situated laterally towards the Waterloo Road, and having a northern front towards an anomalous thoroughfare that runs from Lambeth to Blackfriars, for which I have had, during a long period of years, a great esteem and admiration. This is the Royal Victoria Theatre. To the neophyte in London I frequently point out a brick erection, above the cornice of the pediment, and say, "My friend, in the days when the 'Vic.' (it is popularly termed the 'Vic.') was known as the 'Coburg,' that brick slip was built to contain at its rise—for it could not be rolled up—the famous 'Crystal curtain,' which ruined one management to construct, and half ruined another to demolish. The grand melodramas the Coburg used to give us—real horses, real armour, real blood, almost real water!" Those were the days of "Ginevra the Impaled One" and "Manfroni the One-handed Monk." There are famous dramatists, actors, scene-painters, who would look rather shame-faced (though I cannot see why they should be ashamed) were they reminded, now, of their achievements in the service of transpontine melodrama at the Coburg. How stupidly absurd people are in repudiating their beginnings! Buffel, the millionaire contractor, denies stoutly that he ever carried a hod, although hundreds of us remember him on the ladder. Linning, the fashionable tailor, would poison any one who told him he once kept a beer-shop in Lambeth Walk, and afterwards failed as a tea-dealer in Shoreditch. One of the most accomplished comedians of the day makes a point of cutting me dead, because I can recollect the time, and knew him, when he used to colour prints for a livelihood; and I daresay that Baron Rothschild—with all the philosophy his unbounded wealth should properly give him—would not ask me to dinner, if I reminded him that his grandfather was a pedlar in the Juden-Grasse, at Frankfort. The next Tamworth baronet, I suppose, will strike the beehive and "*Industriâ*" out of the family escutcheon, and assume the three leeches sable on a field gules *semée* or, of his ancestors the De la Pills, who came over with the Conqueror as barber-chirurgeons to the ducal body. And yet a certain Emperor and King was not ashamed to talk of the period when he was a "lieutenant in the Regiment of Lafère;" and the present writer, who is, on one side (the wrong), of the *sangre azul* of Spain, is not above confessing the existence of a tradition in his family, hinting that his maternal grandmother danced on the tight rope.

Although I am a devotee of the opera, and am always glad when Drury Lane doors are open, and mourn over the decadence of the Lyceum, and wish that the Strand would succeed,[10] and longed for the day when the resuscitated Adelphi should open its doors, and rejoice at the prosperity of the Olympic, and think that one of the most rational and delightful night's amusements in Europe, may be attained by the sight of the "Merchant of Venice" at the now closed (so far as Charles Kean is concerned) Princess's, I have yet a tenderness, a predilection, an almost preference, for the Vic. There is a sturdy honesty of purpose, unity of action, sledge-hammer morality about the rubbishing melodramas, which are nightly yelled and ranted through on the Victoria stage, that are productive, I believe, of an intellectual tone, highly healthful and beneficial. Burkins, the garotter, who is now in hold in Pentonville for his sins, and is so promising a pupil of the chaplain, (having nearly learnt the Gunpowder Plot service and the prohibitions of consanguinity by heart,) has confidentially informed his reverend instructor that to the melodramas at the Victoria must be ascribed his ruin. It was the "Lonely Man of the Ocean" that led him to fall on Mr. Jabez Cheddar, cheesemonger, in Westminster Broadway, at two o'clock in the morning, split his skull open with a life-preserver, jump upon him, and rob him of eight pounds twelve, a silver hunting-watch, and a brass tobacco-box; at which confession the chaplain orders him more beef and books, and puts him down in the front rank for his next recommendatory report to the visiting magistrates. Partaking, in company with some other persons, of the opinion that Burkins adds to the characteristics of a ruffian and a blockhead, those of a hypocrite and a Liar, I do not necessarily set much store by the expression of *his* opinions on the British drama. But when I find shrewd police-inspectors and astute stipendiary magistrates moralising over the dreadful effects of cheap theatres, attended as they are by the "youth of both sexes," I deem them foemen worthy of my steel. Good Mr. Inspector, worthy Master Justice, where are the youth and the adults of both sexes to go in quest of that amusement, which I suppose you will concede to them, of some nature, the necessity? Are the churches open on week nights, and to such as they? and would you yourselves like to sit under Doctor Cumming, or even Mr. Spurgeon, from Saturday to Saturday? Are they to go to the Opera, to Almack's, to the Carlton Club, or to the conversaziones of the Geological Society? You object, you say, to the nature of the entertainments provided for them. Come with me, and sit on the coarse deal benches in the coarsely and tawdrily-decorated cheap theatre, and listen to the sorrily-dressed actors and actresses—periwigged-pated fellows and slatternly wenches, if you like—tearing their passion to tatters, mouthing and ranting, and splitting the ears of the groundlings. But in what description of pieces? In dramas, I declare and maintain, in which, for all the jargon, silliness, and buffoonery, the immutable principles of right and justice are asserted; in which virtue, in the end, is always triumphant, and vice is punished; in which cowardice and falsehood are hissed, and bravery and integrity vehemently applauded; in which, were we to sift away the bad grammar, and the extravagant action, we should find the dictates of the purest and highest morality. These poor people can't help misplacing their h's, and fighting combats of six with tin broadswords. They haven't been to the university of Cambridge; they can't compete for the middle-class examinations; they don't subscribe to the "Saturday Review;" they have never taken dancing lessons from Madame Michau; they have never read Lord Chesterfield's Letters; they can't even afford to purchase a "Shilling Handbook of Etiquette." Which is best? That they should gamble in low coffee-shops, break each other's heads with pewter pots in public-houses, fight and wrangle at street corners, or lie in wait in doorways and blind alleys to rob and murder, or that they should pay their threepence for admission into the gallery of the "Vic."—witness the triumph of a single British sailor over twelve armed ruffians, who are about to carry off the Lady Maud to outrage worse than death; see the discomfiture of the dissolute young nobleman, and the restitution of the family estates (through the timely intervention of a ghost in a table-cloth) to the oppressed orphan? And of this nature are the vast mass of transpontine melodramas. The very "blood-and-murder" pieces, as they are termed, always end with the detection of the assassin and his condign punishment. George Cruikshank's admirable moral story of "The Bottle" was dramatised at the "Vic.," and had an immense run. They are performing "Never Too Late to Mend," now, over the water, to crowded houses. If we want genteel improprieties, sparkling immoral repartees, decorously scandalous intrigues, and artful cobwebs of *double entendre*, touching on the seventh commandment, we must cross the bridges and visit the high-priced, fashionably-attended theatres of the West-end. At a West-end theatre, was produced the only immoral version of an immoral (and imbecile) "Jack Sheppard," which is, even now, vauntingly announced as being the "authorised version"—the only one licensed by the Lord Chamberlain; and in that "authorised version" occurs the line, "Jack Sheppard is a thief, but he never told a lie," a declaration than which the worst dictum of howling Tom Paine or rabid Mary Wolstoncraft was not more subversive of the balance of moral ethics. And, at a West-end theatre, likewise, his Lordship the Chamberlain authorised the production of a play, whose story, regarded either as a melodrama or as the libretto of a trashy Italian opera, has not been equalled for systematic immorality: no, not by Wilkes; no, not by Aphra Behn: no, not by Crebillon the younger: no, not by Voltaire in the scandalous "Pucelle."

And have I brought you all the way over Waterloo Bridge in the evening only to sermonise you! I deserve to be mulcted in three times the halfpenny toll; and I must make amends by saying nothing whatsoever about the shot towers, or the Lion Brewery, the London and South-Western Terminus, and Hawkstone Hall. Here we are, at the corner of the New Cut. It is Nine o'Clock precisely (I must have flown rather than walked from the pawnbroker's in that lane on the Middlesex side), and while the half-price is pouring into the Victoria Theatre, the whole-price (there is no half-price to the gallery, mind, the charge for the evening's entertainment being only threepence) is pouring out with equal and continuous persistence, and are deluging the New Cut. Whither, you may ask, are they bound? They are in quest of their Beer.

The English have been a beer-loving people for very many ages. It gives them their masculine, sturdy, truculent character. Beer and beef, it has been before remarked, make boys. Beer and beef won the battle of Waterloo. Beer and beef have built railways all over the world. Our troops in the Crimea languished, even on beef (it was but hard corned junk, to be sure) till the authorities sent them beer. There is a *lex non scripta* among the labouring English, much more potent than many Acts of Parliament, and called the "Strong Beer Act." They have songs about beer with lusty "nipperkin, pipperkin, and the brown beer" choruses; and in village parlours you may hear stentorian baritones, of agricultural extraction, shouting out that "Feayther likes his beer, he does;" that "Sarah's passionately fond of her beer, she is;" and denouncing awful vengeance upon those enemies of the people who would "rob a poor man of his beer." Our fingers were brought to the very hair-trigger of a revolution by the attempted interference of an otherwise well-meaning nobleman, with the people's beer; and did not William Hogarth strike the right nail on the head when he drew those two terrible pictures of Beer Street and Gin Lane? The authorities of the Victoria Theatre have preserved, I am glad to say, a wholesome reverence for the provisions of the Strong Beer Act, and it is, I believe, a clause in the Magna Charta of the management, that the performances on Saturday evenings shall invariably terminate within a few minutes of midnight, in order to afford the audience due and sufficient time to pour out their final libations at the shrine of Beer, before the law compels the licensed victuallers to close.

There are not many gradations of rank among the frequenters of the Victoria Theatre. Many of the occupants of the boxes sat last night in the pit, and will sit to-morrow in the gallery, according to the fluctuation of their finances; nay, spirited denizens of the New Cut will not unfrequently, say on a Monday evening, when the week's wages have not been irremediably dipped into, pay their half-crown like men, and occupy seats in the private box next the stage. And the same equality and fraternity are manifest when the audience pour forth at half-price to take their beer. There may be a few cheap dandies, indeed—Cornwall Road exquisites and Elephant-and-Castle bucks—who prefer to do the "grand" in the saloon attached to the theatre; there may be some dozens of couples sweethearting, who are content to consume oranges, ginger beer, and Abernethy biscuits within the walls of the house; but the great pressure is outwards, and the great gulf stream of this human ocean flows towards a gigantic "public" opposite the Victoria, and which continually drives a roaring trade.

I wish that I had a more savoury locality to take you to than the New Cut. I acknowledge frankly that I don't like it. We have visited many queer places in London together, of which, it may be, the fashionables of the West-end have never heard; but they all had some out-of-the-way scraps of Bohemianism to recommend them. I can't say the same for the New Cut. It isn't picturesque, it isn't quaint, it isn't curious. It has not even the questionable merit of being old. It is simply Low. It is sordid, squalid, and, the truth must out, disreputable. The broad thoroughfare, which, bordered with fitting houses, would make one of the handsomest streets in London, is gorged with vile, rotten tenements, occupied by merchants who oft-times pursue the very contrary to innocent callings. Everything is second-hand, except the leviathan gin-shops, which are ghastly in their newness and richness of decoration. The broad pavement presents a mixture of Vanity Fair and Rag Fair. It is the paradise of the lowest of costermongers, and often the saturnalia of the most emerited thieves. Women appear there in their most unlovely aspect: brazen, slovenly, dishevelled, brawling, muddled with beer or fractious with gin. The howling of beaten children and kicked dogs, the yells of ballad-singers, "death and fire-hunters," and reciters of sham murders and elopements; the bawling recitations of professional denunciators of the Queen, the Royal family, and the ministry; the monotonous *jödels* of the itinerant hucksters; the fumes of the vilest tobacco, of stale corduroy suits, of oilskin caps, of mildewed umbrellas, of decaying vegetables, of escaping (and frequently surreptitiously tapped) gas, of deceased cats, of ancient fish, of cagmag meat, of dubious mutton pies, and of unwashed, soddened, unkempt, reckless humanity: all these make the night hideous and the heart sick. The New Cut is one of the most unpleasant samples of London that you could offer to a foreigner. Bethnal Green is ragged, squalid, woe-begone, but it is quiet and industrious. Here, there is mingled with the poverty a flaunting, idle, vagabond, beggarly-fine don't-care-a-centishness. Burkins in hold in Pentonville for his sins assures the chaplain that the wickedness of the New Cut is due solely to the proximity of the "Wictoriar Theayter, that 'aunt of disypashion and the wust of karackters." For my part, I think that if there were no such safety-valve as a theatre for the inhabitants of the "Cut," it would become a mere Devil's Acre, a Cour des Miracles, a modern edition of the Whitefriars Alsatia; and that the Cutites would fall to plundering, quarrelling, and fighting, through sheer *ennui*. It is horrible, dreadful, we know, to have such a place; but then, consider—the population of London is fast advancing towards three millions, and the wicked people must live somewhere—under a strictly constitutional government. There is a despot, now, over the water, who would make very short work of the New Cut. He would see, at a glance, the capacities of the place; in the twinkling of a decree the rotten tenements would be doomed to destruction; houses and shops like palaces would line the thoroughfare; trees would be planted along the pavement; and the Boulevard de Lambeth would be one of the stateliest avenues in the metropolis. But Britons never will be slaves, and we must submit to thorns (known as "vested interests") in the constitutional rose, and pay somewhat dear for our liberty as well as for our whistle.

In the cartoon accompanying this essay, you will find a delineation of the hostelry—the tavern—bah! it isn't a hostelry—it isn't a tavern; it is an unadulterated gin and beer palace—whither takes place the rush at half-price for malt refreshment. I have kept you lingering at the door a long time; I have digressed, parried, evaded the question; discoursed upon the transpontine drama, and the moot question of its morality; I have wandered about the New Cut, and have even gone back to the last century, and evoked the ghost of Doctor Johnson; I have been discursive, evasive, tedious very probably, but purposely so. I was bound to show you the place, but it is better that the pen should leave the fulness of representation to the pencil in this instance. It is humorous enough, brilliant enough, full of varied life and bustle enough. I could make you very merry with accounts of the mock Ethiopian serenaders at the door, with facetious remarks on the gentleman in the sou'-wester, knee-shorts, anklejacks, and gaiters, who is instructing the lady in the mob-cap in the mysteries of the celebrated dance known as the "Roberto Polveroso," or "Dusty Bob and Black Sal." I might be eloquent upon the subject of the sturdy sailor who is hobnobbing with the negro, the Life Guardsman treating the ladies, like a gallant fellow as he is, and the stream of honest, hardworking mechanics, their wives, and families, who have surged in from the "Vic." to have their "drop of beer." But the picture would still be incomplete. In graver pages—in tedious, solemn journals only—could be told (and I have told, in my time) the truth about a gin-shop in the New Cut. I will not descant upon the crime and shame, the age made hardened, the very babies weaned on gin. Let us take the better part, and throw a veil over this ugly position of the night side of London.

NINE O'CLOCK P.M.: HOUSE OF CALL FOR THE VICTORIA AUDIENCE.

Do you ever read the supplement of the "Times" newspaper? Of course you do; at least, you must diurnally peruse one column at least of that succursal to the monster journal, specially interesting to yourself. Almost every one who can read is anxious to consult the "Times" every morning for one purpose or other. Either he requires information about a ship that is going out, or a ship that should be come home; about a purse he has lost, or a banknote he has found; about a situation he wants, or a clerkship he has advertised for competition; about the wife he has run away from, or the son who has run away from him; about the horse he wishes to sell, or about the Newfoundland pup he wants to buy; about his debtor's bankruptcy, or his own insolvency; about the infallible remedy for all diseases, for which he has promised to send a recipe on the receipt of twelve postage-stamps; or the best curative pills advertised for hypochondriasis and dyspepsia; about the cheapest sherries, and the best second-hand broughams; about pianofortes for the million, sales by auction, money to be lent, or money wanted to borrow; and, chiefest of all, about the "births, deaths, and marriages," which announcements are the prime and favourite reading of the female sex. Indeed, I know one lady—young, comely, accomplished, good-natured, and married—who never even condescends to glance at a line of the colossal "Times" newspaper, beyond the "Births, Marriages, and Deaths;" and very good reading she declares them to be.

There is a portentous column to which my attention is attracted (I know not why, for it has never concerned me in the slightest degree), having reference to dancing. I don't allude to the casinos, or masquerades, or public full-dress balls, to which a man may go, lounge about, stare at the votaries of Terpsichore, and go away again without ever shaking a leg; but to the advertisements of the professors of dancing and "drawing-room deportment," who really mean business, and give instruction in those elegant and graceful arts, and hold their academies daily and nightly all over London, from the farthest East to the extremest West. Now I am myself no dancer. I remember as a boy, in the grim Parisian *pension*, or school boarding-house attached to the College where I had my scant Humanities hammered into me, a certain obese professor, to whom my parents and guardians paid a certain quarterly sum for my instruction in the poetry of motion. I remember him well, for whenever we took our walks abroad in Paris, we could scarcely pass a dead wall without seeing it placarded, or a *porte cochère* without seeing it hung, with a little yellow black framed bill, screened with a wire trellis-work, proclaiming "Boizot" and his *"cours de danse."* This was in '39; yet last winter in Paris the same walls and *portes cochères* still sounded the praises of Boizot. He appears to be immortal, like Cockle of the pills, Grimstone of the eye-snuff, and Elizabeth Lazenby of the sauce. The square *toqued* and black-gowned professors of the College Bourbon—now Lycée Bonaparte—could by dint of locking me up in cellars, making me kneel across sharp rulers and rapping my knuckles with ferulas (for corporal punishment never—oh! never—enters into the scheme of French education), impel me to construe Cæsar indifferently well; but Boizot, in all his *cours de danse*, failed in teaching me the difference between *cavalier seul* and *en avant deux*—between the *pastorale* and the *chaine des dames*. A more incorrigible dunce at dancing than your humble servant, never, I believe, existed. In the attempt to instruct me in the enchanting and vertigo-giving waltz, Boizot made a most lamentable *fiasco*, although he resorted to his famous specific of stamping on the pupil's toes with heavy-heeled shoes till he made the right steps to the right time. But our gyrations always ended in my doing all my waltzing on *his* toes; and he flung me away from him at last, denouncing me as a hopeless *butor, ganache, cretin,* and *cancre*—a Vandal, a Goth, an Ostrogoth, and a Visigoth—the three first being terms perfectly comprehensible to the French schoolboy, but for which it is difficult to find equivalents in this language. I am sure that Boizot left me with the utmost dislike and contempt, and with the most sinister forebodings for my future career. Thenceforth I was released from the dancing-lessons. In after years, I have heard it reported on good authority that I once danced a hornpipe at the wedding-breakfast of a maritime relation of mine; but the exploit, if ever accomplished, was due more, I opine, to the salmon and cucumber of the nuptial feast than to the *certaminis gaudia* of dancing. I essayed seriously once more to waltz at a Kursaal ball at a German watering-place. How I tore a lady's dress, how I tripped myself up, how I was covered with shame, and had the finger of scorn pointed at me, are yet matters of history at Bubbelbingen Schlaggasenberg. Thither I will return no more. Again, when I visited Russia, the first letter of introduction I presented on my arrival at St. Petersburg brought me an invitation to a grand ball. It was—Oh, horror! a diplomatic ball; there were not half a dozen persons in plain clothes in the ball-room; and I stood lonely and forlorn among a crowd of brilliant guardsmen, be-starred and be-ribboned ministers, plenipotentiaries, and embroidered *attachés*, who are proverbially the best dancers in Europe. I had not even the miserable safety-valve of crossing over and talking to the non-dancing dowagers, for, according to Russian custom—one which would delight the irreverent Mr. Spurgeon—the ladies remain at one end of the *salon*, and the gentlemen at the other—a relic of Orientalism—and in strict isolation, during the intervals between the dances. I was in despair, and about either to rush out or to recite "My name is Norval," with a view towards exciting curiosity and inspiring terror, when the gracious lady who did the honours for the ball-giving minister, who was a bachelor, asked me if I didn't dance? I didn't say that I had a sprained ankle, that I was hot, or tired, but I told the truth for once, and said honestly that I couldn't. "Don't you smoke, then?" she continued, glancing at me with a sort of pitying expression, as though she were thinking, "I wonder what this gawky Englishman *can* do?" I replied that I could smoke a little; whereupon, with her own fair hands, she opened a door and inducted me to an apartment, where a score of Boyards and secretaries of legation were smoking Havannahs, playing *préférence*, and sipping whisky-punch, and where I stopped till two o'clock in the morning, became very popular, and positively sang a comic song. At evening parties in England, alas! they seldom have a smoking-room, and so I don't go to them. A non-dancing man becomes speedily known in society, and the women shun him.

I can't help thinking (of course, on the fox and sour grapes principle), whenever I see a very accomplished male dancer, as when I look upon a first-rate amateur billiard-player, on the immense amount of time the man must have wasted to acquire a useless and frivolous art. Yet I remember the fox and the grapes, and suppress my rising sneer. Dancing to those who like it, and can dance gracefully, is an innocent and cheerful recreation. It does my heart good sometimes to see the little tiny children in our crowded London courts and alleys waltzing and polkaing to the Italian organ-grinder's music; and I shall be sorry for the day when some new Oliver Cromwell or Puritan government—we may have another in time—may denounce and put down "public dancing and dancing academies."

But why should the dancing academy column in the "Times" advertisements possess more than general attractions for me? Is it that I have a sneaking inclination to visit one of these establishments as a pupil; take six private lessons from Miss Leonora Geary, or Mrs. Nicholas Henderson—I could never dare to face Madame Mélanie Duval, or the Semiramis of dancing mistresses, Madame Michau Adelaïde—study the fashionable steps in secret, and then burst upon the world as an adept in the *Schottische*, the *Cellarius*, and the *Deux Temps*? Alas! I do not even know the names of the fashionable dances of the day, and very probably those to which I have alluded are by this time old fashioned, out of date, rococo, and pigtaily. But I have a theory that every man must dance before he dies, and that of the choreographic art we may say as of love—

"Whoe'er thou art, thy master see,

Who is, or was, or is to be."

And I shall dance, I suppose, some of these days, although my nerves be shrunk, my blood be cold, and hair white, and Death scrape away on the fiddle, as in Hans Holbein's shudder-giving panorama.

Mr. William M'Connell, however, the young gentleman who is my artistic *fides achates* in this horological undertaking, is, I am given to understand, a complete master of this desirable accomplishment, and a finished adept in its various mysteries. In this case, therefore, the leader has become the led, and I am grateful to him for his service as cicerone in introducing me to the domains of Terpsichore.

Assume, O reader and spectator—to violate no academical privacy—that we are in the *salle de danse* conducted for so many years, and with so much success, by Mrs. Hercules Fanteague, late of the Royal Operas. Throughout each day, from morn till dewy eve, does Mrs. Fanteague—a little woman, who, at no remote period of time, has been pretty—assisted by her husband, Mr. Hercules Fanteague, a diminutive gentleman, with tight pantaloons and a "kit," and a numerous family of sons and daughters, who all appear to have been born dancing-masters and mistresses, give private instruction to ladies and gentlemen, who are as yet novices in the art, or who are too shame-faced to venture upon the ordeal of public instruction. But, at nine o'clock in the evening, commences the public academy—the "hop," as some persons, innocent of the bump of veneration, call it. There, in the tastefully yet cheaply decorated saloon, with its boarded floor and flying cupids and sylphides on the panels—there, where the gas shines, and the enlivening strains of a band, composed of a harp, piano, and violin, are heard—there, in a remote section of the apartment—the *pons asinorum* of the dancing-school—the adult gentlemen, who are as yet in the accidence or rudiments of dancing, are instructed in the mysteries of the "positions" and preliminary steps by Mrs. Hercules Fanteague. The dancing-mistress is obliged to be very firm and decided, not to say severe, with her awkward pupils; for some are inclined to blush, and some to laugh and whisper disparaging jokes to one another, and some to tie their legs into knots and imitate the action of the old shutter telegraphs with their arms, and some to sink into a state of stony immobility and semi-unconsciousness, from which they can only be rescued by sharp words and pushes. When these hopeful ones are sufficiently advanced in the elements, they are handed over to lady partners, who, to the sound of the aforesaid harp, piano, and violin, twirl them about the room till they are pronounced fit to figure in the *soirées* of society, and in the Arabian Night-like scenes of Cremorne and Highbury Barn.

NINE O'CLOCK P.M.: A DANCING ACADEMY.

I once heard a man of the world tell a lady, in gay reproach, that there were three things impossible of accomplishment to her sex. "Women can't throw," he said, "they can't jump, and they can't slide." The lady stoutly denied the third postulate, and adduced in proof her own sliding performances in winter time in the day-room at boarding school. The first assertion she settled by throwing the peeling of an apple at him, which fell deftly over his left shoulder, and formed on the carpet, I am told, the initials of her Christian name. However this may be with other ladies—for she was fair, and good, and wise, as "Sydney's sister, Pembroke's mother," though Time has not thrown a dart at her yet, I know there is one thing a man cannot do. He cannot dance. He may take lessons of Mrs. Hercules Fanteague till his hair grows out of his hat, and his nails grow out of his pumps; he may dance the Crystal Platform at Cremorne to sawdust, but he will never succeed in making himself more than a capering elephant, or an ambling hippopotamus, with the facial expression of an undertaker's man on duty for the funeral of a very rich "party," where extra woe is laid on by Mr. Tressels, regardless of expense.

Of course I except professional dancers, and I bow reverentially before the bust of Vestris, "*Diou de la Danse*" and of the late Mr. Baron Nathan. I do not remember the first. He died years before I was born, yet I see him in my mind's eye on the stage of the Grand Opera in Paris, swelling with peacock-pride and conscious merit—in dancing—in full court-dress, his sword by his side, his laced and plumed *chapeau bras* beneath his arm, his diamond *solitaire* in his laced shirt-frill, leading his son to the footlights, on the night of the first appearance of the youth, and saying, "*Allez*, my son, the Muses will protect you, and your father beholds you." Was it this son, or a grandson I—tell me "Notes and Queries"—that was the Armand Vestris, whom our Eliza Bartolozzi (the famous Madame Vestris) married, and who was hurried at that dreadful hole at Naples? I see the *Diou de la Danse* on a subsequent occasion at rehearsal, when the same son, being committed to the prison as Fort l'Evêque by the lieutenant of police (the whole operatic *troupe*, led by Mademoiselle Guimard, were in a state of chronic revolt) dismissed him with these magnanimous words: "*Allez*, my beloved one. This is the proudest day of your life. Demand the apartments of my friend the King of Poland. Take my carriage. Your father pays for all!" But the poor baron, with his corkscrew ringlets, turn-down collar, and limber legs, I can and do remember. I have seen him dance that undying *pas*, blindfold, among the eggs and tea-things, in the Gothic Hall at Rosherville. But five Sundays since I was at Gravesend, and over my shilling tea in the Gothic Hall, I sighed when I thought of Baron Nathan and of happier days. "Where art thou, my Belinda? There is no one to pull off my shrimp-heads now."

Lo, as I pen these reminiscences of nine o'clock in the evening—pen them in the "quiet street," where I am again for a season—though my boat is on the shore, and my bark is on the sea, and ere you hear from me again there will be a considerable variation of clocks between London and Jericho—a fife and tabour announce the advent of a little dancing boy and girl, with a careworn mother, in the street below. I look from my window, and see the little painted people capering in their spangles and fleshings and short calico drawers. It is against conviction, and against my own written words, and against political economy, and ex-Lord Mayor Carden; but I think on Mr. Carrick's picture of "Weary Life," and must needs take some pence from the clock-case, and throw them out to these tiny mummers. Life is *so* hard, my brother!

TEN O'CLOCK P.M.—A DISCUSSION AT THE "BELVIDERE," AND AN ORATORIO AT EXETER HALL.

Exists there, in the whole world, civilised or uncivilised, a nation of such inveterate grumblers as the English? We grumble at everything. We are five-and-twenty millions of bears afflicted with perpetually sore heads. Are we charged sixpence extra for a bed? is the tail of our mutton-chop underdone? does our mockturtle soup disagree with us? is a railway train late? or the requisite amount of hop deficient in our pale ale? does an Italian itinerant split our ears while we are endeavouring to solve the Seventh Problem in the First Book of Euclid? does the editor or manager refuse to return the manuscript of our poems or our farces? do we buy a silk dress that turns out to be nine-tenths cotton? are we surcharged by the commissioners of income-tax, (*they*) say I make a thousand a year, I say I don't *make* a hundred and fifty; but may difference of opinion never, et cetera)? forthwith we call for pen, ink, and paper, and indite a letter to the "Times," that providential safety-valve for the great legion of grumblers. What are our public meetings but organised arenas of grumbling? what the "leaders" in our Sunday newspapers but extra facilities for grumbling after we have been grumbling all the week? I think it was Mr. Horace Mayhew, in his "Model Men and Women," who told the story of a waiter at a city tavern, who took but one holiday in the course of the year, and then enjoyed himself by paying a visit to another waiter at another tavern, and assisting him in laying the knives and forks. In like manner the ordinarily-understood holiday for the gentlemen of the daily press—there being no diurnals published on Sunday—is Saturday; whereupon, after lying in bed somewhat longer than usual on the sixth day's morning, they indulge in the *dulce desipere in loco*, by writing stinging leading articles in the journals which publish editions on the Sabbath. This is due to their inveterate propensity for grumbling. And, mark me, this licensed and acknowledged grumbling is the surest safeguard of our liberties, and the safest guarantee for our not drifting from our snug roadstead of constitutionalism, where we can ride at anchor, and smile at the timid argosies and caravels of despotism, moored and chained in the grim granite basins of the inner port, and all without launching into the troubled oceans, full of breakers and white squalls, of utter democracy. We seize upon a wrong, and grumble at it, till, after a few months', and sometimes a few years' grumbling, we find that the wrong exists no more, and that we have gained another Right. But we have had no barricades *ad interim*, no fusillades, no bombardment of private houses, no declarations of the "solidarity" of anybody, no confiscations, no deportations, and no guillotinings. Our rulers, grown wise by experience of smashed windows, pelted heads, and occasional (when the people were very hard driven) political annihilation, and hurling into the limbo of red tapism, have of late years placed few or no restrictions upon grumbling. The noble lord at the head of the Government daily receives deputations, who grumble at his measures, or at the measures he won't guarantee to propose, fearfully. In the Parliament House, no sooner does our gracious Queen, in her silver bell-like voice, speak the speech that others have written down for her (I daresay she could write a much more sensible discourse herself), than Lords and Commons begin to grumble about the sense of her words, and move amendments to the address which is to be presented to her. Downstairs, all through the session, parliamentary committees are grumbling at witnesses, and witnesses are grumbling at the committee; and in outlying boroughs vicious electors are grumbling at the members of the Commons' House of Parliament. The country newspapers and the London newspapers grumble. The barristers grumble at the judge, and the judge at the jury. The public grumbles at the way soldiers are treated by the officers, and the soldiers (who are about the only citizens who are not addicted to grumbling) go out and fight and win battles, at which we at home grumble, because so many lives have been lost. And I daresay the Prime Minister grumbles because he has the gout, and the Queen on her throne grumbles because "Punch" caricatures the Prince Consort, and "Punch" grumbles because the Prince Consort does not often enough give occasion to be grumbled at. I grumble at being obliged to write for your amusement, and you grumble because I am not half amusing enough. We grumble at the cold dinners at school, at the price of the marriage license, at the doctor's bill for our first child's measles, at the cost of the funeral of Uncle John, who left us all his money. We grumble because we have to live, and grumble when the physician tells us that we must die. Does it not all resolve itself into our purer, better Fielding's aphorism in "Vanity Fair"—"Ah! *vanitas vanitatum*? Who of us has not his hobby, or, having it, is satisfied?" Yet there is much virtue in having at least liberty to grumble.

These thoughts come over me as I wend my way at Ten o'Clock at night along the New Road—what do they call it now? Euston Road, Pancras Road, Paddington Road—*que scais-je*—towards the suburban district of Pentonville. It won't be suburban much longer; for Clerkenwell and Islington, Somers Town and Finsbury, are hemming it in so closely that it will be engulphed some of these days by a brick-and-mortar torrent, like the first Eddystone Lighthouse. A pleasant spot once was Pentonville, haunted by cheery memories of Sir Hugh Myddleton, the New River Head, Sadlers' Wells Theatre, and the "Angel" at Islington—which isn't (at least now-a-days, and I doubt if it ever was) at Islington at all. They began to spoil Pentonville when they pulled down that outrageously comic statue of George IV., at Battle Bridge. Then they built the Great Northern Railway Terminus—clincher number one; then an advertising tailor built a parody of the Crystal Palace for a shop—clincher number two (I am using a Swivellerism). The pre-ordinate clincher had been the erection of the hideously lugubrious penitentiary. However, I suppose it is all for the best. The next step will be to brick up the reservoir, and take down that mysterious tuning-fork looking erection, which no doubt has something to do with the water supply of London, and the New River Head; then they had better turn the Angel into a select vestry-room or a meeting-house for the Board of Works; and then, after that, I should advise them to demolish the "Belvidere."

Whose connection with grumbling you shall very speedily understand. At this famous and commodious old tavern, one of the few in London that yet preserve, not only a local but a metropolitan reputation, there is held every Saturday evening—ten o'clock being about the time for the commencement of the mimic Wittenagemotte—one of those meetings for political discussion, and the "ventilation" of political questions, whose uninterfered with occurrence, not only here, but in Fleet Street, in Bride Lane, and in Leicester Square, so much did rouse the ire of the *shirri*, and *mouchards*, and unutterable villany of Rue de Jérusalem spydom, in the employ of his Imperial Majesty, Napoleon III.

I have run the gauntlet of most of these harmless symposia of political talk; and with all, save the Westminster Forum, I can claim acquaintance. I have been one of the Alumni of "Cogers" or "Codger's" Hall, Bride Lane, where the gentleman who occupied the chair was addressed as "My Noble Grand" by the speaker. I have attended a meeting at the Forum, held at the Green Dragon,[11] Fleet Street, where visitors are invited to join in the discussion; and where, one evening, joining in the discussion as a stranger, the meeting objected to my political views, and a vote passed the chair that I was to be thrown out of the window; from which ignominious exodus I was only rescued by the advent of a friendly Templar, who had dropped in from chambers to the Forum to oil his rusty eloquence in time for the coming Western Circuit. I have dropped in, too, occasionally, at Mr. Wyld's Reading-Room, in Leicester Square, and have listened to much drouthy eloquence on subjects home and foreign. But nowhere have I seen such tableaux as the governmental journals of Paris have depicted, in the gloomiest of colours, as images of the political discussion meetings of *perfide Albion*. Nowhere have I seen a bowl of blood on the table, the chairman sitting on a barrel of gunpowder—to be subsequently used for the conflagration of the Thames—the orator addressing his hearers from the summit of a pile of ball-cartridges erected on a coffin; or dissentient members launching *abuses*, charged with fulminating mercury, at an unpopular speaker's head. Dark and dangerous meetings, of dark and dangerous men, do certainly take place in London. Oppressed, despairing, starving, outlawed, outraged exiles, do meet in holes and corners, do plot and conspire, do hurl, in speech, denunciation and sarcasm, at despots. But you must not go to Fleet Street, to Bride Lane, to Leicester Square, nor, least of all, to Pentonville, to find them. The doors of those mysterious meeting-places are "tiled" as securely as Freemasons' lodges. Now and then a traitor, by lies and hypocrisy, gains admittance, but woe to the traitor if he be discovered in his treason. He dies within the year.

TEN O'CLOCK P.M.: A DISCUSSION AT THE "BELVIDERE."

The "Belvidere" is distinguished above its kindred discussion halls, by its eminently respectable aspect. The subjects broached are bold enough, and are as boldly treated; but you are puzzled to reconcile the full-blown democracy of some of the speakers, with their mild, bank-account-possessing, rate-and-tax-paying, housekeeping appearance. They bark but do not bite. The usages and prestige of the place, too, demand a certain amenity in discussion and forbearance in reply, which throws an extra tinge of respectability over the whole. Looking at this spacious, handsome room, panelled and pillared, comfortably and brilliantly lit, with its doubled rows of mahogany tables covered with bottles and glasses full of steaming compounds that do comfort the flesh outwardly and rejoice the spirit inwardly—in strict moderation, mind; looking at this burly, substantial auditory, ensconced in their cosy chairs, smoking their cigars, and listening with attentive ears to the orator; looking at the thoughtful waiter slipping from table to table, administering refreshment and receiving orders with a subtle swiftness, yet taking, I will be bound, an ardent mental interest in the discussion; looking at the grave chairman in his comfortable high-raised *fauteuil*—you might fancy this to be one of the parochial "representative councils," as vestries are now queerly christened, or a freemasons' lodge, when, "labour" being over, "refreshment" commences, or an ordinary club of middle-class men accustomed to meet one another, and talk upon the topics of the day over a social glass. And, in truth, were you to suppose this, you would not be so very far out in your calculation. These are, indeed, vestrymen—or representative councillors—freemasons, benefit-club, middle-class men. But the topic of the night is invested with authority, and its discussion is subject to rules; and the highest compliment I can pay to the "Belvidere" is that, if in that other Discussion Hall, held between the months of March and August, in a green-leather and oak-carving furnished chamber, nigh unto the crypt of St. Stephen's Chapel, Westminster, as much sobriety, decorum, and persistence in adhering to the matter in hand were shown, as in this convivial parliament, the business of the nation would progress much better, and we should have much less cause to grumble at most things.

See a speaker on his legs—a fluent speaker, somewhat of a florid speaker, occasionally somewhat of a violent speaker, though his violence is strictly confined to words and gesticulations. What withering sarcasms he hurls at kings and ministers! How eloquently he tells those tyrannical puppets that, when they are forgotten, when the force and direction of personal satire is no longer understood, and measures are felt only in their remotest consequences, his words shall still be found to contain principles worthy of being transmitted to posterity! How sneeringly he assures our rulers that they have but a copyhold interest in the state, that they cannot waste, that they cannot alienate, and that the fee-simple is in us! How menacingly he assures the monarchs of the earth that the crowns which were gained by one revolution may be lost by another! and how much, listening to his impassioned exordium, to his whirlwind argument, to his scathing peroration, I become impressed with a notion that the orator has a capital memory, and has been an assiduous student of certain letters, which were addressed, in our great-grandmothers' time, to Mr. Woodfall, the printer of the "Public Advertiser," by a mysterious correspondent—a correspondent whose motto was, "*Stat nominis umbra*" and who chose to assume the pseudonym of "JUNIUS."

In these orations you are sure to hear a good deal about Catholic Emancipation, the Test and Corporation Acts, the Spa Fields Riots, the Peterloo Massacre, the "Piccadilly Butchers," the "Dorsetshire Labourers," Queen Caroline's Trial, Richmond the Spy, and similar topics. They are not very amusing, perhaps, but they are of infinite service in keeping juvenile politicians *au fait* with the political *memorabilia* of thirty or forty years since. I have even heard an ardent reformer, with scarcely so much as a tuft on his chin, declaim in burning accents upon the great case of Horne Tooke *versus* the House of Commons—"Once a priest forever a priest"—on Jack Wilkes, Number Forty-five, and the question of general warrants, on the cruelty of Lord Ellenborough to William Hone, the trial of Colonel Despard, and the eventualities which might have followed the successful assassination of Lord Sidmouth by Arthur Thistlewood.

A staid, middle-aged gentleman follows the reformer, and proceeds, genteelly, to demolish him. He is a staunch upholder of our ancient institutions, and sneers at the presumptuous and levelling tendencies of the age. He has some neat things to say about the "Pig and Whistle" style of oratory, at which the ardent reformer winces, chews the end of his cigar, and empties his glass indignantly; and he concludes with a glowing eulogium on church and state, our glorious constitution, and our noble aristocracy.

Ere I leave these placid tribunes of Pentonville Hill, discharging their harmless philippics at men high in place and power, I muse a little over the tavern itself, and call to mind a certain story I once heard respecting it, possessing what foundation of truth I know not, but which, if not true, is assuredly *ben trovato*. Thus runs the dubious legend: You remember the fair young daughter of England, the good princess, the virtuous daughter of a wicked father, and in whom, from her cradle to her marriage, the hope and love of this stolid but strong-feeling nation were centred. You remember her husband: he is a king at Brussels now. You remember how, when she died, all England burst into a passionate lament; how thousands went into voluntary mourning; how clergymen wept in the pulpit, when they discoursed on her virtues; how an awful darkness and despair seemed to overshadow the ill-governed land when the news came that the Princess Charlotte was dead. There is little need to say that her husband (who, I am glad to believe, loved her very truly and fondly) was at first inconsolable for her loss, and grieved long and bitterly for her. But time was good to him, and heaven merciful, and by degrees his sorrow wore away. Still he was melancholy, pre-occupied, and loved nothing so much as to be left alone. It was about this time that the then landlord of the Belvidere began to notice that about eleven o'clock almost every forenoon during the week a gentleman in deep mourning, and on horseback, would stop at the door of the tavern, leave his horse in charge of his groom, enter the large room, call for a pipe and a pint of ale, and quietly enjoy those refreshments for about the space of one hour. The room would be at that early hour of the day almost deserted. The one or two tradesmen who would occasionally drop in for a crust of bread and cheese, and a peep at the "Times," would be bidden a civil "good morning"—in a slightly foreign accent—by the stranger; but he never entered into conversation; he never read the newspaper; he "kep hisself to hisself," the waiter said. But he was so punctual and so regular in his attendance, that the people of the house came to look out for his daily visit in his suit of sables, and a special pipe was laid, a special dish of tobacco prepared, and a special chair and spittoon arranged, every day for his use. So things went on for many weeks; till one luckless morning, just after the departure of the black horseman, a customer of the house—I believe he was a commercial traveller, who had just returned from a journey in the west of England, and who had been enjoying his pipe and pint in the society of the taciturn stranger—called the landlord on one side.

"Do you know who that chap is?" he asked.

"Not a bit," answered the host. "Comes here every morning regular. Pint of mild sixpenny; bird's-eye; gives the waiter twopence, and goes away. Groom has a glass of ale sitting on his horse. Pays his way like a gentleman."

"He's somebody," said the commercial traveller, significantly.

"So I should think," returned the landlord, quietly.

"He's a high fellow," added the bagman, mysteriously.

"I shouldn't wonder," said the landlord, tranquilly.

"Why, bless your heart, man alive!" broke out, impatiently, his interlocutor, "can't you guess who he is? He's Prince Leopold of Saxe-Coburg. I have seen his Royal Highness a hundred times, and know him by sight as well as I do you."

The next forenoon, when the sable horseman arrived, he found a roll of crimson baize laid down from the pales before the tavern to the doorway, which was lined by American aloes in tubs. The staircase was freshly carpeted; in the stranger's customary place was a table covered with a crimson cloth, backed by a crimson chair with gilt legs. The landlady, her daughter, and the barmaid, were all in holiday attire, and when the unknown rang the bell, the landlord himself, in a blue coat and brass buttons, and his hair newly powdered, brought him the beer in a silver tankard, and a wax candle at which to light his pipe. The black horseman said nothing, drank his ale, and smoked his tobacco, paid his reckoning, made his way downstairs amidst a profusion of bows and curtsies, mounted his horse, and—never came again. So runs the legend. The commercial traveller may have been wrong in his assertion, or may have been hoaxing the landlord; but I incline to the belief that this was really Prince Leopold. Why not? The incident is trifling enough; yet there is something touching in the picture of the good-natured young German brooding over his bereavement, yet consoling himself in the simple German fashion, over his pipe and beer.

Friend of mine, if you have the slightest hope or thought that whither I am now taking thee is one of the gay and merry scenes of London night-life, prithee dismiss the thought, for thou art in error. Prithee pull up the collar of thy coat, stiffen thy neckcloth as much as possible, take that wicked cigar from thy mouth, cast down thine eyes, and assume a decorum, if thou have it not. We are going to Exeter Hall.

Don't be alarmed: this is not the month of May or the season for meetings in aid of missions to the Quashiboos, the Rumbatumbas, or the Oolalooloo cannibals. We are not going to hear John B. Gough lecture on temperance. We are going to hear an oratorio, conducted by Mr. Costa—an oratorio in which Mr. Sims Reeves, Mr. Weiss, Miss Dolby, and Madame Clara Novello, are to sing—and to listen to a band and chorus brought to a degree of perfection which only the genius of such a conductor could insure, or the gigantic resources of the Sacred Harmonic Society command.

There would seem to be in an oratorio something essentially germane to the English mind and character. The sounding recitative and swelling hymns, the rolling choruses and triumphant bursts of exultant music, have a strange affinity with the solemn, earnest, energetic English people, slow to move to anger or to love, but, when moved, passionately enthusiastic in their love, bloody and terrible in their great wrath. The French can no more understand oratorios than they can understand blank verse. I remember going to see Mendelssohn's "Elijah" once in Paris. It was winter time, and the performances took place in Franconi's great, windy, for-summer-built horse-riding circus in the Champs Elysées. The band and chorus shivered as they scraped and sang; the *prima donna's* nose and lips were blue, and the music paper quivered in her hand; the *contralto* looked exquisitely uncomfortable at not having to wear a page's dress and show her legs. As for the audience, the ladies sat muffled up in shawls and furs—it was a morning performance—and whispered among themselves; the men sucked the knobs of their canes, twirled their moustaches, stared up at the chandeliers, and murmured, *Quelle drôle de musique*! They didn't repeat that oratorio, and I don't wonder at it. To the French it was neither fish nor flesh, neither ecclesiastical nor secular. If the first, they might argue, give us the chanting priests, the swinging censers dispensing fragrant clouds, the red-cassocked altar boys, the twinkling tapers, the embroidered canopies, and the swelling pæans of the concealed choristers. If the last, let us have a drinking chorus, a laughing chorus, and a dagger chorus, a *prima donna* to make her entrance on horseback, a *contralto* in tights, a ballet in the second act, and some red fire at the end. But this is neither mass nor opera.

They think differently in England. To the seriously-inclined middle classes the oratorio supplies the place of the opera. And it behoves you to consider what a vast power in the state those serious middle-class men and women are. It is all very well for us, men and citizens of the world, yet living in a comparatively contracted circle of acquaintances as cosmopolitan as ourselves; it is all very well for us, who see "no harm" in sitting at home and reading the newspaper, while our wives go to church; who support Sunday bands, Sunday steamboats, and Sunday excursion trains, and are agitating now for the opening of museums, and galleries, and palaces on the Sabbath; who talk lightly on serious topics, and call clergymen parsons; it is all very well, I say, for us, travelled, and somewhat cynical as we may be, to pretend that the "serious" world is an amalgam of bigotry, hypocrisy, and selfishness, and to ignore the solemn religious journals that denounce hot dinner on Sundays, or a walk after it, or the perusal of a secular book on the sacred day, as intolerable sins. Yet how many thousands—how many millions—of sober, sincere, conscientious citizens are there, who are honestly persuaded of the sinfulness of many things which we consider harmless recreations! who would shrink back in horror, if they heard a tithe of the conversations that go on every night in hundreds of well-conducted London drawing-rooms! who look upon dancing as an irreligious and Babylonish pastime! whose only light reading consists of tracts, missionary chronicles, and memoirs of sainted cheesemongers, and the beatified daughters of dairymen! I declare that I never see a theatre in a country town—where, at least, two-thirds of the population consist of such as I have described—without wondering at the lunacy of the person who built it, without marvelling at the idiocy of every fresh speculator who enters on the management. We may pretend to despise the Puritan world, write books and farces against them, and quiz the "Record" or the "Wesleyan;" but it is folly to ignore the vast numerical strength of these same Puritans. They purchase such books as "Memorials of Captain Headly Vicars" by thousands; they subscribe thousands of pounds yearly in an almost insane hope of converting heathen barbarians to a better faith; they give away millions of tracts; they flood the platform and the auditory of every public meeting. It won't do to ignore them. Cromwell's Ironsides and Sir Harry Vane's Fifth-Monarchy Men have made too deep a mark upon the people of England to be lightly passed over.

But the serious world, and that section who are worldly, meet on neutral ground at an Exeter Hall oratorio. The religionists see no sin in listening to sacred music; the mundane come to listen with delight to the immortal strains of Handel, of Haydn, and of Mendelssohn. "When shall their glory fade" asked Tennyson, singing of the Six Hundred at Balaclava. When shall the glory of our great oratorio writers decay? Never—I hope.

A resident at Bethlehem Hospital—he wasn't either a doctor or a keeper, but wore, habitually, a strait-waistcoat, took shower-baths very frequently, and kept his head close shaved—once divided the world into two classes: people who were mad, and people who would be mad. I, too—but out of Bedlam, thank heaven!—have made a somewhat analogous classification. I divide the world into people who have and have not seen Ghosts. I belong myself to the first class. I am continually seeing ghosts. I shake hands in the street with friends who have been dead these ten years. A dear dead sister comes and sits by me at night when I read, and tells me, with a kiss, that I am a good boy for coming home so early. I was troubled some years ago with a man with his head off, who, in that unseemly position, and holding his head on his knees, sat continually before me. I dismissed him at last as being an unworthy hallucination, and not a genuine ghost. I meet a good many ghosts now—friendly ghosts, pleasant ghosts—but chiefly do they favour me with their company at places of public entertainment. It may be that I am a bad listener to music or theatrical dialogue, that I am absent in mind, and *distrait*; but so surely as I go to a theatre or concert, so surely do I fall a conjuring up mind-pictures, till the theatre or the hall, and its occupants, quite fade away, and I find myself in entirely different company, talking to people who are mouldering in their graves, or who are thousands of miles away.

And so the oratorio goes on, the assemblage paying a grave and decorous attention to the music, and bearing themselves far more like a congregation than an audience. They are so devotedly rapt in the magnificent performance, that I expect every moment to hear the vast mass of them join in the choruses; and when, at the first bar of the sublime "Hallelujah Chorus," the hearers all *stand up*, the singers in the orchestra seem to me like priests. In truth, I think that to hear an oratorio, chastens and purifies the mind, and that we go away from those grand performances wiser and better men. There is a natural disinclination to return—at least, immediately—to frivolous and trivial pursuits, after listening to those solemn and ennobling strains. I know that some exist upon whom music has no effect whatsoever; but I believe that the vast majority of mankind are influenced for good or evil by the sound of music. The most heartless woman in the world whom I know, cries when she hears "Kathleen ma vourneen." Napoleon could never listen to "*Lascio ch'io piango la cruda sorte*," without crossing himself. How grandly does John Dryden set forth this theory in his immortal St. Cecilian Ode! with what exquisite art has he shown us Alexander moved to alternate joy, pride, shame, weeping, frenzy, as old Timotheus sweeps the lyre in varied strains!

TEN O'CLOCK P.M.: AN ORATORIO AT EXETER HALL.

Now, in sober broughams and in hack-cabs—driven, I hope, by regenerated cabmen, who give tickets before they are asked for them, and never charge more than thirty per cent. above the legal fare—or haply, if the night be fine, on foot, the serious audience, well cloaked and bonneted, leave the hall. For half an hour afterwards, the Exeter Hall side of the Strand, both east and west, is dotted with serious groups in search of the last omnibus, or, perchance, boldly walking home. I wonder how many of the serious ones know anything of the thoroughfare. They may traverse it at noonday, or pass down it every morning for twenty years in omnibuses on their way to the city; but do they know anything of the night aspect of that most mysterious of London thoroughfares? It is better, perhaps, that they should not.

Minute by minute they grow scarcer, and by ten minutes to eleven there are no serious groups in the Strand. They are all gone home to supper—hot ones, very probably, for the serious world is not at all unaddicted to good living—and sober. I, too, have liberty to go and sup, if I so choose; but not, alas! to bed. Still have I work to do, and for some hours.

ELEVEN O'CLOCK P.M.—A SCIENTIFIC CONVERSAZIONE, AND AN EVENING PARTY.

It is Eleven o'Clock post meridian, and I am once more thrown, with my clock on my hands, on the great world of London. The insatiable, restless metropolis is as busy in the night as in the day season; there is no respite, no cessation, in its feverish activity. One set or class of mortals may, quite worn and worried out, cast themselves on beds more or less hard, and sleep; but, forthwith, another section of the population arise like giants refreshed—the last hour of the night to some is the commencement, the opening day, to others; and an innumerable army of conscripts are ready to relieve one another in mounting the guard of London Life.

Eleven o'clock, and thousands are yet in the streets, tens of thousands still in the pursuit of the avocations by which they earn their daily (or nightly) bread, hundreds of thousands awake, busy, and stirring. The children of the aristocracy and some sections of the middle classes are gone to bed—save those who have been so good that their fond parents have taken them to the play, which entertainment they are now enjoying, with delightful prospects superadded of "sitting up" to supper, perchance of oysters, afterwards. But the children of the poor do not dream of bed. They are toddling in and out of chandlers' shops in quest of ounces of ham and fragments of Dutch cheese for father's supper; they are carrying the basket of linen—mother takes in washing—to the residences of clients; they are eliminating the most savoury-looking bits of plaice or flounders from the oleaginous pile in the fried-fish shop; they are fetching the beer and the "clean pipe" from the public-house; nay—not unfrequently, alas! assisted by a lean baby in arms—they are fetching father himself home from the too-seductive establishment of the licensed victualler. Eleven o'clock at night is the great supper-time of the working classes; then, by the steady and industrious mechanic, the final calumet is smoked, the borrowed newspaper read, the topics of the day, the prospects of the coming week, discussed with the cheery and hard-working helpmate who sits by the side of her horny-handed lord, fills his pipe, pours out his beer, and darns the little children's hose.

Eleven o'clock: theatrical audiences are at their apogee, and the last piece is "on." Convivial clubs are in full action, and the waiters at the supper-rooms, very tumbled and drowsy during the day, put on their most highly-starched neckcloths, and begin to rub their eyes, in preparation for the labours of the night. The linen-drapers' shopmen, who have been strolling about Regent Street and Oxford Street since the shops closed at nine, and who "live on the premises," begin to turn in; the proprietors tolerate no gadding about after eleven, and persistence in keeping bad hours to the extent of hearing the chimes at midnight, out of doors, would entail reprimand, and perhaps expulsion, on the offender. At eleven o'clock close the majority of the coffee, chop houses, and reading-rooms. There are some that will remain open all night; but they are not of the most reputable description. At eleven the cheap grocer, the cheesemonger, and the linen-draper, in low-priced neighbourhoods, begin to think of putting up the shutters; and, by half-past eleven, the only symposia of merchandise open will be the taverns and cigar-shops, the supper-rooms and shell-fish warehouses, the night coffee-houses, and the chemists—which last shops, indeed, never seem to be quite open, or quite closed, at all, and may be said to sleep with one eye open.

Eleven o'clock at the West-end is, morally speaking, broad day-light. Midnight will be high noon. Fashionable life's current riots through the veins of West-end streets; mirth, and gaiety, and intrigue, are heard on staircases and at street corners. And pre-eminently wide awake, busy, active, and restless just now is the great and mysterious country of Bohemia, both Upper and Lower. You are beginning to hear of Bohemia, oh, reflective reader! and of its shady denizens. Recondite, half-reluctant allusions are made to it in solemn reviews and portentous magazines. An arch-Bohemian proposed the other day to write a novel concerning the present condition of his country. The book actually appeared, but its author stumbled on the threshold of his own subject. Either he dared not say that which he knew, or he had over-estimated his knowledge of things Bohemian: and he drew, not the real country, but an impalpable region full of monsters. But his was no easy task. After all, who shall say, who can tell, where Bohemia really is, and who really are Bohemians? They are secretly affiliated, and to each other known, like freemasons, like the Illuminati and Brethren of the Rosy Cross of the last century, like Balzac's "Treize;" but the outside world knows them not, and oft-times mistakes for a Bohemian a vile Illyrian, a contemptible Styrian, a worthless Croat, or a base Bezonian. Is there a king of Bohemia? or is it an oligarchy, a theocracy, or a red republic? How does a man become a Bohemian, and can he ever renounce his allegiance to the "friends of Bohemia," and become an ordinary citizen of the world? Yet Bohemianism is ubiquitous. The initiated ones are everywhere. In the House of Commons, at this very moment, a free and accepted Bohemian is pounding away at the ministry, and a past grand-master of Bohemianism is descending the steps of the Carlton. A Bohemian is dancing the Schottische in Westbourne Terrace, and his brother is passing underneath Temple Bar, in a cab and in custody, on his way to Mr. Slowman's caravanserai in Cursitor Street. There is a Bohemian, in white kid gloves and a white cravat, sitting in his opera-stall, and he whispers to his companion to order a Welsh rabbit and a pint of half-and-half for him at the Club. Some Bohemians are drinking claret at the Wellington, and others are sleeping among the vegetable baskets under the tarpaulins in Covent Garden Market. Bohemian No. one has just won a hundred pounds at *écarté*. Bohemian No. two has just pawned his great-coat.

A Bohemian has just gone home to read Plato, and take a basin of arrowroot for supper. Another has let himself out with his latch-key, and is on his way to the Haymarket. Oh, marvellous land! Oh, people yet more marvellous! Despised, derided, abused by men, ye are yet a power in the state. Bootmakers combine against ye; but you can turn out governments. Clerks of county courts issue judgment summonses against ye; but you dine at princes' tables. Lands you have not, nor jewels, nor raiment, nor fine linen, nor pieces of gold, nor pieces of silver; still do ye travel first-class express; still do you clamour for green fat at mighty banquets, and turn up your Bohemian noses if the venison be not hung to your liking; still do you pride yourselves upon being good judges of Rhine wine and Habana cigars. A peculiar race! And the most astonishing thing about the Bohemian is this: that he does not—as the non-Bohemian charitably supposes and reports—die in an hospital, to be saved from dissection, and humbly buried, only by a subscription among his Bohemian associates. If he be an ass and a profligate, he goes to the bad, and serve him right; but the Bohemian, dying, frequently leaves a great deal more money behind him than yonder starched man of business, who professed to regard him, during his lifetime, with a shuddering, pitying horror. The Bohemian, brought, as it would seem, to the lowest and forlornest state of impecuniosity and discredit, suddenly starts up as Attorney-General of Yellow-Jack Island with twelve hundred a year, as Judge-Advocate of the Meridional Quashiboos, or Consul-General to the Tontine Republic.

While thus discoursing to you on things in general, I have been keeping a sharp look-out for the most notable things that are to be seen in London at eleven p.m. But as we shall have to sit up very late to-night—or rather early to-morrow morning—I think it right that we should pass the time till midnight in a quiet and decorous manner. Not but that we have been exceedingly well-behaved ever since the commencement of our peripatetics; but life is life, and one can scarcely go twice round the clock in London without some moral and physical wear and tear. Suppose we drop in at a Conversazione.

This (more or less) social *réunion* is an institution of purely modern invention. It is the latest device of the fantastically despotic organisation we call "society," with the exception of *the dansante*, or dancing tea. It might be alleged, but the allegation would be open to the imputation of hypercriticism, that the first conversazione on English record was the meeting of the Royal Society at which King Charles II. propounded the famous problem of the live fish in the pail of water: and another semblance of a conversazione might be found in the assemblage of antiquaries at the christening of Martinus Scriblerus. But the real conversazione is quite another affair, and wholly modern. It is not much more than twenty years old, its establishment following close on the heels of the fashionable "rout," which again succeeded the "assemblies" of our grandmothers and the "drums" of our great-grandmothers. The modern conversazione means a room or a suite of rooms thrown open for the reception of a miscellaneous mob of fashionables or of celebrities, foreign and native, political, literary, scientific, or artistic. It is a vast menagerie, a "happy family" on a monster scale, a Noah's ark upon dry ground, and the birds, beasts, and fishes crowd and elbow each other, and roar, or yell, or howl, or bark, or low, or grunt, or squeak, or crow, or whistle, or scream, or pipe, to the infinite delectation of the host and hostess. The only sounds proper to the animal or ornithological kingdom are those which might be supposed to be produced by billing and cooing; for the guests are not—or do not in general look—very good-tempered, and a favourite manner of passing the time at a conversazione is to scowl at your neighbour, and wonder who the deuce he is. But one of the chief advantages connected with these bringings-together of celebrities, lies in the moderate sum for which the thing can be done. The conversazione is eminently cheap. They don't give these lions any shinbones of beef; tea, coffee, macaroons, and, at very hospitable houses, sandwiches and wishy-washy negus, are all that you can reckon upon in the way of refreshment at a conversazione.

Of late days, conversaziones, which were ordinarily given by private persons—the Mrs. Leo Hunters of the *beau monde*—have been held by societies literary and learned, nay, even by commercial and financial companies. I remember myself receiving on one occasion an invite to a "conversazione" at which the novel principles of a new life assurance company, and the immense advantages offered to shareholders, assurers, and annuitants, were to be fully developed and explained. The conversazione was held at the bran-new offices of the company, smelling very strongly of recent varnish, putty, and French polish, and of calf ledgers and day-books yet innocent of entries. There were plenty of ladies in evening dress, and plenty of gentlemen in white waistcoats, and flirtation and gallantry were oddly mixed up with the Northampton Tables and the Institute of Actuaries. We had a neat lecture by a stout gentleman, in a blue coat buttoned up to the chin, upon the inestimable blessings of life assurance. Tea and coffee were handed round in the intervals of his discourse upon bonuses, paid-up capital, and the purchase of reversions; and an immense sensation was created at the termination of the lecture by the recitation, on the part of the orator, of a neat little copy of verses, of which the commencing stanzas, so far as my recollection will serve me, ran somewhat thus:—

"When dear papa went up to heaven,

What grief mamma endured!

And yet that grief was softened, for

Papa he was assured.

"He never lodged his policy,

He left it to mamma;

The office paid most cheerfully,

How happy now we are!"

This touching effusion was received with great waving of handkerchiefs, and some sobs, indeed, on the part of the ladies, and I have no doubt that many of those fair ones on returning home did that night incite, command, and compel their liege lords and masters forthwith to assure their lives in the "Amiable and General Fire and Life Assurance Company" (with which are incorporated the "Good-natured and Law Life," the "Equitable and Jocular Fire," and the "Compassionate and Confidential Deposit and Loan Association"). The friendly meeting of the "Amiable and General" was distinguished above other conversaziones by the fact, that when the ladies had taken their departure, a capital cold supper, and abundant libations of champagne, were provided for the directors and their friends, at which repast, which lasted to a very advanced hour, everybody drank everybody else's health with all the honours, and everybody was made a preferential shareholder. I know that I was; though I am not quite aware at the present moment of the exact locality of the "Amiable and General's" offices, or, indeed, whether that most promising company is still in existence.

The strange conversaziones a man may from time to time visit! I have been to one at the Hanover Square Rooms given by the confraternity of dentists. Slim gentlemen of Carker-like dental developement held forth on the transcendant merit of the art of pulling out people's teeth, and fiercely denounced the quacks and impostors who ignorantly tampered with the jaws of her Majesty's subjects; the room itself was hung round with the most hideous coloured cartoons, representative of diverse phases of dental surgery, and I came away haunted by visions of pink beeswax, thin gold plates, morocco easy chairs, springs, *dents osanores*, artificial gums, and those dreadfully clean hands, the wrists garnished by wristbands as clean, which seem to be the exclusive property of dentists. I congratulated myself, too, on my departure, on the fact that no visitor to the conversazione had, for the pure love of art, pulled out one of my few remaining teeth, just as, after dining with a schoolmaster, I felicitate myself for having escaped a caning. There is something in the whiteness of a dentist's hand, and in the twinkling of a schoolmaster's gray eye, that would make me tremble were I Lord Chancellor of Great Britain.

But the oddest conversazione I ever attended was not in this country, but in a foreign land. It was in Paris—and I am speaking seriously—a conversazione of *coiffeurs*, of barbers, hair-dressers, and wig-makers. I declare that I have seldom passed a more agreeable evening in my life. Everything was conducted on the most intensely genteel footing, and everybody was ceremoniously polite; although I must be candid in admitting that a decided odour of pomatum and freshly-frizzled curls pervaded the *salon*, which was, indeed, the upstairs room of a *restaurant* at Montmartre. There were ladies present, too; and after some pleasant little discourse, all tending to the glorification of hair-dressing, an eminent professor of the philocomal art there present proceeded to a series of practical and illustrative experiments on the heads of some of the young ladies, in order to show the different styles of dressing and arranging the head which had prevailed from the time of François, *premier jusqu' à nos jours*, to our own days. The ladies submitted with charming equanimity to the operation, and the experimentalist was enabled to submit to public inspection and admiration a full-blown Ninon d'Enclos, a Mademoiselle de Montpensier, a Duchesse de Longueville, a Madame de Maintenon, together with several Du Barris, De la Vallières, Pompadours, Madame Talliens, Mademoiselle Mars, Charlotte Cordays, and Théroigne de Méricourts. At the conclusion of the experiments, there was a grand procession of the ladies variously *coiffées* round the room, followed by the triumphant hair-dressers, waving their tongs and combs, and redolent of puff-powder; then we had *orgeat* and *anisette*; and then I went and supped in the *restaurant* downstairs with one of the hair-dressers, who went me halves in a bottle of Beaune, and swore eternal friendship to me over a *Mayonnaise de homard*.

But to return to the conversazione world of London. Suppose we take a literary one to begin with: say one of Mrs. Van Umbug's Thursdays. Mrs. Van Umbug lives at that classically severe mansion, the "Arena. Gladiator's Crescent, Nero Square." Mr. Van Umbug is a member of Parliament, and sits on the Liberal side of the House, but nobody takes much notice of him, and he is usually alluded to as Mrs. Van Umbug's husband. If you ask the coachman in the adjacent mews whose horses are those the helper is harnessing to the brougham, he will probably answer, "Mrs. Van Umbug's." The servants in the house in Gladiator Street, talk continually of "Missus" (who makes her presence not only seen but felt), but scarcely ever mention "Master." The tradespeople usually send in their bills to Mrs. Van Umbug; and it is certain that it is that lady who issues the invitations and receives the company at her Thursday conversaziones. Mr. Van Umbug, M.P., is scarcely ever seen at those gatherings, and when he is, rarely, manifest, it is in a very meek and subdued manner. He sneaks in and out as if the house didn't belong to him (which, indeed, it does not), and appears desperately afraid of the portly man in black with the white Berlin gloves who hands round the tea and coffee.

Mrs. Van Umbug's mansion is supposed to be furnished in the highest style of taste and virtu. Hers is quoted as an abode of all that is elegant, *recherché*, and *distingué*. What are taste and virtu, I wonder? what makes things elegant, *distingué*, and *recherché*? Do chairs that you can't sit down upon, and spindled-shanked tables, tottering beneath the weight of gaudily-bound books, containing specimens of chromo-lithography? do a sham pre-Raphaelite picture or two, in which a long-legged swain is courting a lady with yellow hair and a striped dress falling in unnatural folds, under the lee of a marvellously-executed waterbutt—a curiously-manipulated mangold-wurzel, and a minutely finished frying-pan occupying the foreground? do scraps of armour and oak-carvings, supposed to be ancient, but in reality manufactured the week before last in Wardour Street? do odds and ends, and Chinese monsters in porcelain, and a Louis Quinze clock, and the model of a Swiss châlet in box-wood, and an imitation grotto and aquarium in an ante-room? I suppose these things do.

This present Thursday at Mrs. Van Umbug's is a great literary one.

The lions of literature are present in the flesh. Here is the distinguished Snortup, author of "The Common Objects of the Back-yard," "Geology in Joke," "Trigonometry Judged by Taxation," "The Extinct Animals of Eel-pie Island," and other erudite and ponderous scientific works. Snortup, who is a Doctor of Philosophy of the University of Schinckelbrauen, is a heavy man, with a black wig and a huge black satin stock, in which gleams a cameo bearing a curious resemblance to an oyster. He snuffs a great deal, and when he speaks he does not belie his name, but literally snorts. Near him is young Twiddles, with his auburn hair, his turn-down collar, and Byron tie, his speckled silk stockings and low shoes, his baby face and falsetto voice. Twiddles, who writes under the pseudonym of Swedenborg Scanderberg, has just published a volume of poems of the ultra-spasmodic order. In passages replete with burning eloquence, he has spoken of the "moonbeam's frosty rime, that hoars the head of nature, and makes last summer's sapling patriarchal white." His grand passage in "Ladye Babbynetta," in which he alludes to "the hot and rabid ice, that burns and sears by force of congelation," has been enthusiastically spoken of by Sidney Muffins, editor of the "Tomfool" (with which is incorporated the "Pinchbeck News") weekly journal. Muffins is not a poet yet, but he hopes to be one when his whiskers grow and he has read "Cassel's Popular Educator." Meanwhile, he swears by Twiddles, and fiercely abuses, in print and in person, those who can't avoid the conviction that Twiddles is a donkey.

Do you see that man with the enormous red beard, the black velvet cuffs, collars, and facings to his coat, and the fez cap? That is O'Roarer. O'Roarer is a special correspondent to the "Howl" daily newspaper. O'Roarer went to the Crimea for the "Howl," during the war; he quarrelled with a major in a marching regiment, and challenged him to mortal combat. The general commanding the division was compelled to request O'Roarer to select some other locality for his hut, and terrific were the criticisms upon that divisional general's military conduct, which subsequently appeared in the "Howl." Little Eggles, who was a clerk in the Commissariat Department, who hates O'Roarer, declares that he was found in Balaclava once returning from a carouse on board ship, and *Bacchi plenus*, that he was taken to the main-guard, and in the morning, notwithstanding his protestations that it was "all a mistake," and his assertions of his "responsible position," he received the customary hospitality of the main-guard, namely, two dozen lashes. Eggles adds, with a knowing wink, that the provost-marshal was not General —— 's nephew for nothing.

Besides Mr. O'Roarer and his fellows already described, there is the Honourable Simperkin Blushington, that pleasing novelist and Oriental traveller. A little to the left, and scowling at the Honourable Simperkin fearfully, is Leathers, the author of "A Jaunt to Jericho" and "Seven Years in a Penal Settlement." Leathers wears a huge cut-velvet waistcoat, that looks like a fragment from some tapestried window-curtain. He is not at all clever, is Leathers—has no humour, observation, or power of description; but he has got a name among the book-selling trade, somehow, as a "good travelling hand"—a safe man for two volumes royal octavo with plates and a map—and so soon does any foreign country, from Canton to British Columbia, begin, from political or other causes, to attract public attention, so soon is Leathers commissioned to write his two bulky volumes of travels therein. Ill-natured people say that he keeps particulars relative to geography pigeon-holed in his library, and that he never went further than Boulogne, in the days of the five-shilling fares; but Leathers gets his price, and can afford to laugh at the evil-speaking. Bonassus, the publisher, of Bumpus Street, will have Leathers's portrait in the next edition of "Rambles in the Island of Perim."

I am sure it is very ungallant in me to have been so long silent regarding the ladies who grace the literary conversazione with their presence. A man must be, indeed, a brute who could pass over the charms of Miss Withers, aged forty, authoress of "Crackings of the Heartstrings," "Shudderings of the Soul," "Crinklings of the Spirit-skin," "Eyeball Darts," and other pathetic lyrics. Miss Withers once kept a boarding-school, but gradually languished into poetry. She attained considerable celebrity in the time of the Annuals, but on the downfall of those amusing ephemerides, she betook herself to history, and is the writer of "Lives of the Wet Nurses of the Princesses of England," "Memorials of celebrated Bedchamber Women," and "The Silversticks in Waiting before the Conquest"—all works replete with critical acumen, and brimful of historical lore, though following a little too closely in the footsteps of a lady who has written an admirable and genuine History concerning some Queens of England. Miss Withers, however, has done very well for her publishers and for herself. She is one of those authoresses who, dying, would never wish to blot out a line they had written, simply because Heaven has gifted them with a happy mental cecity that prevents them from discerning that nine-tenths of their works should never have been written at all. You may see Miss Withers any day in the British Museum Reading-room, vigorously compiling away at the desk marked "for ladies only." She has piles of books around her; she makes the attendants' lives a torment to them with the flying squadrons of book-tickets she deposits at the bar; she walks about the india-rubber flooring with one pen behind her ear and another in her mouth. She, being tall, bony, severe of aspect, and much given to snuff-taking, is generally feared by the Museum frequenters. She wrenches volumes of the catalogue from mild young clergymen in spectacles and M. B. waistcoats. She follows line after line of the printed page with her heavy inkstained forefinger. Once Dedman the pedigree-hunter, who was filling up his ticket opposite Miss Withers, was venturous enough to ask her the day of the month. She called him, in a hollow voice, "fellow," on the spot, snuffed indignantly, and afterwards spoke of him to the attendant with the red moustache as an "impertinent jackanapes." The only person with whom she condescends to be conversational in the reading-room, is Eglintoun Beaverup, the famous novelist, satirist, poet, traveller, Quarterly Reviewer, essayist, epigrammatist and politician, who stood for the Macbeth district of burghs last general election, and proved in an article in the "Rampant Magazine," that the present Duke of Sennacherib's grandfather was a pork butcher in Liquorpond Street, and that Sir Ranulph De Brie's papa (who was a pawnbroker) owed his baronetcy to a loan of ten thousand pounds, advanced by him to the Prince Regent on the security of a pinchbeck watch, which that improvident scion of royalty, having no other available pawnable property, had borrowed for the nonce from one of the helpers in his stable. Beaverup is himself descended from Brian de Bois Guilbert on the father's side, and from the original Thane of Cawdor, who slew Duncan, on that of the mother. Miss Withers will sometimes exchange deadly whispers with him relative to the mushroom characteristics of our modern peerage, and the departed glories of soccage and villeinage, infang theof and outfang theof.

Ah! and you are there, too, at Mrs. Van Umbug's conversazione, little Fanny Gillytin. Even so! behold Fanny in a black satin dress and a laced *berthe*, and her yellow wavy hair parted on one side like a man, seated on an ottoman in deep conversation with Professor Sventurato, that red-hot republican, formerly one of the tribunes of the Ultramontane Republic; next, under the name of Kibaub Bey, a colonel in the Turkish service, warring against the Moscovs in Anatolia; then deputy-assistant quartermaster-general under the immortal Walker, liberator of Nicaragua; next, an actor at the Variétés Theatre, New Orleans; next, keeper of an oyster and lager bier saloon, in One-Hundred-and-Twenty-seventh Street, Ginslingopolis, in the United States of America; next, of Paris, Milan, Turin, Vienna, and Pesth, travelling as a broom-girl, an old woman, a Jesuit priest, a waiter at a *café*, a Franciscan friar, and a clown to a circus; now of the Whetstone Park College for Ladies (by whom he is adored), professor of modern languages; during the foregoing time, and occasionally, a prisoner in divers cells, wards, casemates, underground dungeons, *oubliettes*, *piombi*, *ergastoli*, and penal colonies, from all of which he has escaped by means little short of miraculous. Fanny, they say, is madly in love with Sventurato, and would marry him, were not the professor already allied to a Moldo-Wallachian lady, the daughter of a Kaïmakan, whose heroism effected his escape from the citadel of Comorn, and who afterwards essayed to poison him in his coffee. Fanny is no less mad after liberty, by which she means universal democracy, universal spoliation, and universal smash. She has some private fortune, which she dispenses liberally among necessitous refugees; and in furtherance of the sacred cause of liberty—as she understands it—she has written piles of books. She is the authoress of that flaming epic, "The Tyrant's Entrails, or a Maiden's Wish;" "Crowns and Coffins, or Oligarchs and Ogres," an historical retrospect; "Mazzini the Shiloh," and "Victory and Vitriol," those soul-stirring pamphlets. She signs revolutionary bank-notes; she applauds regicide; she is in correspondence (in a complicated cipher which every police official from Paris to Petersburg understands and laughs at) with foreign revolutionary committees. She visits the Continent sometimes to distribute funds and ammunition. She would be ready to assume man's clothes for the benefit of her adored liberty—as she understands it. Ah! Fanny, Fanny, pause; ah! rash and foolish girl, for whom to be whipped and sent to bed would be the better portion, forbear to play with these edged tools! No second-sight is necessary for the result of these miserable machinations to be manifest. I see the portico of a theatre brilliantly lighted up; for a Tyrant and his young innocent wife come hither to-night. He is hemmed in by guards and police-agents; yet, for all his escort, desperate men rush forward and throw hand-grenades beneath his carriage-wheels. A horrible explosion, and then scores of peaceful men, women, and children, are borne, dead or frightfully mutilated, to the hospitals; and the Tyrant, safe and sound, bows to a cheering audience from his box. I see four downcast men sitting between gensd'arme on the criminals' bench of a crowded court-house, before stern judges who have doomed them to death before the very reading of the indictment. I see a straight-waistcoated wretch sitting in his chair in a gloomy cell, his head bent down, the governor and the priest standing by, while the executioner cuts off his hair and shaves the back of his neck. I see a grim, gray winter's morning in the fatal Place of the Roquette. A space is kept clear by thousands of horse, foot, artillery, and police; and, thrust to the furthermost limits of the place, is a pale-faced crowd surging like a sea. Then the drums beat, and the dismal procession issues from a prison to a scaffold. Then, tottering between priests and turn-keys, come two bare-footed men, with long white shirts over their garments, and their faces concealed by hideous black veils. But the veils are removed when they mount the scaffold, when one by one a distorted, livid face, with white lips, appears, when the executioner seizes the pinioned criminal, and flings him—yes, flings him, is the word—on the plank. Then I see the horrible gash in the face as the moribund strives to shape his mouth to utter his last words on earth; the last up-turning of the starting eye-balls; but the plank reverses, the rollers revolve, the slide closes, the spring is touched, the KNIFE falls, the blood spouts, and the heads drop into the sawdust of the red basket. Liberty, equality, and fraternity, flaming epics, soul-stirring pamphlets, and complicated ciphers, have come to this miserable end. The Tyrant is borne through the streets, the people shouting, and the maidens strewing flowers at his feet. The telegram has been despatched from the revolutionary committee to the Roquette, and the answer is a corpse that quivers, the parricide's shroud, and the headsman's bloody axe.

Of course there are some titled folks at Mrs. Van Umbug's conversazione: it would not be complete without a literary lord—a harmless nobleman, generally, who has translated Horace, invented a new metre, or discovered a new butterfly; and a literary lady—if separated from her husband all the better, who paints him in the darkest of colours, as the hero of every one of her novels. And, equally of course, Ethelred Guffoon is here. Ethelred Guffoon is everywhere. He is one of Mrs. Van Umbug's special favourites. She calls him by his Christian name. He hunts up new lions for her; occasionally he officiates as peacemaker, and prevents the lions from growling and fighting among themselves. He rushes from Mrs. Van Umbug's conversazione to the Pontoppidan Theatre, to see a new face, which he must criticise; after that he will sit up half the night to review Mr. Gladstone's Homer, for the "Daily Scratcher," and will be at Somerset House by punctual office hours the next morning. A man of the age, Ethelred Guffoon—a man of the time, a good fellow, but frivolous.

I wonder whether the celebrities one sees at this shadowy conversazione really represent the literary world—the real people who write the books and think the thoughts. I am afraid they do not. I fear that to find the princes of the pen, the giants of the land of letters, I must go further afield. Lo, here is Great Tom of Chelsea, sitting cosily, in his back parlour, smoking a pipe of bird's-eye with Eglintoun Beaverup, and telling him he is about having his ceilings whitewashed. Here is Lord Livy poring over Restoration and Revolution broadsides by his reading-lamp in his lonely chambers in the Albany;—no, not lonely, the spirits of the old historic men come from their dusty shelves and clap him on the shoulder, and cry, "Go on and prosper, Thomas Babington, Lord Livy." The great Mr. Polyphemus, the novelist, is bidden to the Duke of Sennacherib's, and as he rolls to Sennacherib House in his brougham, meditates satiric onslaughts on "Tom Garbage" and "Young Grubstreet"—those Tom Thumb foes of his[12]—in the next number of the "Pennsylvanians." Mr. Goodman Twoshoes is reading one of his own books to the members of the Chawbacon Athenæum, and making, I am delighted to hear, a mint of money by the simple process. Goldpen, the poet, has taken his wife and children to Miss P. Horton's entertainment; Bays, the great dramatist, is sitting in the stalls of the Pontoppidan Theatre listening with rapt ears to the jokes in his own farce; and Selwyn Cope, the essayist, is snoring snugly between the sheets, having to rise very early to-morrow morning in order to see a man hanged. And where are the working-men of literature, the conscripts of the pen, doomed to carry Brown Bess, for sixpence a day, all their lives? Where are Garbage and Grubstreet? In the worst inn's worst room, with racing prints half hung, the walls of plaster and the floors of sand, at once a deal table but stained with beer, sits Garbage playing four-handed cribbage with an impenitent hostler, a sporting man who has sold the fight, and a potboy who is a returned convict? Sits he there, I ask, or is he peacefully pursuing his vocation in country lodgings? And Grubstreet, is he in some murky den, with a vulture's quill dipped in vitriol inditing libels upon the great, good, and wise of the day? Wonder upon wonders, Grubstreet sits in a handsome study—listening to his wife laughing, over her crochet work, at Mr. Polyphemus's last attack on him, and dandling a little child upon his knee! Oh! the strange world in which we live, and the post that people will knock their heads against!

ELEVEN O'CLOCK P.M.: A SCIENTIFIC CONVERSAZIONE.

From a literary to a learned or scientific conversazione, at one of which we are about to take a transient peep, there is but one step; indeed, literature is always welcome among the good-natured old Dryasdusts, who are continually raking and rummaging, and rocking the "placers" and "prospects" of knowledge, and turning up huge masses of quartz, from which the nimble-fingered chymists of the pen extract flakes of shining gold. Presto! we leave the Republic of Letters, and are in the handsome rooms of the Royal Inquiring Society. This meritorious association (incorporated by Royal charter) is perpetually asking questions, and, though it often receives insufficient, if not ridiculous responses, yet manages, at the close of every year, to accumulate a highly-respectable stock of information on almost every imaginable topic. The members, I will assume (would that such a society in strict reality existed), are draughts from all the learned, scientific, philosophical, antiquarian, and artistic societies in London; and on the first Thursday in every month during the season, they meet to gloze over curiosities exhibited for their inspection, to shake hands and crack jokes with one another—I have even seen the friendly dig in the ribs, accompanied by the sly chuckle, occasionally administered—and to ask questions and receive answers. They are "Notes and Queries" (chattiest, most quaintly-erudite of periodicals) incarnated. But they abjure not the presence of the gentler, unscientific sex. These rare old boys of learning and science thread their way through the rooms (sometimes almost inconveniently crowded, for the Royal Inquiring Society is very popular) with blooming wives and daughters on their arms. The young ladies delight in these conversaziones—for a change. They are so strange, so peculiar, they say. You don't meet anybody to dance with or to talk about the weather, or the Crystal Palace, or crinoline, or the Botanical Gardens; but you see such nice old gentlemen, with dear, shiny, bald heads, and such wonderful intellectual-looking beings, with long hair, turn-down collars, and large feet, who smell musty bones with unpronounceable names, and make extraordinary instruments to whiz round, and point out places upon maps, and talk *so* cleverly (but so incomprehensibly to you, my dears) about rusty coins and the backbones of fishes, and battered saucepans, which *they* say are helmets. And then there are the nice stereoscopes to peep through, and the beautiful water-colour drawings and photographs to look at, and the old gentlemen are so quiet and so polite, and so different from the young men one meets in society, who either stammer and blush or are superciliously rude and put their hands in their trousers' pockets. Yes, young ladies, the bald-headed old gentlemen, the careworn, long-haired, slovenly-looking men, are quiet and polite. They were, many of them, poor and humble once; but they have hewn out steps from the rock of knowledge, whereby they have mounted to that better fortune—European, Worldwide fame. That quiet man with gray hair, smiles when ministers press upon him a knighthood or a baronetcy: "*Cui bono?*" he says; "I would rather be a corresponding member of the Academy of Honolulu. When I am old and broke, and past work, you may give me enough for a little bread in my old days: I take it as a Right, not as a favour," just as Turner the painter left in his will the simple direction that he was to be buried in the Cathedral Church of St. Paul.—"St. Paul's is for the painters and the warriors, as Westminster Abbey is for the poets and statesmen; but I want not your honours and titles. Such as you have, you bestow on your lawyers and your lacqueys; but your captains are almost ashamed to take the decorations that are shared by footmen and backstairs cringers."

You have readily divined, I hope, why I have instructed the dexterous limner who illustrates these pages to select for his subject the scientific, rather than the literary, conversazione. The men of science do not obtrude their personalities upon the public. Their fame is known, their influence felt from London to Louisiana, but their portraits seldom meet the public eye. Those of General Tom Thumb or the Christy Minstrels would attract more crowds to the print-shop windows, and sell better. But, good lack! what a commotion there would be if the portraits of a series of *littérateurs*, in their habits as they live, appeared in "Twice Round the Clock!" I should be denounced, repudiated, vilified, abused, for the artist's misdeeds. The great Mr. Polyphemus would crush me mercilessly beneath his iron heel; Grubstreet would (threaten to) kick me; Garbage would have me on the hip; O'Roarer smite me beneath the fifth rib; Leathers devise devices against me to make my existence intolerable; and Ethelred Guffoon castigate me terribly in his popular paper, "The Half-penny Cane." No; let me deal only with the shadows; and those that the cobweb cap fits, e'en let them wear it.

At Eleven o'Clock in the evening, the social institutions known as Evening Parties assume their gayest and most radiant aspect. I think that I have already hinted in these pages that I am not a very frequent visitor at these entertainments. The truth must out: the people don't like me. At the last *soirée* I attended, a fashionable physician, coming in very late, and throwing out for general hearing the fact that he had been dining with an earl, I meekly suggested that he should allow me to rub myself up against him, in order to catch some of his aristocracy. All the women laughed, but the men looked as though they would have very much liked to throw me out of the window. There was one exception—a gentleman with one eye, and a face like a glass case full of curiosities, so many different phases of expression were there in it, who came across to me and made friends at once. But I shall never be asked to that house again; and if I am ill, I won't send for the fashionable physician. *Timeo Danäos*, and the pills they give you.

Thus circumstanced, I feel it becoming my degree to stay on the outside of great houses, and, herding among the crowd and the link-men, to witness the setting down and the taking up of the carriages coming to or going from evening parties. It has always been my lot so to stand on the kerb, to be a continual dweller on the threshold. I have stood there to see people married, to see people buried, and have murmured: "My turn must come next, surely;" but my time has not come yet. A king has patted me on the head, and I have sate, as a child, on the knee of the handsomest woman in Europe. I have been on the brink of many a precipice; I have attained the edge of many a cloud. But I have stopped there. I have always been like the recalcitrant costermonger's donkey, "going for to go," but never accomplishing the journey in its entirety.

I spoke of link-men. I might tell you a not uninteresting story regarding those industrials, in these gas-lit days growing day by day rarer and rarer. The tarred-rope made links are indeed, save on extraneous foggy nights, grown quite extinct, and are replaced by neat lanterns; and the time will come when the old red jackets, famous as a class from Grosvenor Square to the Horticultural Gardens at Chiswick, from the club-house fronts, on *levée* days, to the doorways of evening parties, shall become quite obsolete. But there is a grand old admiral living now—titled, high in office, before whom even his equals in rank bow, and who can make post-captains wait in his ante-chambers—who owes at least half his advancement and social position to the services of the link-men. Thirty years ago this officer was a young stripling, cast upon the ocean of London society. He was of good family, but his acquaintances in the fashionable world were few and far between, his influence was *nil*, and his promotion was therefore more than dubious. But at the Opera, then the King's Theatre, he happened to form a shilling-giving on the one side, cap-touching on the other, acquaintance with a link-man— Silver Tom, I think he was called, from a silver badge he always wore, presented to him by a noble marquis whom he had saved from being prematurely scrunched on a certain dark night between his own carriage wheels and those of the equipage of a duchess, his grandmamma. "Silver Tom," moved by gratitude, and experienced by his (outside) knowledge of the fashionable world, put the then young and poor lieutenant up to what is vernacularly known as "a thing or two." Not a grand entertainment could be given in Fashionabledom, but on the lieutenant's arrival in full evening costume, "Silver Tom" bawled up his name to the footman in attendance on the door-step (the *régime* of cards was not so strictly attended to as it is now); he on the door-step halloaed it out to the powdered attendant on the first landing; he, in his turn, gave it to the black-vestmented groom of the chambers, who proclaimed it to the world in general in sonorous tones, and the bold lieutenant was inducted to the saloons of reception. Who was to know whether he had been invited to the feast or not? Not, certainly, the hostess, who, perhaps, did not know two hundred and fifty of her five hundred guests by sight. Some had been asked by her husband, some by herself. Not certainly the guests, who would not have been much surprised if they had met the Hottentot Venus or the King of the Cannibal Islands. The lieutenant made his bow and himself comfortable; was sure to meet some lady or gentleman in society whom he knew, and probably departed with a list of half-a-dozen newly-formed and valuable acquaintances. He went on and prospered. Gradually, from being met and liked at great houses, he received genuine invitations, and, as I have premised, he made a good end of it at the Admiralty. I hope he pensioned "Silver Tom."

ELEVEN O'CLOCK P.M.: AN EVENING PARTY.

Who is dead by this time, most probably; but I can still stand by the side of his successor, at the door of the great house, by the lamp and lantern's glare, and see the gay company pass in and out. How the horses champ! how the dresses rustle! how the jewels shine! and what fair women and brave men are here congregated! Messrs. Weippert's or Collinet's band are upstairs; Messrs. Gunter's men have brought the ices; there are flirtations in the conservatories, and squeezings of hands interchanged on the stairs. Vows of love are spoken, flowers from bouquets are given; and is it not, after all, the same old, old story, that boys and girls will love one another, and that the old people will look on with pretended severity, but with real contentment in their hearts, and that there will be present a few jealous and cankered ones, who will look on to envy the others because they are so happy? Drive envy from your hearts, ye who ride not in gilded chariots, and move not in the "fashionable circles." There is as much truth, love, and gaiety at a "sixpenny hop," between maid-servants and journeymen bakers, as at the most refined evening parties.

MIDNIGHT.—THE HAYMARKET, AND THE SUB-EDITOR'S ROOM.

Midnight: an awful sound. Supposing you were to be hanged at three o'clock in the morning, as I am doomed to be, in a literary sense, how would you like to hear twelve o'clock sound? But three hours more to live! In three hours "the sheriff he will come," and the chaplain, and the hangman, as they came to Mr. Samuel Hall *en route* for Tyburn. In three hours the clock will run down; the pendulum shall oscillate no more; Time shall rest on his scythe; the last grain of sand shall run out, and of these ephemeral papers you shall say *fuit*. We have clomb the hill together, and we will rest together at the foot.

Glancing over my map of London, and retracing the course of our peregrinations, I find, with some complacency, that we have not, after all, left many parts of the metropolis unexplored. We have been to Camberwell and to Hyde Park Corner; to Pentonville and to London Bridge; to Billingsgate and to Euston Square. It is true, that we have not yet penetrated to the interior of Buckingham Palace, or the condemned cell at Newgate, nor do I think that I shall assume the part of the Boy Jones or a visiting magistrate for your amusement; but we have been "behind the scenes" of more places than theatres since this clock was first wound up. It is not without regret now, that I linger over and dally with my few remaining hours. They have been very pleasant ones for me. I shall miss the printer's boy (for, be it known, I am about to abandon literature and go into trade, though I have not yet settled the precise business—corn, or coals, or commission agency). I shall miss, beyond aught else, the daily deluge of letters from anonymous correspondents—praising, blaming, complaining, or inquiring, but all, I am glad to say, very appreciative readers of my shiftless writings.

But we have come to the complexion of midnight, and the hour must be described. It is fraught with meaning for London. You know that in poetical parlance midnight is the time when church-yards yawn (they had need to be weary now, for the Board of Health won't allow them to receive any occupants *intra muros*), and graves give up their dead. And there be other grave-yards in London town—yards where no tombstones or brick vaults are—that at midnight yawn and send forth ghosts to haunt the city. A new life begins for London at midnight. Strange shapes appear of men and women who have lain a-bed all the day and evening, or have remained torpid in holes and corners. They come out arrayed in strange and fantastic garments, and in glaringly gaslit rooms screech and gabble in wild revelry. The street corners are beset by night prowlers. Phantoms arrayed in satin and lace flit upon the sight. The devil puts a diamond ring on his taloned finger, sticks a pin in his shirt, and takes his walks abroad. It is a stranger sight than even the painter Raffet imagined in his picture of Napoleon's midnight review, and it is, I think, a much better thing to be at home and in bed, than wandering about and peeping into the mysteries of this unholy London night life.

I know this book (to my sorrow) well; have conned its grim pages, and studied its unwholesome lore, attentively. But I am not about to make you a too-recondite participant in my knowledge. Were it not that the appointed hours were meted out to me, and that from one of the hours—midnight—the Haymarket is inseparable, the wicked street should find no place here; but I must be faithful to my trust, and the bad thoroughfare must be in part described.

Foreigners have frequently pointed out to me a peculiar aspect of London, and one which appeals strongly to the observant faculties, and which, nevertheless, may escape us Cockneys who are to the metropolitan manner born. It is the duality of the huge city, not so much as regards its night and day side, as in its Sunday and week-day appearance. And this is not wholly to be ascribed to the shop shutters being closed. The Strand on Ash Wednesdays and Good Fridays is still the Strand; but on the Sabbath it would seem as though every house in the West and East ends had put on its special Sunday suit, and had decorated itself with a certain smug spruceness quite marked and distinct. You have a difficulty in recognising your most familiar streets. Regent Street is quite altered. The aspect of Piccadilly is entirely changed; and Cheapside is no more like the Cheapside of yesterday than Hamlet is like Hecuba. The people, too, are not by any means the same people you meet on week-days. Not only their clothes are different, but their faces, their manners, their very gait and bearing, seem changed. You meet people out walking on Sundays, who during the week are confined to places where they are hidden from the public gaze, or are at most but half visible. You see the bar-maids' skirts and the pawnbrokers' legs on Sundays. From Monday to Saturday you can see but their busts. You may nod to a sheriff's officer on Sunday without entertaining any apprehensions as to the piece of paper he may have against you in that dismal black leather pocket-book of his. The omnibus roofs are covered, the steamboats' decks are crowded, the cabs full, the pavement thronged, the very saddle-horses bestridden by men who seem of a different race to the outside world of the previous four and twenty hours. Dirty streets look clean; disreputable streets decorous; and thoroughfares that were as still as mice during the week, become quite noisy on Sundays with carriage and cab wheels, as sinners of wealth and distinction rattle up to the doors of the fashionable chapel.

It is the privilege of the unique Haymarket to be like its week-night self on Sunday; but in the six mundane days to be a totally different Haymarket from the street which it becomes immediately after midnight. True, by daylight, and during the early part of the evening, it is that which it will remain all night: a broad thoroughfare inclining slightly downhill northward; a theatre on its eastern, a colonnaded opera-house on its western side; a thoroughfare containing a sufficiency of shops for the sale of general merchandise, but, predominating above these, a crowd of hotels, *restaurants*, cigar-divans, coffee-houses, and establishments for the sale of lobsters, oysters, and pickled salmon, according to the seasons in which those dainties are considered most fit to be enjoyed. But it is not the same—no, not at all the same—Haymarket to which it will suddenly turn, when the clock of St. Martin's church shall proclaim the hour of midnight. The change, at first imperceptible, is yet in a moment more immense. As though Harlequin had smitten the houses—and the people also—with his wand, the whole Haymarket wakes, lights, rises up with a roar, a rattle, and a shriek quite pantomimic, if not supernatural. The latter image would, I think, be the most *vrai semblant*. "Hey for fun!" "How are you to-morrow?" and "How are you?" are the cries and the pass-words. The painted Clown (in mosaic jewellery, and all-round collar, an astonishing cravat, and a variegated shirt) grins his grin and tumbles on the pavement. He is not above stealing an occasional sausage, bonneting a policeman, overturning an image-boy's stock in trade, or throwing the contents of a fishwoman's basket about. Harlequin in a mask and patchwork-suit is here, there, and everywhere, conjuring money out of people's pockets, and perpetually pursued by a vindictive Sprite, habited in the garb of a police constable. The lean and slippered Pantaloon hobbles over the flags, and grimaces, with his wicked old countenance, beneath the gas-lamps. And Columbine, *Wallah billah!* Columbine in muslins, spangles, and artificial flowers, is here, there, and everywhere, too, and dances her miserable jigs to the sorry music of the fife, viol, and tabor, squeaking, scraping, and thumping at the gin-shop by the corner of the court.

Midnight: the play is over, and the audience pour from the Haymarket Theatre. The aristocratic opera season is concluded by this time of the year, and the lovers of the drama have it all their own way. Crowds of jovial young clerks and spruce law students cluster beneath the portico, yet convulsed by the humours of Mr. Buckstone. Happy families of rosy children, radiant in lay-down collars, white skirts and pink sashes, trot from the entrance to the dress-circle under the wing of benevolent papa and stout good-humoured mamma, with a white burnous, and a tremendous fan; their healthy countenances all beaming and mantling with smiles, and joyously recalling the jokes of that funny old man in the farce, or expatiating on the glories of the concluding *tableau*, with its tinsel and gold leaf, its caryatides of ballet girls, and its red and blue fire, in Mr. Talfourd's last sparkling burlesque. Happy, happy days and frame of mind, when the theatre can give such delights as these. Isn't it better to sit amazed and delighted in the front row of the dress-circle, or on the third row of the pit, roaring at the stalest Joe Millerisms, and clapping the hands at the tomfool feats of tumbling, than to lie *perdu* in a private-box, now scowling, and now sneering, like Stricknine, the great theatrical critic, who will go and sup afterwards at the Albion, on an underdone mutton-chop, and, calling for pen, ink, and paper, slaughter the inoffensive burlesque mercilessly. Stricknine can't write burlesques himself. He can't write books; he can only slaughter, and must have been apprenticed in his youth to Bannister or Slater. And, slaughterer as he is, he is not equal to the manly business of knocking down a bullock with a pole-axe. Give him a long keen knife, and he will puncture the neck of a lamb, and that is all.

Ethelred Guffoon (who has been to three theatres to-night) bustles out from his stall with his lorgnette in its shagreen case. Mr. Kickeroe, Q.C., comes from the pit, shouldering his umbrella. Kickeroe has been a constant visitor to the pit of the Haymarket any time these twenty years, though he could easily afford a private box once if not twice a week. His greatest extravagance is to purchase four upper-box tickets when Mr. Buckstone takes his benefit. He is an ardent admirer of the Haymarket five-act comedies; and people say that many of his most effective and jury-touching perorations have been drawn from the sentimental "tags" of the Haymarket dramatists. Trotting down the box-stairs, too, comes vivacious, learned, chatty, kindly, abusive Mr. Boblink, with his head prematurely white, but his heart as green as it was thirty years since. Mr. Boblink is generally beloved, though regarded with a humorous terror for his vituperative qualities. He expatiates on the necessity of breaking butterflies on the wheel, although, good man, he would not harm a particle of pollen on their wings. His fierce language is but the bellow of the blunderbuss: here is no bullet, not so much as a bit of old hat for wadding in his gun. He strikes with a wooden sword, and scourges malefactors with a knout whose lash is made of floss-silk. He wears the mask of a Gorgon horrible to see; but the mask is transparent as glass, and you may descry the honest genial face of the man wreathed with sly smiles behind it. So he goes through life—a *bourru bienfaisant*—hitting men sounding thwacks with a bladder full of peas, and recording sentence of literary death against culprits, knowing full well that the sentence will never be carried out. To hear Boblink talk, you would think him the most malevolent creature breathing. He is so different from smooth, quiet, smiling Mr. Stricknine, (*he* only scowls when he is alone) who presses your hand warmly, and immediately betakes himself to the Albion, there to make a neat *fricassée* of your reputation, and, in the most polished and classical language, insinuate that you are a hopeless fool with dishonest propensities. And yet Mr. Boblink has a deadly armoury of his own at home, and knows the *tierce* and the *carte* and the "*raison démonstrative*," and has, when exasperated, proved himself so cunning of fence, that I would see him hanged before I would fight with him in earnest.

Supper is now the great cry, and the abundant eating and drinking resources of the Haymarket are forthwith called into requisition. Bless us all! there must be something very dusty and exhaustive in the British drama to make this Haymarket audience so clamorous for supper. By the ravenous hunger and thirst displayed by the late patrons of the theatre, you would imagine that they had gone without dinner for a week. You may sup in the Haymarket as your taste would lead, or as the state of your finances would counsel—if people followed such counsel—you to sup. You may cut your coat according to your cloth. Are you rich—there is Dubourg's, the Hôtel de Paris, and the upstairs department of the Café de l'Europe. There is no lack of cunning cooks there, I warrant, to send you up pheasants and partridges *en papillotte*; *filets*, with mushrooms or truffles, culinary gewgaws that shall cost five shillings the dish. Yea, and cellarers will not be wanting to convey to you the Roederer's Champagne, the fragrant Clos Vougeot, the refreshing Lafitte, and the enlivening Chambertin with yellow seal; smooth waiters to attend to your minutest wishes, and bring you the handsome reckoning on an electro-silver plateau, and, with many bows, return you what odd change there may be out of a five-pound note. I do not say that the Haymarket contains such gorgeous supper-houses as the Maison Dorée, the Café de Paris, the Café Anglais, or Vachette's; but I have seen some notable *parties fines* within its precincts. The Haymarket never was virtuous; so there is never any question about the cakes and ale, and the ginger that is hot in the mouth, to be found therein.

If still your taste leads you towards French cookery—though you wince somewhat at the idea of claret, Burgundy, and Champagne to follow—there exists a second-class French *restaurant* or two where succulent suppers may be obtained at moderate prices. If unpretending chops, steaks, kidneys, sausages, or Welsh rabbit, washed down by the homely British brown stout, and followed perchance by the soothing cigar, and the jorum of hot anything-and-water: if such be your ambition, I should advise you not to sup in the Haymarket at all; but to wait till one o'clock and sup with me. I will show you the whereabouts. Such chops and steaks and *et ceteras*, you may indeed obtain in the neighbourhood, but I like them not. If your funds and your credit be very low, why, you can enter one of the taverns—if you can reach the bar for the crowd of Bacchanalians that are gathered before it, and sup on the quarter of a pork pie, a sausage roll, and a Banbury cake, washed down by a glass of pale ale; nay, if you be yet lower in pocket, and your available wealth be limited to the possession of the modest and retiring penny, you may, at the doors of most of the taverns, meet with an ancient dame, of unpretending appearance, bearing a flat basket lined with a fair white cloth. She for your penny will administer to you a brace of bones, covered with a soft white integument, which she will inform you are "trotters." There is not much meat on them; but they are very toothsome and succulent. It is no business of yours to inquire whether these be sheep's trotters or pigs' trotters, or the trotters of corpulent rats or overgrown mice. They are trotters. Look not the gift-horse in the mouth; for the penny was perhaps a gift, however strictly you may have purchased the trotters. Eat them, and thank heaven, and go thy ways, and take a cooling drink at the nearest pump with an iron ladle chained to it, which is, if I am not mistaken, over-against St. James's Church in Piccadilly. Or, perhaps you are fond of ham-sandwiches. The unpretending dame with the basket will straightway vend you two slices of a pale substance, resembling in taste and texture sawdust pressed into a concrete form, between which is spread a veneer of inorganic matter, having apparently a strong affinity to salted logwood. This is ham! The concrete sawdust is bread! The whole is a sandwich! These luxuries are reckoned very nice by some persons, and quite strengthening.

Or, "another way," as old Mrs. Glasse says in her cookery book. At the Coventry Street extremity of the Haymarket stands that celebrated and long-established institution known as the Royal Albert Potato Can. At that three-legged emporium of smoking vegetables, gleaming with block tin painted red, and brazen ornaments, the humble pilgrim of the Haymarket may halt and sup for a penny. For a penny? What say I? for a halfpenny even, may the belated and impoverished traveller obtain a refreshment at once warm, farinaceous, and nourishing. Garnish your potato, when the Khan of the Haymarket has taken him from his hot blanket-bed, and cut him in two—garnish him with salt and pepper, eschew not those condiments, they are harmless, nay, stimulating; but ho! my son, beware of the butter! it is confusion. Better a dry potato and a contented mind, than dreadful Irish salt grease—for butter I dare not call it, which may give you a bilious attack that will last for a month.

I should like to know what has been the use of my recommending these various grades of supper to you, from the lordly Café de l'Europe to the humble Potato Can, when I should have known all along, and as it were intuitively, that your mind was bent upon oysters, and that oysters after the play you were determined to have. Come along, then, a' goodness' name, and if oysters are to be the order of the night, e'en let us have them.

The London oyster, or rather shell and cured fish shop, for the sale of lobsters, crabs, pickled and kippered salmon, bloaters, and dried sprats, is combined with that of the delicious molluscs of which so many thousands are nightly consumed; the London oyster-shop, and particularly the Haymarket one, stands, and is a thing apart, among the notabilia of this metropolis. You know how the French eat oysters. There is the *belle écaillère*, generally a hideous old woman of about sixty, with a snuffy-looking pocket-handkerchief twisted round her head, who sits at the *restaurant* door amid a grove of oyster-shells and hanks of straw, and, in the intervals of oyster-opening, darns worsted stockings. The nimble *garçons* come skipping from the gilded saloons of the *restaurant* within, and demand their required dozens and half-dozens from the *écaillère* without. The bearded frequenters of the *restaurant* evidently think it an epicurean and fashionable thing to commence, or rather precede dinner, by swallowing so many oysters. There are enterprising *bon vivants* who will even go so far as their two dozen: but I dissent from them, for three reasons: The first, that, in my opinion, oysters should be eaten either alone—of themselves, by themselves, or for themselves—or that they should be consumed full twenty minutes before the repast; for the second, that all French oysters, whether of Ostend, Maremnes, or Canale, are to me utterly abominable, having—even when they are fresh, which is seldom—a certain coppery flavour, superlatively nauseous; for the third, that in the best French *restaurants*, it is difficult, if not impossible, to procure Cayenne pepper; and, without that rubicund condiment, I would give no more for the best "natives" than for a plate of cold boiled veal without salt. The *écaillère* element is the only one prevalent in France relative to the sale of oysters, and the consumers pick them off the shells with little silver pitchforks, squeeze lemon over them, and eat them daintily in many mouthfuls. Fie upon such miminy-piminy ways! Oyster-shops the French don't seem to understand at all. At Chevet's, that vast comestible shop in the Palais Royal, they keep oysters, and lobsters, and prawns, and shrimps—keep them as a show in the windows for a week or two, when, their novelty beginning to wear off, they are disposed of, I presume, to the nobility and gentry. They tell a story of a Frenchman, who hoarded up his money, in order to purchase *un homard magnifique*, which he had seen at Chevet's, and to which he had taken a fancy.

MIDNIGHT: SUPPER-ROOMS IN THE HAYMARKET.

Americans tell me that though the oyster attains high perfection, and is held in culinary reverence as high, in the States, anything resembling our Haymarket oyster-shop is not to be found in New York. But on Broadway Pavement, during the gay night, brilliant lamps, sometimes coloured in fantastic devices, invite you to enter underground temples of oyster-eating. These are called oyster-cellars. Some are low and disreputable enough, and not impassible to imputations of gouging, bowie-knifing, and knuckle-dusting; but others are really magnificent suites of apartments, decorated with mirrors and chandeliers, and glowing with gilding, mahogany, and crimson velvet; and here you may consume oysters as small as periwinkles or as large as cheese-plates—oysters of strange and wondrous flavours—oysters with *bizarre* and well-nigh unpronounceable names—oysters cooked in ways the most marvellous and multifarious: stewed, broiled, fried, scolloped, barbacued, toasted, grilled, and made hot in silver chafing dishes like the delicious preparation known as "despatch lobster." You wash down suppers in oyster-cellars such as these with Hock and Champagne; yet for all the splendour and the rarity of the cooking, and the variety of oysters, I will abide by the Haymarket oyster-shop, rude, simple, primitive as it is, with its peaceful concourse of customers taking perpendicular refreshment at the counter, plying the unpretending pepper-castor, and the vinegar-cruet with the perforated cork, calling cheerfully for crusty bread and pats of butter; and, tossing off foaming pints of brownest stout, (pale ale—save in bottles, and of the friskiest description—is, with oysters, a mistake) contentedly wipe their hands on the jack-towel on its roller afterwards.

As in this real life of ours, Old Age and Infancy often meet on neutral ground, and the prattle of the child goes forth with hand out-stretched to meet the graybeard's maundering: so, oh reader, do I find the beginning and the end of these papers drawing closer and closer together. Ere many hours they will meet; and their conjunction shall be the signal for their decay. You will remember how, when the day was very young, the morning scarce swaddled, and kicking in his cradle with encrimsoned heels (Aurora, the nurse, had chafed them), we visited a great newspaper office, and saw the publication of the monster journal. Now, when midnight itself is fallen into the sere and yellow, we stand once more within the precincts of journalism. This is not, however, the monster journal that has all Printing House Square to roar and rattle in. No: our office is in the Strand. We are free of the charmed domains. We pass up a narrow court running by the side of the office, push aside a heavy door, ascend the creaking staircase, and discreetly tapping at a door, this time covered with green baize, find ourselves in the presence of Mr. Limberly, the sub-editor of the "Daily Wagon."

Let us cast a glance round the room. What a litter it is in, to be sure! what piles of newspapers, home and country ones, mangled and disembowelled by the relentless scissors, cumber the floor! More newspapers on shelves—old files, these—more on the table; letters opened and unopened, wet proof-sheets, files of "copy," books for review, just sent by the publishers, or returned by the reviewers, after they have duly demolished the contents and the authors. And all about the room are great splashes and dried-up pools of ink, and the ceiling is darkened with the smoke of innumerable candles—gas was, until very lately, considered anything but orthodox in a newspaper office, and many sub-editors still find its sharp, harsh, flickering, though brilliant light, far inferior to the honest, though evil-smelling, old tallow-candles, in their tin sconces and japanned shades. The "Daily Wagon," be it understood, is a newspaper of the good old Conservative way of thinking—no Liberal notions, or humbug of that sort: Church and State, strict constitutional and social discipline (including game-laws, religious disabilities, church-rates, unequal taxation, rural justices' justice, and flogging in the army and schools)—the True Blue British line of politics, in fact. Thus situated, the "Wagon," one of whose proprietors is said to be a peer, another a bishop, and a third a brewer—nothing could be more respectable—sticks to its old office, its old rooms, and its old staff. The two former have not been painted within the memory of man; though it must be admitted that the latter wash quite as frequently as the *employés* of the "Morning Cracker," with its bran-new offices, its bran-new furniture, its bran-new type, paper, machines, writers—bran-new everything but ideas. The "Daily Wagoners" affect to sneer at the "Morning Cracker," which, in its turn, laughs the "Wagon" to scorn; but both combine in abusing the monster journal of Printing House Square. "Wagoner" and "Cracker" are both high-priced journals. So, of course, they both feel bound to ignore even the existence of a journal called the "Daily Bombshell," which somehow manages to keep up a better staff of writers, and a larger establishment, to give fresher news, more accurate intelligence, more interesting correspondence, and reflections on public events incomparably more powerful, than its high-priced contemporaries, all for the small sum of one penny. The "Wagon" and the "Cracker" are in a chronic state of rage at the "Bombshell," though they pretend to ignore its existence; but one day the bishop who is interested in the "Wagon," hearing that the circulation of the abhorred "Bombshell" exceeded fifty thousand, while that of his own beloved journal fluctuated between five and seven hundred, drove down in almost delirious excitement to the offices of the "Wagon"—drove down in his own carriage, with his mitre on the panels—and suggested to Mr. Fitzfluke, the editor, that the price of the paper should forthwith come down to one penny. But Mr. Fitzfluke shook his head in respectful deprecation of the proposition, and summoned to his aid Mr. Limberly, who likewise shook his head, and whispered the magic word "advertisements." A grand consultation between the proprietors took place next day, whereat the brewer came out in a rabidly conservative point of view, and declared, striking a leathern-covered table, that he would sooner see his own "Entire" retailed at a penny a pint, than submit to an imitation in price of the "rubbishing prints" of a set of "dam radicals." So the "Daily Wagon" keeps up its price, and manages to crawl on in a tortoise-like manner, supported by its advertisements. It sleeps a good deal, and doesn't want much to eat; and will bear being trodden on, stumbled over, nay, occasionally jumped upon, without seeming in the least to mind it.

MIDNIGHT: THE SUB-EDITOR'S ROOM.

Mr. Limberly sits, then, in his sub-editorial throne—an unpretending cane-bottomed arm-chair—surrounded by his *attachés* and myrmidons, his good men and true. The electric telegraph messenger—a spruce lad in the not unbecoming uniform of that recently-formed corps—has just arrived, bearing a message which may announce either war in the East or Peace in China, either a fluctuation in the funds at St. Petersburg, or a murder at Haverfordwest; either the wreck of a steamer, with all hands lost, on the north-west coast of Ireland, or the arrival in the Mersey of a clipper ship from Australia, with a few score thousand ounces of gold in her treasure-room, to say nothing of the nuggets, the gold dust, and the bankers' receipts in the pockets of her wide-awake-hatted passengers. But all is fish that comes to Mr. Limberly's net. Leading article and literary criticism, theatrical notices and prices of railway and mining shares, advertisements and letters from eulogistic or indignant correspondents, telegrams and foreign tittle-tattle, fires, murders, fatal accidents, coroners' inquests, enormous gooseberries, showers of frogs, the acceptances of the St. Leger, and the prices of hops in the Borough Market: he looks upon all these items but as so much "copy," for which the master printer is waiting, and which are required to fill the ever-yawning columns of the "Daily Wagon." Snipping and pasting, extracting, excising, revising, and correcting, Mr. Limberly will work late into the night and early into the morning; but he will not dream of retiring to rest till the paper itself be "put to bed,"—*i.e.*, laid on the printing machine for the requisite number of copies to be struck off; and even then he will probably go and smoke a cigar at the "Crimson Hippopotamus," in the Strand, hard by—the great house of call for morning journalists—before he hails his matutinal cab, the driver of which waits for him on the stand, and looks out for him quite as a regular customer, and rattles over Waterloo Bridge to his well-deserved bed.

ONE O'CLOCK A.M.—EVANS'S SUPPER-ROOMS, AND A FIRE.

In the bleak, timbery city of Copenhagen, so terribly maltreated at the commencement of the century by Admiral Lord Nelson, K.C.B.; in that anything-but-agreeable capital of Denmark, where raw turnips sliced in brandy form a favourite whet before dinner,—where they blacklead (apparently) the stairs in the houses, and three-fourths of every apartment are sacrificed to the preposterous exigencies of the Stove; where the churches are mostly of wood, and the streets are paved with a substance nearly resembling petrified kidney potatoes; in Copenhagen, then, I formed, some thirty months since, a transient acquaintance with an old gentleman in green spectacles. He was a Dane, formerly commercial, now retired from business. He came every day, and with unvarying regularity, to take his post-prandial coffee and *petit verre* in the *speise saal* of the hotel then afflicted with my custom: he generally indulged in the refreshment by dipping a large lump of sugar in the hot liquid, sucking it, replenishing it, occasionally replacing the lump, till the cup was emptied; and he snuffed eternally. These are not such peculiar characteristics of a foreign gentleman that I have any special cause to dwell upon them here; but as the hotel was very empty, and I was very dull, I made this old gentleman—as my incorrigible habit is—a study and a theme. I converted him into a mental clothes-prop, and hung an infinity of fantastic notions, theories, and speculations upon him. We soon became, thanks to the French language and constant proximity, tolerably good friends. Of course the old gentleman did not delay long in asking me why I had come to Copenhagen. *That* question is invariably asked you—*ad nauseam*, too—throughout the North of Europe. They begin at Hamburg, continue at Berlin, return to it in Denmark and Sweden, and end at St. Petersburg. If a man be not a commercial traveller, or a diplomatist, a spy, or a negotiator of forged bank-notes, these Northern people seem utterly bewildered as to his object in coming to such latitudes. The Rhine, the Mediterranean, the Bosphorus, the Holy Land, Switzerland, the Tyrol, good; but the North: *que diable!* what does he want in that galley? I confess that I was somewhat at a loss to give a straightforward answer to the old gentleman in green spectacles. I might have told him that I had come to see the birthplace of Hans Christian Anderson; but then I was not quite certain as to whether that delightful Danish writer first drew breath in Copenhagen. It would have been equally disingenuous to have adduced a wish to see the famous Thorwaldsen's Museum as the reason for my visit; for with shame I acknowledge that, having no guide-book with me, I had entirely forgotten that the Danish metropolis contained that triumph of plastic art. It is true that, by attentive study of the glorious museum, I subsequently atoned for my mnemonic shortcomings. So, being on the horns of a dilemma, I elected to tell the truth—not a bad plan under any circumstances—and said that I had come to Copenhagen for the simple reason that I did not know what to do with myself, and would have gone with equal alacrity to Nova Zembla or to Katamandu; which candid avowal placed me on a most confidential footing with the old gentleman in green spectacles, and materially assisted the progress of our intercourse.

Now, whatever can this Danish old gentleman and his verdant spectacles have to do with One o'Clock in the morning, and Evans's Supper-rooms? You must have patience, and you shall hear. In subsequent chatty interviews, it came out that the old gentleman had once upon a time—a very long while ago, more than a quarter of a century—been in England. His reminiscences of our country were very dim and indistinct by this time. His knowledge of the English language, I take it, had not at any time been very extensive, and it was reduced now to a few phrases and interjections; some trifling oaths, a few facetious party-cries, current, I presume, at the time of his visit, and having, mainly, reference to Catholic Emancipation and the Reform Bill; these, with some odds and ends of tattered conversation, formed his philological stock in trade. But, even as "single-speech Hamilton" had his solitary oration, Mrs. Dubsy's hen her one chick, and Major Panton his unique run of luck at the card-table, so my old gentleman had his one story which he persisted in delivering in English. It was a mysterious and almost incomprehensible legend; and began thus: "'Ackney Rod! Aha!" Then he would snuff and suck his lump of sugar, and I would look on wonderingly. Then he would explain matters a little. "'Ackney Rod. I live there so long time ago. Aha!" This would lead to a renewed series of snuffings and suckings, and he would proceed—"Vontleroy he not 'ang. He rich man, banquier in America. He 'ang in a sospender basket. Aha!" For the life of me, I could not for a long time understand the drift about "Vontleroy" and the "sospender basket;" but at length a light broke in upon me, and I began to comprehend that this wondrous legend related to Henry Fauntleroy, the banker, who was hanged at Newgate for forgery, and concerning whose apocryphal rescue from strangulation—by the means, according to some, of a silver tube in his windpipe, and, according to others, of an apparatus of wicker-work, which, suspending him from the waist, so took the strain off his neck—rumours were current at the time of his death and for a considerable period afterwards. This cock-and-bull story was well-nigh all the poor man could recollect about England, and he decidedly made the most of it.

And, after all, I have only introduced him as a species of gentleman-usher to another foreign acquaintance—with whom my intercourse was even more transient, for I met him but once in my life, and then had only about seven minutes' conversation with him on the deck of a steamer—whose knowledge of English and recollection of England were even more limited. "Ver fine place," he remarked, referring to my native land. "Moch night plaisir, London. Sing-song ver good. Ev'ns magnifique." There, the secret of my digression is out now, and I land you—somewhat wearied with the journey, it may be—under the Piazza of Covent Garden Market.

Mr. Charles Dickens once declared in print that were he to start a horse for the Derby, he would call that horse Fortnum and Mason: the delightful hampers of edibles and drinkables vended by that eminent firm about the period of Epsom Races being connected with the most pleasurable of his impressions concerning that exciting sporting event. I have no doubt that my steamboat acquaintance was not by any means solitary in his enthusiastic estimate of the "magnifique" nature of Ev'ns, or EVANS'S, and its "sing-song;" and his opinion is, I have reason to believe, shared by many hundreds of English country gentlemen who patronise the Bedford, the Tavistock, the Hummums, and other kindred Covent Garden hotels, and who at Evans's find their heartiest welcome and their most inexhaustible fund of amusement. Nor can I see myself, exactly, how this great town of ours could manage to get on without the time-honoured Cave of Harmony; for be it known to all men—at least to so many as do not know it already—Evans's, though Captain Costigan is no longer permitted to sing his songs there, and even Colonel Newcome, were he to volunteer to oblige the company with a song, would be politely requested to desist by a waiter—is the "Cave," and the "Cave" is Evans's. It is not without a certain sly chuckle of gratulation that I record this fact. Those friends of mine who have adopted the highly honourable pursuit of hiding round corners in order to throw, with the greater security, jagged stones at me as I pass, those precious purists and immaculate precisians who cry hard upon a writer on London life in the nineteenth century, because he describes things and places which every man knows to exist, and whose existence he for one has not the hypocrisy to deny—these good gentlemen will scarcely be angry with their poor servant, Scriblerus, for giving a word-picture of a place of amusement which is immortalised in the first chapter of "The Newcomes." And please to observe, gentlemen, that I am not about to venture on the very delicate ground with respect to the quality of the songs once sung at Evans's, and so boldly trodden by Mr. Thackeray. I have the less need to do so, as that delicate or indelicate ground has long since—and to the honour of the present proprietor, Mr. Green—been ploughed up and sown with salt, and the musical programme rendered as innocuous as the bill of fare of a festival in a cathedral town.

And now for the place itself. About a century since, when the shadowy hero of the "Virginians" was beating the town with my Lords Castlewood and March, and Parson Sampson, and his black man Gumbo was flirting with

Colonel Lambert's servant-maids; about a century since, when in reality Johnson—not so long since emancipated from sleeping on bulks with that other homeless wretch, and man of genius, Savage—was painfully finishing his gigantic work, the "Dictionary;" when Goldsmith was "living in Axe Lane among the beggars," or starving in Green Arbour Court; when honest Hogarth dwelt at the sign of the Golden Head, in Leicester Fields (he had set up his coach by this time, worthy man, was Serjeant-painter to the King, and had his country-house at Chiswick); when the wicked, witty Wilkes was carousing with other "choice spirits" as wicked and as witty as he, at Medmenham Abbey; when the furious Churchill was astonishing the town with his talent and his excesses; when Lawrence Sterne was yet fiddling, and painting, and preaching, while his friend Hall indited the "Crazy Tales;" when George II., hitherto considered as a heavy, morose German king, who did not like "boetry and bainting," and could not see the fun of the "March to Finchley," but now for the first time revealed to us by Mr. Carlyle as a dapper, consequential little coxcomb—the *"mein bruder der comödiant,"* "my brother the playactor" of Friedrich-Wilhelm, was Sovereign of Great Britain, by the grace of the Act of Settlement and the madness of the Stuarts—this town of London was full of choice holes and corners, known under the generic name of "night cellars." You may see in Liverpool to this day—and I am told, also, in New York—some flourishing specimens of these inviting localities, but they have almost died out in London. The White Horse Cellar in Piccadilly is now a booking-office; the Shades in Leicester Square (underneath Saville House), once Pennant's "pouting house for princes," is a *restaurant*; the cellar of the Ship at Charing Cross is yet a tavern, but is used more as a waiting-room for passengers by the Kent Road and Deptford omnibuses; and a whole nest of cellars were swept away by the Adamses when the Adelphi Terrace, with a worse range of cellars beneath, as it afterwards turned out, was constructed. But the night cellars of a hundred years ago! What dens, what sinks, what roaring saturnalia of very town scoundrelism they must have been! We have but two reliable authorities extant as to their manners and appearance: Hogarth's prints, and the pages of the Old Bailey Sessions Papers. The former are the engraven testimony of a man to whose honest nature it was utterly abhorrent and intolerable to bear false witness; the latter is a record that *cannot lie*. I don't mean by these Sessions Papers the collection of trials known as the "Newgate Calendar." In these, crimes are dressed up with all manner of romantic and adventitious details, and occasionally spiced with moral reflections by the ordinary of Newgate. I mean the real Sessions Papers, the *verbatim* reports of the trials—from murder to pot-stealing—taken officially in short-hand by the Gurneys and their predecessors, and which, in their matchless *extenso*, remain, to the inestimable advantage of our historians and our painters of manners. They date from the time of Judge

Jeffreys, to the last session of the Central Criminal Court—it may have been the day before yesterday.

The cellars come out with a perfectly livid radiance in the reports of these trials. You see the "brimstone" woman, whom Hogarth pointed out to his friend and sketched upon his thumbnail, spurting brandy from her mouth at the enraged virago her companion. You see Kate Hackabout passing the stolen watch to Tom Idle, who is under the unseen surveillance of one of Justice de Veil or Harry Fielding's runners, and the luckless Thomas will be laid by the heels by daybreak to-morrow. Kate will go to Bridewell, there to be whipped and to pick oakum. Foote's Mother Cole is here, you may be sure; and Tom Rakewell, spending his last guineas among the gamblers and ruffians. Who else are there? Ferdinand Count Fathom, you may sure; poets and hack-writers—for Grub Street existed then in spirit and in truth—making my lord's gold pieces, which he gave for that last foolishly-fulsome dedication, fly. Yes; Mr. Peregrine Pickle, and you are spending your night in the cellar. And Mr. Thomas Jones, fresh from the western counties,—you, too, are here, with a laced coat bought out of my Lady Bellaston's last bank-note. Ah! Thomas! Thomas! if pure-minded Sophy Western could but see you in this bad place, among these ruffianly companions!—among horse-jockeys, highwaymen-captains, unfrocked parsons; deboshed adventurers, redolent of twopenny ordinaries and Mount Scoundrel in the Fleet; disbanded lieutenants of phantom regiments; scriveners struck off the rolls, ruined spendthrifts, Irish desperadoes enthusiastic for the Pretender and other men's pence, bankrupt traders, French and Italian rascals flagrant from the galleys of foreign seaports, and all, according to their own showing, distressed patriots; German swindlers and card-sharpers, who declare themselves to be Counts of the Holy Roman Empire, Jew coin-clippers and diamond-slicers, riverside vagabonds in the pay of the commanders of press-gangs on the look-out for benighted journeymen, or dissolute lads who have run away from their apprenticeship or quarrelled with their parents, recruiting crimps for both sexes, usurers looking for prodigals who have yet money to lose, bailiffs' followers looking for prodigals who have lost all and owe more; and, scattered among all this scum of frantic knavery and ragabosh, some gay young sprigs of aristocracy, some officers in the regiment of Guards, some noisy young country squires of the Western type. This, all garnished with dirt and spilt liquors, with the fumes of mum, Geneva, punch, wine, and tobacco smoke, with oaths and shrieks and horrid songs, with the clatter of glasses and tankards, the clash of rapiers and verberations of bludgeons—is the London night cellar of a hundred years ago. Round Covent Garden such places positively swarmed. The Strand, the neighbourhood of Exeter 'Change, Long Acre, and Drury Lane, reeked with dens of this description. For hereabouts were the playhouses, and in their purlieus, as in those of cathedrals, you must expect to find, and do find, in every age, the haunts of vice and dissipation. It may be profane to say *ubi apis ibi mel*; but such is the sorry fact.

I am to give you notice that this article was originally intended to be intensely topographical—nay, *sant soit peu*, antiquarian and archæological. It was my desire to give you a minute description of the hostelry called Evans's Hotel, and whose basement contains the saloon known as Evans's supper-room, from the earliest period of authentic research to the present time. How it emerged from a state of brawling night-cellarhood, to the dignity of a harmonic meeting; who first ordered "chops to follow," and what ingenious spirit originally suggested the curious principle now in practice, of paying for your refreshment at the door on quitting the establishment; who instituted the glee-choir, introduced books of the words, and discovered that baked potatoes are necessarily associated with bumpers of stout, poached eggs, and liberally cayenned kidneys; who formed the gallery of portraits which now graces the walls of the ante-saloon, and who first dreamed of such an Arabian Night's succedaneum as a ladies' gallery. All these things it was my firm intention to record, in Roman type, for your amusement, if not your edification. "Who knows," I asked myself enthusiastically, "if I take sweet counsel (hot and strong as well as sweet, sometimes) of Mr. Paddy Green, most urbane of nocturnal Bonifaces, and sit reverentially at the feet of Mr. Peter Cunningham, who, it is rumoured, in the matter of London localities, could, an he chose, rival the marvellous feat of memory ascribed to old Fuller of the 'Worthies,' who could repeat backwards, and without book, the names of all the tavern signs on both sides of the way from Temple Bar to Ludgate: who knows," I repeated, "but that I shall be able to submit to the readers of 'Twice Round the Clock,' a copy of an unpaid score left by Oliver Goldsmith at some Evans's of the past; or put it upon record that Sir Thomas Lawrence and Major Hanger had claret-cup together here, on the night that Thurtell was hanged, or that on the fatal evening when the Catholic Bill passed the Lords, a live bishop—a hackney coachman's many-caped coat over his apron and shorts—descended Evans's well-worn stairs, ordered a Welsh rabbit, partook of two 'stouts,' and, the tears coursing down his right reverend cheeks, murmured—'Britain! oh my country! *Delenda est Carthago!* by way of chorus to Captain Costigan's favourite ditty of 'The Night before Larry was stretched?'"

In the famous gardens of the Villa Pallavicini, near Genoa, there is an artificial piece of water winding between rocks, at the extremity of which the mimic river seems to lose itself in the blue waters of the Mediterranean. Nothing of the sort is the case: the sea is, in reality, more than three hundred yards distant; but the intervening ground has been so dexterously sloped and masked with groups of plants, that the optical delusion is marvellous. Of such are the aspirations of mankind. In such disappointment ended my castles in the air with respect to Evans's. It was from across the ocean that I had to respond to the printers' wail for "copy:" this article was commenced in view of the Castle of Rolandseck, on board a Rhine steamer, whose worn-out engines throbbed as irregularly as though they had palpitation of the heart. It is being continued now at the sea-side, in bed, gruel on the one side, sweet spirits of nitre on the other: and where it will be finished, who can tell? Old Æsop told the soldiers, when they asked him whither he was going, that he did not know, whereupon they arrested him for an impertinent. "Was I not right?" he cried; "did I know that I was going to jail?" "*Sait on où l'on va?*" echoes Diderot. How do I, how do you, how does your lordship, how does your grace, how does your majesty, know what will happen the moment after this? Therefore, take heed of the present time, and make your wills: the best will, in my humble thinking, that a man can make, being that strong will and determination to act as justly as he can in each moment in the which he is permitted to live.

So you understand, now, why I was compelled to dispense with the assistance of Mr. Paddy Green and Mr. Peter Cunningham, and why I am reduced to a dependence on my own personal reminiscences with respect to Evans's, without the adventitious aid of recondite anecdote and historical data. Here is the place as I remember it.

One o'clock in the morning. Of course we are supposed to be spending just a fortnight in town, and putting up at the Bedford, or it would never do to be so early-late abroad. We have been to the play, and have consumed a few oysters in the Haymarket; but the principal effect of that refreshment seems to have been to make us ten times hungrier. The delicate bivalves of Colchester have failed in appeasing our bucolic stomachs. We require meat. So, says the friend most learned in the ways of the town to his companion— "Meat at our hotel we eschew, for we shall find the entertainment of the dearest and dullest. We will go sup at Evans's, for there we can have good meat and good liquor at fair rates, and hear a good song besides." Whereupon we walk, till the piazza, about which I have kept you so long lingering, looms in sight. A low doorway, brilliantly lit with gas, greets our view. We descend a flight of some steps, pass through a vestibule, and enter the "Cave of Harmony."

Push further on, if you please. You are not to linger in this ante-chamber, thickly hung with pictures, and otherwise, with its circular marble tables, much resembling a Parisian *café*, minus the mirrors and the rattle of the dominoes. This ante-chamber will be treated of anon; but your present business is with chops and harmony.

Passing, then, through this *atrium*, the visitor finds himself in a vast music-hall, of really noble proportions, and decorated not only with admirable taste, but with something nearly akin to splendour. You see I am at a loss for authorities again, and I cannot tell you how much of the hall is Corinthian, and how much composite; whether the columns are fluted, the cornices gilt or the soffits carved, and whether the Renaissance or the Arabesque style most prevails in the decorations employed. All I know is, that it is a lofty, handsome, comfortable room, whose acoustic properties, by the way, are far superior to those enjoyed by some establishments with loftier philharmonic pretensions. At the northern extremity of the hall is a spacious proscenium and stage, with the grand pianoforte *de rigueur*, the whole veiled by a curtain in the intervals of performance. As for the huge area stretching from the proscenium to a row of columns which separate it from the ante-chamber *café*, it is occupied by parallel lines of tables, which, if they do not groan beneath the weight of good eatables and drinkables piled upon them, might certainly be excused for groaning—to say nothing of shrieking, yelling, and uttering other lamentable noises, evoked by the unmerciful thumping and hammering they undergo at the conclusion of every fresh exercitation of harmony.

Still, the eatables and drinkables do merit a paragraph, and shall have one. To the contemplative mind they are full of suggestions, and evidence of the vast digestive powers of the English people. To any but a race of hardy Norsemen, sons of Thor and Odin, hammerers of steel, welders of iron, and compellers of adverse elements, men who are sometimes brought to live when on shipboard upon weevily biscuit that breaks the teeth, and salted leather, humorously nicknamed beef; or in trenches, upon rancid pork, toasted on bayonet or ramrod tips; to any but that unconquerable, hard-headed, and strong-stomached people, of whom it is sometimes said that they would eat a donkey if they were allowed to begin at the hind legs, this post-midnight repast at Evans's would be full of menace of perturbed slumbers, distraught dreams, nay, even ghastly nightmares. Your Frenchman, when he sups, takes his cold salad, his appetising fruit, his succulent partridge, his light omelette, or, at most, his thin weak *bouillon*, with a lean cutlet to follow. He drinks sugar-and-water, wine-and-water, or, on high holiday nights, a glass or two of champagne; puffs his mild cigars, and goes to bed, simpering that he has *bien soupé*. And even then, sometimes, your Frenchman has dreams, and rising in bed, with the hair of his flesh standing up, vows that he will sup no more. Your Italian sups on his three-halfpennyworth of maccaroni. Your Spaniard rubs a piece of bread with garlic, and eats it, blesses heaven, and goes to sleep with a cigarette in his mouth. Your gross German affects the lighter kind of cold meats and salads at supper, and washes down his spare repast—to be sure, it is the fourth within the twelve hours—with some frothy beer. The Americans can't be said to sup, any more than they breakfast, lunch, or dine. They are always over-eating, over-drinking, and over-smoking themselves; and were it not for their indomitable pluck and perseverance, their tendency to dyspepsia would be an insurmountable obstacle to their ever becoming a great people. *For the great peoples have always had strong stomachs.* Homer's heroes ate beef undone. When the Romans took to made-dishes and kick-shaws, then came their decadence, and the strong-stomached barbarians of the North overran them. To make an end of foreign wanderings, Russian suppers, among the people, are just no suppers at all. One—or at most two—meals a day, is the rule with the moujik. In elegant society, the cook might as well provide for supper painted chickens and lobster salads made of sealing-wax and cut paper, as any genuine viands. A supper at St. Petersburg, means champagne and gambling till the next morning.

But see the suppers set forth for the strong-stomached supporters of Evans's. See the pyramids of dishes arrive; the steaming succession of red-hot chops, with their brown, frizzling caudal appendages sobbing hot tears of passionate fat. See the serene kidneys unsubdued, though grilled, smiling though cooked, weltering proudly in their noble gravy, like warriors who have fallen upon the field of honour. See the hot yellow lava of the Welsh rabbit stream over and engulf the timid toast. Sniff the fragrant vapour of the corpulent sausage. Mark how the russet leathern-coated baked potato at first defies the knife, then gracefully cedes, and through a lengthened gash yields its farinaceous effervescence to the influence of butter and catsup. The only refreshments present open to even a suspicion of effeminacy are the poached eggs, glistening like suns in a firmament of willow-pattern plate; and those too, I am willing to believe, are only taken by country-gentlemen hard pressed by hunger, just to "stay their stomachs," while the more important chops and kidneys are being prepared. The clouds of pepper shaken out on these viands are enough to make Slawkenbergius sneeze for a fortnight; the catsup and strong sauces poured over them are sufficient to convince Sir Toby Belch that there are other things besides ginger, which are apt to be "hot i' the mouth," and, as humble servitors in attendance on these haughty meats, are unnumbered discs of butter, and manchets of crustiest bread galore.

ONE O'CLOCK A.M.: EVANS'S SUPPER-ROOMS.

Pints of stout, if you please, no puny half-measures, pints of sparkling pale ale, or creaming Scotch, or brownest Burton, moisten these sturdy rations. And when the strong men have supped, or rather before they have supped, and while they have supped, and indeed generally during the evening, there bursts out a strong smell of something good to drink; and presently you perceive that the strong men have ordered potent libations of spirituous liquors, hot whiskey-and-water being the favourite one; and are hastily brewing mighty jorums of punch and grog, which they undoubtedly quaff; puffing, meanwhile, cigars of potency and fragrance—pipes are tabooed—taken either from their own cigar-cases, or else recently laid in from the inexhaustible stores of the complaisant Herr von Joel.

"Who will always be retained on this establishment," the proprietor good-naturedly promises, and more good-naturedly performs. "Why," asks the neophyte, "is it necessary for my well-being, or the prosperity of this establishment, that the services of Herr von Joel should always be retained thereon? Why this perpetual hypothecation of Joel? Can no one else sell me cigars? What am I to Joel, or what is Joel to me? Confound Joel!" To which I answer: "Rash neophyte, forbear, and listen. In the days when thou wert very young and foolish, wore lay-down collars, and had no moustaches, save the stickiness produced by much-sucked sweetstuff on the upper lips—in the days when thou wert familiar, indeed, with Doctor Wackerbarth's seminary for young gentlemen, but not with Evans's—Herr von Joel, young and sprightly then, was a famous Mimic. In imitating the cries of birds, Herr von

Joel was unrivalled, and has never been approached. In the old days, when he was famous, and did the lark and the linnet so well, he brought crowds of visitors to the old supper-rooms, who laughed and wondered at his mimicry, supped and drank, and smoked, and paid fat scores. So Joel, in his generation, was a benefactor to Evans's. And now, when the thorax is rusty, and the larynx no longer supple, the faithful servant rests upon "his well-earned laurels"—of tobacco-leaves—among the old faces of old friends. "His helmet is a hive for bees"—and Havannah cigars, and "his services will always be retained in this establishment." One would shudder to think of Wellington's old charger, Copenhagen, being sent to Cow Cross, to the knackers, instead of ending his days peacefully in a paddock at Strathfieldsaye. No one likes to hear of Sophie Arnould or Mademoiselle Camargo (the ballet-dancer who introduced short petticoats) being brought to indigence in their declining years. Guilbert in the hospital, Camöens starving, blind Belisarius begging for an obolus, these are pitiable; and to this day I think the country might have done something for the widow of Ramo Samee. We give pensions to the families of those who use their swords well, but I should like to know how many can swallow them as Ramo did?

All the while the company have been supping and I have been prosing, the "Cave of Harmony" has not belied its name. A bevy of fresh-coloured youths, of meagre stature, of curly hair, in broad collars and round jackets, such as distinguished you and me, neophyte, when we were pupils at Dr. Wackerbarth's, have made themselves manifest on the stage, and in admirable time and tune have chanted with their silver-bell voices those rare old glees which were written by the honest old masters before the Father of Evil had invented Signor Guiseppe Verdi. Thersites Theorbo (who is an assiduous frequenter of the Cave at hours when men of not so transcendent a genius are in bed) Thersites Theorbo, down yonder in the *café* ante-saloon, glowering over his grog, cannot forbear beating time and wagging his august head approvingly when he hears the little boys sing. May their pure harmony do the battered old cynic good! Honest old glees! though your composers wore pigtails and laced ruffles. And none the worse, either, because we owe some of the most beautiful of them to an Irish nobleman. Do you know who that nobleman was? Go ask Mr. Thackeray, who, in an absurd copy of verses, written in barbarous Cockney slang, has brought the "unaccustomed brine" to these eyes many and many a time. He describes a stately lady sitting by an open window, beside the "flowing Boyne," with a baby on her lap. It is a man child, and not far off is the father,

"... Most musical of Lords,

A playing madrigals and glees

Upon the harpsichords."

And this child's father was old Lord Mornington, whose son was Arthur, Duke of Wellington.

If you scrutinise the faces of these juvenile choristers somewhat narrowly, and happen yourself to be a tolerably regular attendant at the abbey church of St. Peter's, Westminster, it is not at all improbable that you may recognise one or two young gentlemen whom, arrayed in snowy surplices, you may have heard trilling forth in shrill notes their parts of the service among the gentlemen choristers and minor canons of the Abbey. I wonder if it is very wicked for them to be found at Evans's thus late. I don't mean at one o'clock in the morning, for they mostly disappear about midnight. Perhaps not so wicked, for I know there are some people so very religious that they only think of religion on Sundays; and fancy that week-day transactions can't have the slightest connection with the Sabbath. However this may be, I must mention it as a curious fact in relation with the moral economy of Evans's, that in the old days, when Captain Costigan or one of his peers, was about to sing anything approaching to a *chanson grivoise*, the juveniles were invariably marched out of the room by a discreet waiter, in order that their young ears might not be contaminated.

With respect to the remaining harmonic attractions of Evans's, I shall be very brief. I believe that on some evenings individuals of the Ethiopian way of thinking, and accoutred in the ordinary amount of lamp-black, Welsh wig, and shirt-collars, and provided with the usual banjo, accordion, tambourine, and bones, are in the habit of informing the audience that things in general are assuming an appearance of "Hoop de dooden do;" also of lamenting the untimely demise of one Ned, an aged blackamoor, who stood towards them in an avuncular relation, and of passionately demanding the cause of their master effecting the sale of their persons, by auction or otherwise, on the day on which they entered into the state of matrimony. I am given to understand that a gentleman with an astonishing falsetto voice is a great favourite among the *habitués*, and that some screaming comic songs by popular vocalists are nightly given with immense applause; but I candidly confess that I am not qualified to speak with any great degree of certitude with respect to these performances. I go to Evans's generally very late, and as seldom venture close to the proscenium. I am content to bide in the ante-saloon, and to muse upon Thersites Theorbo, glowering over his grog.

This iracund journalist—to borrow an epithet from Mr. Carlyle—is not by any means solitary in his patronage of the marble-tabled, portrait-hung *café*. To tell the honest truth, as, in Paris, if you wish to see the actors in vogue, you must go to the Café du Vaudeville—if the authors, to the Café Cardinal or the Café du Helder—if the artists, to the Café des Italiens—if the students, to the Café Belge—and if the dandies, to the Café de Paris; so in London, if you wish to see the wits and the journalist men about town of the day, you must go to Evans's about one o'clock in the morning. Then those ineffables turn out of the smoking-rooms of their clubs—clique-clubs mostly—and meet on this neutral ground to gird at one another. *Autres temps, autres mœurs.* A century since it used to be Wills's or Button's, or the Rose; now it is Evans's. I should dearly like to draw some pen-and-ink portraits for you of the wits as they sit, and drink, and smoke, at one o'clock in the morning; but I dare not. As for Thersites Theorbo, he is a shadow. You know what I told you about clubs; and this place also is a prison-house to me. It is true, Heaven help me, that I am not affiliated to witcraft myself, that I am neither priest nor deacon. Still I have been one of the little boys in red cassocks, who swing the censers, and I dare not reveal the secrets of the sacristy. But I may just whisper furtively in your ear, that Ethelred Guffoon is never seen at Evans's. It makes his head ache. Mr. Goodman Twoshoes, also, is but a seldom visitor to the Cave of Harmony. He prefers his snug corner-box at the Albion, where he can brew his beloved ginger-punch. It is not that the wits despise the "Cave." Mr. Polyphemus, the novelist, not unfrequently condescends to wither mankind through his spectacles from one of the marble tables; and I have seen the whole "Times" newspaper—proprietors, editors, special correspondents, and literary critics—hob-nobbing together at—— *Will* you hold your tongue, sir?

One trifling indiscretion more, and I have done with Evans's. "It is not generally known," as accurate, erudite, and amusing Mr. John Timbs would say, that the sly gallantry of Mr. Green, the proprietor of the Cave of Harmony, caused him, when his new and sumptuous music-hall was in course of construction, to move the architect to build some cunning loop-holes and points of espial connected with commodious apartments—in other words, with private boxes, somewhat resembling the *baignoires* in the Parisian theatres, whence ladies could see and hear all that was going on without being seen or heard. A somewhat similar contrivance exists, it will be remembered, in our House of Commons; I only wish that the fair ones who there lie *perdues* during a late debate, were doomed to hear as little trash as meets their ears from the secluded bowers overhanging Evans's. What passport is required to ensure admission into these blissful regions I know not; but I have it on good authority that ladies of the "very highest rank and distinction"—to use a "Morning Postism"—have on several occasions graced Evans's with their presence, and with condescending smiles looked down upon the revelries of their lords.

Tell me, you who are so quick of hearing, what is that noise above our heads—it must be in the street beyond—and which dominates the revelry as the sound of the cannon did the music of the Duchess of Richmond's ball before Quatre Bras. It grows louder and louder, it comes nearer and nearer, it swells into a hoarse continually-jarring roar, as I sit smoking at Evans's. The sham blackamoor on the stage pauses in his buffoonery, forbears to smite his woolly pate with the tambourine; his colleague's accordion is suspended in the midst of a phthisic wheeze, and the abhorred bones quiver, yet unreverberate in the nicoto-alcholoicho-charged air. The rattle of knives and forks, the buzzing conversation, cease; a hundred queries as to the cause of the noise rise on as many lips; the waiters forget to rattle the change, the toper forgets to sip his grog: there is intromission even in the inspiration of tobacco fumes: then comes the mighty answer—comes at once from all quarters—caught up, echoed and re-echoed, and fraught with dread, the momentous word—FIRE!

Man, it has been somewhere pertinently observed, is a hunting animal. The delight in having something to run after: whether it be a pickpocket, who has just eloped with a watch or a silk handkerchief; a dog with a kettle tied to his tail, a hare, a deer, a woman, a fugitive hat, a slaver, a *prima donna*, a lord's tuft, an oriental traveller, a deformed dwarf—something to chase, something to scour and scud after, something to run down, and ultimately devour and destroy: such a pursuit enlivens and comforts the heart of man, and makes him remember that he has the blood of Nimrod in his veins. The schoolboys at Eton have their "paper chases," and course miles through the pleasant playing-fields, crossing brooks, and tearing through hedges, after a quire of foolscap torn up into shreds. The child chases a butterfly; the adult exhausts himself and his horse in racing after a much-stinking fox; and the octogenarian frets his palsied old limbs, and bursts into a feverish snail's gallop, after a seat on the Treasury Bench, or a strip of blue velvet embroidered with "*honi soit qui mal y pense*" in gold, and called a garter. There is a wild, engrossing excitement and pleasure in hunting; the fox-hound, the otter, the "harmless necessary cat," would tell you so, were their speech articulate; but of all things huntable, chasable, rundownable, I doubt if there be one that can equal a Fire.

"Fire! fire!" It matters not how late the hour be, how important the avocations of the moment, that magic cry sets all legs, save those of the halt and the bed-ridden, in motion—strikes on every tympanum. "Fire! fire!" as the sound rolls earwards, the gambler starts up from the dicing-table, the bibber leaves the wine-pots, the lover rises from his mistress's feet, the blushing maiden forgets half of that last glowing declaration, the captive runs to his grated window, the sluggard sits up on his couch, the sick man turns his head on his pillow to whence issues the portentous cry. Hundreds of impulses are bound up in the uncontrollable desire that prompts us to run at once after the "Fire!" Fear: it may be our own premises that are blazing, our own dear ones that are in peril. Hope and cupidity: we may be rogues, and there may be rich plunder from a fire. Duty: we may be policemen, firemen, or newspaper reporters. Generous emulation, brave self-devotion: there may be lives at stake and lives to save. Curiosity: it is as good to see a house burned (when it doesn't happen to be your own) as a bear baited or a man hanged. All these may prompt us to follow the howl of the fire-dogs; but, chiefest of all, is the vague, indefinite, yet omnipotent desire to swell a pursuing crowd, to join in a hue and cry, to press to the van of the chasers: to hunt something, in fact.

I never could understand where a London crowd comes from. Be the hour ever so late, were the street ever so deserted a moment before, a man quarrelling with his wife, or cry of Fire, will be sufficient to evoke the presence of a compact and curious crowd, growing instantaneously thicker and noisier. Whether they start from the sewers or the cellar-gratings, or drop from the chimney-pots or the roof-copings, is indeterminate; yet they gather somehow, and jostle, squeeze, yell, stamp, and tear furiously. No conscription, no mustering of the *posse comitatis*, no summoning of ban and *arrière* ban, no "call of the House," no sending forth of the "fiery cross," no beacon signalling, no Vehmgericht convening under penalty of the cord and dagger, could be half so successful in calling multitudes together as the one word—FIRE! A minute past, I was at Evans's, tranquilly conversing with the veteran Herr von Joel, and now I find myself racing like mad up St. Martin's Lane, towards St. Giles's. How I found my hat and donned it I haven't the slightest idea, and I sincerely hope that I didn't forget to pay the waiter for my chop, kidney, stout, and etceteras. All I know is, that I am running after that hoarse cry, and towards that awful Redness in the sky; that I tread upon unnumbered corns; that I hold cheap as air, innumerable punches and thrusts which I receive from my neighbours; and that I will not by any means undertake to make oath that I am not myself also vociferating, "Fire! Fire!" with the full strength of my lungs.

I thought so. There goes the "Country Fire Office." There it goes, dashing, rattling, blazing along—only the very strongest adjective, used participle-wise, can give a notion of its bewildering speed—there it goes, with its strong, handsome horses, champing, fuming, setting the pavement on fire with their space-devouring hoofs, and seeming to participate in the fire-hunting mania. They need no whip; only the voices of the firemen, clustering on the engine like bees, the loose rattle of the reins on their backs, and the cheers of the accompanying crowd. The very engine, burnished and glistening, flashing and blushing in its scarlet and gold in the gaslight, seems imbued with feeling, and scintillating with excitement—(Oh! critics of fishy blood, oyster temperament, and tortoise impulses, pardon my heedless exuberance of epithet)—so gleaming and glittering, and its catherine-like wheels revolving, and the moon just tipping the burnished helmets and hatchets of the firemen, who will have a ruddy glare on those accoutrements shortly, goes screaming through the night, the County Fire-engine. The Northern Express blazing over Chatmoss at speed is a terrible sight to see: that fiery messenger has subdued the wilderness, and made the waste places, whilom the haunts of bats and dragons, tremble; but the fast-tearing fire-engine is nobler and more Human. It cleaves its way through the sleeping city; it bears the tidings of succour and deliverance. Yon express-train may convey but a company of chapmen and pedlars, thirsting to higgle in the cheapest so that they may haggle in the dearest market; but the five-engine is freighted with brave manly hearts, braced—with little lust of lucre, God knows! for their pay is but a pittance—to the noble task of saving human life. That they do so save it, almost every night throughout the year, save it in the midst of peril to their own, in the ever-imminent peril of a sudden, hideous, unrewarded death, Mr. Braidwood and the fire companies know full well. That the best of the young British painting men, John Everett Millais, should have chosen the every-day, but none the less glorious, heroism of a fireman for the theme of a magnificent picture, is good to know; and the very thought of the picture goes far towards making us forgive the painter for his asinine "Sir Isumbrasse," or whatever the abortion was called; but it would be better if the knowledge of our firemen's good deservings were extended beyond Mr. Braidwood and the fire companies. The deeds of those plain men with the leathern helmets and the trusty hatchets, have received neither their full meed of praise, nor a tithe of their meed of reward. I have yet to hear of the Fireman's Order of Valour; I have yet to learn that our bounteous Government, so prompt to recognise diplomatic demerit, to reward political worthlessness, and to ennoble military failure, have thought it worth their while to bestow even the minutest modicum of a pension on a fireman. To be sure, these worldly, unwise men, are, for their own interests' sake, disastrously and inexcusably modest, unobtrusive, and retiring. There is no trumpeter attached *ex-officio* to the fire brigade. Would you believe it, that these unambitious men, their glorious labours over, are content to retire to the sheds where their engines stand at livery, where they eat bread-and-cheese with clasp knives, read cheap newspapers, and teach tricks to their dogs? Their principal recreation is to scrub, polish, tickle, and frictionise the brass and wood work of the fire-engines to a Dutch pitch of cleanliness, and they are much given, I am sorry to say, to the smoking of long clay pipes. This is, in itself, sufficient to ruin them in the estimation of such sages and public benefactors as ex-Lord Mayor Garden. Let us hope that it is not his ex-Lordship's house that is being burned down this November morning.

ONE O'CLOCK A.M.: A FIRE.

No—the fire is in the very thickest part of St. Giles's. Unfaithful topographers may have told you that the "Holy Land" being swept away and Buckeridge Street being pulled down, St. Giles's exists no more. *Ne'n croyez rien.* The place yet lives—hideous, squalid, decrepit—yet full of an unwholesome vitality. Splendid streets have been pierced through the heart of this region—streets full of mansions four and six storeys high—affluent tradesmen display their splendid wares through glistening plate-glass windows. But St. Giles's is behind, round about, environing the new erections, sitting like Mordecai in the gate on the threshold of the brick and mortar and stucco palaces with which cunning contractors and speculative builders have sought to disguise the most infamous district in London. The proof of what I have asserted is very easy. You have but to be invited to dinner in Gower Street, or to have a morning call to make in Bedford Square. Take a walk from young Mr. Barry's bran-new opera-house in Bow Street, and walk straight a-head—nearly a measured mile to the Square of Bedford. You pass the gigantic carriage factory, which I will call by its ancestral name of Houlditch's—for it always seems to be changing proprietors—at the corner of Long Acre. You ascend Endell Street, and greet with satisfaction such signs of advancing civilisation as baths and wash-houses, and a bran-new dispensary. I had forgotten to mention that you might have had a back view of St. Martin's Hall. Then you cross the area of High Street, St. Giles's, or High Street, Holborn, whichsoever you may elect to call it. Then, still straight a-head, you mount Charlotte Street, Bloomsbury, a thoroughfare dignified by any number of churches, belonging to any number of persuasions. And then you are at your journey's end, and are free to call in Bedford Square, to dine in Gower Street, or to go see the Nineveh Marbles in the British Museum, *comme bon vous semble*.

But throughout this pilgrimage, passing by edifices erected in the newest Byzantine, or early English, or Elizabethan, or sham Gothic style, you have had St. Giles's always before, behind, and about you. From a hundred foul lanes and alleys have debouched, on to the spick-and-span-new promenade, unheard-of human horrors. Gibbering forms of men and women in filthy rags, with fiery heads of shock hair, the roots beginning an inch from the eyebrows, with the eyes themselves bleared and gummy, with gashes filled with yellow fangs for teeth, with rough holes punched in the nasal cartilage for nostrils, with sprawling hands and splay feet, tessellated with dirt—awful deformities, with horrifying malformations of the limbs and running sores ostentatiously displayed; Ghoules and Afrits in a travestie of human form, rattling uncouth forms of speech in their vitrified throttles. These hang about your feet like reptiles, or crawl round you like loathsome vermin, and in a demoniac whine beg charity from you. One can bear the men; ferocious and repulsive as they are, a penny and a threat will send them cowering and cursing to their noisome holes again. One cannot bear the women without a shudder, and a feeling of infinite sorrow and humiliation. They are so horrible to look upon, so thoroughly unsexed, shameless. Heaven-abandoned and forlorn, with their bare liver-coloured feet beating the devil's tattoo on the pavement, their lean shoulders shrugged up to their sallow cheeks, over which falls hair either wildly dishevelled or filthily matted, and their gaunt hands clutching at the tattered remnant of a shawl, which but sorrily veils the lamentable fact that they have no gown—that a ragged petticoat and a more ragged undergarment are all they have to cover themselves withal. With sternness and determination one can bear these sights; but, heavens and earth! the little children! who swarm, pullulate—who seem to be evoked from the gutter, and called up from the kennel, who clamber about your knees, who lie so thickly in your path that you are near stumbling over one of them every moment, who, ten times raggeder, dirtier, and more wretched-looking than their elders, with their baby faces rendered wolfish by privation, and looking a hundred years old, rather than not ten times that number of days, fight and scream, whimper and fondle, crawl and leap like the phantoms a man sees during the access of *delirium tremens*. I declare that there are babies among these miserable ones—babies with the preternaturally wise faces of grown up men; babies who, I doubt little, can lie, and steal, and beg, and who, in a year or so, will be able to fight and swear, and be sent to jail for six months' hard labour. Plenty of the children are big enough to be "whipped and discharged." Yes; that is the pleasant tee-totum: "six months' hard labour," "whipped and discharged," the merry prologue to Portland and the hulks, the humorous apprenticeship to the penal settlements and the gallows. And yet people will tell me that St. Giles's is "done away with"—"put down," as the worshipful Sir Peter Laurie would say. Glance down any one of the narrow lanes you like after passing Broker's Row. See the children coming out of the gin-shops and the pawnbrokers'. Ask the policeman whether every court in the vicinity be not full of thieves, and worse. Look at the lanes themselves, with the filthy rags flaunting from poles in the windows in bitter mockery of being hung out to dry after washing; with their belching doorways, the thresholds littered with wallowing infants, and revealing beyond a Dantean perspective of infected backyard and cloacan staircase. Peep, as well as you may for the dirt-obscured window panes, and see the dens of wretchedness where the people whose existence you ignore dwell—the sick and infirm, often the dying, sometimes the dead, lying on the bare floor, or, at best, covered with some tattered scraps of blanketing or matting; the shivering age crouching over fireless grates, and drunken husbands bursting through the rotten doors to seize their gaunt wives by the hair, and bruise their already swollen faces, because they have pawned what few rags remain to purchase gin. But then St. Giles's doesn't exist! It has been done away with! It is put down! "Stunning Joe Banks" and Bamfylde Moore Carew have been subdued by civilisation and the march of intellect! Of course.

Notwithstanding all which there is a terrific fire in the very midst of St. Giles's to-night; and that conflagration may do more in its generation towards the abolition of the district, than all the astute contractors and speculative builders. The fire is at an oilman's shop, who likewise manufactures and deals in pickles, and from the nature of the combustible commodities in which he trades, you may anticipate a rare blaze. Blaze! say an eruption of Mount Vesuvius rather; far high into the air shoot columns of flame, and hanging thickly over all are billows upon billows of crimson smoke, the whole encircled by myriads of fiery sparks that fall upon the gaping crowd and make them dance and yell with terror and excitement.

The police have very speedily made a sanitary *cordon* round about the blazing premises, and let none pass save those who have special business near the place. The firemen are "welcome guests" within the magic *cordon*, as also the fussy, self-important sergeants and inspectors of police, who often do more harm than good with their orders and counter-orders. There are some other gentlemen, too, who slip in and out unquestioned and unchallenged. They don't pump at the fire-engines, and they don't volunteer to man the fire-escape. But they seem to have an undisputed though unrecognised right to be here, there, and everywhere, and are received on a footing of humorous equality by the police, the fire-escape men, the firemen, and the very firemen's dogs. They are not official-looking persons by any means. They wear no uniforms, they carry no signs of authority, such as truncheons, armlets, or the like. They are rather given, on the contrary, to a plain and unpretending, not to say "seedy," style of attire. Napless hats, surtouts tightly buttoned up to the throat and white at the seams, pantaloons of undecided length, unblackened bluchers, and umbrellas, seem to be the favourite wear among these gentlemen. They are, not to mince the matter, what are termed "occasional reporters" to the daily newspapers, and, in less courteous parlance, are denominated "penny-a-liners." It is the vocation of these gentlemen (worthy souls for the most part—working very hard for very little money) to prowl continually about London town, in search of fires, fallings in and down of houses, runnings away of vicious horses, breakings down of cabs, carriages, and omnibuses; and, in fact, accidents and casualties of every description. But especially fires. Fatal accidents are not unnaturally preferred by the occasional reporters, because they lead to coroners' inquests, which have of course also to be reported; and, in the case of a fire, a slight loss of life is not objected to. It entails "additional particulars," and perhaps an inquiry before the coroner, with an examination of witnesses relative to the cause of the fire; nay, who knows but it may end in a trial for arson? There was—and may be now—a gentleman attached to the combustible department of the press, who was so well known and practised a hand at reporting conflagrations, that he was christened, and to some extent popularly known as, the "Fire King." It was facetiously suggested that he was unconsumable, made of asbestos, not to be affected by heat, like Signor Buono Cuore at Cremorne Gardens. According to the legend current in London newspaper circles, the "Fire King" had his abode next door to a fire-engine station in the Waterloo Road, and further to guard against the possibility of missing one of these interesting, and, to him, remunerative events, he caused to be inscribed on the door-jamb, in lieu of the ordinary injunction to "ring the top bell," this solitary announcement on a neat brass plate, "Fire Bell." So, when a fire was signalled within the beat of that portion of the brigade stationed in the Waterloo Road—or, indeed, anywhere else if of sufficient magnitude, for the brigade are not by any means particular as to distances, and would as lief go down the river to Gravesend or up it to Henley if occasion required—a stalwart brigadier, his helmet and hatchet all donned, would pull lustily at the fire-bell, accompanying the tintinnabulation by stentorian shouts of "Wake up, Charley!" Charley, the "Fire King," perhaps at that moment serenely dreaming of new Great Fires of London, Temples of Diana at Ephesus, and Minsters at York, ignited by Erostatratuses and Jonathan Martins yet unborn, would sing out of the window a sonorous "All right!" hastily dress, descend, jump on the ready-harnessed engine, and be conveyed jubilantly, as fast as ever the horses could carry him, to the scene of the fire. But two stains existed on the "Fire King's" otherwise fair escutcheon. It was darkly rumoured that on one occasion—it was a very fat fire at a patent candle manufactory—he had offered to bribe the turncock, so tampering with the supply of water; and that on another, it being a remarkably cold winter's night, he expressed a hope that the main might be frozen. And yet a more tender-hearted man—"additional particulars," and the claim of a wife and large family being put out of the question—than the Fire King, does not exist.

Meanwhile the oil and pickle man's house blazes tremendously. The houses on either side must go too; so think the firemen. Fears are entertained for the safety of the houses over the way, already scorched and blistering, and the adjoining tenements within a circle of a hundred yards are sure to be more or less injured by water, for the street is wretchedly narrow, and the houses lean-to frightfully. One extremity of the thoroughfare has been shored up for years by beams, now rotting. The oil and pickle man is heavily insured, so is the contractor for army clothing over the way, so is the wholesale boot and shoe manufacturer next door. It would be a mercy if the whole decayed stack of buildings were swept away by the devouring, yet purifying element. Yes, a mercy, surely a mercy. But the miserable inhabitants of the crumbling tenements that cling like barnacles to the skirts of the great shops and factories, are they insured? See them swarming from their hovels half naked, frenzied with terror and amazement, bearing their trembling children in their arms, or lugging their lamentable shreds and scraps of household goods and chattels into the open. Are *they* insured? The fire will send them to the workhouse, or, maybe, to the workhouse dead-wall—for they have no legal settlement there, or they are not casual paupers, or they haven't seen the relieving-officer, or they are too early, or too late—there to crouch and die. To be sure, they ought never to have been born. *They* are not necessary for the prosperity of the wholesale trade in boots and shoes, oil, pickles, and army clothing. Why cumber they the earth?

And still the fire leaps up into the cold morning air. The house will be gutted out and out, the police now say authoritatively. Happily there is no danger to be apprehended now for human life within the blazing pile. The oil and pickle chandler does not dwell in his warehouse. He has a snug villa at Highgate, and is very probably now contemplating the motley sky from his parlour-window, and wondering wherever the fire can be. The only living person who had to be rescued was an old housekeeper, who persisted in saying that she had lived in the house "seven and thirty year," and wouldn't leave it while one stone remained on another; which was not so very difficult a task, seeing that the premises were built throughout of brick. She had to be hustled at last, and after much to do, into the fire-escape; but for hours afterwards she led the firemen a terrible life respecting the fate of a certain tom-cat, of extraordinary sagacity, called Ginger, which she averred to have left sitting on the lid of the water-butt, but which very soon afterwards appeared in the flesh, so scorched that it smelt like burnt feathers, and clawing convulsively at the collar of a police-constable of the F. division. It is, perhaps, scarcely worth while to state that in the course of the fire a poor woman is carried from one of the adjoining hovels dead. She was close upon her confinement, and the child and she are gone to a more peaceable and merciful city, where lives, at least, are assured for ever.

Towards two o'clock, the columns of flame begin to grow slenderer, less continuous, more fitful. The clanking of the fire-engines does not decrease, however, in the least, though the firemen joyfully declare that the fire is "got under." The surrounding publicans—who, though they closed at midnight, have all taken down their shutters with marvellous alacrity—are doing a roaring trade in beer, which is distributed to the volunteers at the pumps in sufficiently liberal quantities, a check being kept upon the amount consumed by means of tickets. Where the tickets come from I have no means of judging, but this wonderful fire-brigade seem prepared for everything.

So, feeling very hot and dry, and dazed about the eyes with constant contemplation of the flames, I leave St. Giles's and the oil and pickle vender's warehouse, which, when daylight comes, will be but a heap of charred, steaming ruins, and wander westward, musing over the fires I have seen and the fires I have read of. I think of the great fire of London in Charles's time— the fire that began at Pudding Lane and ended at Pye Corner, and in commemoration of which they built that strange monument, with the gilt shaving-brush at the top—

"... London's column, pointing to the skies,

Like a tall bully, lifts its head and lies."

I think of the great fire at the Tower of London in 1841, of which I was an eye-witness, and which consumed the hideous armouries built by William III. and their priceless contents. I think upon the great scuffle and scramble to rescue the crown and regalia from the threatened Jewel House, such a scuffle and scramble as had not taken place since Colonel Blood's impudent attempt to steal those precious things. Then my mind reverts to the monster conflagration by which the winter palace at St. Petersburg was destroyed in 1839; of the strange discovery then made, that dozens of families lived on the roof of the palace—lived, and roosted, and died, and kept fowls and goats there, of whose existence the court and the imperial household had not the remotest idea; of the sentinel who died at his post, notwithstanding the imperial command to leave it, because he had not been relieved by his corporal; and of the Czar himself watching with compressed lips the destruction of his magnificent palace, and vainly entreating his officers not to risk their lives in endeavouring to save the furniture. One zealous aide-de-camp could not be dissuaded from the attempt to reach a magnificent pier-glass, framed in gold and malachite, from a wall, whereupon his Imperial Majesty, seeing that injunction, entreaty, menace were all in vain, hurled, with the full force of his gigantic arm, his opera-glass at the sheet of crystal, which was shivered to atoms by the blow. Not an uncharacteristic trait of Nicholas Romanoff.

TWO O'CLOCK A.M.—A LATE DEBATE IN THE HOUSE OF COMMONS, AND THE TURNSTILE OF WATERLOO BRIDGE.

I never could understand politics (which difficulty of comprehension of a repulsive topic I share, I am delighted to know, with the whole charming female sex, for a woman who is a politician is to me no woman at all). I never could be consistent in public matters. If my remembrance serve me correctly, I think I began life as a flaming Conservative. I am now as flaming a Radical; but I admit that I am most deplorably deficient in consistency. I find myself, while straining every nerve to defend the cause, to advocate the rights, to denounce the oppressors of that English people of whom I am one, frequently halting on ground where Eglintoun Beaverup, the Conservative *par excellence*, and I can shake hands; I find myself acknowledging that "blood is thicker than water," and that gentle birth will hold its own in the midst of sarcasms against the tenth transmitters of foolish faces. I find myself actuated now (as ever in that I have been consistent) by the same dislike and contempt for the cruel, capricious, ruffian, unteachable Mob—the base *decamisado canaille*, who are not the working classes, or the lower classes, or any other class, but the Father of confusion and anarchy's—the scurvy mob who pelt a Castlereagh to-day and tear a John de Witt in pieces to-morrow; who slaughtered Rienzi, and yelped for joy when Madame Roland went to the guillotine; who cried for "justice" upon Charles Stuart, and danced round the Tyburn tree from which dangled the rotting corpse of Cromwell; who would trample on Henry Brougham or John Russell at the present writing, and rend their vitals, if *their* mobbish majesty were crossed in one of its wild-baboon whims.

With this candid confession of my political shortcomings (I mean to stand some day for the borough of Weathercock), and having thus, I hope, disarmed criticism, I shall now venture into the (to me) perilous region of politics. It is Two o'Clock in the morning; we will even be present in the spirit at a late debate in the "House."

Which august assembly has already been designated by some irreverent wag as a "large house which keeps bad hours." In truth, one needs to be very intimately acquainted, not only with the framework, but with the minuter organisation of English society and institutions—(how sick I am, and you must be, of those eternally-recurring words "institutions" and "society!")—to understand the causes of the immoderately late hours kept sometimes by the Lords, but with much greater frequency by the Commons' House of Parliament. At the first blush, there seems no earthly reason why the legislative business of the nation should not be got over during the day, or, at the outside, before the night were spent. The French Deputies, Conventionalists, or Representatives in the National Assembly, in their stormiest and most prolonged debates, seldom heard the chimes at midnight; and, ardent parliamentarians as are the Americans, it is only towards the immediate close of the session that Congress keeps for two or three days and nights a sort of Saturnalia of untimely sittings. If report speaks true, the members of the United States Legislature are only enabled to bear these unwonted vigils by incessant recurrence to powerful stimulants. "Quislings," "Fiscal Agents," "Stone Fences," "Bullocks' Milk," and the innumerable tribe of "Cocktails," are at a premium during these abnormally protracted debates; the benches of the House and the desks of the members stand in imminent danger of being whittled away during the excitement of discussion; the amount of tobacco masticated is sufficient to ruin the digestive powers of the nation; the spittoons overflow, and the fretfulness and irritation not unnaturally engendered by nervous excitement, occasionally finds relief in cowhiding in the committee-rooms, gouging in the lobbies, and "stand up and drag out" fights on the august floor itself, occupied by the conscript fathers of the republic. Thus I have been informed; but it may be that report tells a fib, after all.

When we arrive, however, at a just understanding and appreciation of the mechanism of this wondrous British constitutional watch, jewelled in ever so many holes as it is, with its levers, and escapements, and unnumbered compensation balances, the lateness of our legislative hours will not be by far so much of a mystery to us. We are altogether a sitting-up late people. The continental theatres are all closed by eleven. We dismiss our audiences sometimes at midnight, oftener at half-past, or a quarter to one in the morning. Our fashionable balls commence when those of other nations are terminating. We may not dine so late, but then we sup heavily, hours afterwards. Night life in London does not condescend to commence till the "small hours;" yet, in dissipated Paris, you may count the *cafés* and supper-rooms on your fingers whose portals are open at one o'clock in the morning. The "Journal des Debats" goes to press at four in the afternoon; eight hours later, there is yet often a leader to be written for the forthcoming number of the "Times." The only capital that can equal London in the faculty of "keeping it up" to any number of hours, is St. Petersburg. There the antipathy which the Russians entertain for going to bed is solely surpassed by their aversion to getting up. They turn night into day; but the sturdy, strong-willed, perverse English work or dissipate nearly "twice round the clock." They make the little children go to bed; yet the ambition even of those younglings is to "sit up late" like the grown people.

A French senator gets a thousand pounds a year for wearing a blue livery coat with a stand-up collar, the whole handsomely embroidered in gold;

kerseymere small clothes, and silk stockings. He drives down to the Luxembourg in his brougham, about three in the afternoon, dozes for a couple of hours on a well-stuffed bench, goes home to dine, drink coffee, play tric-trac, read the "Gazette de France," or receive a select circle of pensioned fogies like himself. He wakes up some fine morning to find himself complimented in the "Moniteur," and the gratified recipient of the grand cross of the Legion of Honour. A member of the French *Corps Législatif* receives his wages in a comparative ratio, and pursues an analogous cycle of "duties." But look at an English member of Parliament. He receives nothing a year, and in many cases has little more than that problematical income, sometimes humorously characterised as "midshipman's half-pay," to live upon. If he be rich, so much the better; but wealth will not take away a tittle from his hard work. In the early morning, over his tea and toast, he has an ocean of correspondence, often frivolous, always wearisome, to wade through. Then he has his blue-books to dive into, his authorities to consult, his statistics to cram, his speeches to "coach," his grievances to hunt up, his exordia to study, his perorations to practise. Comes the hour of morning calls when he must be at home, and give audience to the great army of Askers and the legionary tribe of bores, men who will take no denial, importunate clients, who want berths in the Post-office for themselves, or reversions of tide-waiterships for their cousins' cousins. Happily for the member of Parliament, Mr. Rowland Hill's penny-postage system has abolished the frank-hunting torture, which brought many M.P.'s to death's door, and made more bitterly regret that they had ever been taught to write their own names. And woe be to the legislator if he receive not his visitors with courtesy! They probably are constituents, and a curt answer will frequently send them away charged with the deadliest schemes against that member's vote and interest at the ensuing general election. As a diversion during the morning calls, the M.P. has to receive some dozens of applications for orders of admission to the Strangers' Gallery of the House, he having always a couple at his disposal. After this, he has, perhaps, to wait upon the Prime Minister, in Downing Street, at the head of a deputation respecting the disputed right in a cess-pool; or he may be the chairman of some parliamentary committee, sitting, *de die in diem*, to inquire into the hideous turpitude of a contractor who has sewn so many pairs of soldiers' boots without cobblers' wax. Then, he has to take a cab to attend the great public meeting for the Evangelisation of Chinese beggars, held at the Mansion House. He is due about this time in the board-room of the public company of which he is a director; and at the special committee of the Benevolent Institution in which he takes so much interest. A pretty hard day's work this, you will acknowledge. Add that the English member of Parliament has to be, over and above all this, a man of business or pleasure: with a wife and family very often, with a turn for literature, or art, or science, or natural history. He is a merchant or banker, and must drudge in his counting-house, like the meanest of his clerks, or gabble on 'Change with the nimblest-tongued bill-broker. He is a great counsel: he cannot plead the cause of "Stradlings *versus* Styles," by deputy, or allow his junior to sum up in the great will case. He is a celebrity of the fashionable world: he must pay his morning visits, ride in the Park, show himself at the "Corner," lounge through his clubs, drop in at the opera at night; and, after all this, or rather in the midst of all this, and pervading it like a nightmare, there is the real business of his life—the "House." He possesses some six hundred other colleagues, who are to the full as busily occupied as he is during the day, yet manage, somehow, to find themselves behind the Speaker's chair, or at the gangway, at five o'clock in the afternoon. He had better not be unpunctual or remiss in his attendance. Those constituents of his, at Shrimpington-super-Mare, will call him to a strict account of his stewardship at the end of the session, and it may go hard with him at the Mechanics' Institution or the Farmers' Ordinary. Under all these circumstances, do you think it so very extraordinary that there should be occasionally a late debate in the House of Commons?

You will remark that I have preserved, throughout, a decorous reticence with regard to the House of Lords. Goodness forfend that I should have to judge their Lordships by the same business-like work-a-day standard which I have presumed to apply to the Lower House. Their Lordships meet early and separate early, as becometh their degree; yet even the Lords have their field-days, and their occasions when they sit up late o' nights. Then the right reverend bishops come down, booted and spurred, to vote against the heathen; and paralytic old peers are borne to the House in litters, there to wheeze forth, in tremulous accents, their unalterable attachment to Church and State, so dangerously menaced in "another place," and from their most noble pockets they pull forth "proxies," signed by other peers more paralytic than themselves. But these field-days of the Lords are few and far between, and the *otium cum dignitate* is the easy, comfortable rule with their Lordships. It is but doing them justice to say, however, that many peers have been members of the Lower House in their time, and have sat up as late, and battled in debate as fiercely, as any middle-aged member of her Majesty's Opposition. Nor are they all idle, parliamentarily, in the day time. There are some noblemen—legal peers mostly—who disdain to rest upon their laurels, and are content to spend the long forenoons in listening to dreary disquisitions about the wrongs of Parsee traders, and the visionary pedigrees of claimants to dormant peerages. The Lords' committee hear appeals, and it is a wondrous sight to see those old boys snoozing and twiddling their thumbs on the crimson benches of their golden chamber. They seem not to listen to the elaborate word-entanglements of the bewigged pleaders; yet they make remarks full of sense and pregnant with acumen. You are a young man or woman, dear reader of this, I hope. You have not much time to lose. Go straight down to Palace Yard, pass through Westminster Hall, and up the stone stairs, by the giant brazen candelabra and the great stained-glass window. So on through the Gothic vestibules and corridors—never mind the frescoes of Messrs. Dyce and Company, they are not worth looking at just now. Hie you quickly to a door-way half-screened by crimson drapery, and edge your way into the House of Lords. An you take off your hat and hold your tongue, you may stare about you as much as ever you please, and hear your fill of the edifying, if not amusing, appeals. You may wonder at the Lord Chancellor's wrinkles and at his ruffles; you may listen to Floorem, Attorney-General, and Botherem, Q.C., till your eyes begin to wink, and your head to nod, and your whole mental framework to grow desperately weary; but you must not go entirely to sleep. Somnolence may entail a fall on the floor of the House, which would cause a noise, and would never do; so, unless you are gifted, like a horse, with the power of going to sleep standing, I would counsel you to take a cup of strong green tea before you enter the House, and so string your nerves up to wakefulness. For diversion, turn away your eyes from the verbose barristers in their horse-hair, silk, and bombazine, and look at their Lordships. There are not often more than half-a-dozen of them present—seldom so many as that. You shall scarcely fail, however, to miss that noble senator—a capital working man of business he is too—who is possessed by the curious idiosyncrasy of dressing in the exact similitude of his own butler: blue coat and brass buttons, yellow waistcoat, pepper-and-salt pantaloons—not trousers, mind—and low shoes. I think, even, that his Lordship's head is powdered. You may object that there is no reason why a gentleman of the old school, wedded to traditions and reminiscences of *le bon vieux temps*, should not wear such a costume as this, and yet look every inch a nobleman. Nor is there, indeed; but glance for a moment at Lord Aspendale, and you will confess that, from hair-powder to shoe-string, there is a permeating flavour of the side-board and the still-room. Whether his Lordship likes it, or whether his Lordship can't help it, it matters little; but the fact is there, plain and obvious.

Standing in the narrow Gothic railed-off space reserved for the public—the throne at the opposite extremity of the House—you may see on one of the benches to the right, almost every forenoon—Saturday and Sunday excepted—during the session, a very old man with a white head, and attired in a simple frock and trousers of shepherd's plaid. It is a leonine head, and the white locks are bushy and profuse. So, too, the eyebrows, penthouses to eyes somewhat weak now, but that can flash fire yet upon occasions. The face is ploughed with wrinkles, as well it may be, for the old man will never see fourscore years again, and of these, threescore, at the very least, have been spent in study and the hardest labour, mental and physical. The nose is a marvel—protuberant, rugose, aggressive, inquiring, and defiant: unlovely, but intellectual. There is a trumpet mouth, a belligerent mouth, projecting and self-asserting; largish ears, and on chin or cheeks no vestige of hair. Not a beautiful man this on any theory of beauty, Hogarthesque, Ruskinesque, Winckelmanesque, or otherwise. Rather a shaggy, gnarled, battered, weatherbeaten, ugly, faithful, Scotch-colley type. Not a soft, imploring, yielding face. Rather a tearing, mocking, pugnacious, cast of countenance. The mouth is fashioned to the saying of harsh, hard, impertinent things: not cruel, but downright; but never to whisper compliments, or simper out platitudes. A nose, too, that can snuff the battle afar off, and with dilated nostrils breathe forth a glory that is sometimes terrible; but not a nose for a pouncet-box, or a Covent Garden bouquet, or a *flacon* of Frangipani. Would not care much for truffles either I think, or the delicate aroma of sparkling Moselle. Would prefer onions or strongly-infused malt and hops: something honest and unsophisticated. Watch this old man narrowly, young visitor to the Lords. Scan his furrowed visage. Mark his odd angular ways and gestures passing uncouth. Now he crouches, very doglike, on his crimson bench: clasps one shepherd's plaid leg in both his hands. Botherem, Q.C., is talking nonsense, I think. Now the legs are crossed, and the hands thrown behind the head; now he digs his elbows into the little Gothic writing-table before him, and buries the hands in that puissant white hair of his. The quiddities of Floorem, Q.C., are beyond human patience. Then with a wrench, a wriggle, a shake, a half turn and half start up—still very doglike, but of the Newfoundland rather, now, he asks a lawyer or a witness a question. Question very sharp and to the point, not often complimentary by-times, and couched in that which is neither broad Scotch nor Northumbrian burr, but a rebellious mixture of the two. Mark him well, eye him closely: you have not much time to lose. Alas! the giant is very old; though with frame yet unenfeebled, with intellect yet gloriously unclouded. But the sands are running, ever running. Watch him, mark him, eye him, score him on your mind tablets: then home; and in after years it may be your lot to tell your children, that once at least you have seen with your own eyes the famous Lord of Vaux; once listened to the voice that has shaken thrones and made tyrants tremble, that has been a herald of deliverance to millions pining in slavery and captivity; a voice that has given utterance, in man's most eloquent words, to the noblest, wisest thoughts lent to this Man of Men by Heaven; a voice that has been trumpet-sounding these sixty years past in defence of Truth, and Right, and Justice—in advocacy of the claims of learning and industry, and of the liberties of the great English people, from whose ranks he rose; a voice that should be entitled to a hearing in a Walhalla of wise heroes, after Francis of Verulam and Isaac of Grantham; the voice of one who is worthily a lord, but who will be yet better remembered, and to all time—remembered enthusiastically and affectionately—as the champion of all good and wise and beautiful Human Things—HARRY BROUGHAM.

But I must not forget, as I am sorely tempted to do in Westminster Hall, that it is two o'clock in the morning. This is the last night—the honourable House are positively determined to divide to-night, even if the Ministry go out—of the adjourned debate on the Gulliver Indemnity Bill. The honourable House have been speechifying at a tremendous rate for the last fortnight on the vexed question as to whether Samuel Gulliver, master mariner, is or is not to have an indemnity. Lord Viscount Palmerston, head of the government, says he shall. The Right Hon. Benjamin Disraeli, ex-Chancellor of the Exchequer, and head of the Opposition, says he sha'n't. Honourable members in formidable numbers range themselves on either side. Night after night the House has been ringing with eulogies and denunciations of Gulliver and his indemnity. The country is in a ferment, the press in arms, on the Titanic topic. A monster meeting at Manchester has pledged itself, amid deafening cheers in the Lancashire dialect and rounds of "Kentish fire," to support the indemnification of Gulliver by every legal and constitutional means. The "Times" newspaper, on its part, declares the indemnity an impudent swindle, and plainly announces that if Gulliver be indemnified, Great Britain must be content to remain henceforth and for ever a second-rate Power. The funds are going up and down like a see-saw, all with reference to Gulliver. More bets are made in the clubs and sporting localities *in re* Gulliver than on the coming Derby, or that other vexed question whether Bludgin Yahoo, who murdered the old lady with the crowbar (they say he is beautifully penitent in Newgate, and that the sheriffs cry to see him eat his daily beefsteak) will be hanged or not. The Emperor of Brobdignag is vitally interested in Gulliver, and there were two *attachés* from the Lilliputian embassy in the Speaker's gallery the night before last. Never mind who Gulliver was, or what was the nature of the losses for which he sought to be indemnified. It matters as little now as whether Bolgrad was a hamlet or a town; and even while the conflict was raging, I very much question whether a hundred members of the House of Commons knew anything about Gulliver personally, or cared two pins about him or his indemnity. In some respects politics are like fox-hunting. You want a fast-running, doubling, artful question—the more powerful in odour the better—to start with; but once run down the fox, and the question goes for nothing. Sometimes Reynard is scarce; but even then a red herring will serve at a pinch to bark at and run after.

We are in a spacious chamber, not very vast, not very lofty—for there is a false roof of ground glass, for acoustic reasons—and not very handsome. A sufficiency of oaken panelling, and windows veiled with velvet curtains, brilliant but cunningly tempered light—the absolute lamps invisible. Altogether a comfortable, well-to-do-place—say something like an enlarged edition of the coffee-room of a terminus hotel, as they are building terminus hotels now-a-days, or the newspaper-room of a club fitted up for a general meeting of the members. A tinge of Gothicism pervades the decorations, here and there tending to the Elizabethan, but altogether leaning more to the "convenient" style of ornament. Everything that skill and ingenuity (duly patented) can devise for the promotion of light, warmth, general comfort, &c., are here. Enthroned on high, slender galleries above him, is the Speaker. "Jove in his chair, of the skies lord mayor," is a sufficiently tremendous Pagan image. He must find it a somewhat hard task to keep order on Olympus' top occasionally. Vulcan will be wrangling with Apollo and eyeing Mars askant: Venus will be having high words with Juno, and Minerva boring the celestial company generally with her strongmindedness; to say nothing of Bacchus, in the plenitude of fermented grape-juice, volunteering a stave when nobody wants one; Mercury, labouring under his eternal disability to keep his hands out of the other gods' and goddesses' pockets; and the arch mischief maker, Cupid, wantoning about on his flyflapper wings, and setting everybody by the ears. But Jupiter-Speaker has a thrice more difficult task! Fancy having to preserve discipline among six hundred and a half gentlemen—young, old, and middle-aged gentles, all fond of the sound of their own voices; many of whom have dined copiously, to the making of them noisy; some who have not dined at all, to the making of them fretful and peevish, not to say quarrelsome. Poor Mr. Speaker! how weary he must be of the honourable House and of its honourable members in general, and of the Gulliver's Indemnity Bill in particular! Yet there he sits, the image of urbanity and equanimity, graceful, composed, dignified, though taciturn; his wig unmoved, his bands and ruffles uncrumpled. How devoutly he must wish that the bill were "in committee," when the mace might lie under the table, and he himself "leave the chair!" But, alas! the atrocious measure has not yet been read a second time. The country need be liberal and the House courteous to the Speaker. Surely, if any man deserves a handsome salary, free quarters, and a peerage on retirement, it is that Right Honourable Gentleman. To have to listen, night after night, to drowthy verbosities, phantasm statements, nightmare gibberings of incoherent statistics, inextricable word-chaoses of statements and counter-statements, sham declarations of sham patriotism bellowed forth with sham energy; to have to hear these tales, full of sound and fury, told by honourable idiots full of unutterable "bunkum" (an Americanism I feel constrained to use, as signifying nothingness, ineffably inept and irremediably pin-perforated windbaggery, and sublimated cucumber sunbeams hopelessly eclipsed into Dis)—these must be trials so sore that they need the highest of wages, the best of living, to be endured even. To induce a man to keep a turn-pike or a lighthouse, to work in a gunpowder mill, or to accept the governorship of Cape Coast Castle, you must offer heavy reward. Of old, in France, glass-blowing was considered to be a trade so dangerous, and requiring so much abnegation of self, that its professors were not ranked with the meaner sort of mechanics. Your glass-blower was entitled to wear a sword, a privilege extended since, I believe, to printers: (it is lucky they do not exercise it now, or I should be run through and through a dozen times a day by compositors infuriate at illegible spider manuscript.) He could blow glass without tarnishing his 'scutcheon, and was called "*Gentilhomme Verrier.*" Touching the Speakership, I think that the mere obligation of hearing men who hate each other, bandying the epithet of "honourable friend" so many hundred times in a night, is in itself worth two thousand a year.

The House has commenced. The peers' gallery, ambassadors' seats, strangers', Speaker's gallery, all full of attentive listeners. "Distinguished foreigners" are present. The Emperor of Brobdignag's ex-Minister for Foreign Affairs has come down from the Travellers', where he has been playing whist with the Hospodar of Wallachia's *Chargé d'Affaires*, and lurks in ambush behind the Speaker. The sparkling eyes of ladies, seeing but unseen, look down, as at Evans's, upon the hall. The members' benches—oaken covered with green leather, carved ends—are full. The members' gallery (stretching along both sides of the House) is, to tell the truth, not full, but it is possibly occupied by honourable members who have retired thither to— listen to the debate, of course. Oddly enough, they find that the assumption of a horizontal position is the very best for hearing that which is going on below; or, perhaps, they only imitate in this Fortunio's gifted servant. To turn the face to the wall, also, seems a favourite method of stimulating the auditory nerve; and some honourable gentlemen are so engrossed in the exciting debate proceeding in the House, that, at two o'clock in the morning, they sometimes give vent to their overworked-up feelings in a deep stertorous nasal sound resembling a snore.

Up in the reporters' gallery there, the gentlemen who submit to "work on an intellectual treadmill for three hundred pounds a year," are having hard times of it. The "turns" of stenography are getting shorter and shorter; but, alas! they have been terribly frequent during the debate. How unmerciful have been the maledictions bestowed on Gulliver and his indemnity since five p.m. when the Speaker was at prayers! Gulliver would be a bold man to venture into the cushion-benched chamber behind the gallery where the gentlemen of the Press retire to transcribe their notes. O'Dobbin of the "Flail" has been dying to hear Tamberlik in "Otello" these six weeks past. His chief gave him a stall this morning. Gulliver sits in it like a ghoule on a grave. Dollfus, of Garden Court, Temple, was invited to Jack Tritail, the newly-made barrister's, "call" carouse in Lincoln's Inn Hall. Gulliver is sitting at the hospitable board, gulping down the claret like Garagantua. Little Spitters, who was always a ladies' man, was to have been a "welcome guest" at a neat villa not far from Hammersmith Broadway. The fiend Gulliver is at this moment being called a "droll creature," and is flirting with the eldest Miss Cockletop.

TWO O'CLOCK A.M.: A LATE DEBATE IN THE HOUSE OF COMMONS.

The great chief of the Opposition has spoken. Gloomy, saturnine, isolated, yet triumphant, sits the eloquent and sarcastic Caucasian. Those once brilliant black corkscrew ringlets are growing slightly gray and wiry now, the chin tuft has disappeared, and time and thought have drawn deep lines in the sallow visage of Benjamin Disraeli, ruler of the Opposition. His attire, too, is sober compared with the myriad-hued garb, the flashing jewellery, and vests of many colours, with which Benjamin was wont to dazzle our eyes in the days before he slew Robert Peel, and hired himself to the Protectionists—all in a parliamentary sense. People say, when he wrote "Venetia" and the "Revolutionary Epic," he used to wear laced ruffles at his wrists and black velvet inexpressibles. He is wiser now. He has turned the half century, and only wears a vest of many colours when he dons his gold robe as Chancellor of the Exchequer. He has worn it once, and would very much like to wear it again. He has made a very long, telling, brilliant speech, in which he has said a multitude of damaging things against Gulliver, his indemnity, and especially against the noble Viscount at the head of the Government. He has never been abusive, insulting, coarse, virulent—oh, never! he has not once lost his temper. He has treated the noble Viscount with marked courtesy, and has called him his right honourable and noble friend scores of times; yet, hearing him, it has been impossible to avoid the impression that if any man was ever actuated by the conviction that his right honourable and noble friend was an impostor and a humbug, with a considerable dash of the traitor; and that—without hinting anything in the slightest degree libellous—his right honourable and noble friend had been once or twice convicted of larceny, and had failed in clearing himself from the suspicion of having murdered his grandmother, that man was Benjamin Disraeli, M.P. for the county of Bucks. He did not begin brilliantly. He was not in the slightest degree like Cicero or Demosthenes, Burke or Grattan, or like thee, my Eglintoun Beaverup, when thou descantest upon the "glorious old cocks," the "real tap, sir," of antiquity. He was, on the contrary, slow, laboured, downcast, and somewhat ponderous; nor even at the conclusion of his magnificent harangue, did he throw his arms about, smite his breast, stamp his foot, or cast his eyes up to heaven—and the ceiling. The days of weeping and gesticulation, of crumpling up sheets of paper, cracking slave-whips, flinging down daggers, and smashing the works of watches, seem to have departed from the House of Commons. Yet the eminent Caucasian contrived to create a very appreciable sensation, and certainly shot those barbed arrows of his—arrows tipped with judicious sarcasm and polite malevolence—with amazing dexterity and with murderous success. He has made his noble friend wince more than once, I will be bound. But you cannot see the workings of that stateman's face, for (save while addressing the House) he wears his hat; and the light coming from above causes the friendly brim to cast the vice-comital countenance into shadow.

A noticeable man this Hebrew Caucasian, Benjamin Disraeli, with his byegone literary nonsenses, and black-velvet-trousered frivolities. Not at all an English Man, trustworthy, loveable, nor indeed admirable, according to our sturdy English prejudices. Such statesmen as Shaftesbury, Ximenes, De Retz, any minister with a penchant for "dark and crooked ways," would have delighted in him; but to upright, albeit bigoted, William Pitt, he would have had anything but a sweet savour. Even Tory Castlereagh and Tory Sidmouth would but ill have relished this slippery, spangled, spotted, insincere Will-o'-the-wisp patriot. I should like very much to have known what manner of opinion the late Duke of Wellington entertained of Benjamin Disraeli. It is, of course, but matter of speculation; but I can't help thinking, too, that if Arthur Wellesley had had Benjamin in the Peninsula, he would have hanged him to a certainty.

Hush! pray hush! Silence, ye cackling juniors on the back benches; wake up, ye sluggards—only they don't wake up—the noble Viscount at the head of the Government is speaking. He begins confidently enough, but somewhat wearily, as though he were thoroughly tired of the whole business. But he warms gradually, and he, in his turn, too, can say damaging things about *his* right honourable friend, head of the Opposition. But he never says anything spiteful—is at most petulant (loses his temper altogether sometimes, they say), and flings about some *bon mots* that, were they published in this week's "Punch," would cause a well-grounded complaint of the growing dulness of that periodical. He speaks long, and to the purpose, and you can see at once in what stead have stood to him his long official career, his immense parliamentary experience. Recollect that John Henry Temple, Viscount Palmerston, has sat in Parliament for half a century, was Secretary-at-War while Wellington was yet wrestling with Napoleon's marshals in Spain, was one of the authors of the "New Whig Guide," has formed part of scores of administrations; and—one of the hardest-worked men of his time—has yet found leasure to be a beau and lion of fashion in Grosvenorian circles, and to be called "Cupid"—Grosvenorian circles rather chap-fallen, crow's-footed, rheumy about the eyes by this time, rather fallen into the sere and yellow leaf, now hessians and short waists have gone out, hoops and pegtops come in. Drollest of all, to think that this smug elderly gentleman, voluble in spite of tongue-clogging seventy, and jaunty in spite of evident gout, but quite a decorous, father-of-family, select vestryman-looking ancient, should be the *"terrible Palmerston"* the firebrand of the Continent, the bugbear of foreign oligarchs, the grim *"Caballero Balmerson"* naming whom Spanish contrabandistas cross themselves, the abhorred "Palmerstoni" whom papal gensd'arme imagine to be an emerited brigand who has long defied the pontifical authority from an inaccessible fastness in the Apennines. I need not tell you anything more about his speech. You will find it all in Hansard; and the newspapers of the day gave an accurate summary of the cheers, the counter-cheers, the ironical cheers, the "Hear, hears," and the "Oh, oh's" which accompanied the harangue, together with the "loud and continuous cheering" (from his own side of the House) which greeted its conclusion.

The longest lane, however, must have a turning; and this desperately long drawn-out parliamentary avenue has its turning at last. There have been frenzied shrieks of "Divide—divide!' numerous bores who have essayed to speak have been summarily shut up and coughed down; and at length strangers are ordered to withdraw, and the division bell rings.

"On our re-admission," we quote from the "Times" newspaper of 185—, the results of the division were announced as follows:—

> For the second reading of the bill
>
> Against it
>
> Majority against the Government

The bill was consequently lost.

Next day the Government presided over by the noble Viscount who wears his hat, goes out of office—the "Times" giving it a graceful kick at parting, and hinting that it was never anything more than a disreputable, shameless, abandoned clique, whose nepotism had grown intolerable in the nostrils of the nation. The Right Honourable Caucasian, who doesn't wear his hat, is sent for by a certain friend of his—a noble Earl, who is generally considered a first-rate hand at making up a book for the Derby. He in his turn is sent for by his Most Gracious Sovereign; and, for the next three or four days, there is nothing but running about and getting upstairs between Buckingham Palace, St. James's Square, and Grosvenor Gate; and at the end of that time, the right honourable Caucasian finds himself snugly ensconced in Downing Street, with full liberty to wear his gold robe again.

TWO O'CLOCK A.M.: THE TURNSTILE OF WATERLOO BRIDGE.

Past, long past two in the morning. The much-suffering House of Commons at last shut up, and deserted save by the police and the night watchmen. The last cabs in Palace Yard driven away: the charioteers grumbling horribly on their boxes, for they have members of Parliament inside, who never pay more than the legal fare. Irish members walked round the corner to Manchester Buildings or Victoria Street, there dwelling. Some members do all but sleep in the House. As for the noble and defeated Viscount, he trots cheerily home—scorning either cab or carriage—shouldering his umbrella, as though nothing in the world had happened to ruffle his equanimity.

And now, for the first time since this clock was set in motion, something like a deep sleep falleth over London. Not that the city is all hushed; it never is.

There are night revellers abroad, night prowlers a-foot. There is houseless wretchedness knowing not where to hide its head; there is furtive crime stalking about, and seeking whom it may devour. Yet all has a solemn, ghastly, unearthly aspect; the gas-lamps flicker like corpse candles; and the distant scream of a profligate, in conflict with the police, courses up and down the streets in weird and shuddering echoes.

The Strand is so still that you may count the footsteps as they sound; and the pale moon looks down pityingly on the vast, feverish, semi-slumbering mass. Here we stand at length by Upper Wellington Street; a minute's walk to the right will bring us to the "Bridge of Sighs."

Which never sleeps! Morning, and noon, and night, the sharp, clicking turnstile revolves; the ever-wakeful tollman is there, with his preternaturally keen apron. I call this man Charon, and the river which his standing ferry bridges over might well be the Styx. Impossible, immobile, indifferent, the gate-keeper's creed is summed up in one word—"A halfpenny!" Love, hope, happiness, misery, despair, and death—what are they to him? "A halfpenny for the bridge" is all he asks! but "a halfpenny for the bridge" he must have.

"Please, sir, will you give me a halfpenny for the bridge?" A phantom in crinoline lays her hand on my arm. I start, and she hastens through the turnstile—

"Anywhere, anywhere,

Out of the world,"

perhaps. But I may not linger on the mysteries of the Bridge of Sighs. They are among the "Secrets of Gas," and the pictured semblance of the place here must content you.

HOUR THE TWENTY-FOURTH AND LAST—THREE A.M.—A BAL MASQUE, AND THE NIGHT CHARGES AT BOW STREET.

When the bad Lord Lyttelton lay on his last bed—thorn-strewn by conscience—and haunted by the awful prediction of the phantom which appeared to him in the semblance of a white dove, telling him that at a certain hour on a certain night he should die, some friends who had a modicum of human feeling, and wished that wicked lord well, thinking that his agony was caused by mere terror of an impending event—half nervous, half superstitious—advanced the hands of the clock One Hour, and when the fatal one, as it seemed, struck, his Lordship started up in bed, apparently much relieved, and cried out joyfully that he had "jockeyed the ghost." But when the *real time* arrived, and the *real hour* was stricken on the bell, the prediction of the white dove was verified, and the bad Lord Lyttelton, shrieking, gave up the ghost.

Moral: there is not the slightest use in playing tricks with the clock. Were it otherwise, and were I not deterred by this awful warning in the case of Lord Lyttelton, I would entreat some kindly friend to stand on tiptoe, and just push the hour-hand of this clock of mine back, were it but for one poor *stunde* of sixty minutes. But in vain. As well ask Mr. Calcraft to postpone his quarter-to-eight visit with a new rope, when the law has consigned you to the tender mercies of that eminent functionary. As well may Crown Prince Frederick entreat the Governor of Cüstrin to defer the execution of wretched Lieutenant Katte, "till he can write to the king." As well may the unfortunate little Pants, hopelessly embroiled for the fifth time this morning with his Greek Delectus, implore the terrible Doctor Budd to spare him the rod this once. As well might I write to the Postmaster-General to say that it will not be convenient for me to deposit the last batch of newspapers in the window till half-past six p.m.; or beg the London and North-Western Railway Company to delay the departure of the Manchester night express till I have finished my wine and walnuts at the Victoria Hotel, Euston Square. The fiat has gone forth. *Missa est.* Judgment is over, and execution is come; and I may say, with Lord Grizzle in "Tom Thumb:"

"My bodye is a bankrupt's shop,

My grim creditor is death,"

who, like a stern sergeant, lays his hand on my collar, and bids me follow him to jail in the king's name. I wish I were Punch, for he not only "jockeyed" the ghost, but the hangman, and the beadle, and Mr. Shallabalah, and his wife, and the very deuce himself. I wish I were in a land where time is indeed made for slaves, or where there are no clocks to cast honest men off their hobbies.

"I wish I were a geese,

For they lives and dies in peace,

And accumulates much grease,

Over there."

But I am not a Punch nor a "geese," to endorse the touching transatlantic locution, however much I may merit the singular application of the name. I am only your humble servant to command, and this is the last hour of "Twice Round the Clock," so I must e'en essay to make a good end of it.

We have not been so badly off for public amusements during our journeyings. We have been to the opera, to the theatre, a dancing-academy, and to hear an oratorio. We have supped at Evans's, and "assisted" at a late debate in the House of Commons; yet I acknowledge, mournfully, that scores of places of recreation exist in London to which I could have taken you, and where we might have enjoyed ourselves very rationally and harmlessly. I should have liked to induct you to the mysteries of Canterbury Hall, the Polytechnic, Christy's Minstrels, and Madame Tussaud's waxwork show. For I hold to this creed, sternly and strongly, that public amusements—indoor and outdoor amusements—are eminently conducive to public *morals*, and to the liberty and happiness of the people. Music, dancing, and dramatic representations, free from grossness and turbulence, are as healthful and innocent recreations as Temperance Halls, lectures on the comet's tail, or monster meetings dedicated to the deification of the *odium theologicum*. From my little parlour window at Brighton, I can see a huge yellow placard disfiguring a dead wall with this inscription:—"Protestants! attend the Great Meeting to-night!" Bother the Protestants, (on platforms) I say, and the Pope of Rome too. What have we done that we are to be perpetually set together by the ears by belligerent Protestants and rampant Romanists? Is the whole framework of society to be shaken by controversies about the cardinal's red stockings or the rector's shovel hat? They had best both be swept into the dust-hole, I think, as having no more to do with religion than my poodle, Buffo, has with the Gunpowder Plot. Will all these roaring meetings—Protestants and Romanist, or Mumbo-Jumboical—where blatant stump-orators, paid for their theology by the night, rant, and stamp, and cook up those eternal Smithfield fires, help the sacred cause of Christianity one iota? It is long since Sheridan expressed a hope that there might be no more "scandal about Queen Elizabeth," and now, I see, they can't let that poor old woman rest in her grave. Some zealous people want to get up a sort of rider to "Guy Fawkes's Day," to commemorate the tri-centenary of her accession. You stupid firebrands! Of course "the Reformation was a blessing;" but do you know what will be the result of this raking up of the Elizabethan scandal? Do you know that there are such books as "Cobbett's Legacy to Parsons," and "Lingard's History," besides "Foxe's Martyrs," and a "Thunderbolt for Rome"? Do you know that it may be proved just six of one and half-a-dozen of the other about Queen Bess? that while to some she is the Great Protestant Sovereign, the Egeria of the Reformation, the Heroine of Tilbury Fort, to others she is a vain, cruel, arrogant old beldame, no better than she should be? who butchered Mary Stuart, and had Leicester poisoned; and who for every Protestant her gloomy sister burned, had at least two Papists hanged, drawn, and quartered, with the pleasant addition of their entrails being torn out and consumed before their eyes! *Eh! laissons la* these horrible reminiscences, and thank Heaven that we live under the sway of good Victoria, not that of ruthless Elizabeth or bloody Mary. Did the wise, and merciful, and bounteous Creator, who made this smiling earth, who has gladdened us with an infinity of good things for our solace and enjoyment, and for all quit-rent has laid this law upon us that we should love one another, in testimony of our greatest love for Him, who is all love and tenderness; did He send us here to squabble and fight and predict eternal perdition to one another, because there fall into our hearts a differently-coloured ray of the divine Effulgence? There is a flaming Protestant here with a broad-brimmed hat, and who is a vessel of much consequence among his fellow-bigots, who told an honest butcher some days since that if the Maynooth grant were renewed we should have "the thumbscrews in three months;" whereupon the affrighted butcher plastered all his joints over with handbills of the great Protestant Meeting, thus, of course, losing all his customers of the other persuasion. I wish those bells which are eternally jangling invitations for us to come and thank Heaven that we are not "as that publican," would ring a little tolerance and charity into men's hearts; would ring out a little more oblivion of phylacteries and pew-rents in high places, and of the sepulchral whitewash brushes. If the people who make all this noise and clamour, and who howl out against rational amusements, led pure and virtuous lives, and set good examples to their neighbours, this voice should not be raised; but, alas! here is brother Dolorous at the bar of the court of Queen's Bench for peculation; here is Sister Saintly scourging her apprentice; here are Messrs. Over-righteous in trouble for adulteration of their wares.

It is by no means incompatible, I hope, with the broad line of argument I have striven to adopt in these papers, if I honestly declare that the tableau I am about to describe has not in any way my approval, nay is, in many respects, much to be reprobated and deplored. I describe it—in its least repulsive details—simply because it is a very noticeable feature in modern

London life. To have passed it over would have been dishonest and hypocritical, and I set it down in my catalogue of subjects at the outset of my task, actuated then, as I am now, by a determination to allow no squeamishness to interfere with the delineation of the truth—so long as that truth could be told without offence to good manners and in household language. A modern masquerade in London is, to tell the honest truth, anything but an edifying spectacle. There is certainly no perceptible harm in some hundreds of persons, of both sexes, accoutred in more or less fantastic dresses, meeting together in a handsome theatre, and, to the music of a magnificent band, dancing till three or four o'clock in the morning. But the place is not harmless: people go there to dissipate, and *do* dissipate. The *salle de danse* of a grand masquerade is a re-union of epicurean passions—an epitome of vice painted and spangled. And I take a masquerade triumphantly as an argument against the precisians and sour-faces, who would curtail the amusements of the people, and viciously thwart them in their every effort to amuse themselves. Look you here, gentlemen of the vestry—arch moralists of the parish! look you here, good Mr. Chaplain of Pentonville, who have got your pet garotter safe in hold for his sins! This is no penny-gaff, no twopenny theatre, no cheap concert or dancing academy—not so much as a "free-and-easy" or a "sixpenny hop." Shopboys don't rob the till to come to a *bal masqué* at her Majesty's Theatre. Your pet garotter didn't throttle the gentleman in the Old Kent Road in order to procure funds to dance with Mademoiselle Euphrosine de la Galette, of the Rue Nôtre Dame de Lorette, Paris, and attired in a ravishing *débardeur* costume. There is, to be sure, a floating population of Bohemians—citizens of the world of London, belonging to the theatres, *enfants perdus* of the newspaper press, and so on, who are admitted gratis to a masquerade: these last Zouaves of social life, have free admission to coroners' inquests, public dinners, ship launches, private views of picture exhibitions, night rehearsals of pantomimes, and royal marriages. The modern newspaper man is, in print, the embodiment of Mr. Everybody; in private he is Mr. Nobody, and doesn't count at all. Lord Derby is afraid of the journalist in print, but in the flesh his Lordship's footman would look down upon him. "Honly a littery man, let him knock agin," Jeames would say. So we go everywhere, even as though we were in the "receipt of fern seed." Even the House of Commons has invented a pleasant fiction for the benefit of the gentlemen of the press, and humorously ignores their presence during the debates. The Empress Julia bathed before her male slave. "Call *that* a man," she cried, contemptuously. In the like manner, no account is taken of the journalist's extra card of admission or extra knife and fork. He goes under the head of "sundries," though he makes sometimes a rather formidable figure in the aggregate.

But to the general public—the social Zouaves are but a drop of water in the sea—a *bal masqué* is a very expensive affair, and a luxury not to be indulged in without a liberal disbursement of cash. First, ticket, half a guinea. Mademoiselle de la Galette's ticket, if you be *galant homme*, five shillings more, if she be in costume; half a guinea if in domino. Next, costume for yourself, variable according to its extravagance—a guinea at least. At any rate, if you are content to appear in plain evening dress, there are clean white kid gloves and patent leather boots to be purchased. And the supper; and the wine, for champagne is *de rigueur*, at twelve and fifteen shillings a bottle! (You will observe that whenever I grow fashionably dissipated, I begin to chatter French.) And Mademoiselle de la Galette's *bouquet*, and the intermediate refreshments, ices, coffee, lemonade, and what-not; and the cabs and the wild revelry in the wicked Haymarket purlieus afterwards. You see I have led you to the very end of the chapter, and that a night at a *bal masqué* will make an irremediable hole in a ten-pound note.

For this reason the persons (of the male sex) who visit such a gathering must be divided into three classes: theatrical and literary nobodies, coming there for nothing and not caring much about the place now they are come; young bucks about the town with more money than wit, who will exist, I am afraid, in every civilised age; and lastly and chiefly, the "Swells." I use the term advisedly, for none other can so minutely characterise them. Long, stern, solemn, languid, with drooping tawny moustaches, with faultlessly made habiliments, with irreproachable white neckcloths, with eyes half-closed, with pendant arms, with feet enclosed in mirror-like patent boots, the "swells" saunter listlessly through the ball-room with a quiet consciousness that all these dazzling frivolities are provided for their special gratification—which indeed they are. As it is *l'œil du maître qui engraisse le cheval*, so it is the "swell" who makes the *bal masqué* pay. Never so many orders may Mr. Nugent give away; but if the "swell" be not in town or muster not in force on the eventful night, there will be wailing in her Majesty's Theatre, and woe in M. Jullien's cash-box. It must be somewhat of a strong till that can stand this *tiraillement*. As regards the ladies who are the partners in the mazy dance of these splendid cavaliers, I may say, once for all, that they are Daughters of Folly; Mademoiselle de la Galette and her condisciples, English and French, are there, multiplied five-hundred fold. I don't think your pet garotter, good Mr. Chaplain, would be very successful as a Hercules at the feet of these Omphales.

THREE O'CLOCK A.M.: A BAL MASQUE.

I wonder how many sons and scions, or cousins or nephews, or multitudinous misty offshoots of the titled men who govern us, who own our lands, our waters, and the birds of the air, the beasts of the field, and the fish of the sea, are here. I wonder how many threads of connection there are in this ball-room theatre between these butterflies and the ermine and the lawn of the House of Peers. How many, how much? Bah! There is young Reginald Fitzmitre, the Bishop of Bosfursus's son, talking to that charming *titi* in the striped silk skirt and crimson satin trousers. Reginald is in the Guards. Bishops' sons are fond of going into the Guards. Yonder is little Pulex, whose brother, Tapely Pulex, is Under-Secretary for the Egregious Department. There Lord Claude Miffin has just stalked in with Sir Charles Shakeypegs (who is old enough to know better); and upon my word, here comes that venerable sinner Lord Holloway, with little Fanny Claypainter on his arm. It won't do, my Lord; you may disguise yourself as closely as you will in a domino and a mask with a long lace beard, but I know you by that side-wise waggle of your Lordship's head. The Earl of Holloway has been a very gay nobleman in his time. He married Miss Redpoll, the famous English *contraltro*, drew her theatrical salary with very great punctuality every Saturday afternoon at three o'clock, and beat her, people said. He was the honourable Jack Pilluler then. Years elapsed before he came into the title and Unguenton Park. *She* died. Advance, then—advance then, my noble swells—to adopt the style of the gentlemen with the thimble and pea. Advance, this is all for your delectation. Meanwhile, let your most noble and right reverend fathers, brothers, uncles, and cousins meet in either House of Parliament, meet at Quarter Sessions, or on borough bench, and make or expound laws against the wicked, thriftless, hardened, incorrigibly dissipated Poor. No beer for them, the rogues! No fairs, no wakes, no village feasts, no harvest-homes, no theatres, concerts, dances, no tobacco, no rabbits, no bowls, no cricket—but plenty of law, and plenty of nice hard labour, and wholesome gruel, and strengthening stone-breaking, and plenty of your sweet aristocratic wives and daughters to force their way into poor men's cottages, ask them questions for which I wonder they don't get their ears boxed, pry into their domestic concerns, peep into their cupboards, and wonder at their improvidence in not having more to eat and drink therein.

Stand we in the orchestral hemicycle, and watch the garish, motley scene. Questions of morality apart, one must have jaundiced eyes to deny that, as a mere spectacle, it is brilliant and picturesque enough. All that M. Jullien's *bizarre* taste and fancy could suggest, or the cunning skill of experienced scenic decorators carry out, has been done here to make the place gay, dazzling, and effective. Wreaths of artificial flowers, reflecting the highest credit upon the paper-stainer and the paper-cutter's art, mask the somewhat *fanées* ornaments of the tiers of boxes; homely corridors and staircases are pleasantly disguised under a plentitude of scarlet baize and drugget; the chandelier is of abnormous size, for any number of glittering festoons have been added to its crystal abacot; devices in glass and devices in gas twinkle and radiate on every side: nor is music's voluptuous swell wanting to incite us to "chase the glowing hours with flying feet," and make all things go "merry as a marriage bell."

Truly, that well-packed orchestra deserves a more dignified arena for its exertions than this vulgar dancing-place. A jangling harp, a wheezy flute, and a cracked-voice violin, with perhaps a dingy old drum, with two perpetual black eyes in its parchment cheeks where the stick hits them, like the wife of an incorrigibly drunken cobbler—instruments such as you may hear tortured any night outside the Moguls in Drury Dane: these would be quite good enough for the *ruffiani* (by which I do not at all mean "ruffians") and *bona robas* of a masquerade to dance to. But this orchestra, numerous as it is, is composed of picked men: it is an imperial guard of veterans in fiddling, bassooning, and cornet-à-pistoning. Even the gentleman who officiates at the triangle, is a solo player; and the fierce-looking foreigner who attends to the side-drums, is the most famous *tambour* in Europe. At beating the *chamade* he stands alone, and his roll is unrivalled. With shame I speak it: you shall find among these artists in wind and artists in string instruments, horns, and clarionettes, tenors and second violins, who, during the operatic season, are deemed not unworthy to be ruled by the Prospero wand of the kid-gloved

Costa or swayed by the magic fiddlestick of the accomplished Alfred Mellon. A pretty vocation for them to have to fiddle and blow for the amusement of ne'er-do-weels in tom-fools' costumes, and bold-faced jigs in velvet trousers! Why, they could take their parts in the symphonies of Beethoven and the masses of Mozart. And thou, too, Jullien the Superb, *maestro* of the ambrosial ringlets, the softly-luxuriant whiskers and moustaches, *gracilis puer* of the embroidered body-linen, the frogged pantaloons, the coat with *moire antique* facings, the diamond studs and sleeve buttons! couldst thou not find a worthier tilt-yard for thy chivalrous gambadoes? Alas! to some men, howsoever talented, charlatanism seems to adhere like a burr, and will not depart. Jullien must have caught this stain at the battle of Navarino or at the Jardin Turc, and it has abided by him ever since. There is not the slightest necessity for this clever, kindly, and really accomplished musician—to whom the cause of good and even classical music in England owes much—to be a quack; but I suppose he can't help it. He was born under a revolving firework star, and would introduce blue fire in the Dead March in "Saul." So it is with many. They could be Abernethies, but they prefer being Dulcamaras; they could be Galileos or Copernici, they prefer the fame of Cagliostro or Katterfelto. There was poor dear Alexis Soyer, as kind a hearted Christian as you might find, an admirable cook, an inventive genius, a brave, devoted, self-denying man, who served his adopted country better in the Crimea than many a starred and titled C.B. He had no call to be a quack; there was no earthly reason why he should inundate the newspapers with puffs, and wear impossible trousers, or cloth-of-gold waistcoats, cut diagonally. The man had a vast natural capacity, could think, ay, and *do* things; yet he quacked so continually, that many people set him down as a mere shallow pretender, and some even doubted whether he could cook at all. He was, nevertheless, a master of his difficult art, though in his latter days he did not exercise it much. Grisier grew tired of fencing. Wordsworth did not write much after he was laureate. Sir Edwin's brush is passing idle now. But I have partaken of succulent dainties cooked in their daintiest manner by the cunning hands of the illustrious *chef*; and I tell you that he could cook, when he chose, like St. Zita, the patroness of the Genoese *cuisinières*. And I think I know, and that I can tell, a *compôte* from a cow-heel, having dined as well and as ill, in my time, as any man of my age and standing.

What shall I say of the moving, living, kaleidoscope, twinkling and coruscating in the vast *enceinte*? Indeed, it is very difficult to say anything a bout the outward similitude of a *bal masqué* that has not been said a hundred times before. You have taken for granted the very considerable admixture of plain evening costume, worn by the swells *et autres*, which speckles the galaxy of gay costumes with multitudinous black dots. After this, we all know what to expect, and whom to find. Paint, patches, spangles, and pearl-powder, tawdry gold and silver (more brassy and pewtery, rather, I opine), and sham point lace. Sham fox-hunters, mostly of a Hebrew cast of countenance, in tarnished scarlet coats, creased buckskins, and boots with tops guiltless of oxalic acid, brandishing whips that have oftener been laid across their own shoulders than on the flanks of the "screws" they have bestridden; and screening their mouths with palms covered by dubious white kid gloves, or with bare dirt-inlaid knuckles protuberant with big rings of mosaic jewellery, shouting "Yoicks," and "Hark-away," in nasal accents. Undergraduates, in trencher caps and trailing gowns, worn by jobbernols, who know far more about Oxford Street than the University of Oxford. Barristers, more likely to be pleaded for than to plead. Bartlemy-Fair Field Marshals, in costumes equally akin to his who rides on the lamentable white horse before the Lord Mayor's gingerbread coach, and Bombastes Furioso in the farce. Charles the Seconds, with all the dissolute effrontery of that monarch, but of his wit or merriment none. Red Rovers and Conrad Corsairs, whose nautical adventures have been confined to a *fracas* on board a penny steamboat; Albanian, and Sciote, and Suliote Chiefs, with due fez, kilt, yataghan, and lambrochines, in orthodox "snowy camise and shaggy capote," and who act their characters in a likelier manner than their comrades, for they are, the majority, arrant "Greeks." A few Bedouin Arabs—a costume picturesque yet inexpensive: a pen'north of Spanish liquorice to dye the face withal; a couple of calico sheets, for caftan and burnous, with the tassel of a red worsted bell-pull or so to finish off with, and you have your Abd-el-Kader complete. Half-a-dozen Marquises, of Louis the Fifteenth's time. Plenty of Monks: robes and *cagoules* of gray linen, a rope for a girdle, a pennyworth of wooden beads for a rosary, and slippers cut down into sandals—these are as cheap as effective. A Knight, in complete armour (pasteboard with tin-foil glued thereupon); a Robinson Crusoe, always getting into piteous dilemmas, with his goatskin (worsted) umbrella; a Bear, a Demon, and a Chinese Mandarin. When I have enumerated these, I find that I have noticed the *travestisements* most prevalent among the English male portion of the costumed mob. But there is another very appreciable element in these exhibitions: the foreign one. A century has passed since Johnson told us, in his mordant satire of "London," that England's metropolis was—

"The needy villain's general home,

The common sew'r of Paris and of Rome."

It is astonishing to find how much foreign riff-raff and alien scoundrelry will turn up at a masquerade. Leicester Square and Panton Street, the *cloaques* of the Haymarket and Soho, disgorge the bearded and pomatumed scum of their stale *pot-au-feu*-smelling purlieus on this dancing floor. They come with orders, and don't sup; rather hover about the Daughters of Folly and Sons of Silliness, to wheedle and extort odd silver sums, with which to gamble at atrocious "nicks," and tobacco-enveloped gambling dens in Leicesterian slums, yet unrooted out by lynx-eyed policemen. Homer not unfrequently nods in Scotland Yard. "None are so blind as those that won't see," whisper the wicked. These foreigners—shameless, abandoned rogues, mostly throwing undeserved discredit upon honest, harmless *forestieri*; fellows who are "known to the police" in Paris, and have a second home at the *Depôt de la Prefecture*—affect the cheap, but thoroughly masquerade costume of the *Pierrot*. Very easy of accomplishment, this disguise. About one and ninepence outlay would suffice, it seemeth to me. Jerkin of white calico, with immoderately long sleeves, like those of a *camisole de force* unfastened; galligaskins of the same snowy cheapness, and scarlet slippers; any number of tawdry calico bows of any colour down the sides, a frill round the neck, where the "jougs" of the pillory or the collar of the garotte should be; the face, that should be seared with the hangman's brand, thickly plastered with flour, so that there would be no room for the knave to blush, even if the light hand of a transient conscience smote him on the cheek and bade him remember that he once had a mother, and was not always aide-de-camp in waiting to Beelzebub; a conical cap of pasteboard, like an extinguisher snowed upon; here you have the *Pierrot*. The Englishman sometimes attempts him, but generally fails in the assumption. In order to "keep-up" the character well, it is necessary to play an infinity of monkey-tricks, to bear kicking with cheerful equanimity, to dance furiously, and to utter a succession of shrill screams at the end of every dance. Else you are no true *Pierrot*; and these elegancies are foreign to our phlegmatic manners.

Another favourite costume with the *bal masqué* is that of the "Postillon de Longjumeau." He is as well-nigh extinct in France, by this chiming, as our own old English post-boys. Railways shunted him off on to oblivion's sidings with terrible rapidity. Only, his Imperial Highness Prince Jerome Napoleon—whom the Parisians persist in calling "l'Oncle Tom," because, say they, Napoleon I., his brother, was *"le grand homme"* Napoleon III., his nephew, *"le petit homme"* so this must be necessarily *"l'oncle-t-homme"*—or Tom—this mediocre old gentleman, who throughout his long life has always been fortunate enough to be lodged, and boarded, and pensioned at other peoples' expense (they positively carved out a kingdom for him once), still keeps up a staff of *postillons de Longjumeau*, who, with much bell-ringing, whip-cracking, and "ha! heu hooping!" guide his fat, white, hollow-backed Norman post-horses, when his Imperial Highness goes down to St. Cloud or Chantilly in his travelling carriage. It is a quaint, not unbecoming costume: glazed hat, the brim built at an angle, broad gold band, cockade as big as a pancake, and multicoloured streamers of attenuated ribbon; short wig, with club well powdered; jacket with red facings and turn-up two-inch tails; saucepan-lid buttons, and metal badge on the left arm; scarlet vest, double breasted; buckskins, saffron-dyed; high boots with bucket tops, and greased, mind, not blacked; long spurs, and whip insignificant as to stock and tremendous as to lash. This is his Imperial Highness's postilion, and this, minus the spurs, is the postilion of the *bal masqué*.

And the ladies? I am reticent. I am nervous. I draw back. "I don't like," as the children say. Hie you to the National Gallery, and look at Turner's picture of "Phryne going to the bath as Venus." Among the wild crew of *bacchantes* and *psoropaphæ* who surround that young person, you will find costumes as extravagant of hues, as variegated, as strike the senses here. Only, among the masqueraders you must not look for harmony of colour or symmetry of line. All is jarring, discordant, tawdry, and harlequinadish. You are in error if you suppose I am about to descant at length on the glittering semi-nudities gyrating here. Go to, you naughty queans! you must find some other inventory-maker. Go and mend your ways, buy horsehair corsets, "disciplines" and skulls if you will, and repair to the desert, there to mortify yourselves. Alas! the hussies laugh at me, and tell me that the only manner in which they choose to tolerate horsehair is *en crinoline*. Go to, and remember the fate of a certain Janet Somebody—I forget her surname—condemned by some Scotch elders, in the early days of the Reformation, to stripes and the stocks, for assuming a "pair of breeks." Alack! the *débardeurs* only mock me, and tell me that I am a fogey.

Three quasi-feminine costumes there are, however, that shall be pilloried here. There is the young lady in a riding-habit, who is so palpably unaccustomed to wearing such a garment, who is so piteously ill-at-ease in it, not knowing how to raise its folds with Amazonian grace, and tripping herself up at every fourth step or so, that she is more ridiculous than offensive. There is the "Middy:" a pair of white trousers, a turn-down collar, a round jacket, and a cap with a gold-lace band, being understood to fulfil all the requirements of that costume. The "middy" sneaks about in a most woeful state of sheep-leggedness, or, at most, essays to burst into delirious gymnastics, which end in confusion and contumely. And last, and most abhorrent to me, there is the "Romp." Romps in their natural state—in a parlour, on a lawn, in a swing, at a game of blind-man's-buff, or hunt-the-slipper—no honest man need cavil at. I like romps myself, when they don't pull your hair too hard, have some mercy on your toes, and refrain from calling you a "cross, grumpy, old thing," when you mildly suggest that it is very near bed-time. But a romp of some twenty-five years of age, with a cadaverous face, rouged, with a coral necklace, flaxen tails, a pinafore, a blue sash, Vandyked trousers, bare arms, and a skipping-rope: take away that romp, I say, quickly, somebody, and bring me a Gorgon or a Fury, the Hottentot Venus or the Pig-faced Lady! Anything for a change. Away with that romp, and cart her speedily to the nearest boarding-school where a lineal descendant of Mother Brownrigge yet wields her birchen sceptre.

It is on record that Thomas Carlyle, chiefest among British prose writing men, once in his life was present, in this very theatre, at a performance of the Italian Opera. He stayed the ballet, even, and went away full of strange cogitations. I would give one of my two ears (for be it known to you I am stone-deaf on the left side, like most men who have led evil lives in their youth, and could, wearing my hair long, well spare the superfluous flap of flesh and gristle) if I could persuade Thomas to visit a masquerade. There would be a new chapter in the next edition of "Sartor Resartus" to a certainty. For all these varied fopperies and fineries, dominoes, battered masks with ragged lace, sham orris, draggle-tailed feathers, tin-bladed rapiers, rabbit-skin and rat's-tail ermine, cotton velvet, "pinked" stockings, frayed epaulettes, mended skirts—all suggest pregnant thoughts of the Bag. *Tout cela sent son marchand d'habits.* Not to be driven away is the pervading notion of Old Clothes of Vinegar Yard and the ladies' wardrobe shop, of the ultimate relegation of these sallow fripperies to Petticoat Lane and Rag Fair. Nor without histories—some grave, some gay, some absurd, some terrible—must be these mended shreds of gaudy finery. They have been worn by aristocratic striplings at Eton Montem—defunct saturnalia of patrician "cadging." Those dim brocades and Swiss shepherdess *corsages*, have graced the forms of the fair-haired daughters of nobles at fancy balls. Great actresses, or *cantatrici*, have declaimed or sung in those satins, before they were disdainfully cast by, abandoned to the dresser, sold to the Jew costumier, cut down into tunics or pages' shoulder cloaks, furbished up with new tags and trimmings. Real barristers and gay young college lads have worn those wigs and gowns and trencher caps; real captains have flaunted at reviews in those embroidered tunics and epaulettes; swift horses have borne those scarlet coats and buckskins across country, but with real fox-hunters inside. Where are the original possessors? Drowned, or shot to death, or peacefully mouldering, insolvent, or abroad, gone up to the Lords, or hanged. Who knows? Perhaps they are lounging here as Swells, not recognising their old uniforms and academics, now worn by sham Abraham men and *franc-mitous*. Who can tell? Where is the pinafore of our youth, and the first shooting jacket of adolescence? *"Où sont les neiges d'antan?"* Where are the last winter's snows?

But Thomas Carlyle wouldn't come to this place, at his age and at this time in the morning; and, between you and me, I think it high time that we too should depart. In truth, the place is growing anything but orderly. Champagne and incessant exercise on the "light fantastic toe" have done their work. Dances of a wild and incoherent character, reminding one of the *"Chaloupé"* the *"Tulipe Orageuse,"* and the much-by-municipal-authorities-abhorred *"Cancan"* are attempted. The masters of the ceremonies seem laudably desirous of clearing the *salle*. Let us procure our great-coats, and flee from Babylon before the masquers grew unroarious.

A stream of masquerading humanity, male and female, begins to pour through the corridors and so out beneath the portico. It is time. Cabs and broughams—the "swells" came in the broughams—sly, wicked little inventions; policemen hoarsely shout and linkmen dart about.

I thought so. I knew how it would end. A row, of course. That big *Postillon de Longjumeau* has borne it with admirable temper for hours; but the conduct of the Charles the Second Cavalier has been beyond human forbearance. She—the cavalier is a she—has incited the *Pierrot* (an Englishman, for a wonder, and hopelessly gone in champagne) to knock the postilion down. He wept piteously at first, but, gathering courage, and not liking, perhaps, to be humiliated in the eyes of a *débardeur* in claret-coloured velvet, he kicked up wildly at the aggressor with his boots. Then the cavalier scratched his face; then the claret-coloured *débardeur* fainted; then Mr. Edward Clyfaker, of Charles Street, Drury Lane, thief, cut in cleverly from between the wheels of a carriage, and picked Lord Holloway's pocket of Miss Claypainter's cambric handkerchief; then A 22 drew his truncheon and hit an inoffensive fox-hunter a violent blow on the head; then four medical students called out "Fire!" and an inebriated costermonger, who had not been to the masquerade at all, but was quietly reeling home, challenged Lord Claude Miffin to single combat; then Ned Raggabones and Robin Barelegs, street Arabs, threw "cart-wheels" into the midst of the throng; then the police came down in great force, and, after knocking a great many people about who were not in the slightest degree implicated in the disturbance, at last pitched upon the right parties, and bore the pugnacious *Pierrot* and the disorderly Cavalier off to the station-house. It is but due to the managers of the masquerade to state, that no such scandalous *melées* take place within the precincts of the theatre itself. The masters of the ceremonies and the police on duty take care of that: but such little accidents will happen, outside, after the best-regulated masquerades.

THREE O'CLOCK A.M.: THE NIGHT CHARGES AT BOW STREET.

To the station-house, then, to the abode of captivity and the hall of justice. The complaining postilion and his friends, accompanied by a motley procession of tag-rag and bob-tail, press triumphantly forward. Shall we follow also?

In a commodious gas-lit box, surrounded by books and papers, and with a mighty folio of loose leaves open before him—a book of Fate, in truth—sits a Rhadamanthine man, buttoned up in a great-coat often; for be it blazing July or frigid December, it is always cold at three o'clock in the morning. Not a very pleasant duty his: sitting through the long night before that folio, smoking prohibited, warm alcoholic liquids only, I should suppose, to be surreptitiously indulged in: sitting only diversified by an occasional sally into the night air, to visit the policemen on their various beats, and learn what wicked deeds are doing this night and morning—a deputy taking charge of the folio meanwhile. Duty perhaps as onerous as that of the Speaker of the House of Commons: but, ah! not half so wearisome. For the Rhadamanthine man in the great-coat has betimes to listen to tales of awful murder, of desperate burglaries, of harrowing suicides, of poverty and misery that make your soul to shudder and your heart to grow sick; and sometimes to more jocund narratives—harum-scarum escapades, drunken freaks, impudent tricks, ingenious swindles, absurd jealousy, quarrels, and the like. But they all—be the case murder, or be it mouse-trap stealing—are entered on that vast loose folio, which is the charge-sheet, in fact; Rhadamanthine man in great-coat being but the inspector of police on night duty, sitting here at his grim task for some fifty or sixty shillings a week. Harder task than sub-editing a newspaper even, I am of opinion.

He has had a busy time since nine last evening. One by one the "charges" were brought in, and hour after hour, and set before him in that little iron-railed dock. Some were felonious charges: scowling, beetle-browed, under-hung charges, who had been there many times before, and were likely to come there many times again. A multiplicity of Irish charges, too: beggars, brawlers, pavement-obstructors—all terribly voluble and abusive of tongue; many with squalid babies in their arms. One or two such charges are lying now, contentedly drunken heaps of rags, in the women's cells. Plenty of juvenile charges, mere children, God help them! swept in and swept out; sometimes shot into cells—their boxes of fusees, or jagged broom-stumps, taken from them. A wife-beating charge; ruffianly carver, who has been beating his wife with the leg of a pianoforte. The wretched woman, all blood and tears, is very reluctant, even now, to give evidence, and entreats the inspector to "let Bill go; he didn't mean no harm." But he is locked up, departing to durance with the comforting assurance to his wife that he will, "do for her," at the first convenient opportunity. I daresay he will, when his six months' hard labour are over. There was a swell-mob charge, too, a dandy *de première force*, who swaggered, and twisted his eye-glass, and sucked his diamond ring while in the dock, and declared he knew nothing of the gentleman's watch, he was "shaw." He broke down, however, while being searched, and on the discovery of the watch—for he had missed the confederate who usually "covered" him—subsided into bad language, and the expression of a hope that he might not be tried by "old Bramwell," meaning the learned judge of that name. Short work has been made with some of these charges, while the disposal of others has occupied a considerable time. As the night grew older, the drunk and disorderly and drunk and incapable charges began to drop in; but one by one they have been disposed of in a calm, business-like manner, and the "charges" are either released, or, if sufficient cause were apparent for their detention, are sleeping off their liquor, or chewing the cud of sweet and bitter fancies, in the adjacent cells.

"I thought the *ball masky* would bring us some work," the inspector remarks to the sergeant, as the *Pierrot* is carried, and the cavalier is dragged, and the postilion and his friend stalk indignantly—the whole accompanied by a posse of police, into the station: "Now, then, F 29, what is it?"

F, or X, or Z, or whatever may be his distinguishing letter or numeral, gives a succinct narrative of the row, so far as he is acquainted with its phases, very much in the style of the *Act d'Accusation* of a French *procureur imperial*, which is always as damaging as it conveniently can be made against the person in custody. The postilion follows with *his* statement, the cavalier breaks in with an indignant denial of all he has said, violently insists upon charging the postilion with murder and assault, and ultimately expresses a desire to know what he, the inspector, thinks of himself, a wish to tear F 29's eyes out, and ardent ambition to "polish off the whole lot." "Don't all speak at once," remonstrates the inspector, but they *will* all speak at once, and the *Pierrot*, waking up from an intoxicated trance, asseverates, in broken accents, that he is a "p-p-p-p-pro-f-f-fessional man, and highly res-pe-pe-p-pectable," and then sinks quiescent over the front of the dock, in an attitude very much resembling that sometimes assumed by the celebrated Mr. Punch.

"There, take him away," says the municipal functionary, pointing with sternly contemptuous finger to the *Pierrot*. "And take *her* away," he adds, designating the cavalier. "And you, sir," he continues, to the postilion, "sign your name and address there, and take care to be at the court at ten in the morning. And I should advise you to go straight home, or you'll be here again shortly, with somebody to take care of you. I wonder whether we shall have any more," he says wearily, to his sergeant, as the captives are removed, and the room is cleared.

It does not so much matter, for the third hour is gone and past, and as we emerge into the street, the clock of St. Paul's strikes FOUR. There! the twenty-four hours are accomplished, and we have progressed, however lamely and imperfectly, "Twice Round the Clock." Good-bye, dear readers—pleasant companions of my labours. Goodbye, troops of shadowy friends and shadowy enemies, whose handwriting—in praise, in reproach, in condolence, in sympathy, in jest, and in earnest—is visible enough to me on many pages laying open before me at this moment, but whose faces I shall never see on this side the grave. Your smiles and frowns henceforward belong to the past, for my humble task is achieved, and the Clock is Stopped.

THE END.

FOOTNOTES

[1] A post-prandial paper, called the "Evening Mail," rarely seen in the metropolis, but extensively circulated in the provinces, and especially in the colonies, and in the United States, is published as a species of vesper thunderer at the "Times" office.

[2] "The Chimes."

[3] This old man's name was "Corney," at least I never knew him by any other appellation. He had been a collegian for years; and being a Briton who "stood upon his rights," and was for "freedom of opinion," gave the governor an immense amount of trouble. I think one of the happiest days of Captain Hudson's life must have been the one on which "Corney" (who, it turned out, ought never to have been imprisoned at all) got his discharge. He took lodgings immediately, I have heard, at a neighbouring coal shed, and brought an action (*in formâ pauperis*) against the governor for false imprisonment, and wrongful detention of property, about once a fortnight.

[4] Free-grown sugar in the first two: slave-grown sugar in boxes.

[5] See page 30.

[6] I am afraid that this legend must be regarded as what the "Times" newspaper called, in reference to old Peter Thellusson's delicate sense of honour, in providing for a possible restitution of property left in his charge by the ancient noblesse of France—a "modern myth." An analogous story, relative to the appearance of a *real* demon on the stage, in addition to those forming part of the *dramatis personæ*, is related in connection with Edward Alleyn, the actor; and the supernatural visitation, it is said, caused him to quit the stage as a profession, and found Dulwich College.

[7] The ladies appear in the gallery before dinner, quit it after grace has been said, and are regaled in ante-chambers with ices, coffee, and champagne. They return when the speech-making, wine-bibbing, and song-singing commence.

[8] This absurd remnant of a candle-snuffing age, and which is about as consistent with dramatic proprieties as the performance of the character of Macbeth by Garrick in the costume of a Captain in the Guards, was abolished—so far as his admirable Shakspearian revivals were concerned—by Mr. Charles Kean.

[9] Who married again, and extinguished herself. So did Maria Louisa, so did Mrs. Shelley. They *will* marry again, those unconscionable feminines.

[10] This pretty little theatre has succeeded, thanks to the genius and perseverance of Miss Swanborough, aided by an admirable company.

[11] There is a curious story anent this "Green Dragon" tavern, a dim record, embosomed in the musty records of the "State Trials." In a note to one of those chronicles of crimes and suffering, it is hinted at that the daughter of the executioner of Charles the First was a barmaid at the Green Dragon in the reign of Queen Anne.

[12] "He made the giants first, and then he killed them."—*Fielding's 'Tom Thumb.'*